# Science Fiction Authors

**Recent Titles in the
Author Research Series**
*Jen Stevens, Series Editor*

Fantasy Authors: A Research Guide
*Jen Stevens and Dorothea Salo*

# Science Fiction Authors:
# A Research Guide

Maura Heaphy

Author Research Series
*Jen Stevens, Series Editor*

A Member of the Greenwood Publishing Group

Westport, Connecticut • London

**Library of Congress Cataloging-in-Publication Data**

Heaphy, Maura, 1953–
    Science fiction authors : a research guide / Maura Heaphy.
        p.    cm. – (Author research series)
    Includes bibliographical references and index.
    ISBN 978–1–59158–515–2 (alk. paper)
    1. Science fiction, English—Bio-bibliography—Dictionaries.    2. Science fiction,
American—Bio-bibliography—Dictionaries.    3. Novelists, English—20th century—
Biography—Dictionaries.    4. Novelists, American—20th century—Biography—
Dictionaries.    5. Science fiction, English—Information resources.    6. Science fiction,
American—Information resources.    7. Science fiction—Information resources.    I. Title.
    Z2014.S33H43    2009
    [PR830.S35]
    016.823′08762080914—dc22        2008025708

British Library Cataloguing in Publication Data is available.

Library of Congress Catalog Card Number: 2008025708
ISBN: 978–1–59158–515–2

First published in 2009

Libraries Unlimited, 88 Post Road West, Westport, CT 06881
A Member of the Greenwood Publishing Group, Inc.
www.lu.com

Printed in the United States of America

The paper used in this book complies with the
Permanent Paper Standard issued by the National
Information Standards Organization (Z39.48–1984).

10  9  8  7  6  5  4  3  2  1

FOR Richard, Kate, and Claire

*I fled with it and seized on a student to take it down to the printer's. I'm almost positive I heard a faint voice crying from the window about a footnote on page 97—but I pretended not to hear.*

**—Dorothy L. Sayers, Gaudy Night.**

# Contents

# Acknowledgments

I would like to thank

- Claire Dutton and Adam Taylor, for their help checking URLs,
- Kate Dutton, for bringing the wonderful Sheri Tepper quote to my attention, and
- Richard Dutton, for listening.

Thanks also to Steve Galbraith, for first involving me in this project and to Ken Walton, for his patient feedback on The List, over a pint in the Ring o'Bells, Lancaster.

I would also like to thank Barbara Ittner and Jen Stevens for their feedback, for their patience—and their encouragement.

# Introduction: *Science Fiction Authors: A Research Guide*

## *What Is Science Fiction?*

*"...there is no fully satisfactory definition of sf..."*
—The Encyclopedia of Science Fiction,
*John Clute and Peter Nicholls, 1999*

Depending on your definition, and the stretch of your imagination, science fiction has been with us

- Since 1923, when the phrase "science fiction" was coined by editor Hugo Gernsback for a special fiction issue of his magazine *Science and Invention.*
- Since the late Victorian fashion for "scientific romance" gave authors such as H.G. Wells and Jules Verne a popular forum for working out the challenges associated with "Progress."
- Since the evening Mrs. Mary Wollstonecraft Shelley took pen in hand, and created a Monster.

Or, perhaps, science fiction has always been with us, in the satiric fabulations of Thomas More and Cyrano de Bergerac, and the philosophic metaphors of Plato. Perhaps, Science Fiction was there as the monks illuminating the Gospels with gold leaf and finely ground lapis lazuli sketched fantastic beasts and gargoyles in among the Prophets and Apostles, or as Cro-magnon man, deep in the caves of Lascaux, made *this* wooly mammoth just a little larger than life, or put a particularly knowing gleam in the eye of *that* saber-tooth tiger.

There is no hard and fast definition of "science fiction." (If proof is needed, see *52 Definitions of Science Fiction* http://www.panix.com/~gokce/sf_defn.html.)

There isn't even consensus about what to *call* the genre: science fiction, speculative fiction, SF, sf . . . anything but "scifi" (which itself is sometimes ironically rendered as "sciffy").

> *"Perhaps you like stf [scientific technological fiction], and want to write it, but are scared off by that word 'science . . .'"*
> —*Leigh Brackett*, "The Science-Fiction Field," 1944.

Science fiction can be about interstellar rockets, and Martians, and " . . . discontinuous functions in a four-dimensional space-time grid . . . " (to quote Leigh Brackett again)—*but it does not have to be.* One of the finest science fiction stories of the past fifty years, "The Heat Death of the Universe," by Pamela Zoline, is about a suburban California housewife who is overwhelmed by the angst and loneliness of her bright, modern life, and winds up having a nervous breakdown and trashing her kitchen. That's it: no alien abduction, no time travel, no clever ray guns that get the washing done in half the time. Just one lonely, alienated young mother, a modern individual at the sharp end of "progress."

> *That's really what SF is all about, you know: the big reality that pervades the real world we live in: the reality of change. Science fiction is the very literature of change. In fact, it is the only such literature we have.*
> —*Frederik Pohl*, Pohlemic, May 1992

*Science Fiction Authors: A Research Guide*, part of the *Author Research* series, fills a gap between readers' advisory books on science fiction writers and reference works that provide biographical information and/or critical bibliographies. This volume is intended for those who already know of a given writer and want to learn more about that writer, or find other similar authors. However, you may also wish to simply browse through the guide to see who looks interesting. In addition, close examination of specific authors within a genre can lead to a greater understanding of the genre as a whole.

## Why Do You Need This Book?

There are two ways to read science fiction—to enjoy it and to understand it. The first way is easy: it requires no training, no special equipment, or supplementary material. Pick up a copy of a book that appeals to you, open your mind and *start reading.* The sense of wonder and excitement of your typical science fiction story, the bravura of the ideas, and the glorious dynamic of words and images will do the rest.

The attractions of the second way—reading to understand—may creep up on us slowly. Regular readers of science fiction may find themselves picking up stories of life in far-off galaxies and far-future times for the fun and the excitement, but lingering over the ideas, over the connections that we find to our own lives, to the circumstances of our own time, and the peculiarities of our place in this world. We begin to suspect that, writing this story, the author had something more on his or her mind than spinning a good yarn, and that knowing a little more about what may have inspired this particular story, told in this particular way, would enhance our pleasure in the tale. To enjoy the novels of Gene Wolfe, Cordwainer Smith, James Blish, or Madeleine L'Engle, it isn't absolutely necessary to understand the spiritual world view at the heart of their stories. But it helps. To enjoy the novels of Kurt Vonnegut (*Slaughterhouse Five*), Walter M. Miller (*A Canticle for Liebowitz*), and Joe Haldeman (*The Forever War*), it isn't absolutely necessary to know anything about their wartime experiences in World War II or Vietnam. But knowing something about these things—being in a position to track down interviews, and read essays about the books and profiles of the writers, puts us in a position to make up our own minds about what makes these stories worth reading.

# Science Fiction Timeline

## The Mother (& Fathers) of Invention

| Literary Events | World Events |
|---|---|
| 1818—Mary Wollstonecraft Shelley: *Frankenstein, or, The Modern Prometheus* | 1815—Napoleon defeated at Waterloo |
| | 1831—Electromagnetic induction discovered by Michael Faraday |
| 1835—Edgar Allen Poe: "The Unparalleled Adventure of One Hans Pfaall" | 1859—Publication of *The Origin of the Species* |
| 1864—Jules Verne: *Journey to the Center of the Earth* | 1861–1865—The War Between the States (The American Civil War) |
| 1895—H.G. Wells: *The Time Machine* | 1902—Death of Queen Victoria |

## "Scientifiction"—Beginnings of a New Genre

| Literary Events | World Events |
|---|---|
| 1912—Edgar Rice Burroughs: *A Princess of Mars* | 1912—The sinking of the *Titanic* |
| 1920—Karel Čapek: *R.U.R.* | 1914–1918—World War I |
| 1920—E.E. "Doc" Smith: *The Skylark of Space* | 1915—Albert Einstein publishes General Theory of Relativity |
| 1930—Olaf Stapledon: *Last and First Men* | 1926—The first flight of liquid fueled rocket |
| 1932—Aldous Huxley: *Brave New World* | 1929—Stock Market Crash |
| | 1930—The first all talking, all-color movie |
| 1933—C. L. Moore: "Shambleau" | 1939—Germany invades Poland: World War II begins in Europe |
| 1938—C.S. Lewis: *Out of the Silent Planet* | |

## The Golden Age

*Literary Events*

1948—George Orwell: *Nineteen Eighty-Four*
1950—Isaac Asimov: *I, Robot*
1950—Ray Bradbury: *The Martian Chronicles*
1951—John Wyndham: *The Day of the Triffids*
1956—Alfred Bester: *The Stars My Destination*
1959—Walter M. Miller: *A Canticle for Leibowitz*
1962—Robert Heinlein: *Stranger in a Strange Land*

*World Events*

1945—Nuclear bombs dropped on Hiroshima and Nagasaki
1948—Berlin blockade (Cold War)
1950–1953—Korean War
1954—Brown v. Board of Education ends segregation in US schools
1957—Sputnik 1 launch
1958—FORTRAN developed by IBM
1959—*The Twilight Zone* debuts on CBS television
1959–1975—Vietnam War

## The New Wave

*Literary Events*

1963—Philip K. Dick: *The Man in the High Castle*
1967—Frank Herbert: *Dune*
1969—J.G. Ballard: *The Atrocity Exhibition*
1970—Ursula K. Le Guin: *The Left Hand of Darkness*
1976—Joe Haldeman: *The Forever War*
1979—Octavia E. Butler: *Kindred*

*World Events*

1963—Assassination of President John F. Kennedy
1968—Assassinations of Dr. Martin Luther King Jr. and Senator Robert F. Kennedy
1967—The first heart transplant operation
1968—US lands man on the Moon
1979—Margaret Thatcher becomes Prime Minister of the United Kingdom

## The Next Generation: Cyber Space, the Return of Space Opera, and "Slipstream"

*Literary Events*

1981—Vernor Vinge: "True Names"
1985—William Gibson: *Neuromancer*
1986—Orson Scott Card: *Ender's Game*
1993—Kim Stanley Robinson: *Red Mars*

*World Events*

1980—Former Beatle John Lennon murdered by stalker
1981—Launch of first Space shuttle mission, *Columbia*
1986—Nuclear accident at Chernobyl
1989—Fall of Berlin Wall

1994—Jonathan Lethem: *Gun, with Occasional Music*
2003—Cory Doctorow: *Down and Out in the Magic Kingdom*
2003—Charles Stross: *Singularity Sky*

1990—Iraq invades Kuwait, triggering First Gulf War
2001—Sept. 11, terrorists' attack on World Trade Center, New York, and Pentagon
2006—Pluto downgraded from planet status

## *About the Authors*

Narrowing the list of authors to be included in this volume was an agonizing process. I relied heavily upon various textual and online aids—volumes such as Clute and Nicholls' *The Encyclopedia of Science Fiction* and Barron's *Anatomy of Wonder* (5th edition) became my Vulgate and Apocrypha. There were also helpful Web sites such as,

- *A Basic SF Library*. James Gunn and Chris McKitterick. December 2007. The J. Wayne and Elsie M. Gunn Center for the Study of Science Fiction. http://www2.ku.edu/~sfcenter/sflib.htm—a list begun by the great science fiction scholar James Gunn in the 1970s, but maintained and updated by the Center at the University of Kansas.
- *Classics of Science Fiction*. James Wallace Harris (Data compilation by Anthony Bernardo). August 2007. http://classics.jameswallaceharris.com/—very statistic-based lists (by title, author, year), which throws up some oddities (Connie Willis, but no James Tiptree?), but offers some interesting comparisons of popular versus critical opinion.
- *Famous Science Fiction/Fantasy Authors*. Preston Hunter. January 2006. Adherents.com. http://www.adherents.com/adh_sf.html—a fascinating Web site that uses a number of scientific and statistical criteria to put together a list of the most famous and influential science fiction/fantasy writers of all time.

The above Web sites used the hard facts of years in print, sales, prizes awarded, and "name recognition" to construct their lists, a process I supplemented with my own research, on Web sites such as *The Locus Index to Science Fiction Awards* (Mark R. Kelly, February 2008. http://www.locusmag.com/SFAwards/).

In the end, the choices were mine—and nothing would have been easier than to sit back and watch the 100 available places begin to fill with the familiar, the undeniably notable, and the old favorites. But I was mindful of the words of Sir Arthur C. Clarke . . .

*Nothing is deader than yesterday's science-fiction. . . .*
—*Sands of Mars (1951)*

. . . and I was determined not to allow this to become a "dead list," consisting only of safe names. I wanted to include some of the great names of tomorrow, the individuals who—like the New Wave of the 1960s, and cyberpunk of the 1980s—are rewriting the rule book for the science fiction of the 21st Century. The authors on this list represent—in my personal opinion—the best and the brightest of Science Fiction, yesterday, today, and tomorrow.

## *Organization of Entries*

Authors are listed, in alphabetical order, under the name most likely to be familiar to a reader or bookstore browser (thus, **James Tiptree Jr.** *not* Alice Sheldon, **C.L. Moore** *not* Cyril Kornbluth, her pen name when she collaborated with her husband Henry Kuttner).

---

*About Pen Names:* Many science fiction authors, particularly those of the Golden Age of sf pulp magazines, wrote under *multiple* pen names to give themselves the chance to score more than one short story sale per issue. Authors of all periods have adopted pen names as "escape mechanisms," to allow them to try different styles and subgenres rather than being pegged to one particular type of story by their loyal fans. And authors writing as teams sometimes use a pen name for a collaborative "persona." Important pen names are mentioned in the biographical details or—in the cases where that name is firmly linked with certain titles by the author—in the works listed.

---

Each author entry begins with a **Quotation**, to give a taste of the writer's style, followed by

- a thumbnail **Biography**
- **Subject tags**, modeled closely on the Checklist of Themes in Clute and Nicholls' *The Encyclopedia of Science Fiction*. These tags are indexed at the end of the book. You can use the tags to find other authors who are known for dealing with similar themes.

---

For example, tags in the entry on **Octavia E. Butler** are

ALIENS; GENDER & SEXUALITY; MYTHOLOGY & LEGEND; PSI POWERS; SEX & TABOOS; UTOPIA

Look at any one of these entries in the Subject Index to find other authors who regularly write about these subjects.

---

- **Major Works**—Notable novels and short fiction (including novellas and novelettes) arranged by date of publication. Current short story collections and omnibus editions of multiple-volume works and series.
- **Other Important Works** listed alphabetically, includes critical essays and other nonfiction, and versions of the author's work in other media (film, television, and radio). On the whole, limited to the author's writing on sf in general and their own writing in particular, but occasionally stretching a point to include any work that offers a valuable insight into the author and his or her extracurricular interests, such as Iain M. Banks' guide to whiskey distilleries of Scotland, or Paul Linebarger's ("Cordwainer Smith") volumes on counter-espionage and Chinese history.

---

The Major Works of each author are not intended as a comprehensive bibliography (references and links to comprehensive bibliographies, text, and online, are listed, wherever possible—see below.) Many sf writers are extremely prolific, and "notable" is always a matter of taste.

Where it has been necessary to be ruthless, I have based my selection on

- titles and series with which the author is most closely identified,
- award-winning fiction and collections,
- work which is currently in print,
- short fiction, novel excerpts, and nonfiction that are available (observing copyright) online.

I have, however, tried to include work from across the entire span of an author's career.

---

## Research Sources

The following headings appear for each author:

- **Encyclopedias and Handbooks**
  Abbreviated list of useful online and print resources, which provide basic information about an author and his or her work. Volumes such as Gale's *Contemporary Authors* and Magill's *Survey of Science Fiction Literature* can be found in any substantial library.
- **Bibliographies**
  Lists of works by and/or about a given author, including bibliographic Web sites. Fiction (novels and stories, poetry, drama, screenplays, etc), nonfiction and criticism, interviews, and autobiographical work by the author are *primary* sources; articles and essays that have been written about the author and his or her work or life are *secondary* sources. Authors' official Web sites usually

include a comprehensive bibliography of primary sources, and some include lists or links of key essays and reviews.

The key to abbreviated entries for Encyclopedias and Handbooks and Bibliography are listed at the end of the Introduction.

- **Biographies and Interviews**
  Biographies and profiles are overviews of the writer's life and career; a biographical article or essay may focus on a specific incident that shaped an author's themes and attitudes.

  Interviews provide first hand information about an author's views of his or her own works. Interviews, like autobiographies, and nonfiction articles that the author has written, are "primary sources." The entries in this volume concentrate on the most current interviews available.
- **Criticism and Readers' Guides**
  There is a wide variety of critical material available, ranging from "monographs" (books on a single subject, whether that is the author's career as a whole, or a specific novel or story), to collections of essays. Individual essays and articles appear in scholarly journals and magazines, or may be posted, or self-published, online.

  What distinguishes scholarly essays from popular criticism, or self-published opinion, is not who writes it or where it appears. Essays that appear in scholarly journals are subject to "peer review;" that is, before the essay can be published, it is read by experts in the field, who comment on accuracy and the rigor of the scholarly method. Articles submitted for publication in popular magazines are subject to review by the editor or editorial staff. Articles, which are self-published, or posted online, are not necessarily checked by anyone.
- **Web Sites**
  In general, the more current an author, the more likely you are to find information about them via the Web. Thus, it is much easier to find online information on Neal Stephenson than Alfred Bester. However, this isn't always the case. For various reasons—a pro-active, technologically savvy estate, dedicated fans, or a revival of interest because of movie or TV tie-ins—there are a number of attractive, well-organized Web sites about classic sf writers (for example, Edgar Rice Burroughs, Robert A. Heinlein, Philip K. Dick, Cordwainer Smith, and H.G. Wells).

There are some common types of Web sites that appear, again and again, in the Author entries. Rather than annotate the typical features of each one, again and again, the following should serve as a general guide to each type. Exceptional features will be noted, as necessary.

*Official Web Site:* Usually includes biographical and bibliographical information, and current author news. Some bonus features may be samples of the author's work (full text of short stories and short articles, excerpts from longer work), FAQs, links to interviews, and photo galleries. Author Web sites are usually professionally designed, up-to-date, and easy to navigate.

*Fan Web Sites:* Can vary widely, in both design and content. Some "fan" Web sites are so good that they could be considered honorary "official" Web sites, particularly for deceased authors. An example is David Lavery's Web site on **James Tiptree Jr.** Others are enthusiastic, but obviously amateur efforts. Any Web site listed in this volume will have something useful or unique to offer, regardless of its superficial appearance: there may be especially useful links to articles or interviews that are available nowhere else, glossaries of character or setting, or some particularly original *homage* to the author's work.

*Fan Forums:* A venue where fans can get together to discuss the author's works. Always necessary to register to post and respond to discussion threads, sometimes necessary to register to read postings in full. Fan forums are a good way to read, and get involved in, discussions about an author's work in some depth.

*Blogs:* Online diary, full of news, observations on writing and current events, links to favorite Web pages, and general insights into the writing life. These days, some authors treat their blogs as their official Web site; or authors may have a link to a blog on their official Web site home page, particularly if they are passing on news about the publication or marketing of a new book.

*All URLs for Web sites cited in this volume were checked during April 2008.*

- **Read-Alike Lists:** *But where do I go from here . . .*
  For over twenty popular authors, I have put together "read alike" lists, which will give the reader an idea of where they can go next. These lists, like the volume as a whole, will be a tool to help the nonspecialist reader find something of interest, and place it in context in the genre.

---

**What's Not Included**

Individual book reviews are not included. There are so many reviews available, online and in print, and they tend to be easy to find, particularly if you have the home page of online journals and magazines (see General Bibliography). You can also use indexes such as *Book Review Digest* or *Mostly Fiction: Beyond Reality* (http://mostlyfiction.com/scifi.htm).

The exceptions to this are occasional reviews that use the volume under consideration as a launching point to survey the author's whole career. (This is not uncommon when the volume is a reissue of a less well-known work, or a novel by a "forgotten" author.)

# Alphabetical Listing of Authors

Adams, Douglas
Aldiss, Brian W.
Anderson, Poul
Asimov, Isaac
Atwood, Margaret
Ballard, J.G.
Banks, Iain M.
Baxter, Stephen
Bear, Greg
Bester, Alfred
Bishop, Michael
Blish, James
Bova, Ben
Brackett, Leigh
Bradbury, Ray
Bradley, Marion Zimmer
Brin, David
Brunner, John
Bujold, Lois McMaster
Burgess, Anthony
Burroughs, Edgar Rice
Butler, Octavia E.
Cadigan, Pat
Čapek, Karel
Card, Orson Scott
Charnas, Suzy McKee

Cherryh, C.J.
Chiang, Ted
Clarke, Sir Arthur C.
Delany, Samuel R.
Dick, Philip K.
Disch, Thomas M.
Doctorow, Cory
Ellison, Harlan
Farmer, Philip José
Finney, Jack
Gibson, William
Gloss, Molly
Goonan, Kathleen Ann
Greenland, Colin
Haldeman, Joe
Harrison, Harry
Harrison, M. John
Heinlein, Robert A.
Herbert, Frank
Hoban, Russell
Huxley, Aldous
Jones, Gwyneth [Ann Halam]
Kelly, James Patrick
Keyes, Daniel
Knight, Damon
Le Guin, Ursula K.

# How to Use This Book

## Jen Stevens, Series Editor

This volume is aimed at a variety of audiences and needs.

### Fans (and Other Readers)

You can browse through to scope out potentially interesting authors and books to read. If you'd like to find out more about an author, check the "Biographies and Interviews." Interviews can be an especially fascinating way to get to know your favorite authors. You might also want to check the "Web Sites" section since many authors have their own Web sites and blogs.

For a more in-depth look at a particular novel or story, consult the "Criticism and Readers' Guides." And finally, if you'd like to get a larger perspective on the Fantasy genre, check the "General Bibliography"—the names of major fan and writer organizations are included, as well as general encyclopedias on fantasy. You may also want to consult the "Awards" section at the back of the book.

### Students

You can browse through the book to get ideas for authors to use for your projects and papers. The "Major Works" section will give you a quick idea of what they've published and when.

To find out more about an author's life, check the "Biographies and Interviews." They might include interviews with the author, books and articles about the author's life, or collected letters to or by the author. Some authors have even written autobiographies. There are a number of author Web sites and blogs included under "Web Sites," which can give you even more information about an author (and their opinions!).

To get information about the books that the authors wrote, consult the "Criticism and Readers' Guides" section. There, you'll find discussions and interpretations of the novels and stories. Some of these articles will be formal academic essays while others may be more popular articles and "reader's guides." You can also find brief articles on authors in the "Encyclopedias and Handbooks" section. Incidentally, literary criticism is often referred to as "secondary," as opposed the "primary" novels, short stories, letters, and other things that were written by the authors themselves.

## Teachers

You can browse through the book to find potential authors to use in your curriculum and syllabi planning. More specifically, the "Major Works" will help you select specific novels and short stories for class or to recommend to students for free reading. The "Biographical" and "Criticism and Reader's Guides" sections provide essays and books that you can use in planning lectures and lessons, or directing student research. For shorter articles on authors, you can also check the "Encyclopedias and Handbooks"—major science fiction literature encyclopedias that have short author articles are listed. Although many of the Web sites listed under "Web Sites" may be less academic, they can provide additional perspectives. Students may especially enjoy the immediacy of reading author's blogs.

There is a "General Bibliography" that you can consult for broader sources for the genre as a whole.

## Librarians

The "Major Works" lists provide quick lists of books by authors to consult in Reader's Advisory questions. Some entries even include a "Read Alike" section that you can use to find books for the patron who has read all of their favorite author's books and needs more. These lists may also be helpful for collection development.

In turn, the "Biographical" sections and "Criticism and Reader's Guides" will prove useful for reference questions concerning writers and their works. You can also use these sections as well as the "General Bibliography," for collection development. The "Web Sites" can also be helpful for answering reference questions, or for posting on online pathfinders.

## Book Club Leaders

You can browse through the book to find authors and books that your book club might be interested in. The "Biographical" sections may be especially helpful to you for background information as you prepare for book club discussions. Author Web sites will tell you what your authors are working on now (they can also be a lot of fun to read!).

## Going Beyond This Book

Authors keep writing books, and researchers keep writing books and articles about them. Although the sources listed will remain useful, you may want to look for more current ones. Here are some tips:

– **Check the Bibliography**

There are reference books, indexes, and Web portals that you can use to find additional sources.

– **One Good Source Deserves Another**

If you find a book or Web site that you like (or even halfway like), look in the index, foot notes, bibliography, or "Links" for more sources.

– **Talk to Your Local Reference Librarian**

They may have ideas for further searching, or know about new sources and updates.

Of course, you can also search the Web, which leads us to further sources and updates. . . .

## Going Beyond Google (or Wikipedia)

Doing author research online can be really hard. The first few (or several) pages of Google results are often full of hits from online book vendors, genealogy charts, or, sad to say, Web sites that tend to all say the same thing. And while some Wikipedia articles can be really informative, others can be really sketchy or biased. A variety of techniques to search for more in-depth articles are available.

– **Think about your search terms**
– Try combining various terms such as "interview" or "article" along with the author name (i.e. "Douglas Adams" AND "interview"). Putting the author's name in quotation marks will also tell the search engine to keep the names together (so you don't end up with hits for every "Ursula" when all you wanted was "Ursula Le Guin").
– **Look for links on Web sites**
– Even so-so Web sites or Wikipedia entries can provide links to really great ones. Science fiction association and journal Web sites are often especially helpful for this (i.e. *Locus*). Author Web sites can also be a great source.
– **Check reference books** for recommended links (this also works for finding books and articles!).

- **Check an index**
- Many indexes are starting to include Web sites, i.e., the Modern Language Bibliography (MLA) and Annual Biography of English Language and Literature (ABELL).

---

**Evaluating What You Find**

Anyone can post a Web site, and (almost) anyone can edit a Wikipedia entry. Even books aren't always trustworthy. So as you do research, consider these factors:

- **Currency**

How old is the information? Does it matter? Currency tends to be more important for authors who are still alive (and publishing).

- **Authority**

Who wrote the book, or created the Web site? What makes them qualified to do so? Do they list credentials? When in doubt, check to see if you can find the same information in at least two other sources (this is also known as "triangulation").

- **Point of View**

A publisher's Web site and a *Locus* article may have very different points of view. Publisher sites are generally focused on selling books, while Web sites, books, and articles produced by third parties are more likely to be neutral or even critical. Look for sources from a variety of viewpoints.

- **Audience**

Who is the article written for? Who is the Web site produced for? Web sites and articles directed to fans often differ from those directed toward scholars and critics. In general, *scholarly* Web sites and publications tend to be more focused, and specialized. They may also assume prior knowledge of the author and their books.

---

## *What To Do If the Web Site Links Don't Work*

Every effort has been made to ensure that the Web site links included are current, but Web site URLs do often change over time. If you should come across any URL that doesn't work, try the following:

- First, try a different Web browser. Some pages won't work in particular browsers.

– Next, try looking up the title of the page on the Internet search engine such as www.google.com. Google also caches sites, so try the cache link if the current link doesn't work.
– If it's a page from a publisher's Web site, try doing an internal search in the Web site (publishers have a habit of rearranging their sites and URLs every so often).
– Finally, try looking up the nonworking URL in the Internet Archive (www.archive.org. Last visited May 30, 2007), an online archive for both active and obsolete Web sites. The Archive doesn't have every page that's ever been online, but it has a large number of them.

# Some Notes about the Text

The following major award winners are noted in each author entry:

**Hugo**　　Hugo Awards, Science Fiction Achievement Award, given annually by the World Science Fiction Society (WSFS)

**Nebula**　Nebula Awards, annual ballot of the Science Fiction Writers of America to choose the best novel, novella, novelette, and short story

**Locus Poll**　Locus Poll Awards, presented to winners of *Locus Magazine*'s annual readers' poll

**Tiptree**　The James Tiptree, Jr. Award, panel of judges select "science fiction or fantasy that explores and expands the roles of women and men.... "

**BSF**　　British Science Fiction Awards, presented annually by the British Science Fiction Association (BSFA)

For more details about the history of these awards, and the constituency of the voters who decide the winners, see the **Major Awards** section in the Appendix.

The following abbreviations are used for sources cited in *Encyclopedias and Handbooks* and *Bibliography* headings:

**ARB**　　*Alpha Ralpha Boulevard*. http://www.catch22.com/SF/ARB/.

**AW**　　Barron, Neil. *Anatomy of Wonder*: 5th edition

**BW**　　*Books and Writers*. http://www.kirjasto.sci.fi/wmiller.htm.

**CA**　　*Contemporary Authors*, Original volumes

| | |
|---|---|
| **CAAS** | *Contemporary Authors, Autobiography series* |
| **CANR** | *Contemporary Authors*, New Revision |
| **ESF** | Clute and Nicholls. *The Encyclopedia of Science Fiction.* |
| **FF** | *Fantastic Fiction.* 2003. http://www.fantasticfiction.co.uk/. |
| **MSSF** | Magill, *Survey of Science Fiction Literature.* |
| **NNDB** | *Notable Names DataBase* http://nndb.com/. |
| **SCFW** | *Science Fiction Writers* |
| **SFAN** | *SciFan* http://www.scifan.com/. |
| **SFW** | *St. James Guide to Science Fiction Writers* |
| **WS** | Willick, George C. *Spacelight* http://www.gcwillick.com/Spacelight/. |

*All URLs in the Science Fiction Research Guide were checked during April 2008.*

# Douglas Adams (1952–2001)

*...although it has many omissions, contains much that is apocryphal, or at least wildly inaccurate, it scores over the older, more pedestrian work in two important ways. First, it is slightly cheaper, and second it has the words 'DON'T PANIC' inscribed in large, friendly letters on the cover.*
        —*The Hitch-Hiker's Guide to the Galaxy (1978)*

## Biography

Douglas Adams' classic, *The Hitch-Hiker's Guide to the Galaxy*, first appeared as a BBC Radio 4 series in March 1978. It became a series of best-selling novels, a TV series, record album, computer games, several stage adaptations, and a Hollywood movie. The five books in the "Trilogy" have sold over 15 million copies in Britain, the United States, and Australia and was a best seller in many other languages.

Douglas Noel Adams was born in Cambridge, England, and grew up in Middlesex. In addition to *The Hitch-Hiker's Guide to the Galaxy*, he was involved as writer, script editor, and sometimes performer on TV series such as *Monty Python's Flying Circus* and *Doctor Who*. While living in Santa Barbara, California with his wife and young daughter, and working on the screenplay of the long-awaited movie version of *H2G2*, Adams died on May 11, 2001, suddenly, of a heart attack.

ALIENS; ARTIFICIAL INTELLIGENCE; END OF THE WORLD; FANTASTIC VOYAGES; HUMOR AND SATIRE

## Major Works

*Novels*

The Hitch-Hiker's Guide "Trilogy:" *The Hitch-Hiker's Guide to the Galaxy* (1979), *The Restaurant at the End of the Universe* (1980), *Life, the Universe and Everything* (1982), *So Long, and Thanks for All the Fish* (1984), *Mostly Harmless* (1992)
Dirk Gently novels: *Dirk Gently's Holistic Detective Agency* (1987), *The Long, Dark Tea-Time of the Soul* (1988)

## Collections

*The Salmon of Doubt: Hitchhiking the Galaxy One Last Time.* New York: Ballantine, 2003. A posthumous collection of previously uncollected essays, interviews, and fiction by and about DNA. Includes a 2001 interview with *The American Atheist*, "A Lament for Douglas Adams," by Richard Dawkins (*The Guardian*, May 2001) and short story "The Private Life of Genghis Khan," cowritten with Monty Python member Graham Chapman in 1975.

## Other Important Works

*Douglas Adams at the BBC* (2004) Three-disc BBC Audiobook set covering DNA projects, that appeared on radio or television between 1974 and 2001.
*The Hitchhiker's Guide to the Galaxy* (2005) Screenplay of the Touchstone Pictures film, begun by Adams and completed by Garth Jennings and Karey Kirkpatrick.
"Hyperland" (1990) http://jonhs.net/freemovies/hyperland.htm. BBC documentary on the early internet.
*Last Chance to See* (1992, with Mark Carwardine)
*The Original Hitchhiker Radio Scripts* (1995)
"Parrots, the Universe and Everything" (2001) http://www.uctv.tv/search-details.asp?showID=5779. A talk given by Adams at the University of California, Santa Barbara, shortly before his death.

# Research Sources

*Encyclopedias and Handbooks:* **AW, CA, CAAS, CANR, ESF, NNDB, SFW, WS**

*Bibliographies:* **ARB, FF, SFAN**

## Biographies and Interviews

*Locus Online.* June 2001. Obituary and Appreciations by (among others) Arthur C. Clarke, Neil Gaiman, and Gregory Benford. http://www.locusmag.com/2001/News/News05a.html.
Simpson, M.J. *Hitchhiker: A Biography of Douglas Adams.* Boston, MA: Justin Charles, 2005.
Swaim, Don. *Wired for Books.* WOUB/Ohio University. Audio Interviews with Douglas Adams: 1983 and 1989. http://wiredforbooks.org/douglasadams/.
Webb, Nick. *Wish You Were Here: The Official Biography of Douglas Adams.* New York: Ballantine, 2005.
Wroe, Nicholas. Obituary. *The Guardian*, May 15, 2001. http://books.guardian.co.uk/news/articles/0,6109,490971,00.html.

## Criticism and Readers' Guides

Gaiman, Neil. *Don't Panic: Douglas Adams & The Hitchhiker's Guide to the Galaxy.* London: Titan, 2005.

Hanlon, Michael. *The Science of The Hitchhiker's Guide to the Galaxy*. Basingstoke (UK): Macmillan, 2005.

Johanson, MaryAnn. "Novel Approach: How Douglas Adams Got Defanged by Hollywood." *Internet Review of Science Fiction*. May 2005. http://www.irosf.com/q/zine/article/10148.

Yeffeth, Glenn, ed. *The Anthology at the End of the Universe: Leading Science Fiction Authors on Douglas Adams' The Hitchhiker's Guide to the Galaxy*. Dallas, TX: Benbella, 2005.

## Web Sites

*Douglas Adams.com*. Official Web site, including links to other DNA projects, such as the computer game *Starship Titanic*. http://www.douglasadams.com/.

*HitchhikerFan.com*. Jake Russell. June 2007. Fan Web site dedicated to various incarnations of the series. http://www.hhgttonline.com/.

*Hitchhikers Guide to the Galaxy*. BBC Radio 4 Web site celebrating all things *H2G2*. Includes extensive information about the original radio broadcast, as well as current versions of the saga. Link to *Hitchhikers Guide to the Future*, a radio series by DNA on future technology recorded in Spring 2001. http://www.bbc.co.uk/radio4/hitchhikers/.

*The Hitchhiker's Guide Project*. Sean Connor. May 2006. Complete encyclopedic reference of all the characters, ships, planets, species, and other minutiae that appear in H2G2. http://hhgproject.org/.

*Life, DNA and H2G2*. Nicolas Botti. June 2006. A comprehensive fan Web site covering biographical information about DNA and his work, H2G2 in all of its incarnations from radio to movie. http://douglasadams.info/.

*Vogon.com: The HHGTT*. Patrick Hubbard. September 2004. Amusing H2G2 tribute Web site, very much in the spirit of the Guide. Features Vogon poetry and links to an online encyclopedia of H2G2 lore, presented as a fully interactive, "handheld" Guide. http://www.vogon.com/.

*ZZ9 Plural Z Alpha*. Official Web site of the Hitchhiker's Guide to the Galaxy Appreciation Society. http://www.zz9.org/.

**If you enjoyed Douglas Adams...**
Douglas Adams graduated from writing classic BBC comedies like *Monty Python's Flying Circus* to the inspired madness of *The Hitchhikers Guide to the Galaxy*. Adam's humor is clever, absurd, and, particularly in the later volumes of the five-volume "trilogy," betrays his serious concerns with Life, the Universe, and Everything.

**Then you might like...**
*Harry Harrison*. The author of the "Stainless Steel Rat" novels, the tongue in cheek adventures of Slippery Jim diGriz, con-man, and the 25th century's most famous outlaw. Harrison also wrote and cowrote various novels in the series "Bill

the Galactic Hero," a non-too-gentle spoof of writers like Heinlein and gung-ho sf like *Starship Troopers*.

*Grant Naylor*. Based on the popular 1990s BBC sf comedy, like H2G2, the "Red Dwarf" series mines the comic potential of interstellar craziness. Written by "Grant Naylor" (a dual entity, consisting of writers Rob Grant and Doug Naylor), they may not be for the delicately minded, as most of the humor is scurrilous, scatological, unhygienic, or all of the above.

*Robert Sheckley* is notable for his black humor and social satire, and the unsettling grain of truth within the laugh, in novels such as *Immortality Inc.* (1958) and *Mindswap* (1966). Reality has almost caught up with some of his "outlandish" ideas—such as the TV game show in which the contestants win big cash prizes for evading competitors who are trying to kill them ("The Prize of Peril," 1958).

*John Sladek*. According to the *Encyclopedia of Science Fiction*, "... the most formally inventive, the funniest, and very nearly the most melancholy of modern U.S. sf writers." His novels include *The Muller Fokker Effect* (1970), *Tik Tok* (1983), *Roderick* (1980) and *The Lunatics of Terra* (1984).

*Kurt Vonnegut*. The ultimate sf humorist who, like Adams, combined inspired lunacy with themes that reflect the real-life concerns and challenges of the late 20th Century in novels like *Slaughterhouse-five* and *The Sirens of Titan*.

# Brian W. Aldiss (1925–   )

> *... she reached out and changed the wavelength of her windows. The garden faded; in its place, the city center rose by her left hand, full of crowding people, blowboats, and buildings (but she kept the sound down). She remained alone. An overcrowded world is the ideal place in which to be lonely.*
> —*"Super-Toys Last All Summer Long" (1969)*

## Biography

In a genre which is generously endowed with prolific authors, insightful critics, and writers with strong opinions and big ideas, Brian Aldiss is a stand-out. In addition to his own novels and stories, Aldiss was the editor of anthologies that helped to shape sf's New Wave of the late 1950s and 1960s; after sixty years in the business, his critical essays and histories continue to influence the genre.

Brian Wilson Aldiss was born in Norfolk, England. He ended an unhappy childhood by joining the Royal Signals Corps at the age of 18 and served in Burma and Sumatra—lush, exotic landscapes that were to influence many of his best works. Among his many honors and awards, he received an OBE (Order of the British Empire) in the Queen's Birthday Honours List of 2005 for his ongoing contribution to British literature.

ALIEN WORLDS; ENTROPY; FAR FUTURE; GOTHIC SF; NEW WAVE

## Major Works

*Novels*

*Non-stop* (1958) USA: Starship
*Hothouse* (1962—aka *The Long Afternoon of Earth*): fixup consisting of novellas
　*Hothouse* (**Hugo**), *Nomansland*, *Undergrowth*, *Timberline,* and *Evergreen*
*Greybeard* (1964)
*Report on Probability A* (1968)
*Barefoot in the Head* (1969)
*Frankenstein Unbound* (1973)
The Helliconia Trilogy: *Helliconia Spring* (1982—**BSF**), *Helliconia Summer* (1983),
　*Helliconia Winter* (1985) **BSF**
*White Mars* (2000, with Roger Penrose)

*Collections*

*Man in His Time: The Best Science Fiction of Brian Aldiss* (1988). Cornwall, UK:
　House of Stratus, 2001.
Other Aldiss collections are *Moment of Eclipse* (1970—**BSF**), *Common Clay: 20-Odd*
　*Stories* (1996), *Supertoys Last All Summer Long and Other Stories of Future Time*
　(2001), and *Cultural Breaks* (2005).

*Short Stories*

"Who Can Replace a Man?" (1958)
"The Saliva Tree" (1965) **Nebula**
"Super-Toys Last All Summer Long" (1969) http://www.wired.com/wired/archive/5.
　01/ffsupertoys.html.

*Other Important Works*

*Billion Year Spree* (1973) **BSF** The revised and updated edition, *Trillion Year Spree:*
　*The History of Science Fiction* (1986, with David Wingrove) was also a winner
　of the **Hugo** and **Locus Poll** awards for nonfiction.
*Bury My Heart at W. H. Smith's* (1990)
*The Detached Retina: Aspects of SF and Fantasy* (1995). Includes essays such as
　"Between Privy and Universe: Aldous Huxley (1894–1963)," "The Downward
　Journey: Orwell's *1984*," and "Sturgeon—The Cruelty of the Gods."
*Hell's Cartographers: Some Personal Histories of Science Fiction Writers* (1975,
　edited with Harry Harrison)
"Oh No, Not More Sci-Fi!" *PMLA: Publications of the Modern Language Association
　of America.* 119 (2004): 509–512.

"On the Origin of Species: Mary Shelley." In James Gunn and Matthew Candelaria, eds., *Speculations on Speculation: Theories of Science Fiction*. Lanham, MD: Scarecrow, 2005, 163–204.

"The Sky's No Limit." *Guardian Unlimited*, July 8, 2006. http://books.guardian.co.uk/departments/sciencefiction/story/0,1815451,00.html.

*The Twinkling of an Eye: My Life as an Englishman* (1999)

"Why are Science Fiction's Best Writers So Neglected?" *Times* (London), November 23, 2007. http://entertainment.timesonline.co.uk/tol/arts_and_entertainment/books/article2930342.ece.

## Research Sources

*Encyclopedias and Handbooks:* **AW, CA, CANR, ESF, MSSF, NNDB, SFW**

*Bibliographies:* **ARB, FF, SFAN**

Aldiss, Margaret. The Work of Brian W. Aldiss: An Annotated Bibliography and Guide. San Bernardino, CA: Borgo, 1992.

### Biographies and Interviews

Auden, Sandy. "Aldiss and More: An Interview with Brian Aldiss." *SF Site*. 2005. http://www.sfsite.com/08b/saba206.htm./

Darlington, Andrew. "A Report on Probability AI: The Brian Aldiss Connection." *The Zone Online*. (No date). http://www.zone-sf.com/brianaldiss.html.

Hunt, Stephen. "Brian Aldiss: The Master of Glacial Helliconia." *SF Crowsnest*. January 2003. http://www.sfcrowsnest.com/sfnews2/03_jan/news0103_1.shtml.

*Locus Online.* "Above Ground." January 2008. http://www.locusmag.com/2008/Issue01_Aldiss.html.

Swaim, Don. *Wired for Books*. WOUB/Ohio University. Audio Interviews with Brian Aldiss: 1984 and 1986. http://wiredforbooks.org/brianaldiss/.

### Criticism and Readers' Guides

Gillespie, Bruce. "A Valediction Forbidding Melancholy: Aldiss and the Far Future." In Damien Broderick, ed., *Earth is But a Star: Excursions through Science Fiction to the Far Future*. Crawley: University of Western Australia Press, 2001, 184–196.

Henighan, Tom. *Brian W. Aldiss*. New York: Twayne, 1999.

Jameson, Frederic. "Generic Discontinuities in SF: Brian Aldiss' *Starship*." *Science Fiction Studies*. 1 (1973): 57–68. http://www.depauw.edu/sfs/backissues/2/jameson2art.htm.

Ruddick, Nicholas. "The Brood of Mary: Brian Aldiss, Frankenstein, and Science Fiction." In C.W. Sullivan III. The Dark Fantastic. Westport, CT: Greenwood, 1997, 77–84.

## Web Sites

*BrianAldiss.org*. Official Web site. http://www.brianwaldiss.org/.
Brian W. Aldiss Archive. University of Liverpool Library. Collection of material spanning the years 1943–1995. Fully listed and featuring an online Finding Aid, which includes further biographical information. http://www.sfhub.ac.uk/Aldiss. htm.

# Poul Anderson (1926–2001)

*We will not be gods, or even guides. But we will – some of us – be givers of opportunity. We will see that evil does not flourish too strongly, and that hope and chance happen when they are most needed . . .*

*—Brain Wave (1954)*

## Biography

Poul William Anderson was born in Bristol, Pennsylvania and grew up in Texas, Denmark, and Minnesota. President of Science Fiction and Fantasy Writers of America in 1972, and a founding member of the Society for Creative Anachronism, Anderson also wrote fantasy novels, often collaborating with his wife, Karen. He died on July 31, 2001 at his home in Orinda, California.

Nominated many times for every important sf award available, he was the winner of three Nebula awards and seven Hugos. He was best known for larger-than-life adventure stories, which achieve their impact through a solid, believable grounding in science and are enhanced by his wide-ranging knowledge of Scandinavian languages, literature, and history. Anderson's predominant themes are personal liberty, and the individual's quest to triumph over adversity—or die trying.

GALACTIC EMPIRES; HARD SF; HUMOR & SATIRE; IMMORTALITY; LIBERTARIAN SF; TIME TRAVEL

## Major Works

*Novels*

*Brain Wave* (1954)
*The High Crusade* (1961)
*Tau Zero* (1970)
*There Will Be Time* (1973)
*The Boat of a Million Years* (1979)
*The Stars Are Also Fire* (1995) **Prometheus**
*Genesis* (2000)
The Technic History sequence: Dominic Flandry novels, beginning with *We Claim These Stars* (1959) and *Earthman, Go Home!* (1960)

Nicholas Van Rijn novels: Including *War of the Wing-Men* (1958), *Trader to the Stars* (1969)

Time Patrol series: Including *Time Patrol* (1955) and *Brave to Be a King* (1959)

The Hoka series (with Gordon R. Dickson): Humorous sf, including *Earthman's Burden* (1957) and *Hoka!* (1983)

## Collections

*Going for Infinity.* New York: Tor, 2003. Includes **Hugo** and **Nebula** award winning stories "The Saturn Game" (1981), "Goat Song" (1972), and "The Queen of Air and Darkness" (1971, also **Locus Poll**).

*To Outlive Eternity and Other Stories.* Riverdale, NY: Baen, 2007.

## Notable Short Stories

"The Longest Voyage" (1960) **Hugo**
"No Truce with Kings" (1964) **Hugo**
"The Sharing of Flesh" (1969) **Hugo**
"Hunter's Moon" (1979) **Hugo**

## Other Important Works

"The Creation of Imaginary Worlds: The World Builder's Handbook and Pocket Companion." In *Writing Science Fiction & Fantasy*, edited by The Staff of *Analog & Isaac Asimov's Science Fiction Magazine*. New York: St. Martin's Griffin, 1993, 105–128.

"On Thud and Blunder." *Articles on Writing.* January 4, 2005. Science Fiction and Fantasy Writer's of America. http://www.sfwa.org/writing/thud.htm.

"Star Flights and Fantasies: Sagas Still to Come." *The Craft of Science Fiction*, edited by Reginald Bretnor. New York: Harper&Row, 1976, 22–36.

# Research Sources

*Encyclopedias and Handbooks:* **AW, CA, CAAS, CANR, ESF, MSSF, NNDB, SFW, WS**

*Bibliographies:* **ARB, FF, SFAN**

Benson Jr., Gordon and Phil Stephensen-Payne. *Poul Anderson, Myth-master and Wonder-weaver: A Working Bibliography.* San Bernardino, CA: Borgo, 1990.

## Biographies and Interviews

Barrett, David V. Obituary. *Guardian Online.* August 6, 2001. http://books.guardian.co.uk/news/articles/0,532151,00.html.

*Locus Online.* Interview. April 1997. http://www.locusmag.com/1997/Issues/04/Anderson.html.

*Locus Online*. SWFA obituary and tributes. September 2001. http://www.locusmag. com/2001/News/News08a.html.

Tenn, William. "Poul Anderson." In *Dancing Naked: The Unexpurgated William Tenn*. Framingham, MA: New England Science Fiction Association, 2004. http://dpsinfo.com/williamtenn/poulanderson.html.

### Criticism and Readers' Guides

Blish, James. "Poul Anderson: The Enduring Explosion." In *The Tale That Wags the God*. Chicago, IL: Advent, 1987. 86–92.

*Halfway Down the Danube*. "The PA System is Broken." March 3, 2005. http://www. bookcase.com/~claudia/mt/archives/000585.html. Intelligent blog essay, which pinpoints weaknesses of style and plotting in Anderson's work.

Hellekson, Karen. "Poul Anderson's Time Patrol as Anti-Alternate History." In *The Alternate History: Refiguring Historical Time*. Kent, OH: Kent State University Press, 2001. 97–107.

McDavid, Glenn T. "Religion in the Fiction of Poul Anderson." Radio Free Thulcandra. 1989. http://home.comcast.net/~gmcdavid/html_dir/anderson.html.

Miesel, Sandra. *Against Time's Arrow: The High Crusade of Poul Anderson*. San Bernardino, CA: Borgo, 1978.

### Web Sites

*Baen Books Web Site*. Features excerpts from *Time Patrol* (1955) and *Virgin Planet* (1957), the 1967 short story "To Outlive Eternity" and *Hokas Pokas!* (2000), a compilation of Hoka stories. http://www.baen.com/author_catalog.asp?author= panderson.

# Isaac Asimov (1920–1992)

*A robot may not injure a human being, or, through inaction, allow a human being to come to harm. . . .*

—*The First Law of Robotics, "Runaround" (1942)*

## Biography

Isaac Asimov's family emigrated to Brooklyn, New York, from Russia when he was three years old. After acquiring a PhD in biochemistry from Columbia University, he was a life-long member of the faculty of the Boston University School of Medicine, although his position was nonteaching after 1958. (His writing income had already exceeded his academic salary.) Asimov died on April 6, 1992, having contracted HIV from a blood transfusion he received during a heart bypass operation.

Asimov made a permanent mark on sf conventions with his "Three Laws of Robotics" (in his 1942 story "Runaround"); his story "Night Fall" (1941) has been acclaimed as the "best sf short story ever written," (SFWA, 1968). For many years the popular voice of science fiction, he was the author of nearly 500 books; some volume by Isaac Asimov is represented in every category of the Dewey Decimal System, except philosophy.

ANDROIDS, CYBORGS & ROBOTS; GALACTIC EMPIRES; MARS, MOON & THE PLANETS; SPACE OPERA

## Major Works

*Novels*

The Galactic Empire series: *Pebble in the Sky* (1950), *The Stars, Like Dust* (1951), *The Currents of Space* (1952)

The Robot Series: beginning with the collection *I, Robot* (1950)

The Foundation Series (**Hugo, Best All-Time Series 1966**): *Foundation* (1951), *Foundation and Empire* (1952), *Second Foundation* (1953), *Foundation's Edge* (1982—**Hugo, Locus Poll**), *Foundation and Earth* (1986), *Prelude to Foundation* (1988) and *Forward the Foundation* (1993)

The Lucky Starr series (as Paul French): Beginning with *David Starr: Space Ranger* (1952) and concluding with *Lucky Starr and the Rings of Saturn* (1958)

*The End of Eternity* (1955)

*Fantastic Voyage* (1966)

*The Gods Themselves* (1972) **Hugo, Locus Poll, Nebula**

*Nemesis* (1989)

*Collections*

*The Complete Stories, Volume 1*. New York: Doubleday, 1990. Fifty stories, combining previous collections *Earth Is Room Enough* (1957), *Nine Tomorrows* (1959), and *Nightfall and Other Stories* (1969).

*The Complete Stories, Volume 2*. New York: Doubleday, 1992. Stories from later collections, such as *The Bicentennial Man and Other Stories* (1976).

*Gold: The Final Science Fiction Collection*. New York: Harper Prism, 1995.

*Notable Short Stories*

"Robbie" (1940)

"Nightfall" (1941)

"The Bicentennial Man" (1976) **Hugo, Locus Poll, Nebula**

"Robot Dreams" (1986) **Locus Poll**

"Gold" (1991) **Hugo**

## Other Important Works

*Asimov's Galaxy: Reflections on Science Fiction* (1989)

*It's Been a Good Life* (2002) Edited by Judith Jeppson Asimov; this is a condensed and reedited version of Asimov's three previous volumes of autobiography—*In Memory Yet Green* (1979), *In Joy Still Felt* (1980), and *I, Asimov: A Memoir* (1994)—and excerpts from Asimov's diaries and personal letters.

"Mr. Spock is Dreamy!" *TV Guide.* April 29, 1967. http://www.geocities.com/Area51/Lair/2777/misc/mr_spock.html.

*Our Angry Earth* (1991, with Frederik Pohl)

"The 'Threat' of Creationism." In Ashley Montagu, ed., *Science and Creationism.* New York: Oxford University Press, 1984, 182–193. http://www.stephenjaygould.org/ctrl/azimov_creationism.html.

## Research Sources

*Encyclopedias and Handbooks:* **AW, BW, CA, CAAS, CANR, ESF, MSSF, NNDB, SFW, WS**

*Bibliographies:* **ARB, FF, SFAN**

Green, Scott E. *Isaac Asimov: An Annotated Bibliography of the Asimov Collection at Boston University.* Westport, CT: Greenwood, 1995.

Main, Michael. "Isaac Asimov Fiction Page." 2000. University of Colorado. http://www.storypilot.com/sf/asimov1.html.

### Biographies and Interviews

Freedman, Carl Howard. *Conversations with Isaac Asimov.* Jackson: University Press of Mississippi, 2005.

"Robot Maker: A Talk with the Late Isaac Asimov." *Fresh Air from WHYY.* National Public Radio. September 9, 1987. http://www.npr.org/templates/story/story.php?storyId=3461066.

Swaim, Don. *Wired For Books.* WOUB/Ohio University. Audio Interview, 1987. http://wiredforbooks.org/isaacasimov/.

White, Michael. *Isaac Asimov: A Life of the Grand Master of Science Fiction.* New York: Carroll & Graf, 2005.

### Criticism and Readers' Guides

Abrahm, Paul A. and Stuart Kenter. "Tik-Tok and the Three Laws of Robotics." *Science Fiction Studies.* 5 (1975): 67–80. http://www.depauw.edu/sfs/backissues/14/abrahm14art.htm.

Chastain, Ben B. "Beryllium, Thiotimoline, and Pate de Fois Gras: Chemistry in the Science Fiction of Isaac Asimov." In Jack H. Stocker, ed., *Chemistry and Science Fiction.* Washington, DC: American Chemical Society, 1998, 77–90.

Gunn, James. *Isaac Asimov: The Foundations of Science Fiction.* New York: Oxford University Press, 1996.

Hull, Elizabeth Ann. "Asimov: Man Thinking." In C.W. Sullivan, ed., *Science Fiction for Young Readers.* Westport, CT: Greenwood, 1993, 47–64.

Lee, Tony and Jeff Young. "In the Dark: Isaac Asimov's 'Nightfall': The Ultimate Fable of Millennial Anxiety?" *The Zone.* 9 (Summer 2000).

Munteanu, Nina. "Unexpected Protocol: A Critique of the I, Robot Book and Motion Picture." *Strange Horizons.* February 14, 2005. http://www.strangehorizons.com/2005/20050214/i-robot-a.shtml.

### Web Sites

*Asimov Online.* Official Web site. http://www.asimovonline.com/.

*Laws Unsafe.* July 2004. Singularity Institute for Artificial Intelligence, Inc. Essays by various sf writers and researchers in the theory and practice of robot development and design, using Asimov's Three Laws as a starting point. http://www.asimovlaws.com/articles/.

*Asimov Vault.* Roland Saekow. April 2007. A fan Web site with biography, book reviews and links. http://homepage.mac.com/pockyrevolution/asimov/index.htm.

*Foundation Gallery.* Slawek Wojtowicz. June 2004. Fan Web site focusing on the novels and short stories of the Foundation Series. http://www.slawcio.com/foundation/cover2.html.

*Timeline for the Robots and Foundation Universe.* Sikander Iqbal. May 2003. Painstaking chronology of events in Foundation Series. http://www.sikander.org/foundation.php.

*The Stars like Dust.* Tobbe Hvornum. August 2001. Enthusiastic and beautifully illustrated fan Web site. http://surf.to/the-stars.

# Margaret Atwood (1939–   )

*There is more than one kind of freedom.... Freedom to and freedom from. In the days of anarchy, it was freedom to. Now you are being given freedom from. Don't underrate it.*

*—The Handmaid's Tale (1986)*

## Biography

Margaret Eleanor Atwood was born in Ottawa, Canada. Her father was an entomologist, and much of her childhood was spent in the backwoods of northern Quebec, accompanying him as he did his research. During the late 1960s and early 1970s she began to write award-winning poetry and fiction; following postgraduate work at Radcliffe College, she taught at various universities in Canada, and at New York University, where she was Berg Professor of English.

Atwood is the author of more than thirty books—novels, short stories, poetry, literary criticism, social history, and books for children—and, while she has been very resistant to the labeling of her speculative fiction as science fiction, she has more than once put classic sf conventions to good literary use. Margaret Atwood lives in Canada with her husband and daughter, dividing her time between Toronto and Pelee Island, Ontario.

APOCALYPSE AND AFTER; DYSTOPIAS; GENETIC ENGINEERING & CLONING; FEMINISM

## Major Works

*Novels*

*The Handmaid's Tale* (1986)
*The Blind Assassin* (2000)
*Oryx and Crake* (2003)

*Other Important Works*

"'Aliens have taken the place of angels': Why We Need Science Fiction." *The Guardian.* July 17, 2005. http://arts.guardian.co.uk/fridayreview/story/0,1507718,00.html.
"For God and Gilead." *The Guardian.* March 22, 2003. http://arts.guardian.co.uk/features/story/0,919211,00.html.
"*The Handmaid's Tale* and *Oryx and Crake* in Context." *PMLA: Publications of the Modern Language Association of America.* 119 (2004): 513–517.
"My Life in Science Fiction/Ma Vie et la Science-Fiction." Cycnos. 22 (2005): http://revel.unice.fr/cycnos/document.html?id=616.
"Oryx and Crake Revealed." Lecture, MIT World. April 4, 2004. Massachusetts Institute of Technology. http://mitworld.mit.edu/video/196/.

## Research Sources

*Encyclopedias and Handbooks:* **AW, CA, BW, CANR, ESF, NNDB**

*Bibliographies:* **FF, SFAN**

Alexander, Lynn. "A Working Bibliography." *Women Writers: Magic, Mysticism, and Mayhem.* Spring 1999. University of Tennessee Martin. http://www.utm.edu/staff/lalexand/350/talebib.htm.
Friedman, Thomas B. "Internet Resources on Margaret Atwood and Her Works." December 10, 2001. http://www.cariboo.bc.ca/atwood/internet.htm.

*Biographies and Interviews*

Ingersoll, Earl G., ed. *Waltzing Again: New & Selected Conversations with Margaret Atwood.* Princeton, NJ: *Ontario Review*, 2006.

Potts, Robert. "Light in the Wilderness." *The Guardian.* April 26, 2003. http://books. guardian.co.uk/departments/generalfiction/story/0,6000,943485,00.html.

Richards, Linda. Interview. *January Magazine.* November 2000. http://www. januarymagazine.com/profiles/atwood.html.

Snell, Marilyn. "Interview: Margaret Atwood." *Mother Jones.* July/August 1997. Foundation for National Progress. http://www.motherjones.com/arts/qa/1997/07/ visions.html.

## Criticism and Readers' Guides

Bloom, Harold, ed. *Margaret Atwood: The Handmaid's Tale.* Philadelphia, PA: Chelsea House, 2003.

Bouson, J. Brooks. "'It's game over forever': Atwood's Satiric Vision of a Bioengineered Posthuman Future in *Oryx and Crake*." *Journal of Commonwealth Literature.* 39(3) (2004): 139–156.

Brians, Paul. "*The Handmaid's Tale.*" *Study Guides.* Washington State University. September 24, 2004. http://wsu.edu/~brians/science_fiction/handmaid.html.

Dunning, Stephen. "Margaret Atwood's *Oryx and Crake*: The Terror of the Therapeutic." *Canadian Literature.* 186 (Fall 2005): 86–101.

Gussow, Mel. "Atwood's Dystopian Warning." *New York Times*, June 24, 2003. Profile of Atwood, and her work on the publication of *Oryx and Crake*. Particular focus on Atwood's view that *Oryx and Crake* is not sf, but realistic speculation.

Howells, Coral Ann. "Margaret Atwood's Dystopian Visions: *The Handmaid's Tale* and *Oryx and Crake*." In *The Cambridge Companion to Margaret Atwood.* Cambridge: Cambridge University Press, 2006. 161–175.

Ingersoll, Earl G. "Survival in Margaret Atwood's *Oryx and Crake*." *Extrapolation* 45 (2004): 162–175.

Neuman, Shirley. "'Just a Backlash': Margaret Atwood, Feminism, and *The Handmaid's Tale*." *University of Toronto Quarterly.* 75 (2006): 857–868.

Oates, Joyce Carol. "Margaret Atwood's Tale." *The New York Review of Books.* November 2, 2006. http://www.nybooks.com/articles/19495.

Wilson, Sharon R. "Margaret Atwood and Popular Culture: *The Blind Assassin* and Other Novels." *Journal of American Culture.* 25, Nos. 3/ 4 (2002): 270–275.

## Web Sites

*Margaret Atwood Reference Site.* March 2007. Official Web site. http://www.owtoad. com/.

*Contemporary Women Writers.* Anniina Jokinen. January 2007. Margaret Atwood section created to make sense of the chaos of Web links available, this extensive and extremely well-designed Web site contains biographical information and links to excerpts, synopses, essays, and reviews. http://www.luminarium.org/ contemporary/atwood/atwoodnovels.htm

*Oryx and Crake.* British publishers Web site, which includes excerpts from reviews and a full-length essay by Margaret Atwood, "Perfect Storms: Writing *Oryx and Crake.*" http://www.oryxandcrake.co.uk/.

*Readers' Companion.* May 2006. Random House. Includes an interview with Atwood about the writing of *The Handmaid's Tale*, and suggested topics for contemplation or group discussion. http://www.randomhouse.com/resources/bookgroup/handmaidstale_bgc.html.

### If you enjoyed Margaret Atwood . . .

Famously resistant to having any of her works labeled "science fiction," in recent years, Margaret Atwood seems to have made her peace with the genre. Her sf is notable for a strong literary style, and sharp observations on the current state and future possibilities of the world, using the time-honored tropes of speculative fiction.

### Then you might like . . .

*Anthony Burgess.* Like Atwood, the author of sf classics like *A Clockwork Orange* and *1985* was a mainstream author with a wide range and sharp intelligence, whose speculative and near-future novels are unflinching considerations of big issues such as violence, personal freedom, and the end of all things.

*Thomas M. Disch.* In novels such as *334* and *Camp Concentration*, Disch regularly dealt with the manipulation of the powerless, and reflected the genre's movement away from pulp adventure to stories with more mature and thoughtful themes and content. A poet as well as a mainstream author and critic, Disch is noted for his finely crafted prose.

*Ursula K. Le Guin.* All of her fiction is intelligent and beautifully written and, like Atwood, has a " . . . tradition of challenging deeply held, and poorly reasoned, assumptions . . . " (**NNDB**). In her long career, UKL has tackled the most challenging of sf themes: society (*Always Coming Home*), anarchy (*The Dispossessed*), gender (*The Left Hand of Darkness*), and colonialism (*The Word for World is Forest*).

*Doris Lessing.* Nobel Prize-winning author of the "Canopus in Argos: Archives," a sequence of loosely connected novels that portray future societies, on earth and elsewhere in the galaxy, at different stages of development. The Swedish Academy described her as a writer who " . . . with skepticism, fire and visionary power has subjected a divided civilization to scrutiny."

*George Orwell. Nineteen Eighty-Four* is the classic imaginative take on totalitarianism, to which Atwood's *The Handmaid's Tale* is often compared. Like Atwood, Orwell was a mainstream writer and cultural critic who made use of the tropes of fantasy (*Animal Farm*) and sf to make his readers see how easily the unspeakable could happen.

# J.G. Ballard (1930–   )

*"Being on the moon?" His tired gaze inspected the narrow street of cheap jewelry stores, with its office messengers and lottery touts, the off-duty taxi-drivers leaning against their cars. "It was just like being here."*
                    *—"The Man Who Walked on the Moon" (1985)*

## Biography

James Graham Ballard was born in Shanghai, where he grew up surrounded by luxury. From 1942 to 1945, he and his family were prisoners of the occupying Japanese forces, interned as "enemy aliens." These years of deprivation, uncertainty, and danger—but also a kind of excitement and freedom—form the basis of his autobiographical novel *Empire of the Sun* (1984), and are also reflected in the extremes of his sf works such as *The Atrocity Exhibition* (1969) and *Crash* (1973).

In 1962 he wrote an editorial for the magazine *New Worlds*, "Which Way to Inner Space?" in which he proposed a thematic and stylistic overhaul of the entire science fiction genre, In Ballard's sf, the only alien planet is earth. Recently, he has moved to other genres, rattling the stylistic and narrative cages of the detective story and thriller, as he once did for science fiction.

ECOLOGY; END OF THE WORLD; ENTROPY; NEW WAVE; POP CULTURE; SEX & TABOOS

## Major Works

*Novels*

The Classical Elements ("Global Disaster Quartet"): *The Wind from Nowhere* (1962), *The Drowned World* (1962), *The Burning World* (1965), *The Crystal World* (1966)
*The Atrocity Exhibition* (1969)
*Crash* (1973)
*The Unlimited Dream Company* (1979) **BSF**
*Hello America* (1981)

*Collections*

*The Complete Short Stories of J.G. Ballard*, New York: Picador, 2001. Includes all Ballard short stories from previous collections *Billennium* (1962), *The Terminal Beach* (1964), *Vermilion Sands* (1971), *Memories of the Space Age* (1988), and *Myths of the Near Future* (1994).

*Notable Short Stories*

"Billennium" (1961)
"The Assassination of John F. Kennedy Considered as a Downhill Motor Race" (1973)
    http://www.evergreenreview.com/102/fiction/preduo.html.

## Other Important Works

*Miracles of Life: Shanghai to Shepperton* (2008)
*A User's Guide To The Millennium* (1997) Includes essays on film, literature, history, and popular culture, on Ballard's own writing and sf, such as "Which Way to Inner Space?" (*New Worlds*, May 1962) and "From Shanghai to Shepperton" (1992).

# Research Sources

*Encyclopedias and Handbooks:* **AW, CA, CANR, ESF, MSSF, NNDB**
*Bibliographies:* **ARB, FF, SFAN**

Rossi, Umberto. "The Critical Exhibition: The James Graham Ballard Secondary Literature Online Bibliography." *Saggistica di Umberto Rossi*. February 2004. http://web.tiscali.it/ausonia/saggistica/jgb_bibliography.html.
McGrath, Rick. "The J.G. Ballard Short Story Bibliography." *The Terminal Collection: J.G. Ballard First&Variant Editions*. http://www.rickmcgrath.com/jgballard/jgb_bibliography.html.

## Biographies and Interviews

Behrens, Richard. "J.G. Ballard." *The Modern Word Scriptorum*. December 2003. http://www.themodernword.com/scriptorium/ballard.html.
*Feltrinelli.it*. Audio Interview. January 2004. Giangiacomo Feltrinelli Editore. http://www.feltrinelli.it/IntervistaInterna?id_int=1242. Italian Web site, but the interview is in English.
Hall, Chris. "Entertaining Violence." *Spike Magazine.com*. January 2004. http://www.spikemagazine.com/0104jgballard.php.
Sellars, Simon. "Rattling Other People's Cages." *The Ballardian*. September 29, 2006. http://www.ballardian.com/rattling-other-peoples-cages-the-jg-ballard-interview/.
Vale, V., ed. *J.G. Ballard: Conversations*. San Francisco: RE/Search, 2005.

## Criticism and Readers' Guides

Bukatman, Scott. "J.G. Ballard and the Mediascape." In *Terminal Identity: The Virtual Subject in Postmodern Science Fiction*. Durham, NC: Duke University Press, 1993. 41–46. http://www.rickmcgrath.com/jgballard/jgb_mediascape.html.
Delville, Michel. *J.G. Ballard*. Plymouth (UK): Northcote House, 1998.
Hall, Chris. "Extreme Metaphor: A Crash Course in the Fiction of J.G. Ballard." *Spike Magazine.com*. June 1997. http://www.spikemagazine.com/0697lard.php.
Luckhurst, Roger. *"The Angle between Two Walls": The Fiction of J.G. Ballard*. Liverpool (UK): Liverpool University Press, 1998.
*Moorcock, Michael. "The Atrocity Exhibition." Fantastic Metropolis*. 15 October 2001. http://www.fantasticmetropolis.com/i/atrocity/.

Nicol, Charles. "J.G. Ballard and the Limits of Mainstream SF." *Science Fiction Studies*. 3 (1976): 150–157. http://www.depauw.edu/sfs/backissues/9/nicol9art. htm.

Rossi, Umberto. "Images from the Disaster Area: An Apocalyptic Reading of Urban Landscapes in Ballard's *The Drowned World* and *Hello America*." *Science Fiction Studies*. 21 (1994): 81–97. http://www.depauw.edu/sfs/backissues/62/rossi62art. htm.

Self, Will. "The Ballard Tradition." *Prospect 90* (September 2003). http://www. prospect-magazine.co.uk/article_details.php?id=5696.

Smith, Jeremy Adam. "Evolution of a Moralist: J.G. Ballard in the 21st Century." *Strange Horizons*. July 19, 2004. http://www.strangehorizons.com/2004/20040719/ ballard.shtml.

Stephenson, Gregory. *Out of the Night and into the Dream: Thematic Study of the Fiction of J.G. Ballard*. Westport, CT: Greenwood, 1991.

### Web Sites

*JG Ballard.com*. Chris Hall. Spike Magazine.com. Not official, but extremely comprehensive. Some links do not work. http://www.jgballard.com/index.php.

*The Ballardian*. Simon Sellars. August 2007. Sleepy Brain Online Magazine. Extremely thorough archive of online resources by and about Ballard, including links to articles and interviews available nowhere else. http:// www.ballardian.com/category/features.

*The Terminal Collection*. Rick McGrath. May 2007. Archive of McGrath's extensive collection of Ballard material, with links to many essays and interviews. http:// www.rickmcgrath.com/jgb.html.

# Iain M. Banks (1954–   )

> . . . It is unusual for us to discover an imperial power-system in space. As a rule, such archaic forms of authority wither long before the relevant species drags itself off the home planet.
>
> —The Player of Games (1988)

## Biography

Iain Menzies Banks was born in Dunfermline, Scotland, the son of an admiralty official and a former professional ice-skater. As "Iain Banks" he has published many popular and respected mainstream novels; as "Iain M. Banks," his sf novels—mostly set in the Culture, a post-scarcity, anarchic/socialist society—offer a complex society, and a richly imagined universe. There is always an interesting dynamic between this "utopia" and the characters who are most often at the center of Banks' stories—the mercenaries, spies, and go-betweens who do the Culture's dirty work, and deeply mistrust the Culture's methods and motives.

Banks' fiction (both science fiction and mainstream) is an expression of his own political views: he is a staunch supporter of Scottish independence, a vocal critic of former Prime Minister Tony Blair and his foreign policy, and a recent convert to the Green Party. Banks currently lives in North Queensferry, on the Firth of Forth.

ALIEN WORLDS; ARTIFICIAL INTELLIGENCE; FAR FUTURE; SPACE OPERA; UTOPIAS

## Major Works

### Novels

The Culture novels: *Consider Phlebas* (1987), *The Player of Games* (1988), *Use of Weapons* (1990), *Excession* (1996—**BSF**), *Inversions* (1998), *Look to Windward* (2000), *Matter* (2008)
*Against a Dark Background* (1993)
*Feersum Endjinn* (1994) **BSF**
*The Algebraist* (2004)

### Collections

*The State of the Art* (1989). San Francisco, CA: Nightshade, 2007. Collection containing both sf and mainstream stories. The title novella and two additional stories are about The Culture.

### Other Important Works

"A Few Notes on the Culture." *Culture Shock.* August 10, 1994. Future Hi. http://www. futurehi.net/phlebas/text/cultnote.html.
*Raw Spirit: In Search of the Perfect Dram.* London: Arrow, 2004. A tour of Scotland and its whisky distilleries.

## Research Sources

### Encyclopedias and Handbooks: **AW, CA, CANR, ESF, NNDB, SFW, WS**

### Bibliographies: **ARB, FF, SFAN**

Virtual Library of Author Information. Editor, Lisa Taylor. *Scottish Writers.* March 21, 2001. Scottish Library Association. http://www.slainte.org.uk/scotwrit/.

### Biographies and Interviews

*Die Welten des Iain Banks.* November 2004. http://homepages.compuserve.de/Mostral/ interviews.html. List of links to transcripts of interviews with various sf journals and magazines from 1995 to 2002.

Gatti, Tom. "It's All in the Game: Interview." *Times Online*. February 17, 2007. http://entertainment.timesonline.co.uk/tol/arts_and_entertainment/.

Hoggard, Liz. "Iain Banks: The Novel Factory." *The Independent* (London) February 18, 2007. http://www.independent.co.uk/news/people/iain-banks-the-novel-factory-436865.html.

Leonard, Andrew. "The Future Perfect." *Salon.com*. February 17, 2005. Salon Media. http://dir.salon.com/story/books/int/2005/02/17/banks/index.html?source= search&aim=/books/int.

## Criticism and Readers' Guides

Brown, Carolyn. "Utopias and Heterotopias: The 'Culture' of Iain M. Banks." In Derek Littlewood, ed., *Impossibility Fiction: Alternativity, Extrapolation, Speculation*. Amsterdam, The Netherlands: Rodopi, 1996, 57–74.

Hardesty, William H. "Space Opera without the Space: The Culture Novels of Iain M. Banks." In Gary Westfahl, ed., *Space and Beyond*. Westport, CT: Greenwood, 2000, 115–122.

Horwich, David. "Culture Clash: Ambivalent Heroes and the Ambiguous Utopia in the Work of Iain M. Banks." *Strange Horizons* January 21, 2002. http://www. strangehorizons.com/2002/20020121/culture_clash.shtml.

## Web Sites

*Iain Banks.net*. Official Web site. http://www.iainbanks.net/.

*The Banksoniain: An Iain (M.) Banks Fanzine*. February 2007. Twice yearly publication covering all things to do with the Iain Banks: issues available in PDF format. http://banksoniain.netfirms.com/.

*The Culture FAQ*. Matthew Stanfield. July 2005. FAQ for questions concerning the Culture, posted to the alt.books.iain-banks newsgroup. http://www.i-dig.info/culture/culturefaq.html.

*Culture Shock*. Robert Keogh. September 2006. Future Hi. Includes a definitive list of the names of all Culture vessels, by novel, and links to a great number of Banks interviews prior to 1998. http://www.futurehi.net/phlebas/.

### If you enjoyed Iain M. Banks...

Iain M. Banks writes entertaining and intelligent space opera, set against the backdrop of a multispecies "post-scarcity" civilization, where limitless material wealth has made peace and comfort available to everyone. Banks asks, in his Culture novels, what is the price of utopia and good intentions?

### Then you might like...

*Poul Anderson* is very different from Banks in his political orientation, but has the same space opera joie de vivre. He was fascinated by the fate of empires, both as historical narratives and as templates for the Cold War clash between two would-be empires. His "Technic History" stories are paeans to capitalism, featuring larger-than-life, swashbuckling "entrepreneur heroes."

***David Brin***. In the "Uplift" series, man is a barely tolerated interloper in a galactic hierarchy in which myriad races have been genetically "uplifted" to give them the ability to navigate space. The central clash of these novels—ambitious, energetic humans, versus the corrupt, feudal Patron races—reflects a recurring theme in Brin's work: the clash between Romanticism and the Enlightenment.

***C.J. Cherryh***. About two dozen of Cherryh's novels, such as *Downbelow Station* and *Cyteen*, are part of the "Alliance-Union Universe," an epic future history series extending from the 21st century out into the far future. Her stories feature alien worlds with great realism, characters with real depth and psychological insight, and plots with thoroughly engaging perspectives.

***Ken MacLeod***. In the "Fall Revolution" sequence and the "Engines of Light" trilogy, MacLeod combines space opera spirit with the substance of political ideas, demonstrating how fanaticism, even to a well-intentioned creed, can destroy independence. His heroes are usually anarchist/libertarians, with a skeptical attitude toward authority in general, and government in particular.

***Alastair Reynolds***. With professional expertise in physics and astronomy, Reynolds writes hard sf that is consistent with current science, but makes good use of the tropes of space opera and noir. Reynolds' "Revelation Space" sequence depicts a universe that has not veered to utopian or dystopian extremes, but is all too recognizable in its moral ambiguity.

# Stephen Baxter (1957–   )

*There is no rest. No limit. No end to the Beyond – no Boundaries which Life, and Mind, cannot challenge, and breach.*
*—The Time Ships (1995)*

## Biography

Stephen Michael Baxter was born in Liverpool, England. He has a doctorate in aeronautical engineering from Southampton University. Before he became a full-time writer in 1995, he worked as a teacher of mathematics and physics. In 1991, he applied to become a cosmonaut on the Soviet space station Mir.

Baxter's thirty novels cover a range of hard sf themes: far-future epics of man in a dangerous universe (the Xeelee sequence, Destiny's Children), stories of near future space exploration (the Time's Tapestry series, the NASA Trilogy), and extended considerations of the riddle of intelligent life in the universe (the Manifold trilogy). Baxter has also worked on three collaborations with Sir Arthur C. Clarke, whom he acknowledges as an early influence; he has also written an authorized sequel to H.G. Wells' *The Time Machine* (*The Time Ships*, 1995). A lifetime supporter of Liverpool Football Club, he currently lives in Northumberland, England.

COLONIZATION OF OTHER WORLDS; FAR FUTURE; HARD SF; TIME TRAVEL

## Major Works

*Novels*

The Xeelee sequence: *Raft* (1991), *Timelike Infinity* (1992), *Flux* (1993), *Ring* (1994), *Vacuum Diagrams* (1997), *Reality Dust* (2000), *Riding the Rock* (2002)
*The Time Ships* (1995) **BSF**
The NASA Trilogy: *Voyage* (1996), *Titan* (1997), *Moonseed* (1998)
Manifold Trilogy: *Manifold: Time* (1999), *Manifold: Space* (2001), *Manifold: Origin* (2001), *Phase Space* (2002— Manifold short stories)
Destiny's Children: *Coalescent* (2003), *Exultant* (2004), *Transcendent* (2005), *Resplendent* (2006—short stories)
Time's Odyssey series (with Sir Arthur C. Clarke): *Time's Eye* (2003) *Sunstorm* (2005), *Firstborn* (2007)
Time's Tapestry series: *Emperor* (2006), *Conqueror* (2007), *Navigator* (2007)

*Notable Short Stories*

"Raft" (1989) http://www.infinityplus.co.uk/stories/raft.htm.
"Moon Six" (1997) http://www.infinityplus.co.uk/stories/moon6.htm
"The Gravity Mine" (2000) http://www.infinityplus.co.uk/stories/gravitymine.htm.
"Sheena 5" (2000) http://www.vondanmcintyre.com/squids/Baxter-Sheena5.html

*Other Important Works*

"Baby Boomers: Writers and Their Origins." *Science Fiction Studies*. 30 (2003): 477–482.
"Freedom in an Owned World: Warhammer Fiction and the *Interzone* Generation." *Vector* 229. http://www.vectormagazine.co.uk/article.asp?articleID=42.
"H.G. Wells' Enduring Mythos of Mars." *In The War of the Worlds: Fresh Perspectives on the H.G. Wells Classic*, edited by Glenn Yeffeth. Dallas, TX: BenBella, 2005, 181–188.
"The Real Matrix." In Karen Haber, ed., *Exploring the Matrix: Visions of the Cyber Present*. New York: St. Martin's, 2003, 30–47.
*Revolutions in the Earth: James Hutton and the True Age of the World* (2004).

## Research Sources

*Encyclopedias and Handbooks:* **AW, CA, CANR, ESF, SFW**

*Bibliographies:* **ARB, FF, SFAN**

*Biographies and Interviews*

Auden, Sandy. "A Man in Shorts: An Interview with Stephen Baxter." *SF Site.* 2005. http://www.sfsite.com/06a/sasb201.htm.

*Locus Online.* "Stephen Baxter: The Cusp of Transcendence." August 2004. http://www.locusmag.com/2004/Issues/08Baxter.html.

Palmer, James. Interview. *Strange Horizons.* April 18, 2005. http://www.strangehorizons.com/2005/20050418/1int-baxter-a.shtml.

*Criticism and Readers' Guides*

Benford, Greg. "Stephen Baxter's *Riding the Rock* in Context." *New York Review of Science Fiction.* 15(7) (2003). 13+.

Brialey, Claire. "Visions of the Far Future World: Human Constants and Cosmic Change in Stephen Baxter's Xeelee Sequence." In Damien Broderick, ed., *Earth is But a Star: Excursions through Science Fiction to the Far Future.* Crawley: University of Western Australia Press, 2001, 401–411.

*Web Sites*

*Stephen Baxter.com.* Official Web site. www.stephen-baxter.com.

*Stephen Baxter Archive.* University of Liverpool Library. Typescripts, outlines, proofs and related essays. http://www.sfhub.ac.uk/Baxter.htm.

*The Baxterium.* Simon Bradshaw. February 2007. Interviews, extracts from novels, and short stories ("The Ghost Pit," 2001, "On the Orion Line," 2000) nonfiction such as "The Moon is Hell" (1998), and "After Man," an extract from *Deep Future* (2001). http://www.baxterium.org.uk/.

*The Manifold.* Fan Web site with bibliography, links, information, and news. http://www.themanifold.co.uk/.

# Greg Bear (1951–   )

> *Nothing is lost.*
> *Nothing is forgotten.*
> *It was in the blood, the flesh.*
> *And now it is forever.*
>
> —*Blood Music (1985)*

## Biography

Gregory Dale Bear was born in San Diego, California. His father was in the U.S. Navy and the family traveled widely during his childhood. Before becoming a full-time writer in the 1980s, he worked as a "roving lecturer" for the San Diego School system, speaking on ancient history, the history of science, and science fiction. In recent years he has served on a number of political and scientific action committees, advising government agencies and private corporations on futurist subjects.

Bear's 1985 novel *Blood Music* (expanded from a 1983 short story) has been credited as the first account of nanotechnology in sf. He has also written about galactic conflict (*Forge of God*), artificial universes (*Eon*), and accelerated evolution (*Darwin's Radio*). Greg Bear is married to Astrid Anderson, the daughter of the legendary Poul Anderson. They have two children, and live outside of Seattle, Washington.

GENETIC ENGINEERING & CLONING; HARD SF; LIBERTARIAN SF; NANOTECHNOLOGY; SUPERMAN

## Major Works

*Novels*

*Hegira* (1979)
*Beyond Heaven's River* (1980)
*Blood Music* (1985)
The Eon Series: *Eon* (1985), *Eternity* (1988), *Legacy* (1995)
The Forge of God series: *The Forge of God* (1987), *Anvil of Stars* (1992), *Queen of Angels* (1990)
*Heads* (1990)
*Moving Mars* (1993) **Nebula**
/(aka *Slant*) (1997) Excerpt—"Autopoiesis and the Grand Scheme." http://www.goodreads.ca/gregbear/autopoiesis.html.
*Foundation and Chaos* (1998) Second volume of the Second Foundation Trilogy, an authorized continuation of Asimov's legendary series. Volumes One and Three are by Gregory Benford and David Brin.
The Darwin novels: *Darwin's Radio:* (1999—**Nebula**), *Darwin's Children* (2003)
*Dead Lines* (2004)
*Quantico* (2007)

*Collections*

*The Collected Stories of Greg Bear.* New York: Tor, 2002.

*Notable Short Stories*

"Blood Music" (1983) **Hugo, Nebula**
"Hardfought" (1983) **Nebula**
"Tangents" (1987) **Hugo, Nebula**

*Other Important Works*

"All the Robots and Isaac Asimov." *3 Laws Unsafe.* Singularity Institute for Artificial
   Intelligence, Inc. http://www.asimovlaws.com/articles/.
"Doctors of the Mind: Effective Mental Therapy and its Implications." In Gary Westfahl
   and George Slusser, eds., *No Cure for the Future: Disease and Medicine in Science
   Fiction and Fantasy.* Westport, CT: Greenwood, 2002, 119–126.
Introduction. *Psychoshop*, by Alfred Bester and Roger Zelazny. New York: Vintage,
   1998.

# Research Sources

*Encyclopedias and Handbooks:* **AW, CA, CANR, ESF, NNDB, SFW**

*Bibliographies:* **ARB, FF, SFAN**

*Biographies and Interviews*

Cabot, Myles. Interview. *Aberrant Dreams: Speculative Fiction.* January 2, 2007.
   http://www.hd-image.com/interviews/myles_cabot_09.htm.
Gambuto, Damon. "Science Fiction Friday: Greg Bear." *Correlations.* December 21,
   2007.
Gevers, Nick. "The Opener of the Way: An Interview with Greg Bear." Infinity Plus.
   February 2006. http://www.infinityplus.co.uk/.
Jenkins, Henry. Greg Bear in Discussion at MIT: April 16, 2000. (Edited version)
   *Media in Transition.* June 2002. Massachusetts Institute of Technology. http://
   web.mit.edu/m-i-t/science_fiction/.
Means, Loren. Interview with Greg Bear. *YLEM Journal* March/April 2004. http://
   www.ylem.org/Journal/2004Iss04vol24.pdf.
*Wired Science.* http://www.pbs.org/kcet/wiredscience/blogs/2007/12/science-fiction
   friday-greg-be.html.

*Criticism and Readers' Guides*

Hatfield, Len. "Legitimate Sequels: Character Structures and the Subject in Greg Bear's
   Sequel Novels." In Donald E. Morse et al, eds., *The Celebration of the Fantastic.*
   Westport, CT: Greenwood, 1992, 237–250.
Lynch, Lisa. "'Not a Virus, But an Upgrade': The Ethics of Epidemic Evolution in
   Greg Bear's *Darwin's Radio.*" *Literature and Medicine.* 20 (2001): 71–93.
Wolf, Tim. "Adulthood's Beginning: From Centered Oneness to Centerless Manyness
   in Greg Bear's *Forge of God* and *Anvil of Stars.*" *Journal of the Fantastic in the
   Arts.* 8 (1997): 78–98.

*Web Sites*

*Greg Bear.com.* Official Web site, including author blog. http://www.gregbear.com/.
*Quantico: The Book.* February 2008. Vanguard Press. Publicity site for Bear's near-
   future thriller. http://www.quanticothebook.com/.

# Alfred Bester (1913–1987)

*This was a Golden Age, a time of high adventure, rich living and hard dying . . . but nobody thought so. This was a future of fortune and theft, pillage and rapine, culture and vice . . . but nobody admitted it.*

*—The Stars My Destination (1956)*

## Biography

Alfred Bester was born in New York City and attended the University of Pennsylvania. During the 1940s, his work appeared in magazines like *Astounding Science Fiction* and *Galaxy*; he also worked at DC Comics, and eventually as a scriptwriter for radio and television. In 1953, his novel *The Demolished Man* was awarded the first ever Hugo Award.

Bester's style, using invented slang and a richly imagined future, is fresh and modern, and foreshadows cyberpunk and other avant-garde sf. His work on comics such as *Superman* and *The Green Lantern*, and on classic radio thrillers like *The Shadow* and *Charlie Chan*, foreshadowed the protagonists and themes of his later novels—the unlikely "superhero," and the notion that one man really can create a new reality for the world. Alfred Bester died in 1987, in Doylestown, Pennsylvania.

FANTASTIC VOYAGES; HUMOR & SATIRE; PSI POWERS; PSYCHOLOGY; SUPERMAN

## Major Works

*Novels*

*The Demolished Man* (1951) **Hugo**
*The Stars My Destination* (also published as *Tiger, Tiger*) (1956)
*Golem*$^{100}$ (1980)
*Psychoshop* (1998, with Roger Zelazny)

*Collections*

*Alfred Bester Redemolished.* Edited by Richard Raucci. New York: Ibooks, 2001.
    Includes "A Diatribe against Science Fiction" (1961); interviews with (among others) Woody Allen (1969), Robert Heinlein and Isaac Asimov (1973); various other uncollected stories, introductions, prologues, and essays.
*Virtual Unrealities.* Introduction by Robert Silverberg. New York: Vintage, 1997.

*Notable Short Stories*

"Star Light, Star Bright" (1953)
"Fondly Fahrenheit" (1954)

"The Men Who Murdered Mohammed" (1958)
"The Pi Man" (1959)


*Other Important Works*

"Gourmet Dining in Outer Space." In Damon Knight, ed., *Turning Points: Essays on the Art of Science Fiction.* New York: Harper & Row, 1977, 259–266.
*The Life and Death of a Satellite: A Biography of the Men and Machines at War with Space.* Boston, MA: Little, Brown, 1966.
"My Affair with Science Fiction." In Brian W. Aldiss and Harry Harrison, eds., *Hell's Cartographers.* New York: Harper&Row, 1975, 46–75.


## Research Sources

*Encyclopedias and Handbooks:* **AW, CA, CAAS, CANR, ESF, MSSF, NNDB, SFW, WS**

*Bibliographies:* **ARB, FF, SFAN**

*Biographies and Interviews*

Platt, Charles. "Alfred Bester's Tender Loving Rage" and Obituary. *Loose Canon.* Holicong, PA: Wildside, 2001. 82–94.
Schweitzer, Darrell. "Alfred Bester." *Science Fiction Voices # 1.* San Bernardino, CA: Borgo, 1979. 18–25.


*Criticism and Readers' Guides*

Cramer, Kathryn. Interactive Intoduction. *The Ascent of Wonder*, edited by David G. Hartwell and Kathryn Cramer. New York: Tor, 1994. http://ebbs.english.vt.edu/exper/kcramer/anth/Pi.html.
Kelleghan, Fiona. "Hell's My Destination: Imprisonment in the Works of Alfred Bester." *Science Fiction Studies.* 21 (1994): 351–364. http://www.depauw.edu/sfs/backissues/64/kelleghan.htm.
Langford, David. "On Alfred Bester." *Ansible.* March 2005. http://www.ansible.co.uk/writing/bester.html.
Palumbo, Donald E. "The Monomyth in Alfred Bester's *The Stars My Destination.*" *Journal of Popular Culture.* 38 (2004): 333–368.
Wendell, Carolyn. *Alfred Bester.* Mercer Island WA: Starmont House, 1980.


# *Michael Bishop (1945– )*

*He wasn't no showboat. He had this easy stillness that spoke straight through everybody else's jive and moonshine.*

*—Brittle Innings (1994)*

## Biography

The only recurring theme in Michael Bishop's work—sf, fantasy, horror, and even humorous detective fiction—is a strain of wonderful weirdness, whether he is writing about our earliest hominid ancestors (in his 1982 Nebula winning novel *No Enemy But Time*) or in strange tales such as *Brittle Innings* (1994) in which Frankenstein's Monster survives to become a minor league baseball player in the Deep South. Over four decades and thirty books, Bishop has resolutely refused to be pinned down and "branded."

Michael Lawson Bishop was born in Lincoln, Nebraska. He taught English at his alma mater, the University of Georgia, and at the United States Air Force Academy Preparatory School until 1974 when he gave up teaching to become a full-time writer. He lives with his wife Jeri in Pine Mountain, Georgia. In April, 2007, his son, Jamie Bishop, a professor of German language and a talented artist, was among the victims of the Virginia Tech massacre.

ALIEN WORLDS; ANTHROPOLOGY; CITIES & SOCIETIES; GOTHIC SF; HUMOR & SATIRE; TIME TRAVEL

## Major Works

*Novels*

*A Funeral for the Eyes of Fire* (1975)
*And Strange at Ecbatan the Trees* (1976—aka *Beneath the Shattered Moons*)
Urban Nucleus Series: *A Little Knowledge* (1977), *Catacomb Years* (1978—fix-up of
    linked stories)
*Eyes of Fire* (1979—radically rev. version of *A Funeral for the Eyes of Fire*)
*Transfigurations* (1979)
*No Enemy but Time* (1982) **Nebula**
*Ancient of Days* (1985)
*Philip K. Dick Is Dead, Alas* (1987—aka *The Secret Ascension*)
*Brittle Innings* (1994) **Locus Poll**

*Collections*

*Brighten to Incandescence*. Introduction by Lucius Shepard. Urbana, IL: Golden
    Gryphon 2003.
*A Reverie for Mister Ray: Reflections on Life, Death, and Speculative Fiction*, edited
    by Michael H. Hutchins. Introduction by Jeff VanderMeer. Hornsea, UK: PS Pub-
    lishing, 2005. Includes seventy essays, articles, and reviews from 1975 to 2004.

*Notable Short Stories*

"The Samurai and the Willow" (1976) **Locus Poll**
"O Happy Day" (1981) http://www.michaelbishop-writer.com/.

"The Quickening" (1981) **Nebula**
"Her Habiline Husband" (1983—Part I of *Ancient of Days*) **Locus Poll**
    extract: http://www.infinityplus.co.uk/stories/ddasadi.htm.
"Dogs' Lives" (1984—featured in *Best American Short Stories 1985*)
"Chihuahua Flats" (1995) http://www.infinityplus.co.uk/stories/chihuahuaflats.htm.
"Blue Kansas Sky" (2000) extract: http://www.infinityplus.co.uk/stories/kansas.htm.
"Bears Discover Smut" (2005)

## Research Sources

*Encyclopedias and Handbooks:* **AW, CA, CANR, ESF, SFW**

*Bibliographies:* **ARB, FF, SFAN**

Stephensen-Payne, Phil. *Michael Bishop: A Transfigured Talent, a Working Bibliography*. Albuquerque, NM: Galactic Central, 1992.

### Biographies and Interviews

Brown, Charles N. "Michael Bishop: The Blessing and the Curse" *Locus*. November 2004. http://www.locusmag.com/2004/Issues/11Bishop.html.
Melloy, Killian. Interview. *Infinity Plus*. June 2003. http://www.infinityplus.co.uk/nonfiction/intmb2.htm.
Snider, John C. Audio Interview. *SciFi Dimensions*. February 2001. http://www.scifidimensions.com/Feb01/michaelbishop.htm.

### Criticism and Readers' Guides

Brooke, Keith. "A Reverie for Mister Ray." *Infinity Plus*. May 13, 2006. http://www.infinityplus.co.uk/nonfiction/reverie.htm.
DiFilipi, Paul. "Essay on Michael Bishop." *The Scribner Writers Series: Supernatural Fiction Writers*. 2003. http://community.livejournal.com/theinferior4/96397.html.
Higdon, David Leon. "A Revision and a Gloss: Michael Bishop's Postmodern Interrogation of H.G. Wells *The Time Machine*." In George Slusser et al, eds., *H.G. Wells's Perennial Time Machine*. Athens: University of Georgia Press, 2001, 176–187.
Sanders, Joe. "The Game of Seek and Hide in Michael Bishop's *No Enemy but Time*." *New York Review of Science Fiction*. 12(2) (1999): 1+.
Senior, W.A. "Silence and Disaster in the Novels of Michael Bishop." *New York Review of Science Fiction*. 8(12) (1999): 12+.
VanderMeer, Jeff. Introduction. *A Reverie for Mister Ray: Reflections on Life, Death, and Speculative Fiction*. http://www.sfsite.com/12b/mr214.htm.

### Web Sites

*Michael Bishop—Writer.com*. Official Web site, ed. Michael H. Hutchins. May 2007. Includes a self-interview dated September 2002, "Writing Science Fiction As If It Mattered." http://www.michaelbishop-writer.com/.

# James Blish (1921–1975)

*"If I were a religious man," the pilot said suddenly, "I'd call this a plain case of divine vengeance. . . . It's as if we've been struck down for—is it hubris, arrogant pride?"*
*"Well, is it?" Chatvieux said, looking up at last. "I don't feel exactly swollen with pride at the moment. Do you?"*

—"Surface Tension" (1952)

## Biography

James Benjamin Blish was born in East Orange, New Jersey. A teenage member of the "Futurians," the influential New York sf fan group who included the young Isaac Asimov and Frederik Pohl, he graduated from Rutgers University, and supplemented his writing income for many years as an in-house editor for a pharmaceutical company.

Blish was a writer of big ideas—in his "Cities in Flight" series, whole cities flee the political chaos of a far-future Earth, powered by antigravity devices called "spin-dizzies." But in his hands, the simplest pulp adventure could become a consideration of the nature of good and evil. Writing as "William Atheling," he was also an early and influential critic of science fiction; he was a founder of the Milford SF Writers Conference and the Science Fiction Writers of America. In 1968, James Blish moved to England where he died of lung cancer in Henley-on-Thames, Oxfordshire, on July 30, 1975.

COLONIZATION OF OTHER WORLDS; FANTASTIC VOYAGES; FAR FUTURE; GENETIC ENGINEERING & CLONING; RELIGION

## Major Works

### Novels

The Cities in Flight sequence: *They Shall Have Stars* (1956), *A Life for the Stars* (1962), *Earthman, Come Home* (1955), *The Triumph of Time* (1958)
After Such Knowledge trilogy: *A Case of Conscience* (1953—**Hugo**), *Doctor Mirabilis* (1964), *The Devil's Day* (1980)
*VOR* (1958, with Damon Knight)
*Spock Must Die* (1970) The first full-length, adult Star Trek spin-off.

### Collections

*The Seedling Stars* (1956). London: Victor Gollanz, 2001.
*The Best Science Fiction Stories of James Blish* (1965) A selection made by Blish himself, and published posthumously. Now, unfortunately, out of print.
*Cities in Flight*. Woodstock, NY: Overlook, 2004. Omnibus volume of four novels.

*Notable Short Stories*

"There Shall Be No Darkness" (1950)
"Surface Tension" (1953)
"Beep" (1954)
"Seeding Program" (1956—aka "A Time to Survive")
"How Beautiful with Banners" (1966)
"We All Die Naked" (1970)

*Other Important Works*

"Cathedrals in Space." In Damon Knight, ed., *Turning Points: Essays on the Art of Science Fiction*. New York: Harper & Row, 1977, 144–162.
"The Development of a Science Fiction Writer." In Maxim Jakubowski and Edward James, ed., *The Profession of Science Fiction: SF Writers on Their Craft and Ideas*. New York: St. Martin's Press, 1992, 26–33.
*The Issue at Hand*. (1964) and *More Issues at Hand*. (1970) Critical essays, written as William Atheling.
"On Science Fiction Criticism." In Thomas D. Clareson, ed., *SF: The Other Side of Realism*. Bowling Green, OH: Bowling Green University Popular Press, 1971, 166–170.
*Star Trek Readers I, II, III, IV*—collection of script adaptations, 1976–1978.
*The Tale That Wags the God* (1987) Includes essays on Blish's career as writer and critic, as well as an eighty-page bibliography, compiled by his wife Judith.

## Research Sources

*Encyclopedias and Handbooks:* **AW, CA, CAAS, CANR, ESF, MSSF, NNDB, SFW, WS**

*Bibliographies:* **ARB, FF, SFAN**

Stephensen-Payne, Phil. *James Blish, Author Mirabilis: A Working Bibliography*. Leeds: Galactic Central, 1996.

*Biographies and Interviews*

Ketterer, David. *Imprisoned in a Tesseract: The Life and Work of James Blish*. Kent, OH: Kent State University Press, 1987.

*Criticism and Readers' Guides*

Aldiss, Brian W. "James Blish and the Mathematics of Knowledge." In *This World and Nearer Ones*. Kent, OH: Kent State University Press, 1981, 37–50.
Blackman, S. James. "Cosmic Dust Bowl: James Blish and 'Cities in Flight.'" *Space.com*, 15 April 2000. http://www.space.com/sciencefiction/books/cities_flight_000413.html.

Ruddick, Nicholas. "Breaking Out of the SF Box: Recent Studies of James Blish and Ursula K. Le Guin." *Canadian Review of American Studies* 21 (1990): 101–106.
Stableford, Brian M. *A Clash of Symbols: The Triumph of James Blish*. San Bernardino, CA: Borgo, 1979.

*Web Sites*

*Blish Genealogy.* Charles Benjamin Blish, August 2007. Fascinating Web site, constructed by James Blish's son, which contains information about Blish ancestors, as well as some personal reminiscences of his father. http://www.blish.org/gens/1380I.html.

# Ben Bova (1932–   )

*Up here, you're free. Really free, for the first time in your life. All the laws and rules and prejudices they've been dumping on you all you life ... they're all down there. Up here it's a new start.*

*—"Zero Gee" (1972)*

## Biography

Benjamin William Bova grew up in Philadelphia. In 1971 he succeeded John W. Campbell as editor of *Analog Science Fiction*; subsequently he received the Hugo Award for Best Professional Editor six times for restoring the magazine to its place at the cutting edge of science fiction. A recurring theme in his fiction is the moment when everything changes—impending nuclear holocaust, first contact with more technologically advanced aliens, the first manned flight to Mars.

In fact and fiction, Ben Bova's heartfelt belief is that man's future is in the stars: he is the President Emeritus of the National Space Society, a Fellow of the American Association for the Advancement of Science (AAAS), and a member of the Advisory Board of The Lifeboat Foundation, a nonprofit organization dedicated to research that would enable humanity to survive an extinction-level event. He currently lives in Naples, Florida, with his wife Barbara.

APOCALYPSE AND AFTER; FIRST CONTACT; HARD SF; MARS, MOON & THE PLANETS; SPACE OPERA

## Major Works

*Novels*

Watchmen: *The Star Conquerors* (1959), *Star Watchman* (1964), *The Dueling Machine* (1969)

Exiles: *Exiled from Earth* (1971), *Flight of Exiles* (1972), *End of Exile* (1975)
Voyagers: *Voyagers* (1981), *The Alien Within* (1986), *Star Brothers* (1990)
The Orion series: *Orion* (1984), *Vengeance of Orion* (1988), *Orion in the Dying Time*
    (1990), *Orion and the Conqueror* (1994), *Orion among the Stars* (1995)
*The Kinsman Saga* (1987) A reworked fix-up of two earlier novels, *Kinsman* (1979)
    and *Millennium* (1976).
The Grand Tour of the Universe series: Overlapping novels and short story collections.
    Beginning with *Mars* (1992) and *Empire Builders* (1993), includes the *Moonrise*
    and *Asteroid Wars* series, and *Venus* and *Jupiter* (2000). Recent titles are *Tales of
    the Grand Tour* (2004), *Powersat* (2005), and *Titan* (2006).

## Collections

*Twice Seven: Stories*. Eos, 1998. Includes "Life As We Know It" (1995), "The Great
    Moon Hoax, or A Princess of Mars" (1996), and "Legendary Heroes" (1996).
Sam Gunn stories: *Sam Gunn, Unlimited* (1992), and *Sam Gunn Forever* (1998).

## Notable Short Stories

"Brillo" (1971, with Harlan Ellison)
"Inspiration" (1995)

## Other Important Works

Column. *Naples Daily News*. http://www.naplesnews.com/staff/ben_bova/. Column
    of local interest to Southwest Florida, but often with science and sf themes such
    as cloning, the ecosystem, and the educational value of sf.
*The Craft of Writing Science Fiction That Sells* (1994)
"O Brave New (Virtual) World." In Charles Sheffield et al., eds., *The World of 2044:
    Technological Development and the Future of Society*. St. Paul, MN: Paragon,
    1994, 129–140.
"The Role of Science Fiction." In Reginald Bretnor, ed., *Science Fiction, Today and
    Tomorrow*. New York: Harper & Row, 1974, 3–16.
*Space Travel: Science Fiction Writing Series* (1997)

# Research Sources

*Encyclopedias and Handbooks:* **AW, CA, CANR, ESF, NNDB, SFW**

*Bibliographies:* **ARB, FF, SFAN**

## Biographies and Interviews

Auden, Sandy. "Scurrying over the Rocks: An Interview with Ben Bova." *SF Site*.
    2005. http://www.sfsite.com/map3.htm.

James, Warren W. "Interviews." *Mike Hodel's Hour 25: Science Fiction Radio for Southern California.* November 9, 2001, and June 18, 2005. http://www.hour25online.com/Hour25_Audio_Index.html.

Jenkins, Henry. Ben Bova in Discussion at MIT: (Edited version). *Media in Transition.* 2 April 2000. Massachusetts Institute of Technology. http://web.mit.edu/m-i-t/science_fiction/

Mullen, Leslie. "An Interview with Ben Bova." *Astrobiology Magazine Online,* April 21, 2004. http://www.astrobio.net/news/article933.html.

### Criticism and Readers' Guides

Kilgore, DeWitt Douglas. "Ben Bova: Race, Nation and Renewal on the High Frontier." In *Astrofuturism: Science, Race, and Visions of Utopia in Space.* Philadelphia: University of Pennsylvania Press, 2003, 186–221.

### Web Sites

*Ben Bova.net.* Official Web site. Chronology of the Grand Tour series. http://www.benbova.net/.

## Leigh Brackett (1915–1978)

> *. . . the Red Sea is hardly more than a legend. It lies behind the Mountains of White Cloud, the great barrier wall that hides away half a planet. Few men have gone beyond that barrier, into the vast mystery of Inner Venus. Fewer still have come back.*
> *Stark was one of that handful.*
>
> —*Enchantress of Venus (1949)*

## Biography

Leigh Douglass Brackett was born in Los Angeles, California, and was a freelance writer from the age of twenty-four. Most of her science fiction is unapologetic space opera or planetary romance: Brackett had a unique talent for imagery, for engaging every sense of the reader in the exotic, wondrous worlds of her Mars and Venus.

Brackett was a thorough professional, who wrote detective novels, screenplays, and even a western. She wrote, or cowrote, the screenplays for acclaimed movies such as *The Big Sleep* (1946), *Rio Bravo* (1958), and *The Long Goodbye* (1973), and, shortly before she died in March 1978, in Lancaster, California, submitted a draft screenplay of *The Empire Strikes Back* (1979), based on the notes of *Star Wars* director George Lucas. In 1980, she posthumously received a Hugo Award for her work on that movie.

APOCALYPSE AND AFTER; MARS, MOON & PLANETS; SPACE OPERA

# Major Works

*Novels*

*Shadow Over Mars* (1944)
*The Starmen* (1952)—re-published in unabridged form as *The Starmen of Llyrdis* (1976)
*The Long Tomorrow* (1955)
*The Book of Skaith* (1976): Includes *The Ginger Star* (1974); *The Hounds of Skaith* (1974), and *The Reavers of Skaith* (1976)

*Collections*

*Martian Quest: The Early Brackett.* Introduction by Michael Moorcock. Royal Oak, MI: Haffner, 2002. Includes all of Brackett's early short stories published up to March 1943.
*Stark and the Star Kings.* Royal Oak, MI: Haffner, 2005.
*Sea-Kings of Mars and Otherworldly Stories.* London: Gollanz, 2005.
*Lorelei of the Red Mist: Planetary Romances.* Foreword by Ray Bradbury, Introduction by Harry Turtledove. Royal Oak, MI: Haffner, 2007.
*The Best of Leigh Brackett*, published in 1977, was edited by, and includes an introduction written by Brackett's husband, Edmond Hamilton.

*Notable Short Stories*

"The Jewel of Bas" (1944)
"The Veil of Astellar" (1944)
"The Vanishing Venusians" (1945)
"Lorelei of the Red Mist" (1946, with Ray Bradbury)
"Enchantress of Venus" (1948)

*Other Important Works*

"Barsoom and Myself." *Edgar Rice Burroughs' Fantastic Worlds.* James Van Hise, ed. (1996). An essay in which Brackett acknowledges her debt to Edgar Rice Burroughs' Tarzan and Barsoom novels.

# Research Sources

*Encyclopedias and Handbooks:* **AW, BW, CA, CAAS, CANR, ESF, MSSF, SFW, WS**

*Bibliographies:* **ARB, FF, SFAN**

Arbur, Rosemarie. *Leigh Brackett, Marion Zimmer Bradley, Anne McCaffrey: A Primary and Secondary Bibliography.* Boston, MA: G. K. Hall, 1982.

## Biographies and Interviews

Macklin, Tony, and Nick Pici, eds. Interview. In *Voices from the Set: The Film Heritage Interviews*. Lanham, MD: Scarecrow, 2000. 219–237.

Stableford, Brian. "Edmond Hamilton and Leigh Brackett: An Appreciation." In *Outside the Human Aquarium: Masters of Science Fiction*. San Bernardino, CA: Borgo, 1995, 7–17.

Swires, Steve. "Leigh Brackett: Journeyman Plumber." In Pat McGilligan, ed., *Backstory 2: Interviews with Screenwriters of the 1940s and 1950s*. Berkeley, CA: University of California Press, 1991, 15–26.

## Criticism and Readers' Guides

Carr, J. L. *Leigh Brackett: American Writer*. Polk City, IA: Chris Drumm, 1986.

Connelly, Michael. "Epiphany." (Afterword, *No Good from a Corpse*). http://www.michaelconnelly.com/Other_Words/other_words.html.

DeBlasio, Donna M. "Future Imperfect: Leigh Brackett's *The Long Tomorrow*." In Carl B. Yoke, ed., *Phoenix from the Ashes*. Westport, CT: Greenwood, 1987, 97–103.

Hansen, Terry. "Myth-Adventure in Leigh Brackett's 'Enchantress of Venus.'" *Extrapolation* 23 (1982): 77–82.

Moorcock, Michael. "Queen of the Martian Mysteries: An Appreciation of Leigh Brackett." *Fantastic Metropolis*. June 13, 2002. http://www.fantasticmetropolis.com/i/brackett/.

Sallis, James. "The Unclassifiable Leigh Brackett." *Boston Globe*. December 12, 2005. http://www.grasslimb.com/sallis/GlobeColumns/globe.09.brackett.html.

Valdron, Den. "Colonial Barsoom: Leigh Brackett. Part I: Spaceman's Burden. Part II: Appendices & Cover Gallery." *ERBzine*. Issue 1783. http://www.erbzine.com/mag17/1783.html.

## Web Sites

*Leigh Brackett, Queen of Space*. G. W. Thomas. February 2007. A brief publication history, plus a comprehensive collection of cover art from magazines that featured Brackett's stories, novels, and short story collections. http://www.gwthomas.org/brackett.htm.

"The Connoisseur's Guide to the Scripts of the Star Wars Saga." *Starkiller: The Jedi Bendu Script Site*. Björn Wahlberg. January 2005. Development of the Star Wars series, including Brackett's involvement. http://starwarz.com/starkiller/writings/cguide.htm.

# Ray Bradbury (1920–   )

*"It is good to renew one's wonder, "said the philosopher." Space travel has again made children of us all."*

—*The Martian Chronicles (1950)*

# Biography

Raymond Douglas Bradbury was born in Waukegan, Illinois; while his family settled in Los Angeles when he was thirteen, much of Bradbury's writing draws upon childhood memories of the wonders and terrors of growing up in small-town USA. Since 1941, he has written more than five hundred published works—short stories, novels such as *The Martian Chronicles* and *Fahrenheit 451*, plays, screenplays, television scripts, and verse; hundreds of his short stories have been collected, anthologized, and published in magazines like *The Saturday Evening Post*, *The New Yorker, Amazing Stories,* and *Dime Detective.*

Bradbury's awards and honors include a special citation from The Pulitzer Board "for his distinguished, prolific, and deeply influential career" (2007); the National Medal of Arts, presented at the White House by President George W. Bush and Laura Bush (2004); and the Distinguished Contribution to American Letters Award from the National Book Foundation (2004).

APOCALYPSE AND AFTER; DYSTOPIAS; GOTHIC SF; HUMOR AND SATIRE; MARS, MOON & THE PLANETS

# Major Works

*Novels*

The Martian Chronicles (1950)
The Illustrated Man (1951)
Fahrenheit 451 (1953)

*Collections*

Bradbury Stories: 100 of His Most Celebrated Tales. New York: Harper Perennial, 2005.
A Sound of Thunder and Other Stories. New York: Harper Perennial, 2005. Includes "R is for Rocket" (1943), "Frost and Fire" (1946—aka "The Creatures that Time Forgot"), "The Rocket Man" (1951), "A Sound of Thunder" (1952).

*Notable Short Stories*

"Mars is Heaven!" (1948)
"There Will Come Soft Rains" (1950)
"The Beast from 20,000 Fathoms" (1951—aka "The Fog Horn")
"The Thing at the Top of the Stairs" (1988)

*Other Important Works*

Bradbury Speaks: Too Soon from the Cave, Too Far from the Stars (2006)
"The Great Years Ahead." Commencement Address, CalTech, 2000.
   http://pr.caltech.edu/commencement/00/bradbury_speech.html.

*Icarus Montgolfier Wright.* Produced and directed by Jules Engel and Herbert Klynn. Format Films. 1961. Animated short based on Bradbury's 1956 short story.

*The Illustrated Man.* Screenplay (Warner Brothers/Seven Arts. 1969). Flawed, but interesting film, starring Rod Steiger and Claire Bloom, and hated by both Bradbury and Steiger.

*It Came from Outer Space.* Screenplay (Universal, 1953)

*Match to Flame: The Fictional Paths to Fahrenheit 451* (2007) Letters, short stories, and drafts that Bradbury views as antecedents to his classic 1953 novel.

*Moby Dick.* Screenplay (Moulin Productions, 1956) The classic tale of obsession in a hostile alien environment, directed by John Huston, and starring Gregory Peck and Richard Basehart.

"Ray Bradbury: The Illustrated Spaceman." *Astrobiology,* May 16, 2004. http://www.astrobio.net/news/article974.html. Edited version of Bradbury's testimony before the President's Commission on Implementation on U.S. Space Exploration Policy.

*The Ray Bradbury Theater.* Alliance Atlantis. 1985–1992. Fifty-nine episodes, based on Bradbury stories and scripts; starring, among others, Alan Bates, Drew Barrymore, Jeff Goldblum, Peter O'Toole, and William Shatner.

*Yestermorrow: Obvious Answers to Impossible Futures* (1993)

*Zen in the Art of Writing: Essays on Creativity* (Expanded ed., 1994)

## Research Sources

*Encyclopedias and Handbooks:* **AW, CA, CANR, ESF, MSSF, NNDB, SFW**

*Bibliographies:* **ARB, FF, SFAN**

Hawvermale, Lance. "Ray Bradbury: To the Canon By Rocketship." *Erin O'Rourke Homepage.* http://www.erinorourke.com/bradbury.html. A thorough survey of critical scholarship. "Erin O'Rourke" is the pen name of sf/thriller and women's interest author Lance Hawvermale.

*Biographies and Interviews*

Aggelis, Steven I., ed. *Conversations with Ray Bradbury.* Jackson: University Press of Mississippi, 2004.

Eller, Jonathan R., and William F. Touponce. *Ray Bradbury: The Life of Fiction.* Kent, OH: Kent State University Press, 2004.

Hibberd, James. "Ray Bradbury is on Fire!" *Salon,* August 29, 2001. http://archive.salon.com/people/feature/2001/08/29/bradbury/print.html.

McCarty, Michael. Interview. *Sci Fi Weekly,* March 26, 2007. http://www.scifi.com/sfw/interviews/sfw15376.html.

Swaim, Don. "Audio Interviews with Ray Bradbury: 1992 and 1993." *Wired for Books.* WOUB/Ohio University. http://wiredforbooks.org/raybradbury/.

Weller, Sam. *The Bradbury Chronicles.* New York: William Morrow, 2005.

Zebrowski, George. Interview. *Science Fiction Weekly,* 2004. SciFi.com. http://www. scifi.com/sfw/issue374/interview.html.

*Criticism and Readers' Guides*

Bloom, Harold, ed. *Ray Bradbury.* Introduction by Damon Knight. New York: Chelsea House, 2000. Includes an essay by Bradbury, "Dusk in the Robot Museum: The Rebirth of Imagination," 23–28.

————. *Ray Bradbury's Fahrenheit 451.* New York: Chelsea House, 2000.

Brians, Paul. "Ray Bradbury's Fahrenheit 451 and the Dystopian Tradition," February 21, 2006, Washington State University. http://www.wsu.edu/~brians/ science_fiction/451.htm.

————. *Study Guides: The Martian Chronicles.* March 27, 2003. Washington State University. http://www.wsu.edu/~brians/science_fiction/martian_chronicles.html.

Hoskinson, Kevin. *"The Martian Chronicles* and *Fahrenheit 451:* Ray Bradbury's Cold War Novels." *Extrapolation* 36 (1995): 345–359.

McGiveron, Rafeeq O. "To Build a Mirror Factory: The Mirror and Self-Examination in Ray Bradbury's *Fahrenheit 451." Critique* 39 (1998): 282–287.

————. "What 'Carried the Trick'? Mass Exploitation and the Decline of Thought in Ray Bradbury's *Fahrenheit 451." Extrapolation* 37 (1996): 245–256.

Reid, Robin Anne. *Ray Bradbury: A Critical Companion.* Westport, CT: Greenwood, 2000.

Smith, Jeremy. "The Failure of *Fahrenheit 451." Strange Horizons,* October 13, 2003. http://www.strangehorizons.com/2003/20031013/fahrenheit.shtml.

Tibbetts, John C. "The Illustrating Man: The Screenplays of Ray Bradbury." *Creative Screenwriting* 6(1) (1999): 45–54.

*Web Sites*

*Bradbury Media.* Phil Nichols. October 2007. A Web site specifically devoted to adaptations of Bradbury's work. In addition to interesting Bradbury book and film news (with links), there is an amazing Short Story Finder—a tabulated database (with links to cover art) of magazines where Bradbury's stories first appeared and anthologies where they can be found. http://www.bradburymedia.blogspot. com/.

*The Center for Ray Bradbury Studies.* April 2007. Indiana University-Purdue University Indianapolis. The Web site of the IU-PUI center, director Prof. William F. Touponce. The Center is devoted to the study of Bradbury's work. It maintains a catalog of holdings, including the original manuscripts of Bradbury stories, a database of his correspondence since 1938, and links to Bradbury news. http://www.iupui.edu/~crbs/.

*Ray Bradbury.com.* Official Web site, "... celebrating a lifetime of wonder and imagination." http://www.raybradbury.com.

*Ray Bradbury Immersion.* Attractive Russian Web site, which, since August 2004, has posted "descriptive introductions to some of his most interesting and amazing stories." Thirty-two of Bradbury's stories (including "R is for Rocket," "A Sound of Thunder," and "The Veldt") in English, Russian, and Polish. Extended quotations from the opening paragraphs of some stories. http://immersion.raybradbury.ru/.

*Ray Bradbury Online.* Richard Johnson et al., October 2006. Business-like, but well-organized Web site that includes an extensive bibliography, image and quotation archives, a list of pseudonyms used by Bradbury during his career, and links to reviews and fan articles. http://raybradburyonline.com/bibliography.htm.

## Marion Zimmer Bradley (1930–1999)

*Here do we first touch the new worlds. Let us never again fear to face the unknown, trusting that the Mind of All Knowledge still has many surprises in store for all the living.*

*—The Colors of Space (1963)*

### Biography

Marion Eleanor Zimmer was born on a farm near Albany, New York. Her childhood dream was to be an opera singer, but her family could not afford the training; instead, she qualified as a teacher, married Robert Alden Bradley, and moved to Texas. She sold her first story in 1952 and, while her earliest sf was formulaic "space opera," her reputation was eventually established by her Darkover novels, and her 1983 fantasy epic, *The Mists of Avalon.*

Bradley's protagonists, in her twenty Darkover novels, are strong, heroic women who challenge traditional gender roles, and contend with the consequences of freedom. Marion Zimmer Bradley suffered a series of strokes, beginning in 1987, and died in Berkeley, California, on September 25, 1999. Her ashes were scattered at Glastonbury Tor, the legendary location of Avalon and supposed resting place of King Arthur and Guinevere.

FANTASY; FEMINISM; GENDER AND SEXUALITY; PSI POWERS; WOMEN IN SF

### Major Works

*Novels*

*The Door through Space.* (1961)
*Seven from the Stars* (1962)
*The Colors of Space* (1963)
The Darkover novels: Beginning with *The Planet Savers* (1958) and including titles such as *Winds of Darkover* (1970), *The Shattered Chain* (1976), *Sharra's Exile* (1981), and *Free Amazons of Darkover* (1986). The last book in the series written exclusively by Bradley was *The Heirs of Hammerfell* (1989). Subsequent Darkover novels were coauthored: *Rediscovery* (1993, with Mercedes Lackey), *Exile's*

*Song* (1996), *The Shadow Matrix* (1997), and *Traitor's Sun* (1999, all three with Adrienne Martine-Barnes). Since the death of MZB, the series has been continued by Deborah J. Ross.

## Collections

*Jamie and Other Stories.* (1993) Reissued and revised version of *The Best of Marion Zimmer Bradley* (1985).
Darkover Omnibus Editions: *Heritage and Exile* (2002), *The Saga of the Renunciates* (2002), *Darkover: First Contact* (2004).

## Other Important Works

"Fandom: Its Value to the Professional." In Sharon Jarvis, ed., *Inside Outer Space: Science Fiction Professionals Look at Their Craft.* New York: Ungar, 1985, 69–84.
"One Woman's Experience in Science Fiction." In Denise DuPont, ed., *Women of Vision.* New York: St. Martin's Press, 1988, 84–97.
"Responsibilities and Temptations of Women Science Fiction Writers." In Jane Branham Weedman, ed., *Women Worldwalkers: New Dimensions of Science Fiction and Fantasy.* Lubbock: Texas Tech, 1985, 25–42.

# Research Sources

*Encyclopedias and Handbooks:* **AW, CA, CAAS, CANR, ESF, MSSF, NNDB, SFW, WS**

*Bibliographies:* **ARB, FF, SFAN**

Benson, Gordon. *Marion Zimmer Bradley, Mistress of Magic: A Working Bibliography.* Leeds, UK: Galactic Central, 1994.

## Biographies and Interviews

Baur, Wolfgang, and Steven Kurtz. Interview. *Visions* 4(1) (1989): 20–23.
Wolfson, Jonquil. "Remembering the Queen of Darkover." *Space.com.* October 22, 1999. Imaginova Corp. http://www.space.com/sciencefiction/marion_zimmer_bradley_retro_991022.html.

## Criticism and Readers' Guides

Arbur, Rosemarie. *Marion Zimmer Bradley.* Mercer Island, WA: Starmont House, 1985.
Hornum, Barbara. "Wife/Mother/Sorceress/Keeper, Amazon/Renunciate: Status Ambivalence and Conflicting Roles on the Planet Darkover." In Jane Branham

Weedman, ed., *Women Worldwalkers: New Dimensions of Science Fiction and Fantasy*. Lubbock: Texas Tech, 1985, 153–164.

Shwartz, Susan M. "Marion Zimmer Bradley's Ethic of Freedom." In Tom Staicar, ed., *The Feminine Eye: Science Fiction and the Women Who Write It*. New York: Ungar, 1982, 73–88.

Wood, Diane S. "Gender Roles in the Darkover Novels of Marion Zimmer Bradley." In Jane Branham Weedman, ed., *Women Worldwalkers: New Dimensions of Science Fiction and Fantasy*. Lubbock: Texas Tech, 1985, 237–246.

## Web Sites

*Marion Zimmer Bradley Literary Works Trust*. Links to articles on writing. ("Advice to New Writers," "What is a Short Story?"). http://mzbworks.home.att.net/.

*Gateway to Cottman IV (Darkover)*. An endearingly amateur Web site, based on the conceit of a tourist visiting Darkover. Maps and descriptions of key locations; genealogies of key characters. http://www.geocities.com/Area51/Quadrant/7650/.

**If you enjoyed Marion Zimmer Bradley . . .**

The Darkover sequence—saga of a lost Earth colony, which resists the hegemony of a galactic empire—is "perhaps the most significant planetary-romance sequence in modern sf " (**ESF**). In Darkover, Bradley married sword and sorcery style with a subtext of gender issues and sexual politics. The popularity of Darkover proved that there was still life in the old formula.

**Then you might like . . .**

**C. J. Cherryh**. Cherryh is widely admired for her versatility—she is as comfortable, and readable, in High Fantasy as she is in hard sf, space opera and science fantasy. Like Bradley, she sometimes flavors even her Alliance-Union Universe series with elements of fantasy—psi powers, Arthurian legend.

**Storm Constantine**. In the "Wraeththu" trilogy, beginning with *The Enchantments of Flesh and Spirit* (1987), much of the male portion of the human race has been converted to a new species of hermaphrodite posthumans. A fantasy of the postcyberpunk era, which takes punk *noir* and decadence as its sword and sorcery.

**Mary Gentle**. Beginning with *Golden Witchbreed* (1983), Mary Gentle has made a career of fiction that slips the bonds of sf and fantasy. In *Ash: A Secret History* (2000), a potent blend of sword and sorcery style and alternative history, a female mercenary fights across a Europe where Carthage never fell and Golems man the castle ramparts.

**Anne McCaffrey**. Like Darkover, the "Dragonriders of Pern" series, which now totals fifteen books, is set on a long-lost Earth colony, which survives thanks to a handy symbiosis with bio-engineered time-travelling, telepathic, and telekinetic dragons.

*Sherri Tepper*. From the very start of her career, Tepper has challenged efforts to categorize her writing as sf or fantasy, "either/or." Novels such as *King's Blood Four* (1983, True Game series), *Beauty* (1992), and *A Plague of Angels* (1993) combine time-honored fantasy tropes, such as shape-shifters, necromancers, witches, and giants, with a good science fiction rationale.

# David Brin (1950–   )

*There were times when Robert actually envied his ancestors, who had lived in dark ignorance, before the 21st century, and seemed to have spent most of their time making up weird, ornate explanations of the world to fill the yawning gap of their ignorance. Back then, one could believe in anything at all.*
*—The Uplift War (1987)*

## Biography

A central theme that David Brin returns to again and again, in his fiction and in his critical nonfiction, is the clash between Romanticism and the Enlightenment—a clash that is echoed in his own writing. Brin can handle hard science with the effortless competence one would expect from a writer with degrees in astronomy (CalTech), applied physics, and space science (University of California in San Diego). But in the fiction of David Brin, hard science is jettisoned where necessary to achieve a compulsive and readable narrative.

Glen David Brin was born in Glendale, California. After earning his doctorate, he taught at San Diego State University and various community colleges. A fulltime writer and lecturer, he currently lives near San Diego with his family; he also acts as a futurist consultant for organizations, which, according to his Web site, "know the value of technologically-informed imagination."

APOCALYPSE AND AFTER; GENETIC ENGINEERING & CLONING; HARD SF; LIBERTARIAN SF

## Major Works

*Novels*

The Uplift Universe: *Sundiver* (1980), *Startide Rising* (1983 **Hugo, Locus Poll, Nebula**), *The Uplift War* (1987—**Hugo, Locus Poll**), *Brightness Reef* (1995), *Infinity's Shore* (1996), *Heaven's Reach* (1998)
*The Postman* (1985) **Locus Poll**
*Heart of the Comet* (1986, with Gregory Benford)
*Earth* (1990)

*Glory Season* (1993)
Foundation Universe, Second Foundation Trilogy: *Foundation's Triumph* (1999)
*Kil'n People* (2002)
*Sky Horizon* (2007)

## Collections

*Otherness*. New York: Bantam Spectra, 1994. **Locus Poll**
*Tomorrow Happens*. Framingham, MA: NESFA, 2003. Includes twenty essays, short
    stories, and "little wonders."

## Notable Short Stories

"The Crystal Spheres" (1984) **Hugo**
"Cyclops" (1984)
    "Thor Meets Captain America" (1986) **Locus Poll**
"The Giving Plague" (1988)
"Reality Check" (2000) http://www.concatenation.org/futures/reality_check_brin.pdf.

## Other Important Works

*Contacting Aliens: An Illustrated Guide to David Brin's Uplift Universe* (2002)
"Gaia, Freedom, and Human Nature." *1992 President's Program Presentations*. LITA:
    Library and Information Technology Association. American Library Association.
    http://www.cni.org/pub/LITA/Think/Brin.html.
"Mystery of the Great Silence." In Ben Bova and Byron Preiss, eds., *First Contact:
    The Search for Extraterrestrial Intelligence*. New York: NAL/Penguin, 1990.
    Expanded from two 1980s *Analog* articles "Xenology: The New Science of
    Asking Who's Out There" and "Just How Dangerous is the Galaxy?"
"Our Favorite Cliché: A World Filled with Idiots . . . or, Why Fiction Routinely Depicts
    Society and Its Citizens As Fools." *Extrapolation* 41 (2000): 7–20.
"A Shaman's View." In Maxim Jakubowski and Edward James, eds., *The Profession
    of Science Fiction: SF Writers on Their Craft and Ideas*.New York: St. Martin's
    Press, 1992, 161–168.
"Singularities and Nightmares: Extremes of Optimism and Pessimism about the Hu-
    man Future." *Lifeboat Foundation*, 2006. http://lifeboat.com/ex/singularities.and.
    nightmares.
"Tomorrow May Be Different." In Karen Haber, ed., *Exploring the Matrix: Visions of
    the Cyber Present*, New York: St. Martin's, 2003, 180–199.
"The Transparent Society." *Wired,* December 1996. http://www.wired.com/wired/
    archive/4.12/fftransparent_pr.html.

## Research Sources

*Encyclopedias and Handbooks:* **AW, BW, CA, CANR, ESF, NNDB,
SFW**

*Bibliographies:* **ARB, FF, SFAN**

## Biographies and Interviews

"Evaluating Horizons." *Accelerating Change 2004*. November 2004, IT Conversations. http://www.itconversations.com/shows/detail358.html.

Means, Loren. "Interview with David Brin." *YLEM Journal* 24(4) (2004): 11–14. http://www.ylem.org/Journal/2004Iss04vol24.pdf.

*Orbit.* Interview. July 19, 2002. http://www.sffworld.com/interview/13p0.html.

*The Planetary Society.* Interview. April 30, 2002. http://mmp.planetary.org/artis/brind/brind70.htm.

Stentz, Zack. "Au Contrarian: Brin on Science Fiction, Society and Kevin Costner." *Metro*, February 6, 1997. http://www.metroactive.com/papers/metro/02.06.97/cover/brin2-9706.html.

Westfahl, Gary, ed. "Greg Bear, Gregory Benford, David Brin: Building on Isaac *Asimov's Foundation:* An Eaton Discussion with Moderator Joseph D. Miller." *Science Fiction Studies* 24 (1997). http://www.depauw.edu/sfs/backissues/71/asimovpanel71.htm.

Winter, Bill. "David Brin—Libertarian." *Advocates for Self-Government,* May 2007. http://www.theadvocates.org/celebrities/david-brin.html.

## Criticism and Readers' Guides

De Los Santos, Oscar. "Of Dystopias and Icons: Brin's *The Postman* and Butler's *Parable of the Sower.*" In Martha Bartter, ed., *The Utopian Fantastic.*Westport, CT: Praeger, 2004, 109–122.

Jones, Gwyneth. "*Glory Season*: David Brin's Feminist Utopia." In *Deconstructing the Starships: Science, Fiction, and Reality.* Liverpool: Liverpool University Press, 1999. 153–156.

## Web Sites

*David Brin.com.* Official Web site: "Tomorrow Happens: Explore the Possible Future with David Brin." http://www.davidbrin.com/.

*Brin-L.* Jeroen van Baardwijk, March 2005. Fan forum, focused on Brin, other hard sf authors, and sf in general. http://www.brin-l.com/.

# *John Brunner (1934–1995)*

*Some troubledome just figured out that if you allow for every codder and shaggy and appleofmyeye a space one foot by two you could stand us all on the six hundred forty square mile surface of the island of Zanzibar.*

*—Stand on Zanzibar (1968)*

## Biography

John Kilian Houston Brunner was born in Oxfordshire, in England. His dystopian novels of the late 1960s and 1970s, like *Stand on Zanzibar* (1968), present stylish, plausible, pictures of a future rendered unlivable by overpopulation, militarism, and pollution. In *The Shockwave Rider* (1975), he anticipated the Internet, the blight of computer viruses and spam, and coined the term "worm" to describe software that could wreak havoc by reproducing itself across a computer network.

These grim subjects, and Brunner's resolutely skeptical, left-wing views, may have hurt his sales in the United States. After the mid-1970s, he returned to writing space opera, but with a noticeable lack of enthusiasm as his health began to decline. John Brunner died of a stroke in Glasgow, Scotland, while attending the 1995 World Science Fiction Convention.

ALIEN THREAT; ECOLOGY; DYSTOPIAS; GALACTIC EMPIRES; OVER-POPULATION

## Major Works

*Novels*

Interstellar Empire: *Galactic Storm* (1951, as Gill Hunt), *The Man from the Big Dark* (1958), *Threshold of Eternity* (1959), *The Space-Time Juggler* (1963), *The Altar on Asconel* (1965)
Zarathustra Refugee Planets: *Secret Agent of Terra* (1962), *Castaways' World* (1963), *The Repairmen of Cyclops* (1965), *Victims of the Nova* (1989)
*The Whole Man* (1965)
*Stand on Zanzibar* (1968) **BSF, Hugo**
*The Jagged Orbit* (1969) **BSF**
*The Sheep Look Up* (1972)
*The Shockwave Rider* (1975)

*Collections*

*The Compleat Traveller in Black.* New York: Bluejay, 1986. Contains "Imprint of Chaos" (1960) and "The Things That Are Gods" (1979)
*The Best of John Brunner.* New York: DelRay, 1988. With an Introduction by Joe Haldeman.

*Other Important Works*

*John Brunner Presents Kipling's Science Fiction* (1992).
"Science Fiction and the Larger Lunacy." In Peter Nicholls, ed., *Science Fiction at Large: A Collection of Essays, By Various Hands, About the Interface between Science Fiction and Reality.* London: Gollancz, 1976, 73–103.

"The Science Fiction Novel." In Reginald Bretnor, ed., *The Craft of Science Fiction.*
New York: Harper & Row, 1976, 216–237.
*Tomorrow May Be Even Worse: An Alphabet of Science Fiction Clichés* (1978)

## Research Sources

*Encyclopedias and Handbooks:* **AW, CA, CAAS, CANR, ESF, MSSF, NNDB, SFW, WS**

*Bibliographies:* **ARB, FF, SFAN**

Stephensen-Payne, Phil, and Gordon R. Benson, Jr. *John Brunner: Shockwave Writer, A Working Bibliography.* 3rd. Ed. Albuquerque, NM: Galactic Central, 1989.

### Biographies and Interviews

*The Daily Telegraph* (London). Obituary. September 25, 1995. *Spacelight.* http://www. gcwillick.com/Spacelight/obit/brunnero.html.

Langford, Dave. "Traveller in Black: John Brunner, 1934–1995." *The Skeptic* 9(6) (1995). http://www.ansible.co.uk/writing/brunner.html.

Schweitzer, Darrell. "John Brunner Interview (1993)." In Darrell Schweitzer, ed., *Speaking of the Fantastic.* Holicong, PA: Wildside, 2002, 19–37.

Watson, Ian. "At the Wrong End of Time: An Appreciation of John Brunner (1934–1995)." In Pamela Sargent, ed., *Nebula Awards 31.* New York: Harcourt, 1997, 116–124.

### Criticism and Readers' Guides

Bukeavitch, Neal. "'Are We Adopting the Right Measures to Cope?': Ecocrisis in John Brunner's *Stand on Zanzibar.*" *Science Fiction Studies* 29 (2002): 53–70.

De Bolt, Joe. *The Happening Worlds of John Brunner: Critical Explorations in Science Fiction*, with a Preface by James Blish. Port Washington, NY: Kennikat: 1975.

Gimon, Charles A. "Heroes of Cyberspace: John Brunner." *InfoNation*, August 1995. http://www.skypoint.com/members/gimonca/brunner.html.

Goldman, Stephen H. "John Brunner's Dystopias: Heroic Man in an Unheroic Society." *Science Fiction Studies* 5 (1978): 260–270. http://www.depauw.edu/sfs/backissues/16/goldman16art.htm.

Miller, Ryder A. "Environmental Dystopias Still to Be Avoided: John Brunner's Classic Environmental Science Fiction Diptych As Agent of Social Change." *Internet Review of Science Fiction*, 2004. http://www.irosf.com/q/zine/article/10056.

Stern, Michael. "From Technique to Critique: Knowledge and Human Interests in Brunner's *Stand on Zanzibar, The Jagged Orbit,* and *The Sheep Look Up.*" *Science Fiction Studies* 3 (1976): 112–130. http://www.depauw.edu/sfs/backissues/9/stern9art.htm.

*Web Sites*

*The John Brunner Archive.* Andy Sawyer, SF Hub. 2004. University of Liverpool.
Index to the collection bequeathed to the Science Fiction Foundation in 1995; includes
corrected typescripts of published and unpublished works. http://www.sfhub.ac.
uk/Brunner.htm.

# Lois McMaster Bujold (1949–  )

> *But pain . . . seems to me an insufficient reason not to embrace life. Being
> dead is quite painless. Pain, like time, is going to come on regardless. Ques-
> tion is, what glorious moments can you win from life in addition to the
> pain?*
>
> *—Barrayar (1991)*

## Biography

Lois McMaster Bujold was born in Columbus, Ohio. She attended The Ohio
State University, where her father was a professor of welding engineering, but left
without graduating. She worked as a pharmacy technician, married, and had two
children; in 1985 she sold her first story to the *Twilight Zone Magazine*, and one
year later, saw three of her novels published.

Bujold is best known for Prince Miles Vorkosigan, hero of the Barrayar series, a
brilliant, charming adventurer who was born with severe physical disabilities as a
result of an assassination attempt on his father. Throughout the series, Miles must
deal with the backward attitudes of his home world, Barrayar, toward disability
and physical imperfection; over the years, Bujold has gradually transformed him
from a dashing scamp to an altogether more serious character who matures and
confronts his dark side. Lois McMaster Bujold has won four Hugos, matching
Robert Heinlein's record; she currently lives in Minneapolis.

DISABILITY & SF; GALACTIC EMPIRES; GENETIC ENGINEERING &
CLONING; HUMOR & SATIRE; WAR

## Major Works

*Novels*

The Barrayar Novels: Miles Vorkosigan: *The Warrior's Apprentice* (1986), *Ethan of
Athos* (1986), *Brothers in Arms* (1989), *The Vor Game* (1990—**Hugo**), *Mirror
Dance* (1994—**Hugo, Locus Poll**), *Cetaganda (1996)*, *Memory* (1996), *Komarr*
(1998), *A Civil Campaign* (1999), *Diplomatic Immunity* (2002)
Cordelia Vorkosigan: *Shards of Honor* (1986), *Barrayar* (1991—**Hugo, Locus Poll**)
*Falling Free* (1988) **Nebula**

## Collections

Barrayar compilations: *Cordelia's Honor* (1999), *Miles, Mystery, and Mayhem* (2003), *Miles Errant* (2002), *Miles, Mutants and Microbes* (2007), *Vorkosigan's Game* (1990), and *Young Miles* (2003). All Riverside, NY: Baen. Each volume includes novels, short stories, and novelettes, in the correct narrative order. http://www. baen.com/author_catalog.asp?author=LMBujold.

*The Borders of Infinity*. Riverside, NY: Baen, 2007. Title novella, plus "Labyrinth" (1989), and "The Mountains of Mourning" (1989—**Hugo, Nebula**).

## Other Important Works

*Dreamweaver's Dilemma: Short Stories and Essays* (1995). A volume for "hardcore" fans, with fiction and nonfiction background to the Barrayar series; includes Vorkosigan genealogy by Suford Lewis.

"The Future of Warfare." (Address to St Petersburg Con). Russian Fan Web site. 2000. http://bujold.lib.ru/b_wareng.htm.

"Letterspace: In the Chinks between Published Fiction and Published Criticism," with Sylvia Kelso. In Helen Merrick and Tess Williams, *Women of Other Worlds*. Nedlands: University of Western Australia Press, 1999, 383–409.

# Research Sources

*Encyclopedias and Handbooks:* **AW, CA, CANR, ESF, NNDB, SFW**

*Bibliographies:* **ARB, FF, SFAN**

Bibliography. *Lois McMaster Bujold Web site.* Elisa Kay Sparks, ed. Clemson University. http://hubcap.clemson.edu/~sparks/bujold.html.

## Biographies and Interviews

Aranaga, Carlos. "Interview." *SciFi Dimensions*, October 2006. http://www. scifidimensions.com/archives.htm.

Hennessey-DeRose, Christopher, and Ryan Timothy Grable. "Author Is a Slush-Pile Survivor." *SciFi.com,* November 18, 2002. http://www.scifi.com/sfw/interviews/ sfw9138.html.

"Highlights of a Life." *Ohioana Authors*. WOSU Public Media. http://www.ohioana-authors.org/bujold/index.php.

*Locus Online.* "It's All in the Footnotes–Interview," July 2005. http://www.locusmag. com/2005/Issues/07Bujold.html.

Martini, Adrienne. Interview. *Bookslut,* May 2005. http://www.bookslut.com/features/ 2005_05_005637.php.

## Criticism and Readers' Guides

Bartter, Martha A. "'Who Am I, Really?' Myths of Maturation in Lois McMaster Bujold's Vorkosigan Series." *Journal of the Fantastic in the Arts* 10 (1998): 30–42.

Bemis, Virgina T. "Barrayar's Ugliest Child: Miles Vorkosigan." In *Kaleidoscope: Exploring the Experience of Disability through Literature and the Fine Arts* 34 (Winter-Spring 1997) 20–22.

Haehl, Anne L. "Miles Vorkosigan and the Power of Words: A Study of Lois McMaster Bujold's Unlikely Hero." *Extrapolation* 37 (1996): 224–233.

Kelso, Sylvia. "Lois McMaster Bujold: Feminism and 'The Gernsback Continuum' in Recent Women's SF." *Journal of the Fantastic in the Arts* 10 (1998): 17–29.

———. "Loud Achievements: Lois McMaster Bujold's Science Fiction." *New York Review of Science Fiction* 11(2 & 3) (1998) 1+.

## Web Sites

*The Bujold Nexus.* Michael Bernardi. July 2007. Official Web site. http://www.dendarii.com/frames/index.html.

*MySpace.com.* Author blog. http://blog.myspace.com/loismcmasterbujold.

### If you enjoyed Lois McMaster Bujold...

The "Miles Vorkosigan" series is comic space opera, with a heart. While Bujold's distinctive blend of military saga, coming-of-age story, and romance is consistently less angst-ridden than some variations on the theme, she has never avoided the serious issues at the heart of the story of her charming, damaged hero.

### Then you might like...

*Catherine Asaro.* Unlike Bujold, who follows the adventures of a single heroic character, Asaro's "Saga of the Skolian Empire" unfolds over several generations, as two interstellar powers struggle for dominance. Political intrigue is played out against the backdrop of individual struggle, conflict, and romance.

*C. J. Cherryh.* The novels in Cherryh's "Alliance-Union" series share much of Bujold's space opera bravado and society building, and feature various other themes in common with Bujold: honor, responsibility, family, and the outsider searching for his or her place in the universe.

*Debra Doyle and James D. MacDonald.* Stylish, escapist fun, the novels of the "Mageworld" series, beginning with *The Price of the Stars* (1992), feature interstellar war, swashbuckling space-pirate heroines, and mysterious villain races from beyond the "Gap Between": multiple-volume grand adventure, with nonstop action and intrigue.

*Elizabeth Moon.* In series like "Vatta's War" and the "Familias Regnant" universe, Moon's fiction features strong female protagonists, whose sense of honor and loyalty get them into—and out of—dangerous situations. Moon's active service with the U.S. Marine Corps in the late 1960s contributes to the plausibility of her military themes.

*David Weber*. Like Bujold, Weber's "Honorverse" series, featuring Space Commander Honor Harrington, owes a debt of inspiration to the classic Horatio Hornblower stories. (Weber's character "HH" is a homage to the earlier HH.) Each volume features battles and intrigue, with occasional serious reflections by his naval heroine on the true cost of war.

# Anthony Burgess (1917–1993)

*The night belonged to me and my droogs and all the rest of the nadsats, and the starry bourgeois lurked indoors drinking in the gloopy worldcasts.*
*—A Clockwork Orange (1962)*

## Biography

Anthony Burgess was born John Burgess Wilson, in Harpurhey, a bleak suburb of Manchester, in the North of England. Music and literature offered him an escape from a childhood blighted by poverty and neglect, and Burgess went on to become an incredibly prolific writer, as well as a critic, poet, and composer.

Although Burgess wrote other novels using the tropes of science fiction, *A Clockwork Orange* is probably the best known. (It was filmed by director Stanley Kubrick, in 1971.) The story of a world at the mercy of ultraviolent youth gangs, *A Clockwork Orange*'s brutal slang "nadsat" is a reminder that sf can use language as effectively as technological gimmicks. In 2005, it was included in *Time Magazine*'s list of 100 best English-language novels since 1923. Anthony Burgess died of lung cancer, in London, on November 22, 1993. His ashes were interred in Monte Carlo.

DYSTOPIAS; LANGUAGE; NEAR FUTURE; OVERPOPULATION; PSYCHOLOGY

## Major Works

*Novels*

*A Clockwork Orange* (1962)
*The Wanting Seed* (1962)
*1985* (1978)
*The End of the World News: An Entertainment* (1982)

*Other Important Works*

*A Clockwork Orange*. Screenplay written and directed by Stanley Kubrick. Hawk Films, 1971.

Introduction (excerpt). *A Clockwork Orange*. London: Century Hutchinson, 1987.
   http://home.wlv.ac.uk/~fa1871/burgess.html.
"Juice from a Clockwork Orange." In Mario Falsetto, ed., *Perspectives on Stanley
   Kubrick*. New York: G. K. Hall, 1996, 187–190.
*Little Wilson and Big God: The First Part of the Confession* (1991)
*You've Had Your Time: The Second Part of the Confession* (1991) Excerpt:
   "On *A Clockwork Orange*." http://www.visual-memory.co.uk/amk/doc/burgess.
   html.

## Research Sources

*Encyclopedias and Handbooks:* **AW, BW, ESF, MSSF, NNDB, SFW**

*Bibliographies:* **FF, SFAN**

### Biographies and Interviews

Creative Arts Television. "An Examination of Stanley Kubrick's *A Clockwork Orange*." 1972. http://video.google.com/videoplay?docid=8665044426065479837
   &9=anthony + burgess&hl=en. A half-hour documentary discussion with Anthony Burgess and actor Malcolm McDowell.
Cullinan, John. Interview. *The Paris Review,* Spring 1973. http://www.theparisreview.
   com/literature.php.
Lewis, Roger. *Anthony Burgess*. London: St. Martin's 2004.
Swaim, Don. *Wired for Books*. WOUB/Ohio University. Audio Interview. 1985. http://
   wiredforbooks.org/anthonyburgess/.

### Criticism and Readers' Guides

Aggeler, Geoffrey. *Critical Essays on Anthony Burgess*. Boston, MA: G. K. Hall, 1986.
   Includes essays "Alex Before and After: A New Approach to Burgess' *A Clock-
   work Orange*" (by Philip E. Ray), and "Linguistics, Mechanics, and Metaphysics:
   Anthony Burgess's *A Clockwork Orange*" (by Esther Petix).
Cavanaugh, Tim. "Orange Méchanique." *Reason,* November 14, 2005. http://www.
   reason.com/news/show/34125.html.
Dalrymple, Theodore. "A Prophetic and Violent Masterpiece." *City Journal.* Winter
   2006. The Manhattan Institute. http://www.city-journal.org/html/16_1_oh_to_be.
   html.
Greener, Mark. "Bookspotting: *The Wanting Seed*: A Classic in Waiting?" *Vector.* 231
   (September/October 2003): 11–12.
Mairs, Gary. "An Elegant Trap: Stanley Kubrick's *A Clockwork Orange*." *The High
   Hat* 8 (2007). http://www.thehighhat.com/Potlatch/008/mairs_kubrick.html.
Pearson, Douglas A. "Anthony Burgess's *A Clockwork Orange*." In Nicholas
   J. Karolides et al., eds., *Censored Books: Critical Viewpoints*, Metuchen, NJ:
   Scarecrow, 1993, 185–190.
Stinson, John J. *Anthony Burgess Revisited*. Boston, MA: Twayne, 1991.

*Web Sites*

*Anthony Burgess, A Clockwork Orange. Nadsat Dictionary.* Mattia Vaccari. June 2005.
Imperial College, London. Meanings and possible origins of Burgess' Nadsat polyglot words, slang and jargon. http://astro.imperial.ac.uk/~vaccari/mis/
nadsat.html.

*The Anthony Burgess Center.* January 2005. Universite d'Angers. Collection of Burgess
material donated by Burgess' widow, Liane. Twice-yearly publishes *The Anthony
Burgess Newsletter.* http://bu.univ-angers.fr/EXTRANET/AnthonyBURGESS/.

*A Clockwork Orange Online.* Anthony Burgess reading an excerpt (Audio Files): http://
town.hall.org/radio/HarperAudio/. Excerpt: http://perso.orange.fr/chabrieres/
texts/clockwork_orange.html.

*The International Anthony Burgess Foundation,* February 2008. Nonprofit organization
dedicated to encouraging and supporting public and scholarly interest in Anthony
Burgess's life and works. Includes Discussion Forum and image gallery. http://
www.anthonyburgess.org/.

# *Edgar Rice Burroughs (1875–1950)*

*I opened my eyes upon a strange and weird landscape. I knew that I was on
Mars; not once did I question either my sanity or my wakefulness.*
                                                    *—A Princess of Mars (1917)*

## Biography

Edgar Rice Burroughs, the unsuccessful son of a Chicago businessman, began
reading pulp fiction magazines in 1911, and decided that, if people were being
paid for such stuff, he could write it as well as anyone. His first story "Under the
Moons of Mars" (later retitled *A Princess of Mars*) was serialized in *All-Story*
magazine in 1912 and earned him $400 (roughly the equivalent of $7600 today).

Burroughs' "Barsoom" novels feature the heroic adventurer John Carter, who
is transported by quasi-magical means to Mars where he meets and fights exotic
warriors, and woos the lovely red-skinned, egg-laying Princess. Scientific plausibility is not high on his list of Burroughs' literary virtues, but writers like Leigh
Brackett, Michael Moorcock, and Ray Bradbury found inspiration on his fantastic
Mars. Edgar Rice Burroughs died of a heart attack on March 19, 1950, in Encino,
California, having written almost seventy novels.

ALIEN WORLDS; FANTASTIC VOYAGES; FANTASY; MARS, MOON & THE
PLANETS

## Major Works

*Novels*

Barsoom: *A Princess of Mars* (1912), *The Gods of Mars* (1914), *The Warlord of Mars*
(1918), *Thuvia, Maid of Mars* (1920), *The Chessmen of Mars* (1922), *The Master*

*Mind of Mars* (1928), *A Fighting Man of Mars* (1931), *Swords of Mars* (1936), *Synthetic Men of Mars* (1940), *Llana of Gathol* (1948)

Pellucidar: *At the Earth's Core* (1914), *Pellucidar* (1923), *Tanar of Pellucidar* (1928), *Tarzan at the Earth's Core* (1929), *Back to the Stone Age* (1937), *Land of Terror* (1944)

*The Land That Time Forgot* (1918)

*The Moon Maid* (1926)

Venus: *Pirates of Venus* (1934), *Lost on Venus* (1935), *Carson of Venus* (1939), *Escape on Venus* (1946), *The Wizard of Venus* (1970)

## Collections

*Savage Pellucidar* (1963). Lincoln, NE: Bison, 2007. Unreleased stories from 1942–1963.

*John Carter's Chronicle of Mars*. Radford, VA: Wilder, 2007. Includes the first five books in the Barsoom series.

## Other Important Works

"How I Wrote the Tarzan Books." *The World Magazine* (*Washington Post* and *New York World,* Sunday supplement). October 27, 1929. http://www.erbzine.com/mag0/0052.html.

"Mr. Burroughs Describes His Publishing Methods." (Letter) *Writers' Digest.* 1937. http://www.erbzine.com/mag0/0056.html.

## Research Sources

*Encyclopedias and Handbooks:* **AW, BW, CA, CANR, ESF, MSSF, NNDB, SFW, WS**

*Bibliographies:* **ARB, FF, SFAN**

### Biographies and Interviews

"How Tarzan Kept the Wolf from the Door." *The Literary Digest*, November 11, 1929. http://www.erbzine.com/mag0/0055.html.

Dean, Roselle. "'Just Made a Living in Business;' Now He's Rich." *Los Angeles Times,* June 25, 1922. http://www.erbzine.com/mag13/1358.html.

Fenton, Robert W. *Edgar Rice Burroughs and Tarzan: A Biography*. Jefferson, NC: McFarland, 2003.

Gravatt, Glenn B. "With the Author of Tarzan: An Interview with Edgar Rice Burroughs in Which He Frankly Discusses His Methods and Gives Sound Advice." *Writer's Monthly*, December 1926. http://www.erbzine.com/mag0/0059.html.

Taliaferro, John. *Tarzan Forever: The Life of Edgar Rice Burroughs, Creator of Tarzan*. New York: Simon & Schuster/Scribner 1999.

*Criticism and Readers' Guides*

Brady, Clark A. *The Burroughs Cyclopaedia*. Jefferson, NC: McFarland, 1996.
Darlington, Andrew. "Martian Dreams: Edgar Rice Burroughs Revisited." *Fantasy Commentator* 10(1/2) (2001/2002): 13–20.
Hanson, Alan. *The Wondrous Words of Edgar Rice Burroughs*. Spokane, WA: Waziri, 1998.
Pohl, Frederik. "Edgar Rice Burroughs and the Development of Science Fiction." *Burroughs Bulletin* 10 (1992): 8–14.
Singer, Armand. "Themes and Sources of Star Wars: John Carter and Flash Gordon Enlist in the First Crusade." *Popular Culture Review* 9(2) (1998): 65–77.
Van Hise, James, ed. *Edgar Rice Burroughs' Fantastic Worlds*. Yucca Valley, CA: James Van Hise, 1996.

*Web Sites*

*Edgar Rice Burroughs Listserve*. David Bruce Bozarth. Art, articles, and exhibits that illustrate the life and work of ERB. Includes glossaries of ERB's series, fan fiction, and articles by regular featured critics. http://www.erblist.com/.
*Edgar Rice Burroughs*. John Anthony Miller, Phantom Bookshop, May 2005. Tribute site, with timeline, links, and bibliography. http://edgarriceburroughs. phantombookshop.com/.
*ERBzine*. Bill and Sue-on Hillman. January 2007. Edgar Rice Burroughs, Inc. Official ERB tribute and webzine. Archive of material searchable by theme or chronologically. http://www.erbzine.com/. Includes link to index of *The Burroughs Bulletin*, which has been published quarterly for member of The Burroughs Bibliophiles since January 1990. http://www.erbzine.com/mag6/0650.html.

# Octavia E. Butler (1947–2006)

> *"He's still mine, you know," my mother said suddenly. "Nothing can buy him from me." Sober, she would not have permitted herself to refer to such things.*
>
> *"Nothing," T'Gatoi agreed, humoring her.*
>
> —*"Bloodchild" (1985)*

## Biography

Octavia Estelle Butler was born in Pasadena, California. She was shy and socially isolated as a child (she was later diagnosed as dyslexic); reading science fiction offered her an escape. Butler soon realized that she could write stories as good, if not better. She found a new way to write about the experience of being a black American woman, and demonstrated that science fiction can tell the important stories. Among her many honors, in 1995 she was the first sf writer to receive a MacArthur Fellowship, popularly known as the "genius grant."

At the end of her life, Butler was still one of a few African-American "big names" of sf—but thanks to her, that is changing. Throughout her career she was a tireless campaigner and a generous mentor to young writers. Octavia E. Butler died on February 24, 2006, of complications following a fall at her home in Seattle, Washington.

ALIENS; GENDER & SEXUALITY; MYTHOLOGY & LEGEND; PSI POWERS; SEX & TABOOS; UTOPIA

## Major Works

*Novels*

The Patternist series: *Patternmaster* (1976), *Mind of My Mind* (1977), *Survivor* (1978), *Wild Seed* (1980), *Clay's Ark* (1984)
The Xenogenesis Trilogy: *Dawn* (1987), *Adulthood Rites* (1988), *Imago* (1989).
Earthseed: *Parable of the Sower* (1993), *Parable of the Talents* (1998—**Nebula**)
*Kindred* (1979)
*The Fledgling* (2005)

*Collections*

*Bloodchild and Other Stories* (1995). New York: Seven Stories, 2007. Includes 1985 title story, winner of **Hugo**, **Locus Poll**, and **Nebula** awards, and "Speech Sounds" (1984—**Hugo**). New edition includes two previously unpublished stories, "Amnesty" (2003), and "The Book of Martha" (2004)
*Xenogenesis* (1989), and *Lillith's Brood* (1989) Compilation editions.

*Other Important Works*

"Aha! Moment: Eye Witness, Octavia Butler." *O, The Oprah Magazine.* May 2002. http://www.oprah.com/rys/omag/rys_omag_200205_aha.jhtml.
"Birth of a Writer." (As O.E. Butler) *Essence* 20(1) (1989): 74+.
"*Devil Girl From Mars*: Why I Write Science Fiction." Massachusetts Institute of Technology Media in Transition Project. February 19, 1998. http://web.mit.edu/m-i-t/articles/.
"The Monophobic Response." In Sheree R. Thomas, ed., *Dark Matter: A Century of Speculative Fiction from the African Diaspora.* New York: Warner Books, 2000, 415-416.
"A World without Racism." *NPR Weekend Edition: UN Racism Conference.* September 1, 2001. National Public Radio. http://www.npr.org/programs/specials/racism/.

# Research Sources

*Encyclopedias and Handbooks:* **AW, CA, CAAS, CANR, ESF, NNDB, SFW, WS**

*Bibliographies:* **ARB, FF, SFAN**

Becker, Jennifer. Rev. and updated by Lauren Curtwright. Biography & Bibliography. *Voices from the Gaps: Women Artists and Writers of Color.* August 21, 2004. University of Minnesota. http://voices.cla.umn.edu/vg/Bios/entries/butler_octavia_estelle.html.

## *Biographies and Interviews*

Barnes, Steven. "Octavia Butler, a Rememberance." *Internet Review of Science Fiction.* March 2006. http://www.irosf.com/q/zine/article/10262.

Champion, Edward. Podcast Interview. *The Bat Segundo Show.* December 1, 2005. Wordpress. http://www.edrants.com/segundo/the-bat-segundo-show-15/.

Chau, Jen, and Carmen Van Kerckhove. Podcast Interview. *Addicted to Race.* February 6, 2006, New Demographic. http://www.addictedtorace.com/?p=29.

Cowen, Tyler. "The Outsider Who Changed Science Fiction." *Salon.com.* March 2, 2006. http://www.slate.com/id/2137269/.

Gonzalez, Juan, and Amy Goodman. "Science Fiction Writer Octavia Butler on Race, Global Warming and Religion." *Democracy Now!* November 11, 2005. http://www.democracynow.org/2005/11/11/science_fiction_writer_octavia_butler_on

Jenkins, Henry. Octavia Butler/Samuel Delany in Discussion at MIT: February 19, 1998. Edited version. *Media in Transition.* August 29, 1998. Massachusetts Institute of Technology. http://web.mit.edu/m-i-t/science_fiction/transcripts/butler_delany_index.html.

Saunders, Joshunda. Interview. *In Motion Magazine.* March 14, 2004. NPC Productions. http://www.inmotionmagazine.com/ac04/obutler.html.

Snider, John C. Interview. *SciFi Dimensions.* June 2004. http://www.scifidimensions.com/Jun04/octaviaebutler.htm.

## *Criticism and Readers' Guides*

Anderson, Crystal S. "'The Girl Isn't White': New Racial Dimensions in Octavia Butler's *Survivor.*" *Extrapolation* 47 (2006): 35–50.

Doerksen, Teri Ann. "Octavia E. Butler: Parables of Race and Difference." In Elisabeth Anne Leonard, ed., *Into Darkness Peering: Race and Color in the Fantastic.* Westport. CT: Greenwood, 1997, 21–34.

Hairston, Andrea. "Octavia Butler—Praise Song to a Prophetic Artist." In Justine Larbalestier, ed., *Daughters of Earth: Feminist Science Fiction in the Twentieth Century.* 265–304. Middletown, CT: Wesleyan University Press, 2006, 265–304.

Melzer, Patricia. "'All That You Touch You Change': Utopian Desire and the Concept of Change in Octavia Butler's *Parable of the Sower* and *Parable of the Talents.*" *Femspec* 3(2) (2001): 31–52. http://www.femspec.org/samples/butler.html.

Moylan, Tom. "Octavia Butler's Parables." In *Scraps of the Untainted Sky: Science Fiction Utopia Dystopia*. Boulder, CO: Westview, 2000, 223–246.

Shaw, Heather. "Strange Bedfellows: Eugenics, Attraction, and Aversion in the Works of Octavia E. Butler." *Strange Horizons*. December 18, 2000. http://www.strangehorizons.com/2000/20001218/butler.shtml.

Slonczewski, Joan. "Octavia Butler's *Xenogenesis* Trilogy: A Biologist's Response." SFRA Conference, Cleveland. June 30, 2000. http://biology.kenyon.edu/slonc/books/butler1.html.

White, Eric. "The Erotics of Becoming: *Xenogenesis* and *The Thing.*" *Science Fiction Studies* 20 (1993): 394–408. http://www.depauw.edu/sfs/backissues/61/white61art.htm.

## Web Sites

*Octavia E. Butler Official Web site*. January 2007. Science Fiction and Fantasy Writers of America. As of March 2006, includes obituaries, news reports, and tributes. http://www.sfwa.org/members/butler/.

*Octavia Butler.net*. Fan blog, edited by "Ayana," which brings together links and news, and gives OEB fans a forum for discussing and sharing information. http://www.octaviabutler.net/.

**If you enjoyed Octavia Butler...**

Butler's fiction evokes "... reflections on everything from family romance and sex and feminism to slavery itself..." (**ESF**). At once strange and allegoric, and resolutely down-to-earth, Butler's stories draw on myth and legend, as well as the familiar tropes of sf, for their emotional and intellectual punch.

**Then you might like...**

**Michael Bishop**. Like Butler, Bishop is impossible to pin down. His early novels of the 1970s are "complex and moving analyses of alien cultures" (**ESF**), using anthropology to illuminate relationships and societies. Novels such as *And Strange at Ecbatan the Trees* and *Funeral for the Eyes of Fire* feature societies that are forced to confront the wrongs they have done to alien races they exploited.

**Nalo Hopkinson**. Jamaican-born writer and editor, whose novels, such as *Brown Girl in the Ring* (1998), *Midnight Robber* (2000), and *The Salt Roads* (2003) often draw on African and Caribbean mythology and traditions of storytelling. Like Butler, Hopkinson's work alternates among various sf scenarios: distant worlds, dystopian near-future, and time-slip, in which the membrane between past, present and future is stretched wafer-thin.

**James Tiptree, Jr**. Yet another who shook up traditional ideas about who an sf writer should be, Tiptree (aka Alice Sheldon) wrote about humans who are alienated from their "own kind" and forced into varying degrees of dependence and symbiosis with alien races, with unexpected results for all concerned. Like Butler, Tiptree's work also "squares" various sf circles—"hard" technology with "soft" psychology, the masculine and the feminine.

**Roger Zelazny.** In novels like *Lord of Light*, and shorter works like the novellas "A Rose for Ecclesiastes" and "The Doors of His Face, The Lamps of His Mouth," Zelazny borrowed from mythic traditions such as Greek, Egyptian, Hindu, and Native American, as well as making unapologetic references to the Bible, and classics like *Moby Dick*.

# Pat Cadigan (1953–　)

*The name came up as Shantih Love, which she couldn't decide if she hated or not; the linked profile informed her that the Shantih Love appearance was as protected by legal copyright as the name. No age given; under Sex it said, Any; all; why do you care?*

*—"Death in the Promised Land" (1995)*

## Biography

Pat Cadigan was born in Schenectady, New York, and grew up in Massachusetts. After graduating with a degree in Theater Studies, she worked as a writer and editor for Hallmark Cards. During the late 1970s and early 1980s, Cadigan edited the sf magazines *Shayol* and *Chacal*, earning repeated nominations and several awards for amateur publication and fanzine.

The tough-minded vigor and icy black humor of her fiction places it squarely in the spirit of 1980s cyberpunk. Her more recent novels are detective stories in the *noir* style, in which the tension and mystery hinge on the real-life implications of cyberlife. Cadigan has also done a number of movie and TV tie-ins (*Twilight Zone, Jason X*), as well as "making of" books about the films *Lost in Space* and *The Mummy*. Pat Cadigan moved to England in 1996, and lives in London.

ARTIFICIAL INTELLIGENCE; CYBERPUNK; POP CULTURE; VIRTUAL REALITY

## Major Works

*Novels*

*Mindplayers* (1987)
*Synners* (1991)
*Fools* (1992)
*Tea from an Empty Cup* (1998)
*Dervish Is Digital* (2001)

## Collections

*Patterns* (1989) **Locus Poll**

Other Cadigan collections are *Dirty Work* (1993) and *Home by the Sea* (1993). *Letters from Home* (1991), edited with Karen Joy Fowler and Pat Murphy, includes stories by all three editors, and an introduction by Sarah Lefanu.

## Short Stories

"Angel" (1988) **Locus Poll**
"True Faces" (1992)

## Other Important Works

"Guest Editorial: Ten Years After." *Asimov's SF Magazine* 17(14) (1993): 4–9.
Introduction. In Karen Haber, ed., *Exploring the Matrix: Visions of the Cyber Present.* New York: St. Martin's Press, 2003, 10–15.
"Lateral Genius and the Persistence of *Neuromancer.*" *Nova Express* 4(4) (Winter/ Spring 1998)
*Making of Lost in Space* (1998)
*Resurrecting the Mummy: The Making of the Movie* (1999)
*The Ultimate Cyberpunk.* Ed. And Introduction. (2004)

# Research Sources

*Encyclopedias and Handbooks:* **AW, BW, CA, CANR, ESF, SFW**

*Bibliographies:* **ARB, FF, SFAN**

Information Database. *The Cyberpunk Project*, December 7, 2004. http://project. cyberpunk.ru/idb/pat_cadigan.html.

## Biographies and Interviews

Castellani, Linda. "Pat Cadigan: Dervish is Digital." *The Well.* August 7, 2001. Salon.com. http://www.well.com/conf/inkwell.vue/.
Jenkins, Henry. "Exchange with Pat Cadigan: Queen of Cyberpunk." Massachusetts Institute of Technology, October 10, 1998. (Edited version) *Media in Transition.* November 3, 1998. Massachusetts Institute of Technology. http://web.mit.edu/m-i-t/science_fiction/transcripts/cadigan_index.html.
Mathew, David. "Step Outside: An Interview with Pat Cadigan." *SF Site.* 2000. http://www.sfsite.com/06a/pc82.htm.
Schmidt, Jakob. "An Interview with Pat Cadigan." *SF Site.* 2006. http://www.sfsite.com/05b/pc224.htm.

*Criticism and Readers' Guides*

Heuser, Sabine. "Pat Cadigan's Virtual Mindscapes." In *Virtual Geographies: Cyberpunk at the Intersection of the Postmodern and Science Fiction.* Amsterdam: Rodopi, 2003, 127–170.
Kraus, Elisabeth. "Real Lives Complicate Matters in Schrodinger's World: Pat Cadigan's Alternative Cyberpunk Vision." In Marleen S. Barr, ed., *Future Females, The Next Generation.* Lanham, MD: Rowman & Littlefield, 2000, 129–144.
Mitchell, Kaye. "Bodies That Matter: Science Fiction, Technoculture, and the Gendered Body." *Science Fiction Studies* 33 (2006): 109–128.
Seed, David. "Cyberpunk and Dystopia: Pat Cadigan's Networks." In Rafaella Baccolini and Tom Moylan, eds., *Dark Horizons: Science Fiction and the Dystopian Imagination.* New York: Routledge, 2003, 69–90.

*Web Sites*

*Ceci N'est Pas Une Web site (Cadigan's Photos).* http://www.flickr.com/photos/cadigan/ and *Ceci N'est Pas Une Blog.* http://fastfwd.livejournal.com/.

# Karel Čapek (1890–1938)

*My dear Miss Glory, robots are not people. They are mechanically more perfect than we are, they have an astounding intellectual capacity, but they have no soul.*

—*R.U.R.—Rossum's Universal Robots (1921)*

## Biography

The man who wrote the play that gave us the word "robot" was born in Male Svatonovice, Bohemia (now the Czech Republic). Karel Čapek was a satirist whose tales are vehicles for his deeply felt concerns about freedom, and man's struggle to retain his humanity in the face of overwhelming odds. He died, in Prague, on Christmas Day, 1938, of a lung inflammation, only a few weeks before Adolf Hitler invaded and occupied Czechoslovakia.

The word *robot* comes from the Czech word *robota*, which means "drudgery" or "slave labor." Čapek always modestly credited his brother Joseph with actually coming up with the word for Rossum's fateful invention—and a powerful 20th-century science fiction archetype. Joseph Čapek, who was a noted painter and writer in his own right, was arrested by the Gestapo in 1939 and died in Bergen-Belsen concentration camp in April 1945.

ANDROIDS; CYBORGS & ROBOTS; HUMOR & SATIRE; MYTHOLOGY & LEGEND; POLITICAL SF

## Major Works

*R.U.R.—Rossum's Universal Robots: A Fantastic Melodrama* (1921) English version, translated by David Wyllie, is available at eBooks@University of Adelaide: http://etext.library.adelaide.edu.au/c/capek/karel/rur/. The text of *RUR—Rossumovi univerzální roboti* in the original Czech is available in full at http://www.gutenberg.org/etext/13083
*Krakatit* (1924)
*The Makropoulos Secret* (1925)
*The Absolute At Large* (1927)
*War with the Newts* (1936)

### Collections

*Cross Roads.* Translated by Norma Comrada. North Haven, CT: Catbird, 2002.
*Toward the Radical Center: A Karel Čapek Reader*, Peter Kussi, ed. Highland Park, NJ: Catbird, 1990.

### Other Important Works

"The Author of the Robots Defends Himself." *Lido'vé noviny (People's News).* June 9, 1935. Trans. Cyril Simsa. *Science Fiction Studies* 23 (1996). http://www.depauw.edu/sfs/documents/capek68.htm.

## Research Sources

*Encyclopedias and Handbooks:* **AW, BW, CA, ESF, MSSF, NNDB, SFW, WS**

*Bibliographies:* **ARB, FF, SFAN**

### Biographies and Interviews

Klíma, Ivan. *Karel Čapek. Life and Work.* Translated by Norma Comrada. North Haven, CT: Catbird, 2002.
Mann, Erika. "A Last Conversation with Karel Čapek." The Nation, January 14, 1939: 68–69. Erika Mann was the daughter of German Nobel Prize laureate author, Thomas Mann. She interviewed Čapek shortly before his death in 1938.

### Criticism and Readers' Guides

Abrash, Merritt. "*R.U.R.* Restored and Reconsidered." *Extrapolation* 32 (1991): 184–192.
Bengals, Barbara. "'Read History:' Dehumanization in Karel Čapek's *R.U.R.*" In Thomas P. Dunn and Richard eds., *The Mechanical God: Machines in Science Fiction.* Westport, CT: Greenwood, 1982, 13–17.
Kinyon, Kamila. "The Phenomenology of Robots: Confrontations with Death in Karel Čapek's *R.U.R.*" *Science Fiction Studies* 26 (1999): 379–400.

Maslen, Elizabeth. "Proper Words in Proper Places: The Challenge of Čapek's *War with the Newts*." *Science Fiction Studies 14 (1987)*. http://www.depauw.edu/sfs/review_essays/maslen41.htm.

## Web Sites

*Karel Čapek (1890–1938)*. Dominick Zunt. February 2004. Includes an extensive bibliography, "The Works and Translations of Karel Čapek," and translations of newspaper articles Čapek wrote for Prague newspapers and magazines ("About the Word Robot," from *Lidove Noviny* (People's News), December 24, 1933. Translated by Norma Comrada, and "Why I am Not a Communist," from *Pritomnost* (*Presence* magazine), December 2, 1924. Translated by Martin Pokorny. http://capek.misto.cz/english/.

*Karel Čapek Links*. April 2007. Links to Web sites with personal information about Čapek, and translations of his work. http://www.karelcapek.com/.

*R.U.R.—Rossum's Universal Robots*. Dennis G. Jerz. October 2002. An extremely valuable web site, that includes summary, links and reviews, as well as an Image Archive of photos and drawings from early productions of the play. http://jerz.setonhill.edu/resources/RUR/index.html.

# Orson Scott Card (1951–   )

*At last he came to a door, with these words in glowing emeralds:*

*THE END OF THE WORLD*

*He did not hesitate. He opened the door and stepped through.*

> *—Ender's Game (1985)*

## Biography

Orson Scott Card is an outspoken writer, critic, political essayist, and speaker. But it is his Ender novels that established his reputation with fans and critics: *Ender's Game* (1985) regularly tops the list of popular novels for young readers. *Ender's Game*, and its sequel *Speaker for the Dead* (1986), remain the only sf novels to earn their author both Hugo and Nebula awards two years in a row. The long-awaited film version is reportedly in development, with a screenplay by Card himself.

Card is descended from Charles Ora Card, a Mormon pioneer and son-in-law of Brigham Young, who fled from the United States to Canada to escape religious persecution. Educated at Brigham Young University and the University of Utah, Orson Scott Card is currently "distinguished professor" at Southern Virginia University in Buena Vista, Virginia. He lives with his family in Greensboro, North Carolina.

ALIEN THREAT; CHILDREN IN SF; MESSIAHS; RELIGION; VIRTUAL REALITY; WAR

## Major Works

*Novels*

*Songmaster* (1979)

*The Worthing Chronicle* (1983) "Fix-up" of linked stories from the late 1970s, reissued in a definitive single-volume format.

The Ender saga: *Ender's Game* (1985—**Hugo, Nebula**), *Speaker for the Dead* (1986— **Hugo, Locus Poll, Nebula**), *Xenocide* (1991), *Children of the Mind* (1996), *Ender's Shadow* (1999), *Shadow of the Hegemon* (2001), *Shadow Puppets* (2002), *Shadow of the Giant* (2005)

*Wyrms* (1987)

*The Folk of the Fringe* (1989) A collection of linked post-apocalyptic stories.

The Homecoming Saga: *The Memory of Earth* (1992), *The Call of Earth* (1992), *The Ships of Earth* (1994), *Earthfall* (1995), *Earthborn* (1995)

*Empire* (2006)

*Collections*

*Maps in a Mirror: The Short Fiction of Orson Scott Card.* (1990—**Locus Poll**) New York: Orb, 2004. Combines stories from previous collections such as *The Changed Man* (1992), *Cruel Miracles* (1992), and *Monkey Sonatas* (1993).

*Notable Short Stories*

"Ender's Game" (1977) http://www.hatrack.com/osc/stories/enders-game.shtml.

"Prior Restraint" (1986) http://www.hatrack.com/osc/stories/prior-restraint.shtml.

"Eye for Eye" (1987) **Hugo**

"Dogwalker" (1989) **Locus Poll** http://www.frescopictures.com/movies/dogwalker/ short-story.html.

*Other Important Works*

*Character and Viewpoint: Elements of Writing* (1999)

"Fantasy and the Believing Reader." *Science Fiction Review,* Fall 1982. http://www. hatrack.com/osc/articles/fall82.shtml.

*How to Write Science Fiction and Fantasy* (2001) **Hugo**

"How Tolkien Means." In Karen Haber, ed., *Meditations on Middle Earth.* New York: St. Martin's Press, 2001, 153–174.

"Morality in Videogames." *Forbes.* December 14, 2006. http://www.forbes.com/2006/ 12/10/games-orson-card-tech-cx_mn_games06_1212morality.html.

## Research Sources

*Encyclopedias and Handbooks:* **AW, BW, CA, CANR, ESF, NNDB, SFW**

*Bibliographies:* **ARB, FF, SFAN**

Collings, Michael. *Storyteller: The Official Orson Scott Card Bibliography and Guide.* Woodstock, GA: Overlook Connection, 2001.

## Biographies and Interviews

Allen, Moira. "Orson Scott Card: On Religion in Science Fiction and Fantasy." *Phantastes*. Spring 2000. http://www.writing-world.com/sf/card.shtml.

Gaudiosi, John. "Orson Scott Card Builds an Empire." *Wired*. October 11, 2006. http://www.wired.com/news/technology/0,72093-0.html?tw=rss.index.

*Geeks On*. Interview, August 6, 2005. http://www.geekson.com/archives/archiveepisodes/2005/episode080605.htm.

James, Warren W. Interview. *Mike Hodel's Hour 25*. January 12, 2001. http://www.hour25online.com/Hour25_Previous_Shows_2001-1.html#orson-scott-card_2001-01-12.

Jenkins, Henry. Orson Scott Card and Allen Steele in Discussion at MIT: February 19, 1998. (Edited version). *Media in Transition*. August 29, 1998. Massachusetts Institute of Technology. http://web.mit.edu/m-i-t/science_fiction/transcripts/card_steele_index.html.

Minkowitz, Donna. "My Favorite Author, My Worst Interview." *Salon*. February 3, 2000. http://archive.salon.com/books/feature/2000/02/03/card/.

## Criticism and Readers' Guides

Collings, Michael R. *In the Image of God: Theme, Characterization, and Landscape in the Fiction of Orson Scott Card*. New York: Greenwood, 1990.

Doyle, Christine. "Orson Scott Card's Ender and Bean: The Exceptional Child as Hero." *Children's Literature in Education* 35 (2004): 301–318.

Kessel, John. "Creating the Innocent Killer: *Ender's Game*, Intention, and Morality." *Moment Universe*. North Carolina State University. http://www4.ncsu.edu/~tenshi/Killer_000.htm.

Slusser, George. "The Forever Child: *Ender's Game* and the Mythic Universe of Science Fiction." In Gary Westfahl and George Edgar Slusser, eds., *Nursery Realms: Children in the Worlds of Science Fiction, Fantasy, and Horror*. Athens: University of Georgia Press, 1999, 73–90.

Tyson, Edith S. *Orson Scott Card: Writer of the Terrible Choice*. Lanham, MD: Rowman & Littlefield/Scarecrow, 2003.

Willett, Edward. *Orson Scott Card: Architect of Alternate Worlds*. Berkeley Heights, NJ: Enslow, 2006.

## Web Sites

*Hatrack River. The Official Web site of Orson Scott Card*. Includes links to Card's critical writing and opinion pieces (*The Ornery American*). http://www.hatrack.com/.

*Bean's Place*. "Bean." September 2004. Fan tribute to *Ender's Game*. http://www.angelfire.com/nh/kc/.

*PhiloticWeb*. March 2008. Fan forum on *Ender's Game*. http://www.philoticweb.net/.

**If you enjoyed Orson Scott Card...**

Vivid, action-fueled plots and strong, sympathetic young protagonists, make it natural that novels like *Ender's Game* and its sequels would be very attractive to young readers. But Card's fiction is much more than that: deeply rooted in his strong sense of family and his faith, his rich and varied output achieve a real mythic intensity, based on complicated moral themes and Messianic heroes.

**Then you might like...**

*Sir Arthur C. Clarke*. Early in his long career, Clarke moved away from writing standard sf adventure and "optimistic propaganda for science" (ESF) and moved his storytelling into a more transcendent style that reflected his interest in Asian and alternative philosophies. In *Childhood's End* and *Rendezvous with Rama*, Clarke, like Card, uses the tropes of science fiction to take his characters—and readers—on a journey of the spirit.

*Gordon R. Dickson*. In the "Childe Cycle," beginning with *Dorsai!* (originally, *The Genetic General*, 1959, rev. 1976), genetically isolated colonies have produced fiercely independent warriors who are the most valuable mercenaries in the known universe. Starting as "action-adventure of a superior sort" (**AW**), the series becomes more thoughtful as the Dorsai are revealed to be the first examples of a new kind of humanity: Ethical-Responsible Man.

*Robert Heinlein*. The ultimate master of stories in which the least regarded of society—youngsters, outcasts, and dreamers—harness their superior talents and triumph over adversity and alien threats (often with the aid of a "father-figure" mentor, whose voice came increasingly to resemble Heinlein's own). Novels worth comparing to *Ender's Game* and its sequels are *Starship Troopers*, *Orphans of the Sky*, and *Friday*.

*Frank Herbert*. As with the setting and backstory of Card's Ender stories, *Dune's* desert planet, Arrakis, is fully realized; the struggles and triumphs of his Messianic central character, Paul Atriedes and his dynasty, cannot be disentangled from their landscape and Herbert's message—respect for the ecology and his plea for a sustainable lifestyle.

*Cordwainer Smith*. In the thirty stories and three novels of "Instrumentality of Mankind," Smith (Paul Linebarger) chronicled the exploitation, and eventual liberation, of Scanners and Underpeople, blending sociology and hard science, style and substance that reflect the author's familiarity with Chinese philosophy. Toward the end of his life, when Linebarger became a devout Episcopalian, he began to include layers of Christian allegory in the saga.

# Suzy McKee Charnas (1939–   )

> *The history of the Holdfast teaches one great lesson: Do not underestimate the lowly.*
>
> —*The Conqueror's Child (2000)*

# Biography

Suzy McKee was born in New York City, the daughter of professional illustrators. After completing a Master's degree in education at New York University, she joined the Peace Corps and taught English and History in Africa. She is married to Steven Charnas, and lives in New Mexico.

Charnas' first novel was *Walk to the End of the World* (1974), the first volume in her four-part sf series "Holdfast," about a post-apocalyptic America where women are enslaved and treated as breeding stock, and the nomadic society of free women who live beyond its reach. In addition to the Holdfast novels, Charnas writes fantasy, horror (the Weyland Vampire stories), and juvenile fiction, such as the Sorcery Hall series (1985–1989), the adventures of a trainee wizard dedicated to defending the world from the forces of evil.

APOCALYPSE AND AFTER; FEMINISM; GENDER & SEXUALITY; WOMEN IN SF

# Major Works

*Novels*

The Holdfast Chronicles: *Walk to the End of the World* (1974), *Motherlines* (1978), *The Furies* (1994), and *The Conqueror's Child* (1999—**Tiptree**)

*Collections*

*The Slave and the Free*. New York: Tor: 1999. Omnibus version of *Walk to the End of the World* and *Motherlines*.

*Moonstone and Tiger-Eye* (1992) A chapbook in the Author's Choice Monthly series, which contains an author's preface and two sf stories, "Scorched Supper on New Niger" (1980), and "Evil Thoughts" (1992).

*Stagestruck Vampires: And Other Phantasms* (2006) Horror stories and two essays about her writing.

*Notable Short Stories*

"Boobs" (1989) **Hugo**
"Peregrines" (2004) http://www.scifi.com/scifiction/originals/.
"Heavy Lifting" (2005) http://www.scifi.com/scifiction/originals/.

*Other Important Works*

*My Father's Ghost: The Return of My Old Man, and Other Second Chances* (2002)
"No Such Thing as Tearing Down Just a Little: Post-Holocaust Themes in Feminist SF." *Janus* 6 (1980): 25–28.

"The Problem of Inadequate Amazons." *New York Review of Science Fiction* 2(8) (1990): 11+.
"A Woman Appeared." In Marleen Barr, ed., *Future Females: A Critical Anthology.* Bowling Green, OH: Bowling Green State University Popular Press, 1981, 103–108.

## Research Sources

*Encyclopedias and Handbooks:* **AW, CA, CANR, ESF, SFW**

*Bibliographies:* **ARB, FF, SFAN**

### Biographies and Interviews

Clemente, Bill. "Of Women and Wonder: A Conversation with Suzy McKee Charnas." In Helen Merrick and Tess Williams, eds., *Women of Other Worlds.* Nedlands: University of Western Australia Press, 1999, 60–81.

Gordon, Joan. "Closed Systems Kill: An Interview with Suzy McKee Charnas." *Science Fiction Studies* 26 (1999): 447–468. http://www.depauw.edu/sfs/interviews/charnasinterview.htm.

Grant, Gavin J. Interview. *Booksense.* November 11, 2002. American Booksellers Association. http://www.booksense.com/people/archive/c/charnassuzymckee.jsp.

Mohr, Dunja. "An Interview with Suzy McKee Charnas." *New York Review of Science Fiction* 12(1 & 2) (1999): 1+.

### Criticism and Readers' Guides

Barr, Marleen. "Utopia at the End of a Male Chauvinist Dystopian World: Suzy McKee Charnas' Feminist Science Fiction." In *Genre Fission: A New Discourse Practice for Cultural Studies.* Iowa City: University of Iowa Press, 2000, 43–66.

Calvalcanti, Ildney. "The Writing of Utopia and the Feminist Critical Dystopia: Suzy McKee Charnas' Holdfast Series." In Rafaella Baccolini and Tom Moylan, eds., *Dark Horizons: Science Fiction and the Dystopian Imagination.* New York: Routledge, 2003, 47–68.

Clemente, Bill. "Apprehending Identity in the Alldera Novels of Suzy McKee Charnas." In Martha Bartter, ed., The Utopian Fantastic. Westport, CT: Praeger, 2004, 81–90.

Duchamp, L.Timmel. "Suzy McKee Charnas's *The Conqueror's Child.*" *Mindspring.* March 2000. http://ltimmel.home.mindspring.com/child.html.

Wulf, Elizabeth. "Becoming Heroic: Alternative Female Heroes in Suzy McKee Charnas' *The Conqueror's Child.*" *Extrapolation* 46 (2005): 120–132.

### Web Sites

*Suzy McKee Charnas: Stagestruck Vampires.* Official Web site. http://www.suzymckeecharnas.com/.

# C.J. Cherryh (1942–   )

*...a beautiful people, tall and slim and golden beneath their black robes: golden manes streaked with bronze, delicate, humanoid features, long, slender hands...The mri were at once humanlike and disturbingly alien. Such also were their minds, that could grasp outsiders' ways and yet steadfastly refused to compromise with them.*

*—The Faded Sun (1978)*

## Biography

When her first novels were published in 1976, Carolyn Janice Cherry was advised to use her initials because it would downplay the fact that she was a woman (her first editor also felt that "Carolyn Cherry" sounded too much like a romance writer). Cherryh added the silent "h" to be "unique." Since winning the John W. Campbell Award for Best New Writer in 1977, Cherryh has written over sixty novels; her stories are known for their detailed world building, characters with real depth and psychological insight, and their thoroughly engaging perspectives.

C. J. Cherryh was born in St. Louis, Missouri, and raised in Oklahoma. She was a member of Phi Beta Kappa at the University of Oklahoma, and later did an MA in classics at Johns Hopkins University, where she was a Woodrow Wilson fellow. She lives near Spokane, Washington, with her partner, science fiction/fantasy author and artist, Jane Fancher.

ALIEN WORLDS; ANDROIDS, CYBORGS & ROBOTS; COLONIZATION OF OTHER WORLDS; GENETIC ENGINEERING & CLONING; WAR

## Major Works

*Novels*

*Downbelow Station* (1981) **Hugo**
*Merchanter's Luck* (1982)
*Port Eternity* (1982)
Unionside series: *The Betrayal* (1988—**Hugo**), *The Rebirth* (1988), *Vindication* (1989)
     *Cyteen* (1988), which was also a **Locus Poll** winner, is the omnibus version of
     the Unionside series.
The Chanur novels: including *The Pride of Chanur* (1981), and *The Kif Strike Back*
     (1985)
The Faded Sun Trilogy: *Kesrith* (1978), *Shon'Jir* (1978), *Kutath* (1979)
The Foreigner Universe: First, Second, and Third sequences, beginning with *Foreigner*
     (1994), and *Invader* (1995). The most recent, *Deliverer*, was published in 2007.

## Collections

*The Collected Short Fiction of C. J. Cherryh.* New York: DAW, 2004. This volume combines two previous collections, *Sunfall* (1981), and *Visible Light* (1986), plus fifteen extra stories, including "Cassandra" (1978—**Hugo**) and "The Scapegoat" (1985).

*Glass and Amber.* Cambridge, MA: NESFA, 1987. Includes a selection of short fiction, and essays such as "In Alien Tongues" (1981), "Perspectives in SF" (1987), "Romantic/Science Fiction: The Oldest Form of Literature" (1978), and "The Use of Archaeology in Worldbuilding" (1978).

## Other Important Works

"Goodbye Star Wars, Hello Alley-Oop." In Sharon Jarvis, ed., *Inside Outer Space: Science Fiction Professionals Look at Their Craft.* New York: Ungar, 1985, 17–26.

# Research Sources

*Encyclopedias and Handbooks:* **AW, CA, CANR, ESF, NNDB**

*Bibliographies:* **ARB, FF, SFAN**

## Biographies and Interviews

Carmien, Edward. "C. J. Cherryh Interview." *SFRevu.* June 15, 2004. http://www.sfrevu.com/ISSUES/2004/0406/CJ%20Cherryh%20Interview/Review.htm.
*SFFWorld.* Interview. January 1, 2000. http://www.sffworld.com/interview/21p0.html.

## Criticism and Readers' Guides

Bacon-Smith, Camille. "Military Command in Women's Science Fiction: C. J. Cherryh's Signy Mallory." *The Swan* 1 (2000). http://www.dm.net/~theswan/baconsmith.html.
Carmien, Edward, ed. *The Cherryh Odyssey.* Holicong, PA.: Borgo, 2004.
Eisenhour, Susan. "A Subversive in Hyperspace: C. J. Cherryh's Feminist Transformation of Space Opera." *New York Review of Science Fiction* 9(2) (1996): 1+.
Hamill, Pete. "C. J. Cherryh, Science Fiction, and the Soft Sciences." *At Wanderer's Well.* http://www.dancingbadger.com/c_j_cherryh.htm.
Heidkamp, Bernie. "Responses to the Alien Mother in Post-Maternal Cultures: C. J. Cherryh and Orson Scott Card." *Science Fiction Studies* 23 (1996): 339–354. http://www.depauw.edu/sfs/backissues/70/heidkamp70art.htm.
Jones, Gwyneth. "Consider Her Ways: The Fiction of C. J. Cherryh." In *Deconstructing the Starships: Science, Fiction, and Reality.* Liverpool: Liverpool University Press, 1999, 131–140.
Raffel, Burton. "C. J. Cherryh's Fiction." *Literary Review* 44 (2001): 578–591.
Stinson, J. G. "Going Native: The Human as Other in Selected Works of C. J. Cherryh." *Strange Horizons.* March 18, 2002. http://www.strangehorizons.com/2002/20020318/going_native.shtml.

## Web Sites

*C. J. Cherryh's World.* Official Web site, "under construction," but still features a full range of author information, including a blog on the writer's life, and links to 1995 essays "Writerisms and Other Sins: A Writer's Shortcut to Stronger Writing," and "Strong vs. Weak Characters." http://www.cherryh.com/.

*Shejidan.* February 2004. Curiosity Killed This Cat. Fan forum, with useful links. http://www.shejidan.com/main.html.

# Ted Chiang (1967–   )

> *There is a well-known "proof" that demonstrates that one equals two. . . . Hidden inconspicuously in the middle is a division by zero, and at that point the proof has stepped off the brink, making all rules null and void.*
> *—"Division by Zero" (1991)*

## Biography

Ted Chiang was born in Port Jefferson, New York. He attended Brown University, graduating with a Computer Sciences degree, and has worked as a technical writer, writing software documentation. His stories use offbeat interpretations of historical themes, religious imagery, and philosophical ideas to unsettling and thought-provoking effect. His first novel, *The Merchant and the Alchemist's Gate* (2007), is a time-travel story, which, according to *Publishers Weekly*, is "half lyrical Arabian Nights legend and half old school cautionary SF tale." Ted Chiang lives near Seattle, Washington.

ALTERNATIVE HISTORY; GODS AND DEMONS; MYTHOLOGY & LEGEND

## Major Works

*Novels*

*The Merchant and the Alchemist's Gate* (2007) Excerpt: http://www.sfsite.com/fsf/fiction/tc01.htm.

*Collections*

*Stories of Your Life, and Others* (2002)—**Locus Poll** Each story in this collection is accompanied by an author's note.

*Notable Short Stories*

"Tower of Babylon" (1990) **Nebula**
"Division by Zero" (1991) http://www.fantasticmetropolis.com/i/division/.

"Understand" (1999) http://www.infinityplus.co.uk/stories/under.htm.
"Story of Your Life" (1998) **Nebula**
"Hell Is the Absence of God" (2001) **Hugo, Locus Poll, Nebula**

## Research Sources

*Encyclopedias and Handbooks:* **AW, CA**

*Bibliographies:* **ARB, FF, SFAN**

### Biographies and Interviews

Anders, Lou. Interview. *SFsite.* July 2002. http://www.sfsite.com/09b/tc136.htm.
Graff, Rani. Interview. *Fantastic Metropolis.* December 13, 2003. http://www.fantasticmetropolis.com/i/chiang/.
Grant, Gavin J. Interview. *Booksense.* August 29, 2002. American Booksellers Association. http://www.booksense.com/people/archive/chiangted.jsp.
*Locus Online.* "Science, Language and Magic: Interview." August 2002. http://www.locusmag.com/2002/Issue08/Chiang.html.
Smith, Jeremy. "The Absence of God: Ted Chiang Interviewed." *Interzone* 182: 23–26. September 2002. http://www.infinityplus.co.uk/nonfiction/inttchiang.htm.

### Criticism and Readers' Guides

Beatty, Greg. "The Bridge between Truth/Death and Power/Knowledge: Ted Chiang's 'Seventy-two Letters'" *Strange Horizons.* April 2001. http://www.strangehorizons.com/2001/20010416/ted_chiang.shtml.
Miéville, China. "Wonder Boy." *The Guardian* (London). April 24, 2004. http://books.guardian.co.uk/reviews/sciencefiction/0,6121,1201890,00.html.

### Web Sites

*With Boots.* October 29, 2007. Multiple contributor blog, in which Chiang participates. http://withboots.blogspot.com/.

# Sir Arthur C. Clarke (1917–2008)

*There are no nationalities beyond the stratosphere....We, who have striven to place humanity upon the road to the stars, make this solemn declaration, now and for the future: We will take no frontiers into space.*

*—Prelude to Space (1947)*

## Biography

As a scientist, Arthur C. Clarke worked to translate the "stuff of science fiction"— radar early warning systems, communication satellites, and space elevators—into realities. His fiction is notable for its mystical and cosmic elements, building memorable stories around conceptual breakthroughs that accelerate humanity into the next stage of its evolution. One of his earliest such stories, "The Sentinel" (1948), became the basis of Stanley Kubrick's film *2001: A Space Odyssey*, a classic of transcendence in space.

Arthur Charles Clarke was born in Somerset, England. During his long career, he was a civil servant, a scientist, and an indefatigable commentator on science, technology, and the human spirit. For many years he suffered from post-polio syndrome, and during the 1950s he moved to Sri Lanka, seeking relief from the symptoms of this progressive illness. He was knighted in 2000, in recognition of his contribution to British literature. Sir Arthur C. Clarke died, aged ninety, on March 19, 2008.

ARTIFICIAL INTELLIGENCE; CHILDREN IN SF; GODS & DEMONS; HARD SF; UTOPIAS

## Major Works

*Novels*

*Prelude to Space* (1951)
*The City and the Stars* (1956) Expanded and rewritten version of *Against the Fall of Night* (1953)
*Childhood's End* (1953)
The 2001 sequence: *2001: A Space Odyssey* (1968), *2010: Odyssey Two* (1982), *2061: Odyssey Three* (1987), *3001: The Final Odyssey* (1997)
*Rendezvous with Rama* (1973) **BSF, Hugo, Nebula, Locus Poll**
*The Fountains of Paradise* (1979) **Nebula, Hugo**

*Collections*

*The Collected Stories of Arthur C. Clarke*. New York: Tor: 2001. Among the many classic Clarke stories in this volume are "The Nine Billion Names of God" (1967), and "The Hammer of God" (1992).

*Short Stories*

"The Sentinel" (1948)
"The Star" (1955) **Hugo**
"A Meeting with Medusa" (1971) **Nebula**

*Other Important Works*

*2001: A Space Odyssey*. Metro-Goldwyn-Mayer. 1968. Directed by Stanley Kubrick, with a screenplay by Clarke and Kubrick. Winner of **Hugo** for Best Dramatic Presentation.

*2010: Odyssey Two.* Metro-Goldwyn-Mayer. 1984. Winner of **Hugo** for Best Dramatic Presentation.
*Astounding Days: A Science Fictional Autobiography* (1989).
*Greetings, Carbon-Based Bipeds! Collected Essays, 1934–1998* (2000) Includes "Son of Dr Strangelove" (1977), and other essays on science and sf.
"Presidents, Experts, and Asteroids." *Science Magazine,* June 5, 1998. American Association for the Advancement of Science. http://www.sciencemag. org/cgi/content/full/280/5369/1532.

## Research Sources

*Encyclopedias and Handbooks:* **AW, BW, CA, CANR, ESF, MSSF, NNDB, SFW, WS**
*Bibliographies:* **ARB, FF, SFAN**

Main, Michael. "The Fiction of Arthur C. Clarke: 1937–1951" *Storypilot.* July 2006. http://www.storypilot.com/sf/clarke.html.

### Biographies and Interviews

BBC Radio. Interviews. January 4, 1987 and October 3, 1975. BBC Four. BBC.co.uk. http://www.bbc.co.uk/bbcfour/audiointerviews/profilepages/clarkea1.shtml.
Cherry, Matt. "God, Science, and Delusion: A Chat with Arthur C. Clarke." *Free Inquiry.* February 2004. Secular Humanism. http://www.secularhumanism.org/ index.php?section=library&page=clarke_19_2.
Couper, Heather. "Sir Arthur C. Clarke: The Science and the Fiction." Radio 4. October 5, 2005. BBC.co.uk. http://www.bbc.co.uk/radio4/science/arthurcclarke.shtml.
"Leaving Home: Sir Arthur C. Clarke on Terraforming." *Astrobiology Magazine,* June 22, 2004. National Aeronautics and Space Administration. http://www.astrobio. net/news/article1030.html.
McAleer, Neil. *Arthur C. Clarke: The Authorized Biography.* Chicago, IL: Contemporary, 1992.
McKie, Robin. "Meeting Mr. Universe. (Appreciation)." *Guardian Online.* March 23, 2008. http://books.guardian.co.uk/departments/sciencefiction/story/0,2267484,00. html.
Lilley, Ernest. "2001: Time for a Few Words About Arthur C. Clarke." *SFRevu.* April 2008. http://www.sfrevu.com/ISSUES/2001/0101/9997%20Arthur%20C. %20Clarke/Clarke.htm.

### Criticism and Readers' Guides

Blackford, Russell. "Future Problematic: Reflections on *The City* and *The Stars.*" In Damien Broderick, ed., *Earth Is But a Star: Excursions through Science Fiction to the Far Future.* Crawley, WA: University of Western Australia Press, 2001, 35–46.

DePaolo, Charles. "Arthur C. Clarke's *2001: A Space Odyssey.*" In *Human Prehistory in Fiction.* Jefferson, NC: McFarland, 2002, 79–93.

Fry, Carrol L. "From Technology to Transcendence: Humanity's Evolutionary Journey in *2001: A Space Odyssey.*" *Extrapolation* 44 (2003): 331–343.

Huntington, John. "The Unity of *Childhood's End.*" *Science Fiction Studies* 1 (1974): 154–164. http://www.depauw.edu/sfs/backissues/3/huntington3art.htm.

Miller, Timothy C. "Arthur C. Clarke's *Rendezvous with Rama*: Agent of Evolution." *Journal of the Fantastic in the Arts* 9(4) (1998): 336–344.

Reid, Robin Anne. *Arthur C. Clarke: A Critical Companion.* Westport, CT: Greenwood, 1997.

Samuelson, David N. "Clarke's *Childhood's End*: A Median Stage of Adolescence?" *Science Fiction Studies* 1 (1973): 4–17. http://www.depauw.edu/sfs/backissues/1/samuelson1art.htm.

Seeley, Nicholas. "The Wizard in the Space Station: A Look Back at the Works of the Late Sir Arthur C. Clarke." *Strange Horizons.* April 14, 2008. http://www.strangehorizons.com/2008/20080414/seeley-a.shtml.

Westfahl, Gary. "'He Was Part of Mankind': Arthur C. Clarke's *A Fall of Moondust.*" In *Cosmic Engineers: A Study of Hard Science Fiction.* Westport, CT: Greenwood, 1996, 67–82.

Živković, Zoran. "The Motif of First Contact in Arthur C. Clarke's sf Works." Translated by Ruzica White and John White. *Fantastic Metropolis.* October 15, 2001. http://www.fantasticmetropolis.com/i/clarke/.

## Web Sites

*The Arthur C. Clarke Foundation*, September 2006. The official Web site of the Foundation that exists to "advance [the] insights of ACC" includes links, a quote of the day and other information on Clarke's ideas and achievements. http://www.clarkefoundation.org/.

*Arthur C. Clarke.net.* Official Web site, "Home to all things Clarkean." http://www.arthurcclarke.net/.

**If you enjoyed Arthur C. Clarke...**

Sir Arthur C. Clarke was a writer of science fiction who was equally at home in the world of real life scientific innovation and discovery. He began his sf career writing "scientific puzzles" and "optimistic propaganda for science" (ESF), but stories like "The Sentinel" (1948) made his reputation for a more transcendent style, reflecting his interest in Asian philosophies, alternative possibilities, and the natural world. Clarke used the tropes of science fiction to take his characters   and readers—on a journey of the spirit.

**Then you might like...**

*Stephen Baxter.* Thirty-plus novels include three collaborations with Sir Arthur C. Clarke, whom Baxter acknowledges as an early influence. Like Clarke, Baxter makes good use of his professional science background, and his degrees in Mathematics and Aeronautical Engineering, while also conveying a "sense of wonder" and transcendence in works such as the "Manifold" trilogy.

*Greg Bear.* Credited with the first account of nanotechnology in sf (*Blood Music*), Bear has also written about galactic conflict (*Forge of God*), portals to other universes (*Eon*), and the inner space of the mind (*Queen of Angels*). In his novels about accelerated evolution (*Blood Music* and *Darwin's Radio*), the universes revealed are within the individual characters and their DNA.

*Hal Clement.* While he was not the most elegant stylist, Clement brought to his stories a true sense of wonder at the complexity of the universe—and man's place in it as a scientist and seeker of knowledge. His *Mission of Gravity* (1953), the story of a rescue mission to a super-jovian planet with erratic gravity, is one of the best-loved novels of classic sf.

*Ursula K. Le Guin.* Trained as a historian, UKL has a ". . . tradition of challenging deeply held, and poorly reasoned, assumptions . . ." (**NNDB**). She is more interested in the anthropology than the hardware, even in her most traditional sf stories, such as the "Hainish" novels, but she shares with Clarke the basic assumption that our world—any world—is far more complex and wonderful than our limited intellects can imagine.

*Clifford D. Simak.* Like Clarke, Simak's early work tended toward competent, traditional stories of time travel, aliens, and space engineers. But his work evolved as he blended the tropes of the genre with nostalgic, pastoral attitudes in novels like *Way Station* (1963) and the eight linked stories of *City* (1952). Like Clarke, the message is "trust the unknown, embrace the strange" (**AW**).

# Samuel R. Delany (1942–  )

> *I am suddenly catapulted into a paranoid world where the walls not only have ears, but probably eyes, and long, claw-tipped fingers.*
> —*"Time Considered as a Helix of Semi-Precious Stones" (1969)*

## Biography

In his memoir, *The Motion of Light in Water*, Samuel Delany describes himself as "[a] black man. A gay man. A writer." His work often features those outside society's mainstream, such as slaves or those who have been physically or biologically modified, characters whose marginalized status is on view for all to see. Delany mixes a potent blend of the conventions of space opera and a love of language, demonstrating a keen understanding of the way language and conventions affect our perception of reality.

Samuel Ray Delany, Jr., was born in Harlem, New York, the child of a prosperous and influential African-American family, the grandchild of freed slaves. His first novel was published before his twentieth birthday. Since then, Delany has published many volumes of fiction, memoir, erotica, and criticism and, over the years, has held various academic positions. He currently teaches English at the State University of New York at Buffalo.

FANTASY; GENDER & SEXUALITY; LANGUAGE; MYTHOLOGY & LEG-END; NEW WAVE; SEX & TABOOS; SPACE OPERA

# Major Works

## Novels

*The Jewels of Aptor* (1962)
The Fall of the Towers: *Captives of the Flame* (1963—aka *Out of the Dead City*), *The Towers of Toron* (1964), and *City of a Thousand Suns* (1965)
*Empire Star* (1966)
*Babel-17* (1966) **Nebula**
*The Einstein Intersection* (1967) **Nebula**
*Nova* (1968)
*Dhalgren* (1975)
*Triton* (1976—aka Trouble on Triton)
*Stars in My Pocket Like Grains of Sand* (1984) **Tiptree, Special Mention** for the Twentieth Anniversery edition, 2004
*They Fly at Çiron* (1993)

## Collections

*Aye, and Gomorrah, and Other Stories.* New York: Vintage, 2003. Combines all fiction in the collections *Driftglass* (1971), and *Distant Stars* (1981).
*The Fall of the Towers.* New York: Vintage, 2004. Includes a revised version of *Out of the Dead City.*

## Notable Short Stories

"Driftglass" (1967)
"Time Considered as a Helix of Semi-Precious Stones" (1968) **Hugo, Nebula**
"We, in Some Strange Power's Employ, Move on a Rigorous Line" (1968—aka "Lines of Power")
"Aye, and Gomorrah" (1971) **Nebula**

## Other Important Works

*About Writing: Seven Essays, Four Letters and Five Interviews* (2006)
"Future Shock." *The Village Voice.* December 29, 1999. Village Voice Media Holdings. http://www.villagevoice.com/news/9952,delany,11385,1.html.
*The Jewel-Hinged Jaw: Notes on the Language of Science Fiction.* (1977)

*The Motion of Light in Water: East Village Sex and Science Fiction Writing: 1960–1965* (1993)

"Racism and Science Fiction." In Sheree R. Thomas, ed., *Dark Matter: A Century of Speculative Fiction from the African Diaspora*. New York: Warner/Aspect, 2000, 383–397.

"Science Fiction and 'Literature,' or, The Conscience of the King." In James Gunn and Matthew Candelaria, eds., *Speculations on Speculation: Theories of Science Fiction*. Lanham, MD: Scarecrow, 2005, 95–118. This volume also includes another Delany essay, "Some Presumptuous Approaches to Science Fiction" (289–300).

"The Star Pit." *The Mind's Eye Theater*. November 1967. WBAI-FM. http://www.pseudopodium.org/repress/TheStarPit/index.html. With "Notes on 'The Star Pit,'" by Delany.

*Starboard Wine: More Notes on the Language of Science Fiction* (1984)

## Research Sources

*Encyclopedias and Handbooks:* **AW, CA, CANR, ESF, MSSF, NNDB, SFW**

*Bibliographies:* **ARB, FF, SFAN**

Cooper, Rebecca. "A Samuel R. Delany Checklist." *Review of Contemporary Fiction* 16(3) (1996): 170–171.

Stephens, Christopher P. *A Checklist of Samuel R. Delany* (revised). Hastings-on-Hudson, NY: Ultramarine, 1991. http://www.starshards.org/bibliography/.

### Biographies and Interviews

Blaschke, Jayme L. "Samuel R. Delany," *Voices of Vision*. Lincoln: University of Nebraska Press, 2005, 143–156.

"Interview with Samuel Delany." (Audio) *The Paula Gordon Show*. WGUN, Atlanta. May 23, 2001. http://www.paulagordon.com/shows/delany/.

Jenkins, Henry. Octavia Butler/Samuel Delany in Discussion at MIT: February 19, 1998. Edited version. *Media in Transition*. August 29, 1998. Massachusetts Institute of Technology. http://web.mit.edu/m-i-t/science_fiction/transcripts/butler_delany_index.html.

Means, Loren. "Interview with Samuel R. Delany." *YLEM Journal* 24(4) (2004): 8–11. http://www.ylem.org/Journal/2004Iss04vol24.pdf.

*Silent Interviews: On Language, Race, Sex, Science Fiction, and Some Comics: A Collection of Written Interviews*. Hanover, NH: University Press of New England/Wesleyan University Press, 1994.

Steiner, K. Leslie. "Samuel R. Delany." *Pseudopodium*. 2004. http://www.pseudopodium.org/repress/index.html.

## Criticism and Readers' Guides

Bee, Robert. "We, In Some Strange Genre's Employ: Inner Space, Outer Space, Patterns and Signifiers in Samuel Delany's Science Fiction Short Stories." *Internet Review of Science Fiction*. January 2007. http://www.irosf.com/q/zine/article/10352.

Davenport, Tristan. "So, Your Utopia Needs a Language . . . " *Strange Horizons*. October 24, 2005. http://www.strangehorizons.com/2005/20051024/utopia-lang-a.shtml.

Fox, Robert Elliot. *Conscientious Sorcerers: The Black Postmodernist Fiction of LeRoi Jones/Amiri Baraka, Ishmael Reed, and Samuel R. Delany*. New York: Greenwood, 1987.

Freedman, Carl. "About Delany Writing: An Anatomical Meditation." *Extrapolation* 47 (2006): 16–29.

Moore, John. "Singing the Body Unelectric: Mapping and Modelling in Samuel R. Delany's *Dhalgren*." In Tim Armstrong, ed., *American Bodies: Cultural Histories of the Physique*. New York: New York University Press, 1996, 186–195.

*Review of Contemporary Fiction*. Special Samuel Delany Issue, 16 (Fall 1996). Includes essays on *Babel-17*, *Dhalgren*, and other aspects of Delany's work.

Sallis, James, ed. *Ash of Stars: On the Writing of Samuel R. Delany*. Jackson: University Press of Mississippi, 1996.

Thistle, Karen. "Wandering in Bellona: One Path through Delany's *Dhalgren*." *Internet Review of Science Fiction*. February 2004. http://www.irosf.com/q/zine/article/10022.

Tucker, Jeffrey Allen. *A Sense of Wonder: Samuel R. Delany, Race, Identity, and Difference*. Middletown, CT: Wesleyan University Press, 2004.

## Web Sites

*Samuel R. Delany Information*. Jay Schuster. September 2001. The Physician's Computer Company. Long list of links to various Delany-oriented interviews, reviews, and essays. http://www2.pcc.com/staff/jay/delany/

*Starshards, a Samuel R. Delany Web site*. Forrest L. Norvell. December 2005. Bibliography and links to sites of interest, including a forum for fans. http://www.starshards.org/old-index.html.

# Philip K. Dick (1928–1982)

> The electric things have their life too. Paltry as those lives are.
> —*Do Androids Dream of Electric Sheep? (1968)*

## Biography

Philip Kindred Dick was born, six weeks premature, during a freezing Chicago winter; his twin sister, Jane, died one month later. Throughout his life, Dick identified with his dead sister, and felt haunted by her; his well-documented substance abuse and a breakdown he suffered in the 1970s were linked to his desire to reconnect with her. In this confusion of identity Dick found the narrative dynamic that has come to be labeled "Dickian": the clash of what is real and what is not.

While Philip K. Dick was hardly neglected during his lifetime—in 1973, he came twelfth in the *Locus Poll* for All-Time Favorite Author—posthumously, his reputation has "gone platinum." Part of this is due to the movies: since 1982, the year of his untimely death due to a stroke and the transcendent *Blade Runner* (based loosely on 1968's *Do Android's Dream of Electric Sheep?*), no less than eight of Dick's novels and stories have been filmed.

ALTERNATIVE HISTORY; ANDROIDS, CYBORGS & ROBOTS; DRUGS & ALTERED CONSCIOUSNESS; ENTROPY; HUMOR AND SATIRE; MESSIAHS; POP CULTURE

## Major Works

*Novels*

*Solar Lottery* (1955—aka *World of Chance*)
*Time out of Joint* (1959)
*The Man in the High Castle* (1962) **Hugo**
*The Game-Players of Titan* (1963)
*Martian Time-Slip* (1964)
*The Three Stigmata of Palmer Eldritch* (1964)
*Dr. Bloodmoney: Or, How We Got Along After the Bomb* (1965)
*Do Androids Dream of Electric Sheep?* (1968)
*Ubik* (1969)
*A Maze of Death* (1970)
*Flow My Tears, the Policeman Said* (1974)
*Deus Irae* (1976, with Roger Zelazny)
*A Scanner Darkly* (1977) **BSF**
VALIS: *Valis* (1981)
*The Transmigration of Timothy Archer* (1982)
*Radio Free Albemuth*, (1985)

*Collections*

*The Collected Stories of Philip K. Dick*. New York: Citadel Press.
    This is a series of five volumes, containing over 100 stories; each volume features an introduction by an sf notable. The current edition titles are: *Second Variety* (1999, Intro. Norman Spinrad); *The Father Thing* (1999, Intro. John Brunner); *Minority Report* (2002, Intro. James Tiptree, Jr.); *The Eye of the Sybil* (2002, Intro. Thomas M. Disch), and *The Short Happy Life of the Brown Oxford* (2002, Intro. Roger Zelazny).

*Vintage PKD*. New York: Vintage, 2005. Extracts from novels, stories; essays, and
  letters currently unavailable elsewhere.
*Selected Stories of Philip K. Dick*. New York: Pantheon, 2002. Intro. Jonathan Lethem.
  Twenty-one key Dick stories, including "The Minority Report" (1956), and "We
  Can Remember It for You Wholesale" (1966).
*Four Novels of the 1960s*. Jonathan Lethem, ed. New York: Library of America, 2007.
  Omnibus version, which brings together *The Man in the High Castle* (1962), *The
  Three Stigmata of Palmer Eldritch* (1965), *Do Androids Dream of Electric Sheep?*
  (1968), and *Ubik* (1969).

## Other Important Works

"The Android and the Human." In Peter Nicholls, ed., *Science Fiction at Large: A
  Collection of Essays, By Various Hands, About the Interface between Science
  Fiction and Reality*. London: Gollancz, 1976, 199–224.
*The Dark-Haired Girl* (1988)
"Foreword to *The Preserving Machine*. (Unpublished)" *Science Fiction Studies* 2
  (1975): 22–24. http://www.depauw.edu/sfs/backissues/5/dick5art.htm.
"Man, Android, and Machine." Lecture delivered at London's Institute of Contem-
  porary Art. In Peter Nicholls, ed., *Science Fiction at Large*. London: Gollancz,
  1976.
*The Shifting Realities of Philip K. Dick: Selected Literary and Philosophical Writings*.
  Lawrence Sutin, ed. New York: Vintage, 1995.

# Research Sources

*Encyclopedias and Handbooks:* **AW, BW, CA, CAAS, CANR, ESF,
MSSF, NNDB, SFW, WS**

*Bibliographies:* **ARB, FF, SFAN**

"VALBS: Vast Active Living Bibliographic System, or Secondary Texts on PKD."
  Andrew M. Butler, Salvatore Proietti and Umberto Rossi, eds. February 2004.
  http://web.tiscali.it/ausonia/saggistica/jgb_bibliography.html.

## Biographies and Interviews

Butler, Andrew M. *Philip K. Dick*. London: Trafalgar Square/Pocket Essentials UK,
  2001.
Carrère, Emmanuel. *I am Alive and You are Dead: A Journey into the Mind of PKD*.
  Translated by Timothy Bent. New York: Henry Holt, 2004.
Dick, Anne R. *Search for Philip K. Dick, 1928–1982: A Memoir and Biography of the
  Science Fiction Writer*. Lewiston, NY: Edwin Mellen, 1995.
Gopnik, Adam. "Blows against the Empire." *The New Yorker*, August 20, 2007: 79–83.
Lee, Gwen and Doris Elaine Sauter, eds. *What If Our World is Their Heaven? The
  Final Conversations of PKD*. New York: Overlook, 2001.

Sutin, Lawrence. *Divine Invasions: A Life of Philip K. Dick* (1989). New York: Carroll & Graf, 2005.

## Criticism and Readers' Guides

Aldiss, Brian W. "Dick's Maledictory Web: About and Around *Martian Time-Slip*." *Science Fiction Studies* 2 (1975): 22–47. http://www.depauw.edu/sfs/backissues/5/aldiss5art.htm.

Brians, Paul. "Blade Runner (and *Do Androids Dream...*)" *Study Guides*. February 2006. Washington State University. http://www.wsu.edu:8080/~brians/science_fiction/bladerunner.html.

Brooker, Will. *The Blade Runner Experience: The Legacy of a Science Fiction Classic*. London: Wallflower, 2005.

Butler, Andrew M. "LSD, Lying Ink, and *Lies, Inc.*" *Science Fiction Studies* 32 (2005): 265–280.

DiTommaso, Lorenzo. "Redemption in Philip K. Dick's *The Man in the High Castle*." *Science Fiction Studies* 26 (1999): 91–119. http://www.depauw.edu/sfs/backissues/5/aldiss5art.htm.

Enns, Anthony. "Media, Drugs, and Schizophrenia in the Works of Philip K. Dick." *Science Fiction Studies* 33 (2006): 68–88.

Freedman, Carl. "*The Man in the High Castle*: Philip K. Dick and the Construction of Realities." In *Critical Theory and Science Fiction*. Hanover, NH.: University Press of New England/Wesleyan University Press, 2000, 164–180.

Galvan, Jill. "Entering the Posthuman Collective in Philip K. Dick's *Do Androids Dream of Electric Sheep?*" *Science Fiction Studies* 24 (1997): 413–429.

Jackson, Pamela. "Sing out *Ubik*." In Daniel Rosenberg and Susan Harding, eds., *Histories of the Future*. Durham, NC: Duke Univrsity Press, 2005, 171–184.

Jakaitis, Jake. "The Idea of the Asian in Philip K. Dick's *The Man in the High Castle*." In Wong Kin-Yuen et al., eds., *World Weavers: Globalization, Science Fiction, and the Cybernetic Revolution*. Hong Kong: Hong Kong University Press, 2005, 157–166.

Kerman, Judith B., ed. Retrofitting *Blade Runner*: Issues in Ridley Scott's *"Blade Runner"* and Philip K. Dick's *"Do Androids Dream of Electric Sheep"*? Bowling Green, OH: Bowling Green State University Popular Press, 1991.

Landsburg, Alison. "Prosthetic Memory: *Total Recall* and *Blade Runner*." In David Bell, ed., *The Cybercultures Reader.* London: Routledge, 2002, 190–204.

Lawson, Scott. "Philip K. Dick's Valis: A Critique and Demystification." *Internet Review of Science Fiction*. January 2007. http://www.irosf.com/q/zine/article/10338.

Lem, Stanislaw. "Philip K. Dick: A Visionary amongst Charlatans." In *Microworlds*. San Diego CA: Harvest/Harcourt Brace, 1986, 106–135.

Lethem, Jonathan. "About Philip K. Dick." *The Library of America e-Newsletter.* May 2007. http://www.loa.org/images/pdf/lethem_interview.pdf. An interview with Lethem in which he talks about his editorial work on *Philip K. Dick: Four Novels of the 1960s*.

Miller, Ryder W. "Drugs and *A Scanner Darkly:* Was Philip K. Dick against Drug Use?" *Internet Review of Science Fiction.* August 2006. http://www.irosf.com/q/zine/article/10305.

Mullen, R. D. et al., eds. *On Philip K. Dick: 40 Articles from Science-Fiction Studies.* Terre Haute, IN: SF-TH, 1992. A variety of interesting PKD essays and reviews from before 1992. The Table of Contents can be found at http://www.depauw.edu/sfs/PKD-book.htm. Abstracts are available for all essays, and some of the texts are available in full, online.

Palmer, Christopher. *Philip K. Dick: Exhilaration and Terror of the Postmodern.* Liverpool, UK: Liverpool University Press, 2003.

Rossi, Umberto. "The Game of the Rat: A.E. Van Vogt's 800–Word Rule and P. K. Dick's *The Game-Players of Titan.*" *Science Fiction Studies* 31 (2004): 207–226.

Spinrad, Norman. "The Transmogrification if Philip K. Dick." In *Science Fiction in the Real World.* Carbondale: Southern Illinois University. Press, 1990, 198—216.

Umland, Samuel J., ed. *Philip K. Dick: Contemporary Critical Interpretations.* Westport, CT: Greenwood, 1995.

## Web Sites

*Encyclopedia Dickiana.* David Hyde, ed. November 2, 2003. Extensive reference material about the author's novels, short stories and other writings. http://www.philipkdickfans.com/pkdweb/.

*Philip K. Dick.com.* Official Web site, "...dedicated to his work, his life and his vision...," maintained by his family. http://www.philipkdick.com/.

*Philip K. Dick Bookshelf.* Henri Wintz ed. May 8, 2008. Pictorial bibliography, with more than 1,300 covers of PKD's books. http://www.pkdickbooks.com/.

*Philip K. Dick Fans.com.* April 13, 2008. Portal Web site, with links to critical essays, lost works and news. http://www.philipkdickfans.com/main.htm.

*Philip K. Dick nOde.* Fusion Anomaly. May 11, 2004. Suitably psychedelic, "permanently morphing" Web site, which contains some very interesting links about Dick's work, life, and themes. http://fusionanomaly.net/philipkdick.html

*Philip K. Dick in Science Fiction.* Adherents.com. September 22, 2004. Lists mainstream and science fiction novels or short stories that contain references to PKD, or Dick as a character. http://www.adherents.com/lit/sf_PKD.html.

*The Religious Experience of Philip K. Dick by R. Crumb.* November 2003. Philip K. Dick Fans.com. Graphic art story, from Weirdo comic #17 (Summer 1986) magazine, about Dick's "Valis" experience. http://www.philipkdickfans.com/weirdo.htm.

### If you enjoyed Philip K. Dick...

Philip K. Dick found the narrative dynamic that powered some of his greatest works in the gray zone between what is real, and what is not, and the shock when, like a character in one of his novels, we realize that we have not been told the whole story. Identity depends on memory—and in a PKD story, memory is at best unreliable, and at worst deceptive.

**Then you might like...**

*J. G. Ballard.* A challenging writer who, like Dick, moved sharply away from conventional science fiction to something altogether more rich and strange: in Ballard's sf, such as the four novels of the "Global Disaster Quartet," and *The Atrocity Exhibition* (1970), the only alien planet is earth. Like PKD, also, the power of memory and the lure of the false prophets of popular culture are powerful themes.

*Samuel R. Delany.* Novels such as *Babel-17*, *Triton: An Ambiguous Heterotopia*, and *Dhalgren* are potent blends of the conventions of space opera, high philosophy, mythology, and linguistics. Identity itself is often fluid in a Delany story: in a universe where one can change one's physical appearance, gender, and sexual orientation at will, what can you trust?

*Jonathan Letham.* Like PKD, reality in the novels of Jonathan Lethem reality is filtered through the lens of pop culture references, which, of course, include science fiction. *Amnesia Moon* and *Gun, with Occasional Music* are Lethem's riffs on the sort of absurd, over-the-top dystopias that were the specialty of Phillip K. Dick.

*Jeff Noon.* Novels *Vurt* (1993) and *Pollen* (1997) combine a cyberpunk sensibility (decaying urban setting, nanotechnology, artificial intelligence, and society in retreat) with a Dickian dream world that combines such disparate elements as British folklore and classic mythology, mathematics, hallucinogenic drugs, and world-wide plagues of alienation.

*Norman Spinrad.* A friend of PKD, his recent career could offer clues as to the directions Dick might have taken, had he lived. In recent years, Spinrad has played with the boundaries of genre, blending thriller and near-future speculation about AIDS and ecological disaster in novels like *Journal of the Plague Years* (1995) and *Greenhouse Summer* (1999).

# Thomas M. Disch (1940–2008)

> *Let me tell you about the end of the world. It happened fifty years ago. Maybe a hundred. And since then it's been lovely. I mean it. Nobody tries to bother you. You can relax. You know what? I like the end of the world.*
>
> *—334 (1974)*

## Biography

Thomas M. Disch never spared the feelings of the reader, or the genre: in a Disch novel, the alien invaders win, the price of understanding is death, and ordinary people treat each other no better than the aliens do. Much of his early fiction was published first in *New Worlds*, the London-based *New Wave* magazine edited by Michael Moorcock; his work strains at the boundaries of sf, and made sf better for it.

Thomas Michael Disch was born in Des Moines, Iowa, and grew up in Minneapolis. He moved to New York City after graduating high school, and worked odd jobs while waiting for his writing career to take off. In later years, he moved away from sf, writing horror and literary criticism, and teaching at various university writing programs; as "Tom Disch" he was a well-respected poet. On July 4, 2008, depressed by personal problems and the death of his longtime partner, he took his own life.

ALIEN THREAT; DYSTOPIAS; END OF THE WORLD; ENTROPY; GENDER & SEXUALITY; NEW WAVE

## Major Works

*Novels*

*The Genocides* (1965)
*Mankind under the Leash* (*The Puppies of Terra*) (1966)
*Echo Round His Bones* (1967)
*Camp Concentration* (1968)
*334* (1972)
*On Wings of Song* (1979)

*Collections*

*Fundamental Disch.* New York: Bantam, 1980. Introduction by Samuel R. Delany. Includes essays, and short fiction such as "White Fang Goes Dingo" (1965), "Casablanca" (1967), "Angouleme" (1971), and "Et in Arcadia Ego" (1971).
Other collections of Disch's short fiction are *Getting Into Death and Other Stories* (1976), and *The Man Who Had No Idea* (1982).

*Notable Short Stories*

"Fun with Your New Head" (1968). http://www.art.net/~hopkins/Don/text/head.html.
"The Brave Little Toaster" (1980) **BSF, Locus Poll.**
"Understanding Human Behavior" (1981). *Strange Horizons,* July 30, 2001. http://www.strangehorizons.com/2001/20010730/human_behavior.shtml.

*Other Important Works*

*The Dreams Our Stuff Is Made Of* (1998).
"The Embarrassments of Science Fiction." In Peter Nicholls, ed., *Science Fiction at Large: A Collection of Essays, By Various Hands, About the Interface between Science Fiction and Reality.* London: Gollancz, 1976, 139–156.

"The Road to Heaven: Science Fiction and the Militarization of Space." *The Nation,* May 10, 1986, 650–656.
"Sermonettes." *Strange Horizons.* July 30, 2001. Short commentaries on a variety of subjects, taken from a weekly broadcast Disch did on WNYC radio in New York City, 1999–2000. http://www.strangehorizons.com/2001/20010730/sermonettes.shtml.

## Research Sources

*Encyclopedias and Handbooks:* **AW, CA, CANR, ESF, MSSF, SFW**

*Bibliographies:* **ARB, FF, SFAN**

Stephens, Christopher P. *A Checklist of Thomas M. Disch.* Hastings-on-Hudson, NY: Ultramarine 1992.

### Biographies and Interviews

Hawtree, Christopher. Obituary. *Guardian Online*, July 9, 2008. http://books.guardian.co.uk/obituaries/story/0,2289732,00.html
Heacox, Tom. "The Dish on Tom Disch." *Jump!* magazine. Fall 1995. The College of William and Mary, February 29, 2004. http://web.wm.edu/so/jump/fall95/disch.html.
Horwich, David. Interview. *Strange Horizons.* July 30, 2001. http://www.strangehorizons.com/2001/20010730/interview.shtml.
*Locus Online.* Interview. June 2001. http://www.locusmag.com/2001/Issue06/Disch.html.

### Criticism and Readers' Guides

Bee, Robert. "'Worms Crawling through the Apple': Disch's Bleak Vision in Two Early New Wave Novels." *Internet Review of Science Fiction.* September 2005. http://www.irosf.com/q/zine/article/10183.
Benford, Gregory. "Meaning-Stuffed Dreams: Thomas Disch and the Future of SF." *New York Review of Science Fiction* 11(1) (1998): 10+.
Crowley, John. "The Gothic of Thomas M. Disch." *SF Commentary* 78 (2003): 14–18.
Delany, Samuel R. The American Shore: Meditations on a Tale of Science Fiction by Thomas M. Disch. Elizabethtown, NY: Dragon, 1978.
———. Introduction. Fundamental Disch. New York: Bantam, 1980.
Sladek, John T. "Four Reasons for Reading Thomas M. Disch." *SF Commentary* 77 (2001): 3–10. http://www.ansible-editions.co.uk/authors/sladek-disch.htm.

### Web Sites

*Endzone.* Live Journal. Author's blog, often in poetic form, on current events in the world and TMD's life. http://tomsdisch.livejournal.com/.

# Cory Doctorow (1971–   )

*I lived long enough to see the cure for death; to see the rise of the Bitchun Society, to learn ten languages; to compose three symphonies; to realize my boyhood dream of taking up residence in Disney World; to see the death of the workplace and of work.*

*—Down and Out in the Magic Kingdom (2003)*

## Biography

Cory Doctorow was born in Toronto, Canada, the son of Trotskyite teachers and activists. He attended an alternative SEED School in Toronto, and dropped out of four universities without attaining a degree. For some years, he lived in London; in 2006, he moved to Los Angeles, where he now teaches, researches, and writes about international copyright activism, technology, and the Net. In February 2008, Doctorow and his partner, Alice Taylor, became the parents of a daughter, Poesy.

From an early age, Cory Doctorow has been involved in causes such as nuclear disarmament, liberalized copyright laws, and the environment. Interviews with the author, and summaries of his career, tend to be overwhelmed with this activism, and sometimes miss the fact that Doctorow writes witty, entertaining novels and stories about modern myths, who owns popular culture, post-scarcity economics, and how wonderful it would be to live in Disneyland.

CYBERPUNK; IMMORTALITY; NEAR FUTURE; POLITICAL SF; POP CULTURE; TECHNOLOGY

## Major Works

*Novels*

Almost all of Cory Doctorow's work is available online, with his permission. For a complete, up-to-date list, see http://www.freesfonline.de/authors/Cory_Doctorow.html.
*Down and Out in the Magic Kingdom* (2003) **Locus Poll.** Excerpt available on http://www.infinitematrix.net/
*Eastern Standard Tribe* (2004)
*Someone Comes to Town, Someone Leaves Town* (2005)
*Themepunks* (2005) Online novella, serialized and available in full at Salon.com. http://dir.salon.com/story/tech/feature/2005/09/12/themepunks_1/index.html.
*Little Brother* (2008)

*Collections*

*A Place So Foreign and Eight More*. New York: Four Walls Eight Windows, 2003.
*Overclocked: Stories of the Future Present*. New York: Thunder's Mouth, 2007.

*Notable Short Stories*

"0wnz0red" (2002)
"Visit the Sins" (2003)
"Appeals Court" (2004, with Charles Stross)
"I, Robot" (2005) **Locus Poll**

*Other Important Works*

*The Complete Idiot's Guide to Publishing Science Fiction.* With Karl Schroeder. New York: Alpha, 2000.
"Science Fiction is the Only Literature People Care Enough About to Steal on the Internet." *Locus.* July 2006 http://www.locusmag.com/2006/Issues/07DoctorowCommentary.html.
"Thought Experiments: When the Singularity is More Than a Literary Device (Interviews Futurist-Inventor Ray Kurzweil)." *Asimov's Science Fiction.* May 2005. http://www.asimovs.com/_issue_0506/thoughtexperiments.shtml.
"Wikipedia: A Genuine H2G2—Minus the Editors." In Glenn Yeffeth, ed., *The Anthology at the End of the Universe: Leading Science Fiction Authors on Douglas Adams' The Hitchhiker's Guide to the Galaxy.* Dallas, TX: Benbella, 2005, 25–34.

## Research Sources

*Encyclopedias and Handbooks:* **AW, CA, NNDB**

*Bibliographies:* **ARB, FF, SFAN**

*Biographies and Interviews*

Adams, John Joseph. "Interview: Information Wants to Be Free." *SciFi Weekly.* September 18, 2006. http://www.scifi.com/sfw/interviews/sfw13669.html.
*Locus Online.* "Everywhere, All at the Same Time: Interview." January 2005. http://www.locusmag.com/2005/Issues/01Doctorow.html.
Ernest, Lilley. Interview. *SFRevu.* January 2007. http://www.sfrevu.com/php/Review-id.php?id=4785.
Harris, Bascha. "A Very Long Talk with Cory Doctorow, Part 1." *Red Hat Magazine.* January 2006. http://www.redhat.com/magazine/015jan06/features/doctorow/.
Koman, Richard. "An Interview with Cory Doctorow." *The O'Reilly Network.* March 4, 2005. http://www.oreillynet.com/pub/a/network/2005/03/04/corydoctorow.html.
Macdonald, Katherine. Interview. *Strange Horizons.* March 31, 2003. http://www.strangehorizons.com/2003/20030331/doctorow.shtml.
Poynder, Richard. "NetGen Cyber Activist." *Open and Shut?* April 20, 2006. http://poynder.blogspot.com/2006/04/interview-with-cory-doctorow.html.

*Criticism and Readers' Guides*

Emsley, Iain. "The Microchips of Wonder: Virtual Communities and Contemporary Cyberpunk." *Internet Review of Science Fiction.* April 2004. http://www.irosf.com/q/zine/article/10040.

Mason, Eric. "Remediating the Magic Kingdom: Notes toward a Poetics of Technology." *Currents in Electronic Literacy* 8 (2004). http://www.cwrl.utexas.edu/currents/fall04/mason.html.

## Web Sites

*BoingBoing.net*. March 2008. "A Directory of Wonderful Things." Author blog of the weird and wonderful. http://www.boingboing.net/.
*Cory Doctorow's Craphound.com*. Official Web site, and author's blog. http://www.craphound.com/.

# Harlan Ellison (1934–   )

*"Get Stuffed!" the harlequin replied, sneering.*
*—"'Repent, Harlequin!' said the Ticktockman" (1965)*

## Biography

Harlan Jay Ellison was born in Cleveland, Ohio. He moved to New York City in 1955 and began his writing career with vivid, violent accounts of city life. His work on TV series, in the 1960s, earned him many accolades—his teleplay for *Star Trek*, "The City on the Edge of Forever" is regularly cited by critics and fans as one of the best of all Star Trek episodes.

As of 1994, Ellison had published some 1,300 stories, essays, scripts, and reviews. As in his life, his fiction rejects technology as a cure for all ills, and reflects his belief in the importance of myth, both personal and universal, and the value of strong emotions. Ellison lives in Los Angeles, California, with Susan, his fifth wife. In 1994, he suffered a heart attack and was hospitalized for quadruple coronary artery bypass surgery.

APOCALYPSE AND AFTER; ENTROPY; MYTHOLOGY & LEGEND; NEW WAVE; POLITICAL SF; SEX & TABOOS

## Major Works

*Novels*

*The Man with Nine Lives* (1960—orig. *The Sound of a Scythe*)
*Doomsman* (1967)
*The Starlost #1: Phoenix without Ashes* (1975, with Edward Bryant)

*Collections*

*Slippage: Previously Uncollected, Precariously Poised Stories*. **Locus Poll**. New York: Mariner, 1998.
*Troublemakers: Stories by Harlan Ellison*. New York: Ibooks, 2001.

*The Essential Ellison: A 50 Year Retrospective.* Beverly Hills, CA: Morpheus, 2005. Most recent revised and expanded edition of a volume that began as a thirty-five-year retrospective, and includes most of Ellison's classic and award-winning stories.

## Notable Short Stories

"Soldier" (1957)
"'Repent, Harlequin!' said the Ticktockman" (1965) **Hugo, Nebula**
"I Have No Mouth, and I Must Scream" (1967) **Hugo**
"The Beast That Shouted Love at the Heart of the World" (1969) **Hugo**
"A Boy and his Dog" (1969) **Nebula**
"The Deathbird" (1973) **Hugo, Locus Poll**
"Adrift Just Off the Islets of Langerhans: Latitude 38° 54' N, Longitude 77° 00' 13" W" (1974) **Hugo, Locus Poll**
"Jeffty Is Five" (1977) **Hugo, Locus Poll, Nebula**
"Paladin of the Lost Hour" (1985) **Hugo, Locus Poll** http://harlanellison.com/ iwrite/paladin.htm,
"With Virgil Oddum at the East Pole" (1985)
"The Function of Dream Sleep" (1988) **Locus Poll**
"Susan" (1993) http://harlanellison.com/iwrite/susan.htm.

## Other Important Works

*A Boy and His Dog.* Dir. L.Q. Jones. LQ/JAF. 1975. Hugo, Best Dramatic Presentation.
"The City on the Edge of Forever." *Star Trek.* Episode #28, April 6, 1967. Hugo, Best Dramatic Presentation.
"Goodbye to All That." In Marleen S. Barr, ed. *Envisioning the Future: Science Fiction and the Next Millennium.* Middletown, NJ: Wesleyan University Press, 2003, 99–110.
*Harlan Ellison's "The City on the Edge of Forever": The Original Teleplay That Became the Classic Star Trek Episode* (1996)
*Harlan Ellison's Dream Corridor.* Volume 1: 1996; Volume 2: 2007. Graphic art adaptations of some of Ellison's stories.
*The Harlan Ellison Hornbook.* Edgeworks. Vol. 3 (1997)
*The Outer Limits.* "Soldier" (Episode 2.1, televised September 19, 1964) and "Demon with a Glass Hand." (Episode 2.5, televised October 17, 1964). The movie *The Terminator* had striking similarities to these two Ellison *Outer Limits* episodes. Ellison eventually sued James Cameron, writer and director of *The Terminator*. The film's end credits now include the statement: "Acknowledgment to the works of Harlan Ellison."
*Sleepless Nights in the Procrustean Bed: Essays* (1984)
"With the Eyes of a Demon: Seeing the Fantastic as a Video Image." *The Craft of Science Fiction.* Reginald Bretnor, ed. New York: Harper & Row, 1976, 236–291.

## Research Sources

*Encyclopedias and Handbooks:* **AW, CA, CANR, ESF, MSSF, NNDB, SFW**

*Bibliographies:* **ARB, FF, SFAN**

*Fingerprints on the Sky: The Authorized Harlan Ellison Bibliography: The Fully Illustrated Reader's Guide.* Hiram, GA: Overlook, 2007.

### Biographies and Interviews

Blaschke, Jayme L. "The Event That Is His Life: Harlan Ellison Interviewed." In *Voices of Vision.* Lincoln: University of Nebraska Press, 2005, 165–184. http://www.sfsite.com/07a/he107.htm.

*Dreams with Sharp Teeth: A Film About Harlan Ellison.* Dir. Erik Nelson. Creative Differences. 2007. http://www.creatvdiff.com/harlan_ellison.php.

Lengel, Kerry. "Grand Master of Fabulism." *The Arizona Republic*, April 28, 2006. http://www.azcentral.com/ent/arts/articles/0428nebula28.html.

Salm, Arthur. "Harlan Ellison is Fearless, and a Fearless Writer." *San Diego Union-Tribune*, March 20, 2005. http://www.signonsandiego.com/news/features/20050320-9999-1a20harlan.html.

Thompson, John. "Dangerous Visionary: An Interview with Harlan Ellison." *Fantastic Metropolis*, January 11, 2002. http://www.fantasticmetropolis.com/i/ellison/.

### Criticism and Readers' Guides

Brosin, Eric Joel. "Reevaluating Ellison's Infamous Fable." *Internet Review of Science Fiction.* July 2006. http://www.irosf.com/q/zine/article/10294.

Francavualla, Joseph. "The Concept of the Divided Self and Harlan Ellison's 'I Have No Mouth and I Must Scream' and 'Shatterday.'" *Journal of the Fantastic in the Arts* 6(2/3) (1994): 107–125.

Kimmel, Daniel M. "Ironic, Isn't it? (*A Boy and His Dog*)." *Internet Review of Science Fiction.* April 2008. http://www.irosf.com/q/zine/article/10410.

Parker, Martin. "'Repent Harlequin,' said the Ticktockman: Digesting Science Fiction." In M. Higgins ed. *Science Fiction and Organization.* London: Routledge, 2001, 193–203.

Priest, Christopher. *The Book on the Edge of Forever.* Seattle, WA: Fantagraphics, 1994.

Russ, Joanna. "A Boy and His Dog: The Final Solution." In *To Write Like a Woman: Essays in Feminism and Science Fiction.* Bloomington: Indiana University Press, 1995.

Weil, Ellen, and Gary Wolfe, eds. *Harlan Ellison: The Edge of Forever.* Columbus: Ohio State University Press, 2002.

*Web Sites*

*Ellison Webderland.* Official Web site. http://harlanellison.com/home.htm.
*Islets of Langerhans: A Literary Topography.* March 2008. A thorough and well-designed survey of Ellison's fiction, nonfiction, and work in other media. http://www.islets.net/.

# Philip José Farmer (1918–   )

*Death, the Destroyer of Delights and the Sunderer of Society, had arrived at last. Blackness. Nothingness. He did not even know that his heart had given out forever. Nothingness. Then his eyes opened.*

*—To Your Scattered Bodied Go (1971)*

## Biography

Farmer is probably best-known for his Riverworld novels, which take historical figures, such as the explorer and adventurer Sir Richard Burton, author Samuel Clemens (Mark Twain), and even Nazi playboy Herman Goering, and resurrect them along the banks of a multimillion mile-long river. Riverworld is an example of one of Farmer's favorite tricks—taking characters from history, and from other people's novels, and tying them together into "vast, playful mythologies (ESF)." His attempt to "recruit" Kurt Vonnegut's character, Kilgore Trout, resulted in some serious unpleasantness between the two authors.

Phillip José Farmer was born in North Terre Haute, Indiana. His novella "The Lovers" (1952), shattered the taboo on sex in sf, and earned him one of the first Hugo Awards as most promising new talent of 1952. The *Farmerphile*, a quarterly magazine created by his fans, is entirely devoted to his impish, anarchic work. Since 1970, Farmer has lived in Peoria, Illinois.

FANTASTIC VOYAGES; GODS & DEMONS; IMMORTALITY; MYTHOLOGY; SEX & TABOOS

## Major Works

*Novels*

*The Green Odyssey* (1957)
*A Woman a Day or The Day of Timestop* (1960)
*The Lovers* (1961) An extended "fix-up," combining the 1952 **Hugo**-winning novella of the same name and its sequel, "Moth and Rust" (1953)
World of Tiers: *The Maker of Universes* (1965), *The Gates of Creation* (1966), *A Private Cosmos* (1968), *Behind the Walls of Terra* (1970), *The Lavalite World* (1977), *Red Orc's Rage* (1991), *More Than Fire* (1993)

Riverworld: *To Your Scattered Bodies Go* (1971—**Hugo**), *The Fabulous Riverboat*
   (1971), *The Dark Design* (1977), *Riverworld and Other Stories* (1979, short
   fiction), *The Magic Labyrinth* (1980), *Riverworld War* (1980, short fiction), *Gods
   of Riverworld* (1983), *River of Eternity* (1983)
Dayworld: *Dayworld* (1984), *Dayworld Rebel* (1987), *Dayworld Breakup* (1990), *The
   Gate of Time* (1966)
*The Stone God Awakens* (1970)
*Venus on the Half-Shell* (1975, as "Kilgore Trout")
*Jesus on Mars* (1979)
*The Unreasoning Mask* (1981)
*The Caterpillar's Question* (1992, with Piers Anthony)

## Collections

*The Classic Philip José Farmer, 1952–1964* and *1964–1973*. New York: Crown, 1984.
*Pearls from Peoria*. Burton, MI: Subterranean, 2006. Over sixty pieces of fiction and
   nonfiction, reviews, and essays.
*Strange Relations*. Riverdale, NY: Baen, 2006. An omnibus version of Farmer's taboo-
   breaking novellas *Mother* (1953), *My Sister's Brother* (1960—aka *Open to Me,
   My Sister*), with novels *The Lovers* and *Flesh* (1960).
*Venus on the Half-Shell*. Burton, MI: Subterranean, 2008. For the first time, this
   volume brings together the best of Farmer's "borrowed character" fiction. Includes
   "Introduction: Why and How I Became Kilgore Trout."

## Short Stories

"Riders of the Purple Wage" (1967) **Hugo**
"The Sliced-Crosswise Only-on-Tuesday World" (1971)
"After King Kong Fell" (1973).

# Research Sources

*Encyclopedias and Handbooks:* **AW, BW, CA, CANR, ESF, MSSF,
NNDB, SFW**

*Bibliographies:* **ARB, FF, SFAN**

Nuninga, Zacharias L.A. "Philip José Farmer International Bibliography." November
   27, 2006. http://www.xs4all.nl/~rnuninga/.

## Biographies and Interviews

Bibo, Terry. "A Conversation with Philip José Farmer." *Peoria Journal Star,* January
   10, 1999. http://www.pjstar.com/services/special/legacyproject/farmerqa.html.
Vernon, William D. Interview. Daryl Lane et al. eds. *The Sound of Wonder: Interviews
   from "The Science Fiction Radio Show." Volume 2*. Phoenix, AZ: Oryx, 1985.

## Criticism and Readers' Guides

Adams, Danny. "A Brobdingnagian Education: Or, How Philip José Farmer Saved My Life in Four Easy Steps." *Some Fantastic* 4(1) (2005): 1–5. http://www. somefantastic.us/Issue_Archive/Issue_No_4.pdf.

Brizzi, Mary T., and Roger C. Sclobin. *Philip José Farmer: Starmont Reader's Guide 3*. Mercer Island, WA: Borgo, 1981.

Carey, Christopher Paul. "The Grand Master of Peoria: Philip José Farmer's Immortal Legacy." The Zone November 2006. http://www.zone-sf.com/philfarm.html.

Chapman, E. L. "From Rebellious Rationalist to Mythmaker and Mystic: The Religious Quest of Philip José Farmer." In Robert Reilly ed., *The Transcendent Adventure: Studies of Religion in Science Fiction/Fantasy*. Westport, CT: Greenwood, 1984, 127–144.

———. *The Magic Labyrinth of Philip José Farmer*. San Bernardino, CA: Borgo, 1985.

Rottensteiner, Franz. "Playing around with Creation: Philip José Farmer." *Science Fiction Studies* 1 (1973): 94–98. http://www.depauw.edu/sfs/backissues/2/rottensteiner2art.htm.

Wolfe, Gary K. "The Dawn Patrol: Sex, Technology, and Irony in Farmer and Ballard." In Nicholas Ruddick ed., *State of the Fantastic: Studies in the Theory and Practice of Fantastic Literature and Film*, Westport, CT: Greenwood, 1992, 159–167.

## Web Sites

*The Official Philip José Farmer Home Page*. Official Web site. " . . . the Brobdingnagian collection of all things Farmerian . . . ;" includes news, links, and messages from PJF. Also link to *Farmerphile,* quarterly magazine completely dedicated to works by and about PJF (index, not contents). http://www.pjfarmer.com/.

*Philip José Farmer's Wold Newton Universe*. Win Scott Eckert. August 2007. Web site devoted to Farmer's classic "biographies" of fictional characters, including Tarzan and "Doc" Savage. http://www.pjfarmer.com/woldnewton/Pulp. htm.

# Jack Finney (1911–1995)

> . . . the sun edging up over the horizon as we stared, I took Julia's arm, and we walked around our little railed circle. On the other side Julia stopped to stand stock-still, her breath suddenly caught motionless in her chest as she stared out across the harbor at the astonishing, soaring skyscrapers filling the tip of Manhattan Island, their tens of thousands of windows flashing orange in the dawn.
>
> —*Time and Again (1965)*

# Biography

Walter Braden Finney, who was known all his life as "Jack," was born in Milwaukee, Wisconsin. For some years he lived in New York and worked in advertising, and many of his stories draw upon that experience. His status as a writer of science fiction is guaranteed by two novels—*Time and Again* (1970) and *Body Snatchers* (1954).

*Body Snatchers* is well known from the four movie versions of pod-people taking over American suburbia. In *Time and Again*, the hero uses autohypnosis to transport himself back to the New York City of the 1980s. *The New York Times*, in Finney's obituary, described it as "beloved especially by New Yorkers for its rich, painstakingly researched descriptions of life in the city more than a century ago." From the 1950s, Jack Finney lived in Marin County, California, and he died there, of pneumonia and emphysema, shortly after producing a long-awaited sequel to *Time and Again*.

ALIEN THREAT; END OF THE WORLD; TIME TRAVEL

# Major Works

*Novels*

*Body Snatchers*. (1954—aka *Invasion of the Body Snatchers*)
*Time and Again* (1970)
*From Time to Time* (1995)

*Collections*

*3 by Finney*. New York: Simon & Schuster/Fireside, 1987. Omnibus which includes lesser-known novels, with time travel themes, *The Woodrow Wilson Dime* (1968), *Marion's Wall* (1973), and *The Night People* (1977).
*About Time*. New York: Simon & Schuster/Fireside, 1986. Stories, previously uncollected and from earlier collections *Third Level (1957)* and *I Love Galesburg in the Springtime* (1963), all with a time-travel theme.

*Other Important Works*

*Forgotten News: The Crime of the Century and Other Lost Stories* (1983). Contains the true-crime story that inspired, and provided the research for, *Time and Again*.

# Research Sources

*Encyclopedias and Handbooks:* **AW, CA, CAAS, CANR, ESF, MSSF, NNDB, SFW, WS**

*Bibliographies:* **ARB, FF, SFAN**

## Biographies and Interviews

Willick, George C. Obituaries. *Spacelight.* June 2006. http://www.gcwillick.com/ Spacelight/obit/finneyo.html.

## Criticism and Readers' Guides

Burns, Ric. "Why *Time and Again* Casts So Powerful a Spell." *New York Times,* January 28, 2001.

Collins, Michael J. "Version/Inversion: Paranoia in Three Cases of Bodysnatching." In Michael A. Morrison, ed., *Trajectories of the Fantastic.* Westport, CT: Greenwood, 1997, 195–202.

De Villo, Sloan. "The Self and Self-less in Campbell's *Who Goes There?* and Finney's *Invasion of the Body Snatchers.*" *Extrapolation* 29 (1988): 179–188.

Hendershot, Cyndy. "The Invaded Body: Paranoia and Radiation Anxiety in *Invaders from Mars, It Came from Outer Space,* and *Invasion of the Body Snatchers.*" *Extrapolation* 39 (1998): 26–39.

Kimmel, Daniel M. "Sleep No More: Why the Pod People Won't Go Away." *Internet Review of Science Fiction.* October 2005. http://www.irosf.com/q/zine/article/ 10202.

McCarthy, Kevin, and Ed Gorman, eds. *Invasion of the Body Snatchers, A Tribute.* Eureka, CA: Stark House, 2006.

Seabrook, Jack. *Stealing Through Time: On the Writings of Jack Finney.* Jefferson, NC: McFarland, 2006.

## Web Sites

*Jack Finney: Time Traveler.* Al Teich. January 2004. Tribute to the book, which includes a photo tour of New York City locations from Jack Finney's *Time and Again* as they appeared in late 2003. http://www.alteich.com/tidbits/t010104.htm.

**If you enjoyed Jack Finney ...**

Finney tapped into a powerful human yearning for tranquility and nostalgia in his time-travel stories. His time-travelers aren't elite Time Police, or mad scientists, but ordinary people, trying to cope or seeking peace and safety in a simpler, better time. In *Time and Again,* the effect was enhanced by Finney's careful research, and his eye for the look and feel of the past.

**Then you might like ...**

***L. Sprague De Camp.*** In *Lest Darkness Fall* (1941) an archaeologist is transported to 6ᵗʰ century Rome; *Rivers of Time* (1993) reprints a series of "shock of the old" stories written from 1956. De Camp wrote in response to what he saw as logical lapses and absurdities in the time travel of those who preceded him; he had a formative influence on authors like Harry Turtledove.

*Eric Flint.* In the "1632 Universe" (motto: "Get your pickup truck and deer rifle— We're joining the Thirty Years' War."), the inhabitants and environs of Grantville, West Virginia, are spirited back in time over 300 years to Central Germany . . . with no way back. Flint's popular and successful series has grown as a collaborative venture, with authors such as David Weber, and a web phenomenon.

*Ward Moore.* The author of a number of books with sf themes, Moore's most famous by far is *Bring the Jubilee* (1953), set in a much-changed 1950s New York, in a world in which the Confederacy won the Civil War. Moore's "fine historical sense" (**AW**) of the unexpected ways the present might be different make this a true classic of the alternative history subgenre.

*Jo Walton.* *Farthing* (2006) is the first volume in the "Small Change" trilogy, a clever and effective "country house murder mystery" set in an England that has made peace with Hitler. Walton's previous novels are re-imaginings of Roman Britain (*The King's Peace*, 2000), and Victorian melodrama, with dragons (*Tooth and Claw*, 2004).

*Connie Willis.* For all their wit and dry humor, Connie Willis' time travel stories like "Fire Watch" (1982) and *Doomsday Book* (1992) are populated with characters who are very real, living, breathing people, and resonate with memorable melancholy. Science fiction has given her the means to say what she wants about "big themes," without being oversentimental or patronizing.

# William Gibson (1948–   )

*The sky above the port was the color of television, tuned to a dead channel.*
*—Neuromancer (1984)*

## Biography

William Ford Gibson was born on March 17, 1948 in Conway, South Carolina. In 1967, he fled to Canada to avoid the draft for the Vietnam War, living first in the "hippie" district of Toronto, and later settling in Vancouver, where he did a BA in English at the University of British Columbia.

Gibson's first novel, *Neuromancer* (1984), was an immediate success: it swept the three major prizes that year—Hugo, Nebula, and Philip K Dick—and, since then, has sold more than 6.5 million copies worldwide. Gibson is credited with "inventing" cyberpunk, although he was drawing on themes and style developed by authors as different as Alfred Bester and Vernor Vinge. He continues to experiment, and push the boundaries of sf; his focus remains advertising, the media, and modern paranoia. Although he is still a U.S. citizen, William Gibson has spent most of his adult life in Canada, and still lives in the Vancouver area.

ARTIFICIAL INTELLIGENCE; CYBERPUNK; NANOTECHNOLOGY; NEAR FUTURE; POP CULTURE

## Major Works

*Novels*

*Neuromancer* (1984) **Hugo, Nebula**
*Count Zero* (1986)
*Mona Lisa Overdrive* (1988)
*The Difference Engine* (1990, with Bruce Sterling)
*Virtual Light* (1993)
*Idoru* (1996)
*All Tomorrow's Parties* (1999)
*Pattern Recognition* (2003)
*Spook Country* (2007)

*Collection*

*Burning Chrome* (1986). New York: Eos, 2003.

*Notable Short Stories*

"The Gernsback Continuum" (1981)
"Johnny Mnemonic" (1981) http://project.cyberpunk.ru/lib/johnny_mnemonic/.
"Burning Chrome" (1982) http://web.bentley.edu/empl/c/rcrooks/courses/350s96/
    gibson.html.
"The Winter Market" (1985)
"Dogfight" (1985, with Michael Swanwick)
"Rocket Radio" (1989) http://www.voidspace.org.uk/cyberpunk/gibson_rocketradio.
    shtml.

*Other Important Works*

*Agrippa (A Book of The Dead)* (1992, with Dennis Ashbaugh) http://www.
    antonraubenweiss.com/gibson/gibson3.html.
*Johnny Mnemonic: The Screenplay and the Story* (1995)
"Modern Boys and Mobile Girls." *The Observer*, April 1, 2001. http://observer.
    guardian.co.uk/life/story/0,6903,466391,00.html.
*Neuromancer.* Audiobook. Read by William Gibson. Music by U2 and Black Rain.
    Time Warner Audiobooks, 1994.
*No Maps for These Territories.* Documentary film. Mark Neale, ed. Docurama. 2003.
    http://www.nomaps.com/.
"The Road to Oceania." *The New York Times,* June 25, 2003. http://www.netcharles.
    com/orwell/articles/col-rtoceania.htm.

"Time Machine Cuba. (2004)" *Infinite Matrix,* January 23, 2006. http://www.infinitematrix.net/faq/essays/gibson.html.
*Wired.* http://www.wired.com/.Regular column on topics such as popular culture, Asia, computers, and technology.
*The X-Files.* Teleplays for "Kill Switch" (February 15, 1998, with Tom Maddox) and "First Person Shooter" (February 27, 2000). Fox TV.

## Research Sources

*Encyclopedias and Handbooks:* **AW, BW, CA, CANR, ESF, NNDB, SFW**

*Bibliographies:* **ARB, FF, SFAN**

Bibliography. Centre for Language and Literature. May 17, 2007. Athabasca University. http://www.athabascau.ca/writers/wgibson_biblio1.html.
*William Gibson Bibliography/Mediagraphy.* S. Page, ed. October 2004.http://www.skierpage.com/gibson/biblio.htm.

### Biographies and Interviews

Barker, Clive. Interview. *Next Theatre,* December 13, 1997. Burning City. http://burningcity.com/CB_WG_P1.html.
Gunn, Moira. Interview. *Tech Nation,* February 10, 2004. GigaVox Media Inc. http://www.itconversations.com/shows/detail389.html.
Parker, T. Virgil. "Sci-Fi Icon Becomes Prophet of the Present." *College Crier.* Summer 2007. http://www.collegecrier.com/interviews/int-0040.asp.
Poole, Steven. "Tomorrow's Man." *Guardian Online,* May 3, 2003. http://www.guardian.co.uk/.
*This Week in Science.* Interview. September 12, 2006. KDVS—University of California, Davis. http://www.twis.org/audio/2006/09/12/.

### Criticism and Readers' Guides

Brande, David. "The Business of Cyberpunk: Symbolic Economy and Ideology in William Gibson." In Robert Markley ed., *Virtual Realities and Their Discontents.* Baltimore, MD: Johns Hopkins University Press, 1996, 79–106.
Brians, Paul. *Study Guide.* August 29, 2005. Washington State University. http://www.wsu.edu:8080/~brians/science_fiction/neuromancer.html.
Cavallaro, Dani. *Cyberpunk and Cyberculture: Science Fiction and the Work of William Gibson.* London: Athlone, 2000.
Csicsery-Ronay, Istvan, Jr. "Antimancer: Cybernetics and Art in Gibson's *Count Zero.*" *Science Fiction Studies* 22 (1995): 63–86. http://www.depauw.edu/sfs/backissues/65/icr65art.htm.
Delany, Samuel R. "Zelazny/Varley/Gibson—and Quality." *Shorter Views: Queer Thoughts & the Politics of the Paraliterary.* Hanover, NH: University Press of New England/Wesleyan University Press, 1999, 271–291.

Hellekson, Karen. "Looking Forward: William Gibson and Bruce Sterling's *The Difference Engine*." In *The Alternate History: Refiguring Historical Time*. Kent, OH: Kent State University Press, 2001, 76–86.

Heuser, Sabine. "William Gibson's Construction of Cyberspace." In Mike Crang ed., *Virtual Geographies*. London: Routledge, 1999, 99–126.

Jones, Christine Kenyon. "SF and Romantic Biofictions: Aldiss, Gibson, Sterling, Powers." *Science Fiction Studies* 24 (1997): 47–56. http://www.depauw.edu/sfs/backissues/71/kenyonjones71art.htm.

Kneale, James. "The Virtual Realities of Technology and Fiction: Reading William Gibson's Cyberspace." In Mike Crang, ed., *Virtual Geographies*. London: Routledge, 1999, 205–221.

Olsen, Lance. *William Gibson*. Mercer Island, WA: Starmont Reader's Guide, 1992.

## Web Sites

*William Gibson Books*. Official Web site. http://www.williamgibsonbooks.com.

*The Difference Dictionary*. Eileen Gunn. February 2003. *sff net*. "Dr. Gunn's Organic History Supplement for *The Difference Engine* . . . ," a Web site that promises to "restore" historical perspective after Reading Gibson and Sterling's *The Difference Engine*, without spoiling its surprises. http://www.sff.net/people/gunn/dd/.

*Paragon-Asia Dataflow*. June 2007. Cosanti Foundation. Visually sophisticated and interesting fan Web site. Links to interviews, TV and movie links, and quotations. http://paragonasia.warp0.com/.

*William Gibson Aleph*. Manuel Derra. August 2007. Essential information collection fan page. http://www.antonraubenweiss.com/gibson/.

*William Gibson nOde*. January 2004. Very busy and imaginative Web site, "permanently morphing," as you follow links related to Gibson quotes and ideas. Hypnotic: only access if you have time to spare. http://fusionanomaly.net/williamgibson.html.

**If you enjoyed William Gibson...**

While the groundwork for cyberpunk was laid by writers like Alfred Bester and Vernor Vinge, *Neuromancer* will always be associated with the style and substance of that particular moment in science fiction: noir thrillers, set in the exotic landscape of virtual reality and peopled with dark, edgy characters, wired-up and "enhanced," who walk the mean streets of cyberspace.

**Then you might like...**

*Pat Cadigan*. "Visionary explorer of high technology, pop culture, and cyborg consciousness" (**AW**), Cadigan specializes in inventive scenarios that find the drama in "practical applications" of cyber-life. In *Synners,* brain-socket implants result in a crippling virus unleashed on the 'Net; in her more recent *Tea from an Empty Cup*, a serial killer stalks his victims in virtual reality.

*George Alec Effinger*. A stylish and surreal writer, whose short stories presented a "dazzling . . . dervish of alternating realities" (**ESF**), Effinger readily channeled this style into cyberpunk with the "Budayeen" stories. In the first, *When Gravity Fails* (1987), a bleak murder mystery set in a future Arab-dominated world, individuals can enhance their skill and personalities with cybernetic modifications.

***Norman Spinrad.*** *Bug Jack Barron* (1969) and *Little Heroes* (1987) are two examples of the manipulation of pop culture (television and rock music, respectively) by a corrupt and greedy corporate and political elite. In style and attitudes, Spinrad could be described as a proto-cyberpunk, even when he isn't writing about cyberspace.

***K.W. Jeter.*** Whether he is writing sf or horror, Jeter's work displayed the tell-tale cyberpunk marks of corruption (of society, of spirit and character) and obsession with noir style. In *Noir* (1998), a futuristic thriller, the detective has had his eyes surgically altered so that he sees the world as if he were in an old Bogart movie.

# *Molly Gloss (1944–   )*

*On that day, the go-down day, Juko Ohaši stood at the head of the weathermast— stood with her feet on the spindly seven-yard and her arms spread wide in the windless glare looking sunward for her husband.*
*—The Dazzle of Day (1997)*

## Biography

Molly Gloss was born in Portland, Oregon, a fourth-generation, working class Oregonian. She graduated from Portland State College (now University) with a BA and a secondary teaching certificate in 1966. She lives in Portland, Oregon, where she teaches writing and literature of the American West at Portland State University.

Molly Gloss writes about the past and she writes about the future, and her talent is in making both seem very strange, wonderful, and important. Only one of her novels is, strictly speaking, science fiction: *The Dazzle of Day* (1997), the story of a Quaker community that escapes the dying planet Earth, so that their children's children can find a new home planet, on their own terms. Her subsequent novel, *Wild Life*, marries the traditions of early sf and boys' own adventure pulp fiction with rural legends of the Pacific Northwest, and won the James Tiptree, Jr. Award in 2001.

ANTHROPOLOGY; COLONIZATION OF OTHER WORLDS; SUSTAINABLE ALTERNATIVES; MYTHOLOGY & LEGEND; RELIGION

## Major Works

*Novels*

*Outside the Gates* (1986)
*The Dazzle of Day* (1997)
*Wild Life* (2000) **Tiptree**

*Notable Short Stories*

"Interlocking Pieces" (1983)
"Personal Silence" (1990)
"Lambing Season" (2002) http://www.asimovs.com/_issue_0401/Lambing.shtml.

*Other Important Works*

"On Becoming a Writer." *Official Web site.* May 2007. http://www.mollygloss.com/
writer.html.

## Research Sources

*Encyclopedias and Handbooks:* **AW, BW, CA, CANR**

*Bibliographies:* **FF, SFAN**

*Biographies and Interviews*

Grant, Gavin J. Interview. *Booksense.com.* August 10, 2001. American Booksellers
Association. http://www.booksense.com/people/archive/glossmolly.jsp.
"Molly Gloss." In Gregory L. Morris ed., *Talking up a Storm: Voices of the New West,*
Lincoln: University of Nebraska Press, 1994.

*Criticism and Readers' Guides*

Abbott, Carl. "Homesteading on the Extraterrestrial Frontier." *Science Fiction Studies*
32 (2005): 240–264.
Attebery, Brian. "Myth and History: Molly Gloss's *Wild Life* and Alan Garner's *Strand-
loper.*" *New York Review of Science Fiction* 13(10) (2001): 1+.
Davis, Ray. "*The Dazzle of Day* by Molly Gloss." *Pseudopodium,* January 4, 2004.
http://www.pseudopodium.org/search.cgi?Molly+Gloss.
Golub, Alex. "*The Dazzle of Day* by Molly Gloss." *Gapers Block,* March 19, 2004.
http://www.gapersblock.com/airbags/archives/the_dazzle_of_day/.
Mills, Katherine. "*The Dazzle of Day* by Molly Gloss." *SF Site.* 1998.http://
www.sfsite.com/07a/daz36.htm.

*Web Sites*

*Molly Gloss.com.* Official Web site. http://www.mollygloss.com/.
Nathan Georgitis ed.,*Guide to the Molly Gloss Papers 1979–2003.* The Northwest
    Digital Archives. 2004. Collection comprising author's papers, including notes,
    planning documents, research materials, and drafts, written between 1979 and
    2003. http://nwda-db.wsulibs.wsu.edu/findaid/ark:/80444/xv25658.

# *Kathleen Ann Goonan (1952–    )*

> *Her entire body hummed as the Bee halted and hovered near her . . . Soft gold
> and brown bands circled its body and glowed in the sun. Its front was a black
> complication of shiny parts. The eyes which stared at her reminded her of the
> heart of a Black-eyed Susan. Pictures hummed in the air between them . . .*
> —*Queen City Jazz (1994)*

## Biography

Goonan's love of music, particularly jazz, informs the structure, tone, and imagery
of all her work, particularly the "Nanotech Cycle," which began with *Queen
City Jazz* in 1994. Her novels also reflect her keen, and self-taught, interest in
nanotechnology, biology, and chemistry. Her work is sometimes grouped with
cyberpunk, as she explores the virtual space that is the consciousness, but Goonan
is more interested in the bright, musical notes of the transcendent, rather than the
trademark cyberpunk *noir*.

Kathleen Ann Goonan was born in Cincinnati, and spent some of her childhood
in Washington, DC. She attended Virginia Polytechnic Institute, earning a degree
in English Literature and Philosophy and, after graduation, trained as a Montessori
teacher. She lives with her husband in Lakeland, Florida.

ALTERNATIVE HISTORY; ANDROIDS, CYBORGS & ROBOTS; ARTIFI-
CIAL INTELLIGENCE; NANOTECHNOLOGY

## Major Works

*Novels*

The Nanotech Cycle: *Queen City Jazz* (1994), *Mississippi Blues* (1997), *Crescent
City Rhapsody* (2000), *Light Music* (2002—excerpt: http://www.infinitematrix.
net/stories/excerpts/light_music1.html).
*The Bones of Time* (1996)
*In War Times* (2007)

*Notable Short Stories*

"The Day the Dam Broke" (1995). http://www.goonan.com/dam.html.
"The String" (1995). http://www.goonan.com/string.html.
"Angels and You Dogs" (2003)

*Other Important Works*

"The Biological Century and the Future of Science Fiction." The Library of Congress.
    December 13, 2001. http://www.goonan.com/loc.html.
"Cities of the Future?" *Paradoxa* 2(1) (1996): 30–35.
"Consciousness, Literature, and Science Fiction" *Iowa Review*, August 2005. Text
    available on http://www.goonan.com/.
"First Sale." In David H. Borcherding ed., *Science Fiction and Fantasy Writer's
    Sourcebook*, Cincinnati, OH: Writer's Digest, 1996, 403–406.
"More Than You'll Ever Know: Down the Rabbit Hole of *The Matrix*." In Karen Haber
    ed., *Exploring The Matrix: Visions of the Cyber Present*. New York: St. Martin's
    Press, 2003, 98–111.
"Science Fiction and All That Jazz" *Borders.com*. June 19, 2001. http://www.goonan.
    com/essay.html.

## Research Sources

*Encyclopedias and Handbooks:* **AW, CA**

*Bibliographies:* **ARB, FF, SFAN**

*Biographies and Interviews*

*Locus Online.* "Make it New." September 2007. http://www.locusmag.com/2007/
    Issue09_Goonan.html.
Martini, Adrienne. "Sunsphere City Solo: . . . How Knoxville Shaped Her Futuristic
    Fiction." *Knoxville Weekly Wire,* March 20, 2000. http://weeklywire.com/ww/03-
    20-00/knox_gamut.html.
Prisco, Giulio. Interview. *Transhumanism.org.* May 12, 2002. World Transhumanist
    Association. http://www.transhumanism.org/index.php/th/more/291/.
Sisson, Kate. Interview. *The Frankenstein Project.* February 2004. Georgia Tech.
    http://frankenstein.lcc.gatech.edu/GoonanInterview.html.

*Criticism and Readers' Guides*

Collins, Graham P. "Shamans of Small." *Scientific American* 285(3) (2001): 86–91.

*Web Site*

*Goonan.com.* Official Web site. http://www.goonan.com/.

# Colin Greenland (1954– )

*Picture her, Tabitha Jute: not as the net media show her, heroine of hyperspace, capable, canny and cosmetically enhanced, smiling confidently as she reaches with one hand for the spangled mist of the Milky Way; but a small, weary young woman in a cracked foil jacket and oil-stained trousers . . .*

*—Take Back Plenty (1990)*

## Biography

Colin Greenland was born in Dover, England. *The Entropy Exhibition* (1983), a scholarly study of Michael Moorcock and the British New Wave, and still considered the foremost critical resource on the subject, was developed from the PhD thesis he did at Pembroke College, Oxford. Greenland's early novels were firmly in the tradition of classic New Wave: exotic, *serious* fabulations, heavy on the entropy, and light on the sf hardware—and the fun.

In 1990, all that changed with the publication of *Take Back Plenty*, a jolly space romp that took a new look at the conventions of old-fashioned genre science fiction and paid the space opera the ultimate tribute of taking it seriously. *Take Back Plenty* was the winner of all three major British sf awards (Eastercon, Clarke Award, and BSF Association), a record that still stands. Colin Greenland lives in London with his partner, the fantasy writer Susanna Clarke.

ALIEN WORLDS; FANTASY; SPACE OPERA; WOMEN IN SF

## Major Works

*Novels*

*Daybreak on a Different Mountain* (1984)
*The Hour of the Thin Ox* (1986)
*Other Voices* (1988)
The Tabitha Jute Trilogy: *Take Back Plenty* (1990—**BSF**), *Seasons of Plenty* (1995), *Mother of Plenty* (1998)
*Harm's Way* (1993)

*Collections*

*The Plenty Principle.* London: Voyager, 1997. A collection of the adventures of Tabitha Jute and her motley crew,

*Short Stories*

"Miss Otis Regrets" (1982)
"A Passion for Lord Pierrot" (1990) http://www.infinityplus.co.uk/stories/pierrot. htm.

*Other Important Works*

*The Entropy Exhibition: Michael Moorcock and the British "New Wave" in Science Fiction.* London: Routledge, 1983.

"The 'Field' and the 'Wave': The History of *New Worlds.*" In James Gunn and Matthew Candelaria eds., *Speculations on Speculation: Theories of Science Fiction.* Lanham, MD: Scarecrow, 2005.

"Images of *Nineteen Eighty-Four*: Fiction and Prediction." In George E. Slusser, Colin Greenland, and Eric S. Rabkin eds., *Storm Warnings: Science Fiction Confronts the Future.* Carbondale: Southern Illinois University Press, 1987, 124–134.

*Michael Moorcock: Death is No Obstacle.* Manchester, UK: Savoy, 1992.

"Writer's Talk: Michael Moorcock with Colin Greenland." VHS Videocassette. Northbrooke, IL: The Roland Collection. 1989.

# Research Sources

*Encyclopedias and Handbooks:* **AW, CA, CANR, ESF, SFW**

*Bibliographies:* **FF, SFAN**

Profile and Bibliography. *Infinity Plus.* 1998. http://www.infinityplus.co.uk/misc/cg. htm.

*Biographies and Interviews*

Beagle, Peter. Interview. Paradoxa 5(13–14) (1999–2000): 288–302.

Bould, Mark, and Andrew M. Butler. "Voices on the Boom." *Science Fiction Studies* 30 (2003): 483–491.

Chester, Tony (moderator). "More than Human: Panel Discussion with Charles Stross, Colin Greenland and Norman Spinrad." *Mexicon 5*: The Science Fact and Science Fiction Concatenation, May 1994. http://www.concatenation.org/interviews/morethanhuman.html.

Hendrick, Dave. Interview. *Fractal Matter.* March 2006. http://fractalmatter.com/main/?p=124.

Kletcha, Anne M. Profile. Phoenix Convention, Dublin. March 12, 2006. http://www.slovobooks.com/phoenix/2006_guest_greenland.php.

*Criticism and Readers' Guides*

Robson, Justina. "The Wild Ride (*Take Back Plenty*)." Paul Kincaid and Andrew M. Butler eds., *The Arthur C. Clarke Award: A Critical Anthology.* Daventry, UK: Serendip Foundation, 2006.

*Web Sites*

*The Colin Greenland Archive.* The SF Hub. University of Liverpool Library. The Archive spans the period from 1972 to 1998, and comprises annotated manuscripts, typescripts, and proofs of his published works and related correspondence. http://www.sfhub.ac.uk/Greenland.htm.

# Joe Haldeman (1943–   )

*I had to stifle an impulse to laugh. Surely 'cowardice' had nothing to do with
his decision. Surely he had nothing so primitive and unmilitary as a will to live.*
                                                              *—The Forever War (1974)*

## Biography

Joe William Haldeman (*not* Joseph) was born in Oklahoma City, and as a child
lived in Puerto Rico, New Orleans, and Anchorage, Alaska. He is a graduate of
the University of Maryland, with a degree in physics and astronomy. He served
as a combat engineer in Vietnam, where he was severely wounded and received a
Purple Heart.

The impact of his wartime experiences, combined with his easy understanding
of the possibilities and consequences of the science, makes for intriguing narratives
such as *The Forever War* (1975), in which soldiers "jump" from one future conflict
to another. Haldeman earned a "trifecta" of Hugo, Nebula, and Campbell awards
in 1998 for *Forever Peace* (1997), the first novel in twenty-two years to sweep
all three prestigious prizes. Joe Haldeman currently divides his time between
Gainesville, Florida, and Cambridge, Massachusetts, where he teaches science
fiction and creative writing at MIT.

ALIEN THREAT; FIRST CONTACT; GENETIC ENGINEERING & CLONING;
HARD SF; VIRTUAL REALITY; WAR

## Major Works

*Novels*

The Forever Wars: *The Forever War* (1975—**Hugo, Locus Poll, Nebula**), *Forever
        Peace* (1997–**Hugo, Nebula**), *Forever Free* (1998)
*Mindbridge* (1976)
*All My Sins Remembered* (1977)
Star Trek: *Planet of Judgment* (1977)
Star Trek: *World without End* (1979)
The Worlds series: *Worlds* (1981), *Worlds Enough and Time* (1992), *Worlds Apart*
        (1983)
*There Is No Darkness* (1983) Three linked Young Adult novellas, written with his
        brother, Jack C. Haldeman.
*The Coming* (2000)
*Guardian* (2002)
*Camouflage* (2004) **Nebula, Tiptree**
*Old Twentieth* (2005)

## Collections

*None So Blind.* New York: Morrow/Eos, 1996. Includes the **Hugo** and **Locus Poll**-winning title story, "Graves" (1993—**Nebula**), and the original version of "The Hemingway Hoax" (1990—**Hugo, Nebula**).
*A Separate War and Other Stories.* New York: Ace, 2007.
Earlier collections by Haldeman include *Infinite Dreams* (1978) and *Dealing in Futures* (1985).

## Notable Short Stories

"Hero" (1973)
"Tricentennial" (1977) **Hugo, Locus Poll**
"None So Blind" (1994) **Hugo, Locus Poll** Excerpt: http://home.earthlink.net/~ haldeman/story1.html.
"Angel of Light" (2005) http://www.cosmosmagazine.com/node/42.

## Other Important Works

"*The Matrix* as Sci-Fi." In Karen Haber ed., *Exploring The Matrix: Visions of the Cyber Present.* New York: St. Martin's Press, 2003, 168–179.
"Point of View." In Robin Wilson ed., *Paragons: Twelve Master Science Fiction Writers Ply Their Craft.* New York: St. Martin's Press, 1996, 273–279.
*Vietnam and Other Alien Worlds.* Framingham, MA: NESFA, 1993. Includes short fiction, poetry, and essays such as "Confessions of a Space Junkie," "War Stories," and "Photographs and Memories."

## Research Sources

*Encyclopedias and Handbooks:* **AW, CA, CANR, ESF, MSSF, NNDB, SFW**

*Bibliographies:* **ARB, FF, SFAN**

### Biographies and Interviews

Bowlin, W. Scott. Interview. *SciFi.com.* January 21, 2003. http://scifi.com/sfw/ issue300/interview.html.
*The Future and You.* Podcast Interviews: January-June 2006. http://www.thefutureand you.libsyn.com/?search_string=haldeman&Submit=Search&search=1.
*Hard Science Fiction.* Interview. July 4, 2006. http://www.hardsf.net/?mode=8&id=3.
Jenkins, Henry. "What Happens to the Body in Cyberspace?" (Roundtable discussion with Gregory Benford)." *Media in Transition.* MIT October 15, 1997. http://web. mit.edu/m-i-t/science_fiction/transcripts/benford_haldeman_index.html.
McShane, Shamrock. "Joe Haldeman's Cosmological Adventure." *The New Moon Rising.* January 18, 2007. http://www.thenewmoonrising.com/archives/haldeman. htm.

Mead, Donald. Interview. *Strange Horizons.* February 23, 2004. http://www.
  strangehorizons.com/2004/20040223/haldeman.shtml.
Rand, Ken. Profile. *Internet Review of Science Fiction.* June 2004. http://www.irosf.
  com/zine/article/10061

## Criticism and Readers' Guides

Blackmore, Tim. "Warring Stories: Fighting for Truth in the Science Fiction of Joe
  Haldeman." *Extrapolation* 34 (1993): 131–146.
Clute, Judith, and Ellen R. Weil. "Joe Haldeman's "For White Hill": A Dual Perspec-
  tive." *New York Review of Science Fiction* 9(10) (1997): 1+.
Gordon, Joan. "Joe Haldeman: Cyberpunk Before Cyberpunk Was Cool?" In Donald
  E. Morse ed., *The Celebration of the Fantastic.* Westport, CT: Greenwood, 1992,
  251–257.
———. *Joe Haldeman.* Mercer Island, WA: Starmont House, 1980.
Jason, Philip K. "Joe Haldeman and the Wounds of War." In *Acts and Shadows: The
  Vietnam War in American Literary Culture.* Lanham, MD: Rowman & Littlefield,
  2000.
Morse, Donald E. "Hoaxing Hemingway: Ernest Hemingway as Character and Pres-
  ence in Joe Haldeman's *The Hemingway Hoax* (1990)." *Extrapolation* 45 (2004):
  227–236.

## Web Sites

*Joe Haldeman.* Official Web site. http://home.earthlink.net/~haldeman/.
*Joe's Place.* Author's blog. http://joe-haldeman.livejournal.com/.

**If you enjoyed Joe Haldeman . . .**
The impact of Haldeman's experiences in the Central Highlands of Vietnam makes
for intriguing narratives of futuristic war. In *The Forever War,* for example, soldiers
doomed to "jump" from one interplanetary conflict to another have nothing to
depend on but their loyalty to each other, which is ruthlessly exploited by those
they serve.

**Then you might like . . .**
*Jack Campbell.* The pen name of author John G. Hemry, a retired US Navy officer,
who has a number of "Navy in space" series, including (as Hemry) "Stark's War,"
and "JAG in Space." The "Lost Fleet" series, beginning with *Dauntless* (2006),
are the adventures of Captain "Black Jack" Geary—a "dead" hero who's just
emerged from a century-long hibernation—returning as the last, best hope to end
an interstellar war that has killed millions.

*David Drake.* Another Vietnam veteran who has become a popular, and immensely
prolific, author of military sf, the author of the "Hammer's Slammers" series. The
typical Drake hero is individualistic, iconoclastic, and politically conservative.

Villains tend to be drawn from the ranks of bureaucrats, politicians, academics, and political leftists.

*John Scalzi*. His first traditionally published novel, *Old Man's War* (2005), is a clever twist on the callow youth, coming of age, story: elderly humans are given a new lease on life—literally—battling aliens in the Colonial Defense Force. A number of sequels and stand-alone novels in the series have followed in rapid succession.

*Lucius Shepard*. Often described as a "futuristic *Apocalypse Now*," *Life During Wartime* (1989) is a fix-up of a number of Shepard's short stories in which secret forces battle it out in the jungles of 21st century Guatemala. Shepard's writing is notable for exotic settings, drugs, and magic realism, as well as (like Haldeman), exceptionally fine writing.

*Walter Jon Williams*. **AW** describes the "Hardwired" series as "excellent examples of the fusion of military sf with Cyberpunk." The "Dread Empire" series is lively and well-written military space opera, while *Hardwired* (1986) and *Voice of the Whirlwind* (1987) feature cyberpunk flourishes like cybor-ized mercenaries and vengeful clones.

# Harry Harrison (1925–   )

> *"You're a criminal," I muttered through clenched teeth, and spat on a NO SPITTING sign. "You hate the law and live happily without it. You are a law unto yourself, and the most honest man in the galaxy."*
> *—The Stainless Steel Rat (1961)*

## Biography

Harry Harrison was born Henry Maxwell Dempsey, in Stanford, Connecticut. His father changed the family's surname to Harrison shortly after the birth of his son. After serving in World War II, Harrison worked as a commercial artist, and during the 1950s and 1960s he was the main writer of the *Flash Gordon* comic strip. His short stories first appeared in magazines under house pseudonyms such as "Wade Kaempfert."

Harrison is best known from the irreverent humor of the Stainless Steel Rat and Bill the Galactic hero (a non-too-gentle spoof of gung-ho space opera such as *Starship Troopers*). His 1966 novel *Make Room! Make Room!* was the basis for the 1973 cult classic *Soylent Green*, starring Charlton Heston, although Harrison's futuristic noir plot was greatly "Hollywood-ized." In the 1970s, Harrison and his wife settled in Ireland, which is where he continues to make his home today.

ALTERNATE HISTORY; COLONIZATION OF OTHER WORLDS; ECOLOGY; HUMOR AND SATIRE; OVERPOPULATION

## Major Works

*Novels*

*Deathworld* (1960), *Deathworld Two* (1964), *Deathworld Three* (1968)

The Stainless Steel Rat series: *The Stainless Steel Rat* (1961), *The Stainless Steel Rat's Revenge* (1970), and, among others, *The Stainless Steel Rat Saves the World* (1972), *You Can Be the Stainless Steel Rat* (1985), and *The Stainless Steel Rat Joins the Circus* (1999).

To the Stars Trilogy: *Homeworld* (1980), *Starworld* (1981), *Wheelworld* (1981)

*Planet of the Damned* (1962—aka *A Sense of Obligation*)

*Bill, the Galactic Hero* (1965) Since 1990, volumes in the Bill, the Galactic Hero series have been written in collaboration with Robert Sheckley, David Bischoff, and Jack C. Haldeman II. The final volume in the series, so far, is *Bill, the Galactic Hero: The Final Incoherent Adventure* (1991, with David Harris).

*Make Room! Make Room!* (1966)

*Captive Universe* (1969)

*Tunnel Through the Deeps* (1972—aka *A Transatlantic Tunnel, Hurrah!*)

*Star Smashers of the Galaxy Rangers* (1974)

*The Jupiter Plague* (1982)

The Eden series: *West of Eden* (1984), *Winter in Eden* (1986), *Return to Eden* (1988)

*Collections*

*The Adventures of the Stainless Steel Rat.* New York: Ace, 1996. Compilation volume, containing the first three volumes in the series.

*50 in 50: Fifty Stories for Fifty Years!* New York: Tor, 2002. Marking Harrison's fiftieth anniversary as a published science fiction writer. Contains classic favorites, as well as stories that have never been anthologized before.

*A Stainless Steel Trio.* New York: Tor, 2003. Compilation volume, which brings together *A Stainless Steel Rat Is Born* (1985), *The Stainless Steel Rat Gets Drafted* (1987), and *The Stainless Steel Rat Sings the Blues* (1994)

*Notable Short Stories*

"The Stainless Steel Rat" (1957; later served as prologue to the first novel)
"By the Falls" (1970)
"The Mothballed Spaceship" (1973)
"The Golden Years of the Stainless Steel Rat" (1993)
"Bill, the Galactic Hero's Happy Holiday" (1995)

*Other Important Works*

"A Cannibalized Novel Becomes *Soylent Green*." In Danny Peary ed., *Omni's Screen Flights Screen Fantasies: The Future according to SF Cinema.* New York: Doubleday, 1984. http://www.harryharrison.com/.

*Great Balls of Fire! A History of Sex in Science Fiction.* New York: Grosset & Dunlap, 1977.

*Hell's Cartographers.* With Brian W. Aldiss, ed. New York: Harper & Row, 1975. Includes Harrison's essay, "The Beginning of the Affair" (76–95), which can be found on his official Web site. http://www.harryharrison.com/.

"Introducing the Future: The Dawn of Science-Fiction Criticism." In Alan Sandison and Robert Dingley eds., *Histories of the Future: Studies in Fact, Fantasy and Science Fiction.* Basingstoke, UK: Palgrave, 2000, 1–7.

*Spacecraft in Fact and Fiction.* With Malcolm Edwards. New York: Exeter, 1979.

"Worlds Beside Worlds." In Peter Nicholls ed., *Science Fiction at Large: A Collection of Essays, By Various Hands, about the Interface between Science Fiction and Reality.* London: Gollancz, 1976, 105–114. http://www.iol.ie/~carrollm/hh/n13-tt-worlds.htm.

## Research Sources

*Encyclopedias and Handbooks:* **AW, CA, CANR, ESF, MSSF, NNDB, SFW**

*Bibliographies:* **ARB, FF, SFAN**

Tomlinson, Paul. *Harry Harrison: An Annotated Bibliography.* Holicong, PA: Wildside/Cosmos, 2002. http://www.harryharrison.com/.

### Biographies and Interviews

Goldsmith, Jeff. "Harry Harrison Invades Hollywood!" *Eon Magazine.* No date. http://www.harryharrison.com/.

"Science Fiction Should be Humane: A Talk with Harry Harrison." *Soviet Literature* 12 (1987): 178–180.

Shreeve, John. "A Stainless Steel Rap: Harry Harrison Interviewed." *Interzone,* June 1993: 23–26.

Walker, Paul. "Harry Harrison on John W. Campbell." In *Speaking of Science Fiction.* Oradell, NJ: Luna, 1978, 208–212.

### Criticism and Readers' Guides

Carter, S. R. "Harry Harrison's *The Adventures of the Stainless Steel Rat*: A Study in Multiple Interfaces." *Extrapolation* 21 (1980): 139–145.

Stover, Leon. *Harry Harrison.* Boston, MA: Twayne, 1990.

### Web Sites

*Harry Harrison.* Official Web site. http://www.harryharrison.com/.

# M. John Harrison (1945–   )

*"Let's see what it does, shall we?"*

—*The Centauri Device (1974)*

## Biography

Michael John Harrison was born in Warwickshire, England. From 1968 to 1975 he was literary editor of the New Wave sf magazine *New Worlds*. He is a keen rock climber, and his 1989 autobiographical novel *Climbers* won the Boardman Tasker Prize for Mountain Literature.

For forty years, Harrison has been at the cutting edge of every important development in science fiction: New Wave, the revival of the intelligent space opera, the transmigration of sf sensibilities to mainstream themes, and, most recently, the melding of the tropes of fantasy and science fiction into a seamless whole, which some call "the Weird." M. John Harrison is a regular fiction reviewer for the *Times Literary Supplement*, and London newspapers *The Guardian* and *The Daily Telegraph*, and he has collaborated with Jane Johnson on a number of more traditional fantasy novels under the name "Gabriel King." He currently lives in West London, near the River Thames.

APOCALYPSE AND AFTER; CITIES AND SOCIETIES; ENTROPY; FANTASY; FAR FUTURE; NEW WAVE

## Major Works

*Novels*

*The Committed Men* (1971)
The Virconium sequence: *The Pastel City* (1971), *A Storm of Wings* (1980), *In Viriconium* (1982—aka *The Floating Gods*)
*The Centauri Device* (1974)
*The Course of the Heart* (1992)
*Signs of Life* (1997)
*Light* (2002) **Tiptree**
*Nova Swing* (2006)

*Collections*

*Things That Never Happen*. London: Gollancz, 2002. Two UK collections, *The Ice Monkey* (1983) and *Travel Arrangements* (2000) combined, with some additional stories. Introduction by China Mieville.
*Viriconium*. New York: Spectra, 2005. Viriconium omnibus; that includes two newer shorts, "The Dancer from the Dance" and "A Young Man's Journey to Viriconium." Introduction by Neil Gaiman.

*Notable Short Stories*

"Isobel Avens Returns to Stepney in the Spring" (1994) http://www.infinityplus.co.uk/stories/isobel.htm.
"The East" (1996) http://www.mjohnharrison.com/archive/east.htm.
"Entertaining Angels Unawares" (2002) excerpt: http://www.conjunctions.com/webconj.htm.
"I Did It" (2003) http://www.mjohnharrison.com/archive/ididit.htm.

*Other Important Works*

"A Literature of Comfort." In Michael Moorcock, ed. *New Worlds Quarterly*. New York: Berkeley, 1971, 182–190.
*Parietal Games: Critical Writings by and on M. John Harrison*. Eds. Mark Bould and Michelle Reid. Liverpool, UK: Science Fiction Foundation, 2005. Comprehensive collection of reviews and essays that Harrison has written over his career, such as, "By Tennyson out of Disney" and "The Chalk Won't Stay on the Biscuits."
"The Profession of Fiction." In Maxim Jakubowski and Edward James eds., *The Profession of Science Fiction: SF Writers on Their Craft and Ideas*. New York: St. Martin's Press, 1992, 140–153.
"What It Might Be Like to Live in Viriconium." *Fantastic Metropolis*. October 15, 2001. http://www.fantasticmetropolis.com/i/viriconium/.
"How I Write." *Time Out*. December 2006. http://www.mjohnharrison.com/archive/tointerview.htm.

## Research Sources

*Encyclopedias and Handbooks:* **AW, CA, CANR, ESF, MSSF, SFW**

*Bibliographies:* **ARB, FF, SFAN**

*Biographies and Interviews*

Chouinard, Gabriel. "A Conversation with M. John Harrison." *SF Site*. September 2002. http://www.sfsite.com/12b/mjh142.htm.
Hudson, Patrick. "Disillusioned by The Actual." *The Zone Online*. November 2002. Pigasus Press. http://www.zone-sf.com/mjharrison.html.
*Locus Online*. "No Escape." December 2003. http://www.locusmag.com/2003/Issue12/Harrison.html.
Mathew, David. Interview. *Infinity Plus*. November 2002. http://www.infinityplus.co.uk/nonfiction/intmjh.htm.
Morgan, Cheryl. Interview. *Strange Horizons*. June 9, 2003. http://www.strangehorizons.com/2003/20030609/harrison.shtml.
Nussbaum, Abigail. "Is There Someone at the End of This Rope? A Long Day's Struggle with M. John Harrison." *Asking the Wrong Questions*. September 17,

2005. http://wrongquestions.blogspot.com/2005/09/is-there-someone-at-end-of-this-rope.html (blog review of *Light*, which includes extended response and discussion with MJH).

### Criticism and Readers' Guides

Freeman, Nick. "An Appreciation of M. John Harrison." *Henry Street: A Graduate Review of Literary Studies* 5(2) (1995): 16–32.
Hughes, Rhys. "Climbing to Viriconium: The Work of M. John Harrison." *Fantastic Metropolis*, October 15, 2001. http://www.fantasticmetropolis.com/i/harrison/.
Langan, John. "Significant Stories, Stylishly Told." *Science Fiction Studies* 33 (2006): 348–352.
Lewis, Martin. "No More New World Orders." *Vector* 245 (2005). http://www.vectormagazine.co.uk/article.asp?articleID=14.
Mieville, China. "The Limits of Vision(aries): Or M. John Harrison Returns to London and it is Spring." *Vector* 226 (2002): 10–13.
Morgan, Cheryl. "In Search of Viriconium." *Emerald City*, March 2006. http://www.emcit.com/emcit127.php?a=23.

### Web Sites

*Uncle Zip's Window: The M. John Harrison News Page.* Official Web site and author's blog. http://www.mjohnharrison.com/.

# Robert A. Heinlein (1907–1988)

*The universe will let us know—later   whether or not Man has any 'right' to expand through it.*

*—Starship Troopers (1959)*

## Biography

Robert Heinlein's prolific output shaped the 20th century's perception of space and the universe, both the fiction and the fact. His scrupulous attention to technical detail, as well as his efforts to maintain plausibility in both plot and character, "raised the bar" for the whole genre. Words and phrases from his work have entered the language, such as "grok" (*Stranger in a Strange Land*) and TANSTAAFL ("there ain't no such thing as a free lunch," *The Moon is a Harsh Mistress*).

Heinlein was born in Butler, Missouri. He graduated from the US Naval Academy in 1929, but had to retire from the service on medical grounds, and turned to writing science fiction. On July 20, 1969, he joined Walter Cronkite and Arthur C. Clarke to provide television commentary as Neil Armstrong set foot on the surface of the moon. Robert A. Heinlein died of cardiovascular disease and emphysema in Carmel, California, on May 8, 1988.

CHILDREN IN SF; IMMORTALITY; MARS, MOON & THE PLANETS; LIB-
ERTARIAN SF; MESSIAHS; SEX & TABOOS; WAR

## Major Works

*Novels*

*The Farmer in the Sky* (1951)
*Double Star* (1956) **Hugo**
*Methuselah's Children* (1958)
*Starship Troopers* (1959) **Hugo**
*Stranger in a Strange Land* (1961) **Hugo**
*Podkayne of Mars* (1963)
*Glory Road* (1963)
*Farnham's Freehold* (1964) Chapters 1–6 of this novel can be found on the
     Web site of Baen Books—http://www.webscription.net/chapters/1416520937/
     1416520937_c_.htm.
*The Moon Is a Harsh Mistress* (1966) **Hugo**
*Time Enough For Love* (1973)
*The Number of the Beast* (1980)
*The Cat Who Walks Through Walls* (1985)
*To Sail Beyond the Sunset* (1987)

*Collections*

*The Past through Tomorrow* (1967) Science Fiction Book Club, 2000. All twenty-
     one stories, novellas, and novels of Heinlein's Future History series. Includes
     "Life-Line" (1939), "Methuselah's Children" (1941), "The Green Hills of Earth"
     (1947), "The Man Who Sold the Moon" (1951).
To read all of Heinlein's short fiction you would also need *Expanded Universe*
     (1980), *The Fantasies of Robert A. Heinlein* (1999), and *Off the Main Sequence*
     (2005).

*Notable Short Stories*

"The Roads Must Roll" (1940)
". . . And He Built a Crooked House" (1941)
"Universe" (1941)
"Waldo" (1942)
"All You Zombies . . . " (1959)

*Other Important Works*

*Destination Moon*. Dir. Irving Pichel. George Pal Productions. 1950.
     Film version of *Rocket Ship Galileo* (1947). Heinlein is credited for the screenplay,
     and as technical advisor.

*Grumbles from the Grave* (1989)

"On the Writing of Speculative Fiction." In The Staff of *Analog & Isaac Asimov's Science Fiction Magazine* eds., *Writing Science Fiction & Fantasy*. New York: St. Martin's Griffin, 1993, 5–12.

"Science Fiction: Its Nature, Faults and Virtues." In Damon Knight ed., *Turning Points: Essays on the Art of Science Fiction*. New York: Harper & Row, 1977, 3–28.


## Research Sources

*Encyclopedias and Handbooks:* **AW, BW, CA, CAAS, CANR, ESF, MSSF, NNDB, SFW, WS**

*Bibliographies:* **ARB, FF, SFAN**

Gifford, James. *Robert A. Heinlein: A Reader's Companion*. Sacramento. CA: Nitrosyncretic, 2000.

Main, Michael. "The Fiction of Robert A. Heinlein." *Storypilot*. July 2007. http://www.storypilot.com/sf/heinlein.html.


### Biographies and Interviews

Pace, Eric. Obituary. *The New York Times*, May 10, 1988.

Platt, Charles. "Heinlein Speaks?" In *Loose Canon*. Holicong, PA: Cosmos/Wildside, 2001, 100–111.

Slusser, George Edward. *Robert A. Heinlein: Stranger in His Own Land*. San Bernardino, CA: Borgo, 1977.

Stimson, Thomas E. Jr. "A House to Make Life Easy." *Popular Mechanics*, June 1952. http://www.nitrosyncretic.com/rah/pm652-art-hi.html.
   Article and photographs of Robert and Virginia Heinlein in the "futuristic" house they designed.

Stover, Leon *Robert Heinlein*. Boston, MA: Twayne, 1987.


### Criticism and Readers' Guides

Dolman, Everett Carl. "Military, Democracy, and the State in Robert A. Heinlein's *Starship Troopers*." In Donald M. Hassler and Clyde Wilcox, *Political Science Fiction*. Columbia: University of South Carolina Press, 1997, 196–213.

Franklin, H. Bruce. *Robert A. Heinlein: America as Science Fiction*. New York: Oxford University Press, 1980.

Hines, Jim C. "Sleeping with the Bug-Eyed Monster: Sexuality in the Novels of Anthony, Heinlein, and Le Guin." *Strange Horizons*, December 17, 2001. http://www.strangehorizons.com/2001/20011217/bug-eyed_monster.shtml.

Lord, M. G. "Heinlein's Female Troubles." *New York Times Book Review* October 2 (2005): 35.

McGiveron, Rafeeq O. "From Love to the Free-Fire Zone: Heinlein's Mars, 1939–1987." *Extrapolation* 42 (2001): 137–149.

————. "Heinlein's Inhabited Solar System, 1940–1952." *Science-Fiction Studies* 23 (1996): 245–252.

Parkin-Speer, Diane. "Almost a Feminist: Robert A. Heinlein." *Extrapolation* 36 (1995): 113–125.

Patterson, William H., Jr. and Andrew Thornton. *The Martian Named Smith: Critical Perspectives on Heinlein's "Stranger in a Strange Land."* Sacramento, CA: Nitrosyncretic, 2001.

Scalzi, John. "Lessons from Heinlein." *New York Review of Science Fiction* 17(9) (2005): 13+.

Sullivan, C. W. "Heinlein's Juveniles: Growing Up in Outer Space." In *Science Fiction for Young Readers*. Westport, CT: Greenwood, 1993, 21–36.

Vonnegut, Kurt. "Heinlein Gets the Last Word." *New York Times Book Review*, December 9, 1990.

Westfahl, Gary. "'You Don't Know What You're Talking About': Robert A. Heinlein and the Racism of American Science Fiction." In Elisabeth Anne Leonard, *Into Darkness Peering: Race and Color in the Fantastic*. Westport. CT: Greenwood, 1997, 71–84.

## Web Sites

*Expanded Universe: More Worlds of Robert A. Heinlein*. Baen Books. Stories, with introductory comment, online in full, from the 1980 Baen Books collection. http://www.webscription.net/chapters/0743471598/0743471598.htm?blurb.

*The Heinlein Society*. Society dedicated to preserving the legacy of RAH. As well as news about public service activities, the Web site has readers' forums and a Concordance of the works. http://www.heinleinsociety.org/.

*Robert A. Heinlein: The Dean of Science Fiction Writers*. Carlos Angelo, ed. April 2002. Enthusiastic fan site that collects links and interesting information, such as an archive of RAH cover art. http://www.wegrokit.com/index.htm.

*Site RAH: The Home Page for Science Fiction's Grand Master*. James Gifford, ed. Nitrosyncretic Press. 2005. http://www.nitrosyncretic.com/rah/.

**If you enjoyed Robert Heinlein...**
As a writer, Heinlein is almost impossible to pin down—the radical and the conservative coexist comfortably together, and just when you think you have his number, he surprises you. He can simultaneously be perceived as patron saint of militarism (*Starship Troopers*) and Free Love (*Stranger in a Strange Land*); at his best, he was a storyteller who created an environment in which readers believed that it could all really happen.

**Then you might like...**
*Poul Anderson*. His predominant themes are personal liberty, and the ability of the individual to triumph over adversity—or die trying. A tireless proponent of the space program; in novels like *Tau Zero* (1970), and series like the Technic History

sequence, his "...cultural style could...be regarded as a form of romantic, Midwestern, libertarian individualism" (**ESF**).

*David Gerrold.* A great admirer of Heinlein, Gerrold borrowed—and made his own—many of Heinlein's best-loved scenarios: the existential problems of time travel (*The Man Who Folded Himself*, 1973), alien invaders (the "War against the Chtorr" sequence), and resourceful youngsters (the "Dingilliad" trilogy).

*Larry Niven.* Like Heinlein, Niven is an all-rounder: he has written comic sf, and science fantasy; he has been very successful working in collaboration with other authors. With the stories that became "Tales of Known Space," Niven established himself in the forefront of a hard science fiction renaissance, an author who is easily able to dramatize the big ideas.

*Spider Robinson.* In addition to the Callahan's Bar series of comic novels, and a number of Heinlein-esque sf adventures, Robinson has recently written *Variable Star* (2006), a novel expanded from a 1955 novel outline by Heinlein: "...his punchy optimism about the human condition...seemed to have established him as a legitimate heir" (**ESF**).

*John Varley.* In novels like *Steel Beach* and the "Gaea" trilogy, Varley effortlessly rejuvenated many tropes that Heinlein had made his own: the independent minded hero/heroine (sometimes the same character), strong female protagonists, compulsive narrative hooks, and gender-bending, free-for-all sexuality.

## *Frank Herbert (1920–1986)*

> *Fear is the mind-killer. Fear is the little death that brings total obliteration. I will face my fear. I will permit it to pass over me and through me. And when it has gone past I will turn the inner eye to see its path. Where the fear has gone there will be nothing. Only I will remain.*
>
> *—Dune (1965)*

## Biography

Frank Patrick Herbert was born in Tacoma, Washington. For most of his working life, he was a professional journalist, writing about issues relating to sustainable lifestyles, and the flora, fauna and preservation of the Pacific Northwest. In 1965, he introduced an entirely different kind of science fiction with *Dune,* in which technology comes second to character, philosophy, and world-building. *Dune's* desert-planet Arrakis is fully realized, and its characters' struggles and triumphs cannot be disentangled from their landscape and Herbert's message.

*Dune* enabled Herbert to put into practice his ecological concerns, writing about, lecturing on, and living the sustainable lifestyle. It is the single work that will always be associated with his name. He was working with his son, Brian

Herbert, on a seventh volume in the Dune saga, when he died on February 11, 1986, in Madison, Wisconsin, the result of a pulmonary embolism brought on by surgery to treat pancreatic cancer.

ECOLOGY; FAR FUTURE; GALATIC EMPIRES; GENETIC ENGINEERING & CLONING; MESSIAHS; PSI POWERS; RELIGION

## Major Works

*Novels*

*The Dragon in the Sea* (1955)
Dune: *Dune* (1965—**Hugo, Nebula**), *Dune Messiah* (1969), *Children of Dune* (1976), *God Emperor of Dune* (1981), *Heretics of Dune* (1984), *Chapterhouse: Dune* (1985)
ConSentiency: "The Tactful Saboteur" (short story, 1964), *Whipping Star* (1970) *The Dosadi Experiment* (1977)
Destination: Void: *Destination: Void* (1966), and (with Bill Ransom) *The Jesus Incident* (1979), *The Lazarus Effect* (1983), *The Ascension Factor* (1988)

*Other Important Works*

*Dune*. Universal Pictures, 1984. Directed by David Lynch, this is a movie that can provoke fisticuffs between the most mild-mannered sf fans. A brilliant failure or a disgraceful mess. Your call.
*Dune* Excerpts. (Read by Frank Herbert.) *HarperAudio!* May 1994. Internet Town Hall. http://town.hall.org/radio/HarperAudio/.
"Dune Genesis." *Omni Magazine* July 1980. http://www.dunenovels.com/news/ genesis.html.
"Listening to the Left Hand." *Harper's Magazine* 1973. http://www.aeriagloris.com/ Resources/FrankHerbertEssay/index.html.
The Maker of Dune. Tim O'Reilly, ed. New York: Berkeley, 1987. A collection of essays and introductions written for a variety of publications; two interviews with the editor.
"Men on Other Planets." In Reginald Bretnor, ed., *The Craft of Science Fiction*. New York: Harper and Row, 1976, 121–132.
"Science Fiction and a World in Crisis." In Reginald Bretnor, ed., *Science Fiction, Today and Tomorrow; A Discursive Symposium*. New York: Harper & Row, 1974, 69–97.

## Research Sources

*Encyclopedias and Handbooks:* **AW, BW, CA, CAAS, CANR, ESF, MSSF, NNDB, SFW, WS**
*Bibliographies:* **ARB, FF, SFAN**

Kahl, Kris. Bibliography. May 2007. *Cave of Birds*. http://www.caveofbirds.com/bib. html.

## Biographies and Interviews

Herbert, Brian. *The Dreamer of Dune: A Biography of Frank Herbert*. New York: Tor, 2003.

McNelly, Willis E. Transcript of an interview recorded with Frank Herbert in Sexek, Turkey. February 2, 1969. July 2005. Plan B. http://www.sinanvural.com/seksek/inien/tvd/tvd2.htm.

Merritt, Byron. "Frank Herbert Lives." *The Zone Online*, November 2005. Pigasus Press. http://www.zone-sf.com/frankherbert.html.

*Mother Earth News*. The Plowboy Interview: Frank Herbert. May/June 1981. http://www.motherearthnews.com/Modern-Homesteading/1981-05-01/The-Plowboy-Interview-Frank-Herbert.aspx.

O'Reilly, Timothy. *Frank Herbert*. New York: Frederick Ungar, 1981. http://tim.oreilly.com/herbert/. Online text of this out-of-print biography, written with Herbert's full cooperation.

Turner, Paul. "Vertex Interviews Frank Herbert." *Vertex*, October 1973. http://members.lycos.co.uk/Fenrir/ctdinterviews.htm.

## Criticism and Readers' Guides

Aylott, Chris. "What's So Great About Dune?" *Space.com*, January 27, 2000. Imaginova Corp. http://www.space.com/sciencefiction/dune_intro_991019.html.

DiTommaso, Lorenzo. "History and Historical Effect in Frank Herbert's *Dune*." *Science Fiction Studies* 19 (1992): 311–325. http://www.depauw.edu/sfs/backissues/58/ditom58art.htm.

Feehan, Ellen. "Frank Herbert and the Making of Myths: Irish History, Celtic Mythology, and IRA Ideology in *The White Plague*." *Science-Fiction Studies* 19 (1992): 289–310. http://www.depauw.edu/sfs/backissues/58/feehan58art.htm.

McNelly, Willis E., ed. *The Dune Encyclopedia*. New York: Berkeley Trade, 1987.

Miller, D. M. *Frank Herbert*. Starmont Reader's Guide, 5. Mercer Island, WA: Starmont, 1981.

Minowitz, Peter. "Prince versus Prophet: Machiavellianism in Frank Herbert's *Dune* Epic." In Donald M. Hassler and Clyde Wilcox, eds., *Political Science Fiction*, Columbia: University of South Carolina Press, 1997, 124–147.

Palumbo, Donald E. *Chaos Theory: Asimov's Foundations and Robots, and Herbert's Dune: The Fractal Esthetic of Epic Science Fiction*. Westport, CT: Greenwood, 2002.

Stratton, Susan. "The Messiah and the Greens: The Shape of Environmental Action in Dune and Pacific Edge." *Extrapolation* 42 (2001): 303–316.

Touponce, William F. *Frank Herbert*. Boston, MA: Twayne, 1988.

## Web Sites

*Dune: The Official Web site*. http://www.dunenovels.com/. Web site chronicling the Dune saga, continued by Brian Herbert and Kevin J. Anderson.

*Dune Index.* March 2007. Fan Web site covering books, films, and TV mini-series, Herbert's life, and other fiction and action figures. http://www.arrakis.co.uk/.

# Russell Hoban (1925–  )

*On my naming day when I come 12 I gone front spear and kilt a wild boar he parbly ben the las wyld pig on the Bundel Downs any how there hadn't ben non for a long time befor him nor I ain't looking to see none agen.*

*—Riddley Walker (1981)*

## Biography

Russell Hoban was the author of about fifty books for children, some illustrated with charming, witty pencil drawings by his wife Lillian, when, in the early 1970s, he began to write adult fiction. He began with *Riddley Walker*, the story of a worn-down, post-apocalyptic future, told in a style and language to match. Hoban's adult stories, some of which have sf themes, are dark, strange, and altogether different, blending allegory and wordplay with the humor that made his children's books such a pleasure for both parent and child.

Russell Conwell Hoban was born just outside of Philadelphia, the son of Jewish Ukrainian immigrants. He has lived in London since 1969. While he has never been a best seller, he has definitely achieved cult status: in 2005, fans organized an international convention, to celebrate his eightieth birthday.

ANTHROPOLOGY; APOCALYPSE AND AFTER; CHILDREN IN SF; FANTASY; LANGUAGE; MYTHOLOGY & LEGEND.

## Major Works

*Novels*

*Lion of Boaz-Jachin* (1973)
*Riddley Walker* (1980)
*Pilgermann* (1983)
*The Medusa Frequency* (1987)
*Fremder* (1996)

*Collections*

*The Moment under the Moment: Stories, a Libretto, Essays, and Sketches.* Philadelphia, PA: Trans-Atlantic, 1993.

*A Russell Hoban Omnibus.* Bloomington: Indiana University Press, 1999. Contains *Lion of Boaz-Jachin* and *Pilgermann*, as well as two mainstream novels, and a selection of short stories, essays, and poetry.

## Research Sources

*Encyclopedias and Handbooks:* **AW, CA, CANR, ESF, SFW**

*Bibliographies:* **FF, SFAN**

### Biographies and Interviews

Martin, Tim. "Russell Hoban: Odd, and Getting Odder." *The Independent*, January 22, 2006. http://arts.independent.co.uk/books/features/article340500.ece.

Myers, Edward. Interview. *The Literary Review: An International Journal of Contemporary Writing* 28(1) (1984): 5–16. http://www.ocelotfactory.com/hoban/rhint1. html.

Swaim, Don. Interview. *Wired for Books.* 1987. http://wiredforbooks.org/russellhoban/.

Wroe, Nicholas. "Secrets of the Yellow Pages: Profile." *Guardian Online*, November 23, 2002. http://books.guardian.co.uk/departments/generalfiction/story/0,845568,00.html.

### Criticism and Readers' Guides

Branscomb, Jack. "Knowledge and Understanding in *Riddley Walker*." In Nancy Anisfield, ed., *The Nightmare Considered: Critical Essays on Nuclear War Literature.* Bowling Green, OH: Bowling Green University Popular Press, 1991, 106–113.

Cowart, David. "The Terror of History: *Riddley Walker*." In *History and the Contemporary Novel.* Carbondale: Southern Illinois University Press, 1989, 83–105. http://www.ocelotfactory.com/hoban/cowart1.html.

Porter, Jeffrey. "'Three Quarks for Muster Mark': Quantum Wordplay and Nuclear Discourse in Russell Hoban's *Riddley Walker*." *Contemporary Literature* 31 (1990): 448–469.

Steinberg, Theodore L. "Bernard Malamud and Russell Hoban: Manipulating the Apocalypse." In Carl B. Yoke, ed., *Phoenix from the Ashes: The Literature of the Remade World.* New York: Greenwood, 1987, 165–172.

Wilkie, Christine. *Through the Narrow Gate: The Mythological Consciousness of Russell Hoban.* Rutherford, NJ: Farleigh Dickinson University Press, 1989.

### Web Sites

*The Head of Orpheus: A Russell Hoban Reference Page.* Dave Awl. September 2007. Not an "official" site, but encouraged and supported by Mr. Hoban; devoted and extremely attractive, with all the features of an official site. http://www.ocelotfactory.com/hoban/index.html.

*Riddley Walker Annotations.* Eli Bishop, ed. April 2007. Graphesthesia. This is a collaborative project devoted to analysis of *Riddley Walker*: online annotations, including maps and "translations." http://www.graphesthesia.com/rw/.

*The Russell Hoban Some-Poasyum.* February 2005 A celebration of the author's work on his eightieth birthday. http://www.hoban2005.co.uk/.

*The Slickman A4 Quotation Event.* Since 2002, Russell Hoban fans around the world have celebrated his birthday (February 4) by leaving their favorite Hoban quotes in public places. A Web site that celebrates and chronicles this annual tribute. http://www.sa4qe.com/.

# Aldous Huxley (1894–1963)

*"But I don't want comfort. I want God, I want poetry, I want real danger, I want freedom, I want goodness. I want sin."*

*"In fact," said Mustapha Mond, "you're claiming the right to be unhappy."*
*—Brave New World (1932)*

## Biography

Aldous Leonard Huxley was born in Surrey, England, into a family of prominent naturalists, scientists, and educators. He studied English at Balliol College, Oxford, and, during the 1920s and early 1930s, earned his living writing social satires, such as *Chrome Yellow* (1921), and *Antic Hay* (1923). His 1932 novel *Brave New World* presents a chilling picture of a "perfect" future in which humankind has been drugged and genetically manipulated into infantile hedonism.

Huxley moved to California in 1937, and lived in the United States for the rest of his life. He worked on the scripts for productions such as *Pride and Prejudice* (1940), and *Jane Eyre* (1944). As time passed, however, his writing became more mystical, reflecting his interest in higher states of consciousness, and Huxley experimented with mescaline and LSD in his efforts to achieve this transcendence. He died of cancer at his home in Los Angeles on November 22, 1963.

DRUGS & ALTERED CONSCIOUSNESS; DYSTOPIA; GENETICS & CLONING; HUMOR AND SATIRE; SEX & TABOOS; UTOPIAS

## Major Works

*Novels*

*Brave New World* (1932)
    Online text in full: http://huxley.net/bnw/index.html
*After Many a Summer* (1939)

*Ape and Essence* (1948)
*Island* (1962)


## Collections

*The Collected Short Stories of Aldous Huxley.* Chicago, IL: Ivan R. Dee, 1992.
*Huxley and God: Essays.* New York: Crossroad General Interest, 2003.


## Other Important Works

*Brave New World Revisited* (1958). A nonfiction work in which Huxley considered
the change, progress, and the accuracy of his predictions in 1932.
"Chemical Persuasion." In Damon Knight, ed., *Turning Points: Essays on the Art of
Science Fiction.* New York: Harper & Row, 1977, 231–237.
"Culture and the Individual." *Playboy* 1963. http://www.psychedelic-library.org/
huxcultr.htm.
"The Doors of Perception." http://www.mescaline.org/huxley.htm. *Literature and Sci-
ence* (1963)
"On Self-Transcendence: Epilog." *The Devils of Loudun* (1953) http://www.
psychedelic-library.org/loudun.htm.
"The Ultimate Revolution." University of California, Berkeley. March 20, 1962. http://
sunsite.berkeley.edu/VideoTest/hux1.ram.


# Research Sources

*Encyclopedias and Handbooks:* **AW, BW, CA, CANR, ESF, MSSF,
NNDB, SFW**

*Bibliographies:* **FF, SFAN**

Bradshaw, David. "A New Bibliography of Aldous Huxley's Work and Its Reception,
1912–1937." *Bulletin of Bibliography* 51(3) (1994): 237–256.


## Biographies and Interviews

Bedford, Sybille. *Aldous Huxley: A Biography.* Chicago, IL: Ivan R. Dee, 2002. Bed-
ford's readable 1974 biography, based on her forty-year friendship with Huxley.
Cooper, Nigel. "Aldous Huxley." *Life Stories.* June 2003. Channel 4, UK. http://www.
channel4.com/science/microsites/S/science/life/biog_huxley.html.
Dunaway, David K. *Aldous Huxley Recollected: An Oral History.* New York: Carroll
& Graf, 1995.
Fraser, Raymond, and George Wickes. "Aldous Huxley: The Art of Fiction." *The
Paris Review* 23 (Spring 1960). http://www.theparisreview.org/viewinterview.
php/prmMID/4698.

Hockenhull, Oliver, dir. *Aldous Huxley: The Gravity of Light*. Documentary. Cinéma Esperança International Inc., 2005.
Hofmann, Albert. "Meeting with Aldous Huxley." *LSD, My Problem Child*. New York: McGraw Hill, 1980. http://www.lycaeum.org/books/books/my_problem_child/chapter8.html.
Huxley, Laura Archera. *This Timeless Moment: A Personal View of Aldous Huxley* (1968). Berkeley, CA: Celestial Arts, 2000.
Melechi, Antonio. "Aldous Huxley." *Fortean Times*, February 2004. http://www.forteantimes.com/features/profiles/168/aldous_huxley.html.
Murray, Nicholas. *Aldous Huxley: A Biography*. New York: St. Martin's Press, 2003.

## Criticism and Readers' Guides

Aldiss, Brian. "Between Privy and Universe: Aldous Huxley (1894–1963)." In *The Detached Retina: Aspects of SF and Fantasy*. Syracuse, NY: Syracuse University Press, 1995, 31–36.
The Aldous Huxley Annual: *A Journal of Twentieth-Century Thought and Beyond*. Bernfried Nugel and Jerome Meckier, eds. Univ. of Kentucky, Aldous Huxley Society. http://www.anglistik.uni-muenster.de/huxley/.
Bloom, Harold. *Aldous Huxley's Brave New World*. Philadelphia, PA: Chelsea House, 1999.
de Koster, Katie, ed. *Readings on Brave New World*. San Diego, CA: Greenhaven; 1999.
Derbyshire, John. "What Happened to Aldous Huxley?" *The New Criterion*, February 2003. http://www.newcriterion.com/archive/21/feb03/huxley.htm.
Matter, William W. "The Utopian Tradition and Aldous Huxley." *Science Fiction Studies* 2 (1975): 146–151. http://www.depauw.edu/sfs/backissues/6/matter6art.htm.
Meckier, Jerome, ed. *Critical Essays on Aldous Huxley*. New York: G. K. Hall, 1996.
Miller, Tom. "H. G. Wells and Aldous Huxley." *The Wellsian* 17 (Winter 1994): 3–10.
Pijnenborg, Robert. "Manipulating Human Reproduction: A Retrospective View on Aldous Huxley's *Brave New World*." *Gynecologic & Obstetric Investigation* 61 (2006): 149–154.
Posner, Richard A. "Orwell Versus Huxley: Economics, Technology, Privacy, and Satire." *Philosophy and Literature* 24(1) (2000): 1–33.

## Web Sites

*Aldous Huxley Papers, 1916–1963*. Texas Archival Resources Online. University of Houston. Collection contains signed letters and manuscripts written by Aldous Huxley between 1916 and 1963. http://www.lib.utexas.edu/taro/uhsc/00008/hsc-00008.html.
*Centre for Aldous Huxley Studies*. Dr. Bernfried Nugel, ed. Aldous Huxley Society. June 2004. Department of English, Westfälische Wilhelms-Universität Münster. Web site of the international organization that aims to promote the study of

the works of Aldous Huxley. http://www.anglistik.uni-muenster.de/Huxley/ahs. html.

*Erowid Character Vaults.* August 1998. Erowid.org. Profile of Huxley on a Web site that provides access to reliable, nonjudgmental information about psychoactive plants and chemicals and related issues. Links to articles, interviews, and other information. http://www.erowid.org/culture/characters/huxley_aldous/huxley_aldous. shtml.

*Soma Web.org.* January 2008. "The intellectual, satirical, spiritual, hypnotic, and philosophical world of Aldous Huxley . . . " A wide range of links to items of interest on Huxley and *Brave New World.* http://somaweb.org/.

# Gwyneth Jones (1952–   )

*But in our time we are ready for Tunguska. It can happen to us immediately. We have the technology. We have the anticipation: what they call in my country the longing, the* hiraeth.

— *"Identifying the Object" (1990)*

## Biography

Gwyneth Ann Jones was born in Manchester, England, and graduated from the University of Sussex with a degree in European History of Ideas. In addition to the sf and fantasy novels she writes under her own name, she has been writing fantasy, horror, and ghost stories for young readers since 1980 under the name "Ann Halam."

Jones' fiction has always been an interesting combination of science fiction and high fantasy—sometimes in the same novel, as with her first book for adults, *Divine Endurance,* which was inspired by her time living in Singapore. Her latest series, the "Bold As Love" cycle, examines a near-future Britain in which ecological and social disasters lead to the ascendance of a Green, counterculture government of rock musicians. Gwyneth Jones' critical writing and reviews have appeared in a wide range of periodicals, as well as online. She lives with her family in Brighton, England.

ALIENS; ARTIFICIAL INTELLIGENCE; MYTHOLOGY & LEGEND; NEAR FUTURE; POLITICAL SF; SEX & TABOOS

## Major Works

*Novels*

*Divine Endurance* (1984)
*Kairos* (1988)
*The Hidden Ones* (1988)
The Aleutian Trilogy: *White Queen* (1991—**Tiptree**), *North Wind* (1994), *Phoenix Café* (1997)

The Bold As Love Cycle: *Bold As Love* (2001), *Castles Made of Sand* (2002), *Midnight Lamp* (2003), *Band of Gypsies* (2005), *Rainbow Bridge* (2006) Excerpts from *Bold As Love, Castles Made of Sand*, and *Rainbow Bridge* are available at http://www.infinityplus.co.uk/.

*Life* (2004)

"Ann Halam" novels with sf themes: *King's Death's Garden (1986), Dr. Franklin's Island* (2002), *Dinosaur Junction* (1992)

## Short Stories

"Identifying the Object" (1990)
"La Cenerentola" (1998) **BSF**

## Other Important Works

*Deconstructing the Starships: Science, Fiction and Reality.* Liverpool, UK: Liverpool University Press, 1998. http://homepage.ntlworld.com/gwynethann/Essays.htm.

"Flight into Fancy." *Insanity: WisCon*, May 29, 2005: 27–30. http://www.wiscon.info/downloads/jones.pdf.

"The Icons of Science Fiction." In Edward James and Farah Mendelsohn eds., *The Cambridge Companion to Science Fiction.* Cambridge: Cambridge University Press, 2003, 163–173.

"Kairos: The Enchanted Loom." In Veronica Hollinger and Joan Gordon eds., *Edging into the Future: Science Fiction and Contemporary Cultural Transformation.* Philadelphia: University of Pennsylvania Press, 2002, 174–189.

"Metempsychosis of the Machine: Science Fiction in the Halls of Karma." *Science Fiction Studies* 24 (1997): 1–10.

"The Neuroscience of Cyberspace: New Metaphors for the Self and Its Boundaries." In Brian D. Loader, ed., *The Governance of Cyberspace: Politics, Technology and Global Restructuring.* London: Routledge, 1997, 46–63.

"Riddles in the Dark." In Maxim Jakubowski and Edward James eds., *The Profession of Science Fiction: SF Writers on Their Craft and Ideas.* New York: St. Martin's Press, 1992, 169–181.

"Secret Characters: The Interaction of Narrative and Technology." Keynote Talk. *Computers and Writing Conference 2001.* Ball State University, May 19, 2001. http://english.ttu.edu/Kairos/6.2/coverweb/jones.htm.

## Research Sources

*Encyclopedias and Handbooks:* **AW, BW, CA, CANR, ESF, SFW**

*Bibliographies:* **ARB, FF, SFAN**

Bould, Mark. "Gwyneth Jones: An Introduction." *Femspec* 5(1) (2004): 190–196.

*Biographies and Interviews*

Auden, Sandy. "Winning with a Bold Streak: An Interview with Gwyneth Jones." *SF Site*. 2005. http://www.sfsite.com/10b/sagj210.htm.

"Building Sandcastles: Gwyneth Jones Interviewed." *Cold Print*, March 10, 2002. http://www.cold-print.freeserve.co.uk/gjones.htm.

Butler, Andrew. "Going Up Hill: An Interview with Gwyneth Jones." *Femspec* 5(1) (2004): 216–233.

Emsley, Iain. Interview. *Infinity Plus*. 2003. http://www.infinityplus.co.uk/nonfiction/intgj.htm.

Soyka, David. "Playing the Power Chords of SF: A Conversation with Gwyneth Jones (Parts 1 & 2) *SF Site*. January 2004. http://www.sfsite.com/02a/gj169.htm.

VanderMeer, Jeff. "Gwyneth Jones Walks the Plank: Interview." *VanderWorld*, July 16, 2006. http://vanderworld.blogspot.com/2006/07/gwyneth-jones-walks-plank.html.

*Criticism and Readers' Guides*

Attebery, Brian. "'But Aren't Those Just . . . You Know, Metaphors?' Postmodern Figuration in the Science Fiction of James Morrow and Gwyneth Jones." In Veronica Hollinger and Joan Gordon eds., *Edging into the Future: Science Fiction and Contemporary Cultural Transformation*. Philadelphia: University of Pennsylvania Press, 2002, 90–107.

Csicsery-Ronay Jr., Istan. "The Lost Child: Notes on *White Queen*." *Femspec* 5(1) (2004): 234–253.

Hollinger, Veronica. "'Prefutural Tension': Gwyneth Jones's Gradual Apocalypse." In Justine Larbalestier, ed., *Daughters of Earth: Feminist Science Fiction in the Twentieth Century*. Middletown, CT: Wesleyan University Press, 2006, 305–339.

Sawyer, Andy. "Gwyneth Jones: Anxieties of Science Fiction." In David Seed, ed., *A Companion to Science Fiction*. Malden: Blackwell, 2005, 420–430.

*Web Sites*

*GwynethAnn*. Official Web site. Links to extracts, author essays, and reviews on the "Books" page. http://homepage.ntlworld.com/gwynethann/.

*Bold as Love*. December 2006. Official Web site for the series. http://www.boldaslove.co.uk/.

# James Patrick Kelly (1951– )

*But what struck me most was the darting strangeness in her eyes. This place, so familiar to me, seemed almost to shock her. It was as if she doubted the walls and was skeptical of air.*

*—"Think Like a Dinosaur." (1995)*

## Biography

James Patrick Kelly was born in 1951 in Mineola, on Long Island, New York; he is a graduate of the University of Notre Dame, and an alumnus of the Clarion Science Fiction Workshop. He began publishing sf in 1975, and is primarily known for stunning short stories, which toy skillfully with the conventions of classic, hard sf, as well as more contemporary themes such as genetic manipulation, identity, and the "corporatization" of life. His work has been translated into eleven languages, and he has adapted a number of his short stories as radio plays.

Currently, Kelly lives in New Hampshire, and teaches in the Stonecoast Creative Writing MFA program at the University of Southern Maine. He is a member of the New Hampshire State Council on the Arts, and served as Chair from 2003–2006. He has also served on the Board of Directors of the New England Foundation for the Arts.

ALIENS; CHILDREN IN SF; GENETICS & CLONING; LOW TECH ALTERNATIVES; TECHNOLOGY; VIRTUAL REALITY

## Major Works

*Novels*

*Planet of Whispers* (1984)
*Freedom Beach* (1985, with John Kessel)
*Heroines* (1990)
*Wildlife* (1994)
*Burn* (2005) **Nebula**
    http://www.infinitematrix.net/downloads/burn/Burn.pdf.

*Collections*

*Think Like a Dinosaur and Other Stories.* New York: Golden Gryphon, 1997. Includes "Mr. Boy (1990), the **Hugo**-winning 1995 title story, and "Itsy Bitsy Spider" (1997—**Locus Poll**).
*Strange But Not a Stranger.* New York: Golden Gryphon, 2002.

*Notable Short Stories*

"The Propagation of Light in a Vacuum" (1990) http://www.infinityplus.co.uk/stories/jpklight.htm.
"Monsters" (1992) http://www.infinityplus.co.uk/stories/monsters.htm.
"Why the Bridge Stopped Singing" (1996) http://www.fantasticmetropolis.com/i/bridge/
"$10^{16}$ to 1" (1999) Hugo
"The Ice Is Singing" (2003) http://www.fantasticmetropolis.com/i/icesinging/.

"The Edge of Nowhere" (2005) http://www.infinityplus.co.uk/stories/edgeofnowhere. htm.
"Why School Buses are Yellow" (2005) http://www.infinitematrix.net/stories/short shorts/kelly-yellow.html.

## Other Important Works

"Making Monsters." In Robin Wilson, ed., *Paragons*. New York: St. Martin's Press, 1997. http://www.sfwa.org/writing/.
"Meditation on the Singular Matrix." In Karen Haber, ed., *Exploring the Matrix: Visions of the Cyber Present*. New York: St. Martin's Press, 2003, 222–234.
"Murder Your Darlings." *Writer's Digest*, July 1995. http://www.sfwa.org/writing/.
"On the Net." Regular column for *Asimov's Science Fiction* magazine. Excerpt from the current column is available at http://www.asimovs.com/.
"The Pyramid of Amirah." *Audio Fun* 2004. Mind Mined Productions. http://www. mindmined.com/audiofun/jamespatrickkelly/the_pyramid_of_amirah.html.
"Slipstream." In James Gunn and Matthew Candelaria, eds., *Speculations on Speculation: Theories of Science Fiction*. Lanham, MD: Scarecrow, 2005, 343–351.
"A Swim in the Laughing Soup." (Play) *Fantastic Metropolis*, July 25, 2003. http://www.fantasticmetropolis.com/i/laughsoup/.
"You and Your Characters." In Gardner Dozois et al., eds. *Writing Science Fiction and Fantasy*. New York, St. Martin's Press, 1991. http://www.sfwa.org/writing/.

# Research Sources

*Encyclopedias and Handbooks:* **AW, CA, CANR, ESF, SFW**

*Bibliographies:* **ARB, FF, SFAN**

## Biographies and Interviews

Adams, John Joseph. "A Genre That . . . Well . . . *Isn't.*" *Sci Fi Weekly*, June 12, 2006. SciFi.com. http://www.scifi.com/sfw/interviews/sfw12963.html.
Jenkins, Henry. Frederik Pohl and James Patrick Kelly. Discussion at Massachusetts Institute of Technology, September 18, 1997. Edited version. *Media in Transition*, August 29, 1998. Massachusetts Institute of Technology. http://web.mit.edu/m-i-t/science_fiction/transcripts/pohl_kelly_index.html.
*Locus Online.* "James Patrick Kelly: Explorer." September 2006. http://www.locusmag.com/2006/Issues/09Kelly.html.
McManus, Victoria. Interview. *Strange Horizons*, May 15, 2006. http://www.strangehorizons.com/2006/20060515/kelly-int-a.shtml.
Slusher, Dave. "Voices in Your Head. Audio Interview." *IT Conversations*, October 11, 2004. GigaVox Media. http://www.itconversations.com/shows/detail219.html.

## Criticism and Readers' Guides

Borsch, Frank. "Information Technology New and Old: James Patrick Kelly's 'Big Guy' and E. M. Forster's *The Machine Stops.*" *Erfurt Electronic Studies in*

*English.* November 1996. Niedersächsische Staats- und Universitätsbibliothek Göttingen. http://webdoc.sub.gwdg.de/edoc/ia/eese/eese.html.

Cox, F. Brett. "We Mean It, Man: Nancy Kress's 'Out of All Them Bright Stars' and James Patrick Kelly's 'Rat.'" *New York Review of Science Fiction* 5(2) (1992): 15+.

Kessel, John. "Cutting Up An Ox: Introduction to *Think Like a Dinosaur.*" February 5, 1997. http://www4.ncsu.edu/~tenshi/Oxcutting.html.

### Web Sites

*Jim Kelly.net.* Official Web site. http://www.jimkelly.net/.

*Free Reads—James Patrick Kelly Reads Himself.* http://freereads.blogspot.com/. Author reading a wide variety of his own work, including the complete novels *Freedom Beach* (1985) and *Look into the Sun* (1989), short story "Barry Westphall crashes the singularity" (2002—also available in print at http://www.infinitematrix.net), and an assortment of "On the Net" columns.

# Daniel Keyes (1927–   )

> "Dr Strauss says I shud rite down what I think and evrey thing that happins to me from now on . . ."
>
> —"Flowers for Algernon" (1959)

## Biography

Daniel Keyes was born in Brooklyn, New York. His novella "Flowers for Algernon," the story of Charlie Gordon, a janitor with an IQ of 70, who volunteers to be the subject of an experimental treatment to enhance his intelligence, won the 1960 Hugo Award for Best Short Fiction. Keyes went on to develop the story into a full-length novel that was adapted into the Academy award-winning 1968 film *Charly. Flowers for Algernon* has been published in thirty countries, and it is studied in schools all over the world.

Daniel Keyes went on to teach creative writing and English literature in Michigan and Ohio. He retired in 2000, and lives in Boca Raton, Florida, where he continues to write and give freely of his time at science fiction conventions and public reading projects.

DISABILITY & SF; PSYCHOLOGY; SUPERMEN

## Major Works

*Novels*

*Flowers for Algernon* (1966) Won **Hugos** for the original short story in 1960, and for the novel in 1967.

*The Touch* (1968)
*The Fifth Sally* (1980)

## Collections

*Daniel Keyes Collected Stories*. Tokyo: Hayakawa, 1993. This collection includes a preface by the author and the novella version of "Flowers for Algernon" (1959), as well as other examples of Keyes' short fiction, such as "Robot—Unwanted" (1952), "The Trouble with Elmo" (1958), "Crazy Maro" (1960), and "Mama's Girl" (1992).

## Other Important Works

*Algernon, Charlie and I: A Writer's Journey*. Boca Raton, FL: Challcrest, 1999.
*Charly*. ABC Pictures. 1968. Starring Claire Bloom and Cliff Robertson, who won an Oscar for his portrayal of Charly Gordon.
"How Much Does a Character Cost?" In Robin Scott Wilson, ed., *Those Who Can: A Science Fiction Reader* (1973). New York: St. Martin's Press, 1996, 101–104.

## Research Sources

*Encyclopedias and Handbooks:* **AW, CA, CAAS, CANR, ESF, MSSF, SFW**

*Bibliographies:* **ARB, FF, SFAN**

### Biographies and Interviews

Hoover, Bob. "Seeds of Inspiration." *Pittsburgh Post-Gazette*, March 20, 2004. http://www.post-gazette.com/pg/04080/288526.stm.
Kurz, David, and Connie Stevens. "Audio Interview with Daniel Keyes." No date. *Wired for Books*. http://www.wiredforbooks.org/danielkeyes/.
*Locus Online*. "Daniel Keyes: 40 Years of Algernon." June 1997. http://www.locusmag.com/1997/Issues/06/Keyes.html.
Malzberg, Barry N. "Author Emeritus 2000: Daniel Keyes." In Robert Silverberg, ed., *Nebula Awards Showcase 2001*. New York: Harcourt, 2001.

### Criticism and Readers' Guides

Cassedy, Patrice. *Understanding Flowers for Algernon*. San Diego, CA: Lucent, 2001.
Ford, Paul. "Notes: *Flowers for Algernon*." fTrain.com, August 28, 2002. http://www.ftrain.com/notes_algernon.html.
Owen, John D. Review. *Infinity Plus*. 2000. http://www.infinityplus.co.uk/nonfiction/flowers.htm.
Palumbo, Donald. "The Monomyth in Daniel Keyes's *Flowers for Algernon*: Keyes, Campbell, and Plato." *Journal of the Fantastic in the Arts* 14 (2004): 427–446.

Small. Robert, Jr. "*Flowers for Algernon.*" In Nicholas J. Karolides et al, eds., *Censored Books: Critical Viewpoints*. Metuchen, NJ: Scarecrow, 1993, 249–255.

*Web Sites*

*Algernon's Pad.* Official Web site. Includes an extensive bibliography, and FAQs about his most famous book. http://www.danielkeyesauthor.com/.

# Damon Knight (1922–2002)

*TO YOU WHO CAN SEE, the first sentence said, I OFFER YOU A WORLD . . .*

*Anyone. Someone. Anyone.*

           —*"The Country of the Kind" (1955)*

## Biography

Damon Francis Knight was born in Baker, Oregon. He was a friend, and sometimes collaborator, with a whole generation of great sf writers of the 1940s and 50s, and more or less single-handedly invented modern science fiction criticism. With his wife, the distinguished sf author Kate Wilhelm, he founded the Milford SF Writers Conference and the Clarion Writers' Workshop, making possible the careers of whole generations of sf writers unborn.

For his own writing, Damon Knight may not be a household name, but his wicked humor made a lasting impression in classic stories like "To Serve Man" (1950) and "The Country of the Kind" (1955). Shortly after he passed away, at the age of eighty-nine, the SWFA Grand Master award (which he had won in 1994) was renamed the Damon Knight Memorial Grand Master Award in his honor.

ALIENS; END OF THE WORLD; DYSTOPIA; HUMOR & SATIRE; NEAR FUTURE; PSYCHOLOGY

## Major Works

*Novels*

*Hell's Pavement* (1955)
*VOR* (1958, with James Blish)
*A for Anything* (1959, aka *The People Makers*)
*The Rithian Terror* (1965)
The CV sequence: *CV* (1985), *The Observers* (1988), and *A Reasonable World* (1991)
*Why Do Birds* (1992)
*Humpty Dumpty: An Oval* (1996)

*Collections*

*The Best of Damon Knight.* New York: Pocket Books, 1976. Includes "To Serve Man" (1950), the wonderful story that became a classic episode of *The Twilight Zone*, "Not with a Bang" (1950), and "Thing of Beauty" (1958)

*One Side Laughing: Stories Unlike Other Stories.* New York: St. Martins Press, 1991.

*Other Important Works*

"Beauty, Stupidity, Injustice, and Science Fiction." *Monad: Essays on Science Fiction* 1 (September 1990): 67–88.

*Creating Short Fiction.* (Rev. Ed. 1997) Excerpt: "Plot," http://www. theroseandthornezine.com/Article/33Plot.html.

*The Futurians: The Story of the Great Science Fiction "Family" of the 30s that Produced Today's Top SF Writers and Editors* (1977)

*In Search of Wonder.* Rev. Ed. (1967)

"Knight Piece." In Brian W. Aldiss and Harry Harrison, eds., *Hell's Cartographers.* New York: Harper & Row, 1975, 96–143.

*Turning Points: Essays on the Art of Science Fiction* (1977) Edited by Knight, and featuring his essays "What is Science Fiction?" (62–69) and "Writing and Selling Science Fiction" (218–228).

"When I Was in Kneepants: Ray Bradbury." In Harold Bloom, ed., *Ray Bradbury.* Philadelphia, PA: Chelsea House, 2001, 3–8.

*Will the Real Hieronymus Bosch Please Stand Up?* 2000. http://fictionwise.com/ knight/.

## Research Sources

*Encyclopedias and Handbooks:* **AW, BW, CA, CANR, ESF, MSSF, SFW**

*Bibliographies:* **ARB, FF, SFAN**

*Biographies and Interviews*

Barrett, David V. Obituary. *Guardian Online*, April 25, 2002. http://books.guardian. co.uk/news/articles/0,6109,687293,00.html.

Haldeman, Joe. "Damon Knight: To Serve Writing." *Locus* 48(6) (2002): 87–88.

Hartwell, David G. Appreciation. *Locus* 48(5) (2002): 66–67.

Nielsen Hayden, Teresa. "Damon Knight 1922–2002." *Making Light*, April 19, 2002. http://nielsenhayden.com/makinglight/archives/000189.html.

McIntyre, Vonda N. "Remembering Damon Knight." In *Nebula Awards Showcase 2004.* New York: Roc, 2004, 85–106.

What, Leslie. Obituary. *SFWA News*, April 17, 2002. http://www.sfwa.org/News/ knight.htm.

*Criticism and Readers' Guides*

Robillard, Douglas. "Uncertain Futures: Damon Knight's Science Fiction." In Thomas
    D. Clareson, ed., *Voices For the Future. Vol. 3*. Bowling Green, OH: Bowling
    Green University Popular Press, 1984, 30–51.
Sleight, Graham. "Putting the Pieces Together Again: Making Sense of Damon
    Knight's Humpty Dumpty." *New York Review of Science Fiction* 17(1) (2004):
    1+.

# Ursula K. Le Guin (1929–  )

> *I'll make my report as if I told a story, for I was taught as a child on my
> homeworld that Truth is a matter of the imagination. The soundest fact may fail
> or prevail in the style of its telling . . .*
>
> —The Left Hand of Darkness (1969)

## Biography

Born Ursula Kroeber in Berkeley, California, Le Guin is the daughter of noted
scholars and writers, and a graduate of Radcliffe and Columbia University. She
met and married her husband, historian Charles Le Guin, while in France on a
Fulbright Scholarship for postgraduate study in the literature and the languages of
the Middle Ages and Renaissance. Beginning in the mid-1960s, Ursula K. Le Guin
began writing science fiction and fantasy, combining sophisticated story telling
with themes inspired by Taoism, feminism, and ecological concerns. She currently
lives in Portland, Oregon.

In fifty years as a writer, Ursula K. Le Guin has been the recipient of over fifty
awards, honors, and honorary degrees. Among her many claims to fame, in her
1966 novel, *Rocannon's World*, she coined the word "ansible" for a device that
allows its users to send and receive messages over vast interstellar distances. This
neat solution has since been adopted by many other sf authors.

ANTHROPOLOGY; COLONIZATION OF OTHER WORLDS; FEMINISM;
GENDER & SEXUALITY; POLITICAL SF; UTOPIAS

## Major Works

*Novels*

Novels of the Ekumen (Hainish sequence): *Planet of Exile* (1966), *Rocannon's World*
    (1966), *City of Illusions* (1967), *The Left Hand of Darkness* (1969—**Nebula,
    Hugo**), *The Dispossessed: An Ambiguous Utopia* (1974—**Hugo, Locus Poll,
    Nebula**), *The Telling* (2000—**Locus Poll**)
*The Lathe of Heaven* (1971) **Locus Poll**
*The Word for World Is Forest* (1972) **Hugo**

*Eye of the Heron* (1978)
*Always Coming Home* (1985)

## Collections

*The Wind's Twelve Quarters* (1975) **Locus Poll**
*The Compass Rose: Stories* (1982) **Locus Poll**
*A Fisherman of the Inland Sea: Science Fiction Stories* (1994)
*Four Ways to Forgiveness* (1995) **Locus Poll**
*The Birthday of the World and Other Stories* (2003)
*Changing Planes: Stories* (2003) **Locus Poll**

## Short Stories

"Vaster Than Empires and More Slow" (1970)
"The Ones Who Walk Away from Omelas" (1974) **Hugo**
"The Day Before the Revolution" (1975) **Locus Poll, Nebula**
"The New Atlantis" (1975) **Locus Poll**
"Sur" (1983) **Locus Poll**
"She Unnames Them" (1985)
"Buffalo Gals, Won't You Come Out Tonight" (1987) **Hugo**
"Forgiveness Day" (1994) **Locus Poll**
"The Matter of Seggri" (1994) **Tiptree**
"Solitude" (1994) **Nebula**
"Coming of Age in Karhide" (1995)
"Mountain Ways" (1996) **Locus Poll, Tiptree**
"The Birthday of the World" (2000) **Locus Poll**
"The Bones of the Earth" (2001) **Locus Poll**
"The Wild Girls" (2002) **Locus Poll**
"The Seasons of the Ansarac" (2002)
   http://www.infinitematrix.net/stories/shorts/seasons_of_ansarac.html.

## Other Important Works

"American SF and the Other." *Science Fiction Studies* 2 (1975): 208–210. http://www.
   depauw.edu/sfs/backissues/7/leguin7art.htm.
*Dancing at the Edge of the World: Thoughts on Words, Women, Places* (1989)
*The Language of the Night: Essays on Fantasy and Science Fiction* (1980)
*Steering the Craft: Exercises and Discussions on Story Writing for the Lone Navigator
   or the Mutinous Crew* (1998)
*The Wave in the Mind: Talks and Essays on the Writer, the Reader, and the Imagination*
   (2004)
"A Whitewashed Earthsea: How the SciFi Channel Wrecked my Books." *Slate*, De-
   cember 16, 2004. http://www.slate.com/id/2111107/.

## Research Sources

*Encyclopedias and Handbooks:* **AW, BW, CA, CAAS, CANR, ESF, MSSF, NNDB, SFW**

*Bibliographies:* **ARB, FF, SFAN**

### Biographies and Interviews

Interviews. *Ursula K. Le Guin.com.* http://www.ursulakleguin.com/Interviews.html# Interviews. Links to the most up-to-date interviews online.

Justice, Faith L. "Ursula K. Le Guin." *Salon,* January 23, 2001. http://archive.salon. com/people/bc/2001/01/23/le_guin/.

Philips, Julie, ed. "Dear Starbear: Letters between Ursula K. Le Guin and James Tiptree Jr." *Fantasy & Science Fiction* 111(3) (2006): 77–115.

Platt, Charles. "The Teflon Fantasist." In *Loose Canon.* Holicong, PA: Wildside, 2001.

Reid, Suzanne Elizabeth. *Presenting Ursula K. Le Guin.* New York: Twayne, 1997.

### Criticism and Readers' Guides

A Partial List of Secondary Sources. *Ursula K. Le Guin.com.* http://www. ursulakleguin.com/SecondarySources.html.

Baccolini, Rafaella. "'A Useful Knowledge of the Present is Rooted in the Past': Memory and Historical Reconciliation in Ursula K. Le Guin's *The Telling.*" In Rafaella Baccolini and Tom Moylan, eds., *Dark Horizons: Science Fiction and the Dystopian Imagination.* New York: Routledge, 2003, 113–134.

Barr, Marleen. "Ursula Le Guin's 'Sur' as Exemplary Humanist and Antihumanist Text." *Lost In Space: Probing Feminist Science Fiction and Beyond.* Chapel Hill: University of North Carolina Press, 1993, 154–170.

Bernardo, Susan M., and Graham J. Murphy. *Ursula K. Le Guin: A Critical Companion.* Westport, CT: Greenwood, 2006.

Brians, Paul. *Study Guides: The Dispossessed,* April 2, 2003. Washington State University. http://www.wsu.edu:8080/~brians/science_fiction/dispossessed.html.

Burns, Tony. "Marxism and Science Fiction: A Celebration of the Work of Ursula K. Le Guin." *Capital & Class* (Winter 2004): 139–149.

Cadden, Mike. *Ursula K. Le Guin Beyond Genre: Fiction for Children and Adults.* New York: Routledge, 2005.

Davenport, Tristan. "So, Your Utopia Needs a Language . . . " *Strange Horizons* October 24, 2005. http://www.strangehorizons.com/2005/20051024/utopia-lang-a. shtml.

Davis, Laurence and Peter Stillman, eds. *The New Utopian Politics of Ursula K. Le Guin's The Dispossessed.* Lanham, MD: Lexington, 2005.

Delany, Samuel R. "To Read *The Dispossessed.*" In *The Jewel-Hinged Jaw.* New York: Dragon, 1977.

Erlich, Richard D. "Coyote's Song: The Teaching Stories of Ursula K. Le Guin." *Science Fiction Research Association,* 2000. http://wiz.cath.vt.edu/sfra/Coyote/ CoyoteHome.htm.

————. "Le Guin and God: Quarreling with the One, Critiquing Pure Reason." *Extrapolation* 47(3) (2006): 351–379.

Hines, Jim C. "Sleeping with the Bug-Eyed Monster: Sexuality in the Novels of Anthony, Heinlein, and Le Guin." *Strange Horizons,* December 17, 2001. http://www.strangehorizons.com/2001/20011217/bug-eyed_monster.shtml.

Jones, Gwyneth. "No Man's Land: Feminised Landscapes in the Utopian Fiction of Ursula Le Guin." In *Deconstructing the Starships: Science, Fiction, and Reality.* Liverpool, UK: Liverpool University Press, 1999, 199–208. http://homepage.ntlworld.com/gwynethann/LeGuin.htm.

Kincaid, Paul. "Founded on the Shambles: A Look at Ursula K. Le Guin's 'The Ones Who Walk Away From Omelas'" *Vector* 249, British Science Fiction Association. http://www.vectormagazine.co.uk/article.asp?articleID=44.

LeFanu, Sarah. "The King is Pregnant." *The Guardian*, January 3, 2004 http://books.guardian.co.uk/departments/sciencefiction/story/0,1115134,00.html.

McAllister, Mick. *Ursula K. Le Guin: Housewives in Space. The Dancing Badger.* March 2007. http://www.dancingbadger.com/ursula_k_le_guin.htm.

McBride, Margaret. "Approaches to Teaching Le Guin's *The Lathe of Heaven.*" *The Science Fiction Research Association Review* 271(1) (2005): 6–11. http://wiz.cath.vt.edu/sfra/sfra-review/271.pdf.

*Web Sites*

*The Ekumen: An Ursula K. Le Guin Reference Page.* Dave Awl. January 2002. Business-like site, but seriously out-of-date. http://www.ocelotfactory.com/leguin/.

*Le Guin's Future History.* Elisa K. Sparks. Clemson University. Internal chronology of the Hainish stories, from "The Dowry of Angyar" (1964) to "Mountain Ways" (1996). http://hubcap.clemson.edu/~sparks/leguinfh.html.

*Le Guin's World.* Fredrik Petersson. February 2003. Enthusiastic Swedish fan site, most useful for links to a Hainish encyclopedia and essays outlining a history of the Hainish Worlds. http://hem.passagen.se/peson42/lgw/.

*Ursula K. Le Guin.com.* Vonda N. McIntyre. March 23, 2008. Beautiful Web site, designed by fellow author, McIntyre; contains everything that could possibly be required by researchers, committed fans, or scholars. Includes thorough bibliographies (primary and secondary), full text essays, "rants," reviews, interviews, and news. http://www.ursulakleguin.com/.

**If you enjoyed Ursula K. Le Guin...**

Intelligent and beautifully written, all of Ursula Le Guin's work has a "... tradition of challenging deeply held, and poorly reasoned, assumptions..." (**NNDB**). The Taoism that pervades it serves to emphasize balance in all things, and the fact that our world—any world—is far more complicated than our limited intellects could imagine.

**Then you might like . . .**

*Michael Bishop*. Like Le Guin, Bishop uses anthropology to illuminate relationships and cultures, whether those cultures are on an alien planet (*Transfigurations*), our own Pleistocene era of prehistory (*No Enemy But Time*), or 21st century Atlanta, Georgia (*Catacomb Years*). Like Le Guin, Bishop is equally adept at fantasy, and sometimes the boundaries are difficult to detect.

*Molly Gloss*. A writer who will not be pinned down: Gloss writes about the past and she writes about the future, and, like UKL, her talent is in making both seem very strange, wonderful, and important. In *The Dazzle of Day* (1997), a Quaker community temporarily establishes a perfectly balanced world for itself on a generation starship escaping the dying planet Earth.

*Doris Lessing*. Nobel Prize-winning author of *The Canopus in Argos: Archives*, a sequence of loosely connected novels that portray future societies, on earth and elsewhere in the galaxy, at different stages of development. The Swedish Academy described her as a writer who " . . . with skepticism, fire and visionary power has subjected a divided civilization to scrutiny."

*Joanna Russ*. Like Le Guin, Russ is respected as a writer, feminist, critic, and scholar; she is also a sharp observer of the trends and assumptions in which sf—or writing of any kind—is created. *The Female Man* is one of her works that have been given retrospective or "classic" Tiptree Awards as fiction that "expands or explores our understanding of gender."

*Joan L. Slonczewski*. A professor of genetic biology, Slonczewski writes exciting and believable stories such as *A Door into Ocean* (1986), the first of the "Elysium Cycle," in which biology *is* destiny, used to control ecology, and to enable alternative forms of reproduction. Slonczewski, like UKL, uses sf to examine issues such as pacifism, the environment, and the rhetoric of violence.

# Stanislaw Lem (1921–2006)

*Man has gone out to explore other worlds and other civilizations without having explored his own labyrinth of dark passages and secret chambers, and without finding what lies behind doorways that he himself has sealed.*

*—Solaris (1961)*
*—Trans. Joanna Kilmartin and Steve Cox (1970)*

## Biography

Stanisław Lem was born in Lvov, in eastern Poland. He survived the Nazi occupation of Poland during World War II with false papers, and used his privileged access as an automobile mechanic to sabotage German vehicles. He was unable to qualify as a doctor after the War because of doctrinaire Communist requirements, and began writing to help support his family. His fame and popularity gave him a degree of immunity from censorship, and his fantastic sf allegories worried away at the hard-line Communism that held Poland in its grip since 1945.

Lem left Poland, and lived in Vienna during the early 1980s. He enjoyed the freedom and physical comforts of life in the West, but found the commercialism and foreignness distracting. In 1988, he returned to Krakow and spent his final years in the company of fellow Polish writers, and his family; he died there on March 27, 2006, at the age of eighty-four.

ALIEN WORLDS; ANDROIDS, CYBORGS & ROBOTS; HUMOR & SATIRE; POLITICAL SF; PSI POWERS; PSYCHOLOGY

## Major Works

*Novels*

*Eden* (1959)
*The Investigation* (1959)
*Memoirs Found in a Bathtub* (1961)
*Return from the Stars* (1961)
*Solaris* (1961)
*The Invincible* (1964)
*His Master's Voice* (1968)
*The Futurological Congress [from the Memoirs of Ijon Tichy]* (1971)
*The Chain of Chance* (1975)
*Fiasco* (1986)
*Peace on Earth* (1986)

*Collections*

*The Cyberiad: Fables for the Cybernetic Age* (1974). New York: Harvest, 2002.
*Memoirs of a Space Traveler: Further Reminiscences of Ijon Tichy* (1982). Chicago,
    IL: Northwestern University Press, 2000.
*Tales of Pirx the Pilot* (1979). New York: Harcourt, 1990. (Also *More Tales of Pirx
    the Pilot*. New York: Harvest, 1983.)

*Other Important Works*

"H. G. Wells' *War of the Worlds*." In Rhys Garnett and R. J. Ellis, eds., *Science Fiction
    Roots and Branches*. Basingstoke, UK: Macmillan, 1990.
*Highcastle: A Remembrance*. (1975)
*Microworlds: Writings on Science Fiction and Fantasy* (2006) Includes "On the Struc-
    tural Analysis of Science Fiction" (1973), "The Time Travel Story and Related
    Matters of SF Structuring" (1974), "Philip K. Dick: A Visionary among the Char-
    latans" (1975; also available online at http://www.depauw.edu/sfs), and "About
    the Strugatskys' *Roadside Picnic*" (1983).

"On Stapledon's *Last and First Men.*" *Science Fiction Studies* 13 (1986): 272–291.
"On Stapledon's *Starmaker.*" Trans. Istvan Csicsery-Ronay, Jr. In Damien Broderick, ed., *Earth is But a Star: Excursions through Science Fiction to the Far Future.* Crawley: University of Western Australia Press, 2001, 412–421.
"Robots in Science Fiction." In Thomas D. Clareson, ed., *SF: The Other Side of Realism.* Bowling Green, OH: Bowling Green University. Popular Press, 1971, 307–325.
*Summa Technologiae.* 4th Polish ed. Lublin, Poland: Wydawnictwo Lubelskie, 1984. Trans. Frank Prengel. http://www.frankpr.net/Lem/Summa/contents.htm

## Research Sources

*Encyclopedias and Handbooks:* **AW, BW, CA, CANR, ESF, MSSF, NNDB, SFW, WS**

*Bibliographies:* **ARB, FF, SFAN**

Graefrath, Bernd. "Taking Science Fiction Seriously: A Bibliographic Introduction to Stanislaw Lem's Philosophy of Technology." *Research in Philosophy and Technology* 15 (1995): 271–285.

### Biographies and Interviews

Csicsery-Ronay, Istvan, Jr. "Twenty-Two Answers and Two Postscripts: An Interview with Stanislaw Lem." *Science Fiction Studies* 13 (1986): 242–260. http://www.depauw.edu/sfs/interviews/lem40interview.htm.
Federman, Raymond. Interview. *Science Fiction Studies*, March 1983. http://www.depauw.edu/sfs/interviews/federman29.htm.
Heer, Jeet. "Stanislaw Lem." *Boston Globe Ideas*, December 15, 2004. http://www.jeetheer.com/culture/lem.htm.
*The Polish Science Voice*, "Life After Lem." April 5, 2006. http://www.warsawvoice.pl/view/11034.
Sisario, Ben. Obituary. *New York Times* March 28, 2006. http://www.timesonline.co.uk/tol/comment/obituaries/article1082652.ece.
Suvin, Darko. "To Remember Stanislaw Lem." *Extrapolation.* March 22, 2006
Swirski, Peter, ed. *A Stanislaw Lem Reader (Rethinking Theory).* Chicago, IL: Northwestern Univ. Press, 1997.
Ziegfeld, Richard E. *Stanislaw Lem.* New York: Ungar, 1985.

### Criticism and Readers' Guides

Balcerzan, Edward. "Language and Ethics in Solaris." Trans. Konrad Brodzinski. *Science Fiction Studies* 2 (1975): 152–156. http://www.depauw.edu/sfs/backissues/6/balcerzan6art.htm.
Brians, Paul. "Solaris." *Study Guide.* November 29, 2002. Washington State University. http://www.wsu.edu:8080/~brians/science_fiction/solaris.html.
Davis, J. Madison. *Stanisław Lem.* Mercer Island, WA: Starmont, 1990.

Helford, Elyce Rae. "'We Are Only Seeking Man': Gender, Psychoanalysis, and Stanislaw Lem's Solaris." *Science Fiction Studies* 19 (1992): 167–177. http://www.depauw.edu/sfs/backissues/57/helford57art.htm.

Parker, Jo Alyson. "Gendering the Robot: Stanislaw Lem's 'The Mask.'" *Science Fiction Studies* 19 (1992): 178–191. http://www.depauw.edu/sfs/backissues/57/parker57art.htm.

*The Philosopher Zone.* "To Solaris and Beyond." April 29, 2006. Australian Broadcasting Corporation. http://www.abc.net.au/rn/philosopherszone/stories/2006/1622605.htm.

Swirski, Peter., ed. *The Art and Science of Stanislaw Lem.* Montreal, Canada: McGill-Queen's University Press, 2006.

Ust, Daniel. "Communication Breakdown: The Novels of Stanislaw Lem." *The Thought.* May/June 2001. http://uweb.superlink.net/~neptune/Lem.html.

Wolf, Gary. "Solaris, Rediscovered." *Wired.* December 2002. http://www.wired.com/wired/archive/10.12/solaris.html.

*Web Sites*

*Solaris: The Official Stanislaw Lem Site.* Tomasz Lem and Wojciech Zemek. November 2007. http://www.lem.pl/.

# Madeleine L'Engle (1918–2007)

*Just because we don't understand doesn't mean that the explanation doesn't exist.*

*—A Wrinkle in Time (1962)*

## Biography

Madeleine L'Engle Camp was born in New York City. Following her graduation from Smith College, she was a published author and a professional actress, but it was as a full-time mother that she wrote *A Wrinkle in Time* (1962), the opening story of a family's quest across time and space. Winner of the Newbery Medal, *A Wrinkle in Time* is one of the best-selling children's books of all time and, like many of her books, equally popular with adults and children.

L'Engle was closely involved with the Cathedral of St. John the Divine, in New York, eventually becoming writer in residence. She was made a Dame of the order of St. John by Queen Elizabeth II in 1977. Well into the 1990s, Madeleine L'Engle was lecturing, traveling, and corresponding with fans all over the world. She passed away on September 6, 2007, at age eighty-eight, near her home in Goshen, Connecticut.

ARTIFICIAL INTELLIGENCE; CHILDREN IN SF; FANTASTIC VOYAGES; MYTHOLOGY & LEGEND; RELIGION

## Major Works

*Novels*

The Time Quartet: *A Wrinkle in Time* (1962), *A Wind in the Door* (1973), *A Swiftly Tilting Planet* (1978), *Many Waters* (1986)
*The Arm of the Starfish* (1965)
*An Acceptable Time* (1989)


*Other Important Works*

Acceptance Speech. (The Margaret Edwards Award) June 27, 1998. http://gos.sbc. edu/l/lengle.html.
"Aslan's Kin: Interfaith Fantasy and Science Fiction." In *Walking on Water: Reflections on Faith and Art*. Wheaton, IL: H. Shaw, 2001. http://greenbelt.com/news/aslan/ lengle.htm.
"The Expanding Universe: Newbery Award Acceptance Speech." August 1963. http:// www.madeleinelengle.com/reference/newberyspeech.htm.
Foreword. *Companion to Narnia*. By Paul F. Ford. San Francisco: Harper, 1994.
*The Rock That Is Higher: Story as Truth* (1993)
"Tell Me a Story." In Katherine Ball Ross, ed., *The Quiet Center: Women Reflecting on Life's Passages*. New York: Hearst, 1997, 163–168.
*Trailing Clouds of Glory: Spiritual Values in Children's Literature* (1985, with Avery Brooke)


## Research Sources

*Encyclopedias and Handbooks:* **AW, CA, CANR, ESF, NNDB, SFW**

*Bibliographies:* **FF, SFAN**


*Biographies and Interviews*

Gonzales, Doreen. *Madeleine L'Engle: Author of A Wrinkle in Time*. New York: Dillon, 1991.
Henneberger, Melinda. "'I Dare You:' Madeleine L'Engle on God, 'The Da Vinci Code' and Aging Well." *Newsweek Online*. May 7, 2006. http://www.msnbc. msn.com/id/4926262/.
Horowitz, Shel. "Madeleine L'Engle: Faith during Adversity." *Writer's Digest*, 1992. http://www.frugalfun.com/l'engle.html.
Scaperlanda María Ruiz. "Madeleine L'Engle: An Epic in Time." *St. Anthony Messenger*. June 2000. http://www.americancatholic.org/Messenger/Jun2000/feature1. asp.
Webb, Heather. "A Conversation with Madeleine L'Engle." *Mars Hill Review 4 (1996): 51–65*. http://www.leaderu.com/marshill/mhr04/lengle1.html.
Zarin, Cynthia. "The Storyteller." *The New Yorker,* April 12, 2004. http://www. newyorker.com/archive/2004/04/12/040412fa_fact_zarin.

## Criticism and Readers' Guides

Chase, Carole F. *Suncatcher: A Study of Madeleine L'Engle and Her Writing.* 2nd ed. Philadelphia, PA: Innisfree, 1998.

Hettinga, Donald. *Presenting Madeleine L'Engle.* New York: Twayne, 1993.

Hein, Rolland. *Christian Mythmakers: C. S. Lewis, Madeleine L'Engle, J. R. R. Tolkien, George MacDonald, G. K. Chesterton, and Others.* Chicago: Cornerstone, 1998.

Shaw, Luci, ed. *The Swiftly Tilting Worlds of Madeleine L'Engle.* Wheaton, IL: Harold Shaw, 1998.

Smedman, M. Sarah. "'The "Terrible Journey' Past 'Dragons in the Waters' to a 'House like a Lotus': Faces of Love in the Fiction of Madeleine L'Engle." In C.W. Sullivan, ed., *Science Fiction for Young Readers.* Westport, CT: Greenwood, 1993, 65–82.

Soares, Manuela. *A Reading Guide to "A Wrinkle in Time" by Madeleine L'Engle.* New York: Scholastic, 2003.

## Web Sites

*Madeleine L'Engle 1918–2007.* Official Web site. http://www.madeleinelengle.com/.

*The Tesseract: A Madeleine L'Engle Bibliography in 5 Dimensions.* Karen Funk Blocher. January 2008. Fan Web site, with some interesting links. http://members. aol.com/kfbofpql/LEngl.html.

*The Madeleine L'Engle Collection.* Buswell Library: Wheaton College Archives & Special Collections. January 2006. The Buswell Library holds a variety of materials, dating from 1919 to the present, and including correspondence, manuscripts, articles, photos, papers written by L'Engle, awards, interviews, book announcements and reviews, biographical and family information, some art work, and a number of miscellaneous items, all donated by L'Engle or her family. http://www.wheaton.edu/learnres/ARCSC/collects/sc03/bio.htm.

**If you enjoyed Madeleine L'Engle . . .**

In the "Time Fantasy" quartet, Madeleine L'Engle uses science fiction and fantasy to tell a story of love and family—and hope. With her optimism and imagination, L'Engle is a writer who has managed to bridge the divide between young adult fiction and the more mature themes of science fiction.

**Then you might like . . .**

*Ray Bradbury.* Not a writer for young readers, or even a writer who particularly focuses on young protagonists, but Bradbury, like L'Engle, draws upon childhood memories of the wonders and terrors of growing up, and translates them into sf tales such as The Martian Chronicles, or horror and fantasy, often with a sf twist, such as *The Illustrated Man.*

*John Christopher.* As well as adult novels about civilization-threatening disaster, Christopher wrote a number of novels for and about resilient young people—coping with worldwide earthquakes (*The Prince in Waiting*, 1970), over-population (*The Guardians*, 1970), and alien invasion ("Tripod" series, beginning with *The White Mountain*, 1967).

***Robert Heinlein***. Master of stories in which the least regarded of society—youngsters, outcasts, and dreamers—harness their superior talents and triumph over adversity (often with the aid of a "father-figure," whose voice increasingly resembles Heinlein's own). Worth comparing to L'Engle are *Have Space Suit—Will Travel* (1958), *Citizen of the Galaxy* (1957), and *Time for the Stars* (1956).

***Zenna Henderson***. Like L'Engle, and like Bradbury, Henderson is a writer from the time before irony was king. Her stories are simple, and sometimes even sentimental, but always sharply aware of injustice, and the danger of hiding who you really are. *Ingathering: The Complete People Stories of Zenna Henderson* contain her stories about a race of peaceful, psychically gifted extraterrestrials who have become stranded on Earth.

# Jonathan Lethem (1964–   )

*"I've been working on her murder," I said.*

*His eyes shot back to mine. "That's a long time ago," he said.*
*"Couple of days, to me. I've still got her blood on my shoes."*
> —*Gun, with Occasional Music (1994)*

## Biography

A recent profile of Jonathan Lethem was entitled "The Borrower," and it is as a writer who makes free use of the storylines and genre conventions of other times and other artists, and makes them uniquely *his,* and uniquely *now,* that he has made his mark on science fiction. Lethem's most recent novels have been more mainstream, but, as in *Fortress of Solitude* (2005), reality is filtered through pop culture references, including sf.

Jonathan Allen Lethem grew up in Brooklyn, New York. He attended Bennington College in Vermont, but dropped out to hitchhike to San Francisco, where he lived for a decade, working in bookstores and writing. Lethem is a tireless essayist, and a past editor of magazines *Para∗doxa* and *Fence*. In 1996, he moved back to Brooklyn, where he currently lives with his family. In 2005, he was awarded a MacArthur Fellowship, often referred to as the "genius grant."

ALIENS; COLONIZATION OF OTHER WORLDS; DRUGS & ALTERED CONSCIOUSNESS; NEAR FUTURE; POP CULTURE; SEX & TABOOS

# Major Works

*Novels*

*Gun, with Occasional Music* (1994) **Locus Poll**
*Amnesia Moon* (1995)
*As She Climbed Across the Table* (1997)
*Girl in Landscape* (1998)
*This Shape We're In* (2000)

*Collections*

*The Wall of the Sky, the Wall of the Eye.* New York: Harcourt Brace, 1996.
*Men and Cartoons.* New York: Doubleday, 2004.
*How We Got Insipid.* Burton, MI: Subterranean, 2006.

*Notable Short Stories*

"The Happy Man" (1991)
"Ninety Percent of Everything" (2000, with James Patrick Kelly and John Kessel)
"The Glasses" (2004, audio file) http://dir.salon.com/story/books/feature/2004/11/01/
    lethem/index.html.
"Super Goat Man" (2004) http://www.newyorker.com/fiction/content/articles/
    040405fi_fiction?040405fi_fiction.
"Phil in the Marketplace" (2006) http://www.vqronline.org/articles/2006/fiction/
    lethem-phil-marketplace/

*Other Important Works*

"Alone at the Movies." *The New Yorker,* June 17, 2002. http://www.newyorker.com/
    talk/content/articles/020617ta_talk_lethem?020617ta_talk_lethem.
"The Amazing . . . " *London Review of Books,* June 2002. http://www.lrb.co.uk/v24/
    n11/leth01_.html.
*The Disappointment Artist* (2005). Includes, among other essays on popular culture,
    "Defending *The Searchers*" (2001).
"The Ecstasy of Influence: A Plagiarism." *Harpers,* February 2007. http://www.
    harpers.org/archive/2007/02/0081387.
"Hitchhiking in Nevada Is Illegal." *Rolling Stone,* July 6, 2000. http://www.verysilly.
    org/lethem/hitching.html.
*Kafka Americana* (1999, with Carter Scholz)
"The Many Dimensions of Rod Serling." *Gadfly,* September–October 1999. http://
    www.gadflyonline.com/archive/SepOct99/archive-serling.html.
"My Marvel Years." *London Review of Books* 26(8) April 15, 2004. http://www.lrb.
    co.uk/v26/n08/leth01_.html.
"Nine Failures of the Imagination." *New York Times,* September 23, 2001.

"The Squandered Promise of Science Fiction." *Village Voice*, June 1998. http://www.
verysilly.org/lethem/lethems_vision.html.
"You Don't Know Dick." *Bookforum* Summer, 2002. http://www.verysilly.org/lethem/
lethemBF.html.

## Research Sources

*Encyclopedias and Handbooks:* **AW, CA, CANR, NNDB, SFW**

*Bibliographies:* **FF, SFAN**

*Lethem in Landscape.* October 26, 2004. http://www.verysilly.org/lethem/.

### Biographies and Interviews

Links to Interviews to 2004. *Lethem in Landscape* October 26, 2004. http://www.
verysilly.org/lethem/interviews.html.
"Chapter and Verse: Rick Moody, Jonathan Lethem and John Darnielle on the
Crossbreeding of Literature and Pop." *LA Weekly,* February 28, 2006. http://
www.brassland.org/ahb/writing/archives/2006/02/chapter_and_ver.html.
Edemariam, Aida. "The Borrower." *Guardian Online,* June 2, 2007. http://books.
guardian.co.uk/departments/generalfiction/story/0,2093368,00.html.
Flannagan, Sean, and Andrew Krucoff. Interview. *92Y Blog,* November 14, 2005.
http://blog.92y.org/index.php/item/jonathan_lethem_interview/.
Kelleghan, Fiona. "Private Hells and Radical Doubts: An Interview with Jonathan
Lethem." *Science Fiction Studies,* July 1998. http://www.depauw.edu/sfs/
interviews/letheminterview.htm.

### Criticism and Readers' Guides

Bredehoft, Thomas A. "Cosms and Lacks: Baby Universes in Lethem and Benford."
*New York Review of Science Fiction* 11(1) (1998): 9+.
Duchamp, L.Timmel. "Denaturalizing Authority and Learning to Live in the Flesh:
Jonathan Lethem's *Amnesia Moon." New York Review of Science Fiction,* Septem-
ber 1998. http://ltimmel.home.mindspring.com/moon.html.
Rossi, Umberto. "From Dick to Lethem: The Dickian Legacy, Postmodernism, and
Avant-Pop in Jonathan Lethem's *Amnesia Moon." Science Fiction Studies* 29
(2002): 15–33.

### Web Sites

*Jonathan Lethem.com.* Official Web site. http://www.jonathanlethem.com/.
*BoldType.* May 2006. Random House. Online magazine feature, including an interview
with the author, essay by Lethem on *Girl in Landscape,* an author reading from the
novel and a print excerpt. http://www.randomhouse.com/boldtype/0598/lethem/.

*Lethem in Landscape*. David Myers. October 26, 2004. A well-organized collection of links to essays, interviews, and reviews. http://www.verysilly.org/lethem/.

# C.S. Lewis (1898–1963)

*He became able to know (and simultaneously refused the knowledge) that he had been wrong from the beginning, that souls and personal responsibility existed. He half saw: he wholly hated. The physical torture of the burning was not fiercer than his hatred of that.*

*—That Hideous Strength (1945)*

## Biography

Clive Staples Lewis was born in Belfast, Northern Ireland. As a Fellow of Magdalen College, Oxford for twenty-nine years, he was a friend and confidant of J.R.R. Tolkien, and other Oxford writers known collectively as "the Inklings." His Space Trilogy was his response to the philosophy of contemporary humanist, irreligious science fiction masters of his day, such as Olaf Stapledon and H.G. Wells. Using narrative effects and imagery from the Bible and *Paradise Lost*. Lewis' fantasy and science fiction make powerful arguments on faith and philosophy available to a wider public.

In 1955, C.S. Lewis became a professor at Magdalene College, Cambridge. His late-life marriage to Joy Gresham was dramatized in the 1993 movie *Shadowlands*. After her death in 1960, his health deteriorated, and he died at his home in Cambridge on November, 22, 1963.

ALIENS; GODS AND DEMONS; MARS, MOON & THE PLANETS; RELIGION

## Major Works

*Novels*

The Cosmic Trilogy: *Out of the Silent Planet* (1938), *Perelandra* (1943), *That Hideous Strength* (1945)

*Other Important Works*

"The New Men." *Beyond Personality*—BBC Broadcast Talks March 21, 1944. http://www.bbc.co.uk/religion/. The only surviving tape of a series of talks that Lewis did for BBC radio. The transcript was eventually published as *Mere Christianity*.
*Of Other Worlds: Essays and Stories* (1966) Includes essays such as "On Science Fiction," "A Reply to Professor Haldane," and "Sometimes Fairy Stories May Say Best What's To Be Said."
*Surprised By Joy: The Shape of My Early Life.* (1955)

# Research Sources

*Encyclopedias and Handbooks:* **AW, BW, CA, CANR, ESF, MSSF, NNDB, SFW**

*Bibliographies:* **ARB, FF, SFAN**

Hooper, Walter. "Bibliography of the Writings of C.S. Lewis, Supplement and Alphabetical Index." In James T. Como, ed., *C. S. Lewis at the Breakfast Table and Other Reminiscences* (1979). New York: Harvest, 1992, 245–320.

## Biographies and Interviews

Adey, Lionel. *C.S. Lewis: Writer, Dreamer & Mentor.* Grand Rapids, MI: Eerdmans, 1998.

Biography. *Religion & Ethics: People.* April 2007. BBC.co.uk. http://www.bbc.co.uk/religion/religions/christianity/people/cslewis_1.shtml.

Bratman, David. "Biographies of C.S. Lewis." *Mythprint.* August 1997. http://home.earthlink.net/~dbratman/lewis.html.

Duriez, Colin. *Tolkien and C.S. Lewis: The Gift of Friendship.* Mahwah, NJ: Hidden Spring/Paulist, 2003.

Hooper, Walter. *C.S. Lewis: A Complete Guide to His Life & Works.* New York: HarperOne, 1998.

Myers, Doris T. *C.S. Lewis in Context.* Kent, OH: Kent State University Press, 1994.

Obituary. *The New York Times.* November 25, 1963. http://www.gcwillick.com/Spacelight/obit/cslewiso.html.

Poe, Dr. Harry Lee, ed. *C.S. Lewis Remembered.* Grand Rapids, MI: Zondervan, 2006. It includes interview from *SF Horizons*, Spring 1964, "C.S. Lewis Discusses Science Fiction with Kingsley Amis and Brian Aldiss."

White, Michael. *C.S. Lewis: A Life.* New York: Carroll & Graf, 2004.

## Criticism and Readers' Guides

Downing, David. *Planets in Peril: A Critical Study of C.S. Lewis's Ransom Trilogy.* Amhurst: Univ. of Massachusetts Press, 1995.

Filmer-Davies, Cath. "That Hideous 1984: The Influence of C.S. Lewis' *That Hideous Strength* on Orwell's *1984*." *Extrapolation.* 26 (1985): 160–169.

Hein, Rolland. *Christian Mythmakers: C.S. Lewis, Madeleine L'Engle, J.R.R. Tolkien, George MacDonald, G. K. Chesterton and Others.* Chicago, IL: Cornerstone, 1998.

Lobdell, Jared. *The Scientifiction Novels of C.S. Lewis: Space and Time in the Ransom Stories.* Jefferson, NC: McFarland, 2004.

Markos, Louis. "Apologist for the Past: The Medieval Vision of C.S. Lewis's 'Space Trilogy and Chronicles of Narnia." *Mythlore.* 23(2) (2001): 24–35.

Miller, Ryder W. *From Narnia to A Space Odyssey: The War of Ideas Between Arthur C. Clarke and C. S. Lewis.* New York: Ibooks, 2003.

Mills, David, ed. *The Pilgrim's Guide: C.S. Lewis and the Art of Witness*. Grand Rapids, MI: Eerdmans, 1998.

Schwartz, Sanford. "Cosmic Anthropology: Race and Reason in *Out of the Silent Planet.*" *Christianity & Literature*. 52(4) (2003): 523–556.

### Web Sites

*The Chronicle of The Oxford University C.S. Lewis Society*. A peer-edited journal dedicated to the thought of C.S. Lewis and his intellectual and literary peers. http://www.cslewischronicle.org/.

*CSL: The Bulletin of the New York C. S. Lewis Society*. 1969–2005. List of contexts of the bimonthly bulletin, since 1969. http://www.nycslsociety.com/backissues.htm.

*Frequently Asked Questions about C.S. Lewis*. Rick Miesel. January 1999. Biblical Discernment Ministries. Addresses questions about the nature of Lewis' faith, and how it was reflected in his work. http://www.rapidnet.com/~jbeard/bdm/exposes/lewis/cs-lewis.htm.

*Further Up & Further In: A C.S. Lewis and the Inklings Resource Blog*. Bruce L. Edwards. April 2008. Pseudobook. "... incisive commentary on all matters Lewisian ... " http://www.pseudobook.com/cslewis/.

*Into the Wardrobe: A C. S. Lewis Web Site*. John Visser. April 2008. Attractive Web site, with a comprehensive bibliography, biographical material, and a long list of useful links. Mostly focused on Narnia, but does have some information about the Silent Planet trilogy. http://cslewis.drzeus.net/.

# Ken MacLeod (1954– )

*Marx was wrong—we aren't alienated from our humanity, alienation is human ity. We're always capable of stepping back and looking at what we're doing, from the outside as it were – we have an outside, inside and it's as infinite as space.*

—*The Cassini Division (1998)*

## Biography

Kenneth Macrae MacLeod was born in Stornoway, on the island of Lewis in the Outer Hebrides of Scotland, and grew up in Greenock, on the south bank of the River Clyde. After graduating from Glasgow University with a degree in zoology, he pursued a career as a computer programmer until 1997, when he was able to become a full-time writer. He currently lives in West Lothian, Scotland.

MacLeod combines space opera spirit with the substance of political ideas best described as techno-utopian socialist. His heroes are usually anarchist/libertarians, with a skeptical attitude toward authority in general, and government in particular. He is resolutely pro-technology, and his anarcho-primitivist characters are often (but not always) villains. He is well known for the jokes and puns that he manages to construct from the head-on clash of futuristic drama, socialist ideology, and computer programming.

ARTIFICIAL INTELLIGENCE; FIRST CONTACT; LIBERTARIAN SF; NANOTECHNOLOGY; POLITICAL SF; TECHNOLOGY

## Major Works

*Novels*

Fall Revolution series: *The Star Fraction* (1995—**Prometheus**), *The Stone Canal* (1996—**Prometheus**), *The Cassini Division* (1998), *The Sky Road* (1999—**BSF**) Excerpt from *The Cassini Division*: "The Downloadable Boy" http://www.salon. com/books/feature/1999/07/27/macleod_excerpt/.
Engines of Light trilogy: *Cosmonaut Keep* (2000), *Dark Light* (2001), and *Engine City* (2002)
*Learning the World: A Novel of First Contact* (2005) **Prometheus**
*The Highway Men* (2006)
*The Execution Channel* (2007)

*Collections*

*Giant Lizards from Another Star*. Framingham, MA: NESFA, 2006. Introduction by Jo Walton. Includes short stories, novellas, and essays such as "The Falling Rate of Profit, Red Hordes, and Green Slime: What the Fall Revolution Books are About" (2001) and "Does Science Fiction Have to Be About the Present?" (2003).

*Other Important Works*

"Does Science Fiction Have to Be About the Present?" *New York Review of Science Fiction*. 16(5) (2004): 14+.
"History in SF: What (Hasn't Yet) Happened in History." In Alan Sandison and Robert Dingley, eds., *Histories of the Future:Studies in Fact, Fantasy and Science Fiction*. Basingstoke (UK): Palgrave, 2000, 8–14.
"Libertarianism, the Looney Left and the Secrets of the Illuminati." *Matrix*. September/October 1997. http://www.libertarian.co.uk/lapubs/persp/persp010.pdf.
"Politics and Science Fiction." In Edward James and Farah Mendelsohn, eds., *The Cambridge Companion to Science Fiction*. Cambridge (UK): Cambridge Univ. Press, 2003, 230–240.
"Science Fiction after the Future Went Away." *Revolution*. 5 (1998). http://www. infinityplus.co.uk/nonfiction/kensf.htm.
*SF Crowsnest*. Regular Features Column. http://www.sfcrowsnest.com/.
    Articles such as "2001 and All That, (or, Life Before and After the End of History)" (June 2003); "Where I Get My Other Ideas From" (April 2006).

## Research Sources

*Encyclopedias and Handbooks:* **AW, CA, ESF**

*Bibliographies:* **ARB, FF, SFAN**

*Biographies and Interviews*

Doran, Kevin. "Blogging Interview with Ken MacLeod." *Mannequin Guillotine*. October 27, 2006. http://kevindoran.blogspot.com/2006/10/blogging-interview-with-ken-macleod.html.

Lawie, Duncan. "Ken MacLeod—A Veritable People's Palace." *The Zone Online*. 2001. http://www.zone-sf.com/kenmacleod.html.

Leonard, Andrew. "An Engine of Anarchy." *Salon*. July 27, 1999. http://www.salon.com/books/feature/1999/07/27/macleod_interview/.

Lilley, Ernest. "Interview with Ken Macleod." *SFRevu* March 2006. http://sfrevu.com/Review-id.php?id=3776.

*Socialist Worker*. "Interview: Science Fiction Can Help Us Learn to Change the World." November 12, 2005. http://www.socialistworker.co.uk/article.php?article_id=7729.


*Criticism and Readers' Guides*

Butler, Andrew M. and Farah Mendlesohn. *The True Knowledge of Ken MacLeod*. Cambridge (UK): Science Fiction Foundation, 2003.

Walker, Jesse. "Anarchies, States and Utopias: The Science Fiction of Ken MacLeod." *Reason*. November 2000. http://www.reason.com/news/show/27843.html.


*Web Sites*

*The Early Days of a Better Nation*. Author's Blog. http://kenmacleod.blogspot.com/.

Ken MacLeod Issue. *Emerald City: Fantasy and Science Fiction*. May 2000. Short fanzine, with two interviews, plus reviews of his four novels. http://www.emcit.com/emcitS01.shtml.

# Anne McCaffrey (1926–  )

> *"Did they remember to program a sense of humor, young lady?"*
>
> *"We are directed to develop a sense of proportion, sir, which contributes the same effect."*
>
> —*"The Ship Who Sang"* (1961)

## Biography

Anne Inez McCaffrey was born in Cambridge, Massachusetts. She studied Slavonic languages at Radcliffe, and later became a character actress and stage director. In 1950, she married, and began to write. Her first sf novel, *Restoree* (1966), was written as a parody of the "damsel in distress" portrayal of women in sf. She was the first woman to win both the Hugo and Nebula Awards, in 1968 and 1969, for the stories that launched her immensely popular series, "Dragonriders of Pern." Most of McCaffrey's work is science fiction—even the Dragonriders series has its feet firmly on the sf ground of a long-lost Earth colony, complete with bio-engineered time-travelling, and telepathic, telekinetic dragons.

After her marriage ended in 1970, McCaffrey and her children moved to Ireland, where she lives today, in County Wicklow. At her home, "Dragonhold-Underhill," which she designed herself, she raises horses.

COLONIZATION OF OTHER WORLDS; DISABILITY & SF; FANTASY; PSI POWERS; TECHNOLOGY; POST-HUMAN; WOMEN IN SF

## Major Works

*Novels*

*Restoree* (1967)

The Brain & Brawn Ship Series: *The Ship Who Sang* (1969) Fix-up which began with the short story "The Ship Who Sang" (1961). Subsequent volumes are collaborations with Margaret Ball, Mercedes Lackey, S.M. Stirling, and Jody Lynn Nye

*The Coelura* (1987)

The Crystal Singers series: *Crystal Singer* (1982), *Killashandra* (1985), and *Crystal Line* (1992)

The Dinosaur Planet Series: *Dinosaur Planet* (1984), *Dinosaur Planet Survivors* (1984) Subsequent volumes are collaborations with Jody Lynn Nye and Elizabeth Moon.

The Dragonriders of Pern: *Dragonflight* (1969) was a fix-up consisting of novellas "Dragonrider" (1967—**Nebula**) and "Weyr Search" (1967—**Hugo**). Some subsequent volumes are *Dragonquest* (1971), *The White Dragon* (1978), *Dragon's Fire* (2006), and *Dragon Harper* (2007), written with her son, Todd McCaffrey.

*Nimisha's Ship* (1999)

The Catteni Series: *Freedom's Landing* (1995), *Freedom's Choice* (1997), *Freedom's Challenge* (1998), *Freedom's Ransom* (2002)

*Other Important Works*

"Hitch Your Dragon to a Star: Romance and Glamour in Science Fiction." In *Science Fiction, Today and Tomorrow*. Ed. Reginald Bretnor, 278–292. New York: Harper & Row, 1974.

# Research Sources

*Encyclopedias and Handbooks:* **AW, CA, CANR, ESF, MSSF, NNDB, SFW**

*Bibliographies:* **ARB, FF, SFAN**

## Biographies and Interviews

Jamneck , Lynne. "An Interview with Anne McCaffrey." *Writing World.* 2004. http://www.writing-world.com/sf/mccaffrey.shtml.

*Locus Online.* "Heirs to Pern." November 2004. http://www.locusmag.com/Archives.html.

McCaffrey, Todd. *Dragonholder: The Life and Dreams (So Far) of Anne McCaffrey.* New York: Ballantine/Del Rey, 1999.

Swaim, Don. Audio Interview. *Wired for Books.* 1988. http://wiredforbooks.org/annemccaffrey/.

## Criticism and Readers' Guides

Brizzi, Mary T. *Anne McCaffrey.* Starmont Reader's Guide. San Bernardino, CA: Borgo, 1986.

Greeley, Andrew. "Anne McCaffrey: Romance as Talent User." In *God in Popular Culture,* 201–209. Chicago, IL: Thomas More, 1988.

Roberts, Robin. *Anne McCaffrey: A Critical Companion.* Westport, CT: Greenwood, 1996.

Salmonson, Jessica Amanda. "Gender Structuring of Shell Persons in *The Ship Who Sang.*" *New York Review of Science Fiction.* 1(10) (1989): 15+.

Schellenberg, James. "My Year of McCaffrey." *Strange Horizons.* February 4, 2008. http://www.strangehorizons.com/2008/20080204/schellenberg-c.shtml.

Trachtenberg, Martha P. *Anne McCaffrey: Science Fiction Storyteller.* Berkeley Heights, NY: Enslow, 2001.

van der Boom, Hans. *40 Years of Pern: A Liber Fanorum for Author Anne McCaffrey.* Van der Boom & Slijkerman, 2007. Essays by fans, with introduction by Anne McCaffrey. Excerpts are available online, including part of the introduction, at http://mccaffrey.srellim.org/.

## Web Sites

*Cheryl's Anne McCaffrey Triad.* Cheryl B. Miller. August 2007. http://www.srellim.org/pern/. Portal to *The Many Works of Anne McCaffrey* and *A Meeting of Minds— An Anne McCaffrey Discussion Forum.* A compendium of information on Anne McCaffrey and all her work, and a bulletin board for fans, with separate forums for series, one-off works, events, and collections.

*The Pern Museum and Archives.* Hans van der Boom. April 2008. Lavish fan site, with the usual news and book information; of particular interest, Pernese Bloodlines and Pern Encyclopedia. http://www.pern.nl/general/about.html.

*The Worlds of Anne McCaffery.* Official Web site. http://www.annemccaffrey.net/index.php.

# Maureen F. McHugh (1959–   )

*"We're using mathematics as metaphors," I explain. "Science filters into the general public as metaphors that describe our world, our history."*
                                        —*China Mountain Zhang (1992)*

## Biography

Maureen F. McHugh was born and grew up in Loveland, Ohio, near Cincinnati. She holds a BA from Ohio University, and a master's degree in English Literature from New York University. After she completed her education, she spent some years in technical writing and temping, and a year teaching in Shijiazhuang, China.

Her first novel, *China Mountain Zhang*, made a great impression when it first appeared in 1992. McHugh has been compared to Ursula K. Le Guin, with her character-driven fiction, her careful construction of believable futures, and her sensitive use of world cultures. In November 2004, McHugh was diagnosed with Hodgkin's Lymphoma. Her blog *No Feeling of Falling* is an ongoing account of her treatment and recovery. She lives with her husband Bob Yeager in Austin, Texas.

ALIEN WORLDS; CITIES AND SOCIETIES; GENDER & SEXUALITY; SUS-TAINABLE ALTERNATIVES; NEAR FUTURE

## Major Works

*Novels*

*China Mountain Zhang* (1992) **Tiptree, Locus Poll**
*Half the Day Is Night* (1994)
*Mission Child* (1998)
*Nekropolis* (2002)
        Excerpt: http://www.booksense.com/chapters/

*Collections*

*Mothers and Other Monsters.* Northampton, MA: Small Beer, 2005. Includes "Nekropolis" (1994), "The Lincoln Train" (1995—**Hugo, Locus Poll**), "In the Air" (1995), and "Frankenstein's Daughter" (2003).

*Short Stories*

"Makeover" (2002) http://www.infinitematrix.net/.
"Eight-Legged Story" (2005) http://www.lcrw.net/trampoline/stories/mchugheight. htm.
"Oversite" (2005) http://www.ruminator.com/.
"Wicked" (2005) http://www.anglemagazine.org/.

## Other Important Works

"The Anti-SF Novel." Talk given to the Philadelphia SF Society. September 12, 1997. http://my.en.com/~mcq/antisf.html.
"Creating and Using Near Future Settings." In David H. Borcherding, ed., *Science Fiction and Fantasy Writer's Sourcebook*. Cincinnati, OH: Writer's Digest, 1996, 18–25.
"Why I Am Not Post-Modern." *Book Sense*. September 28, 2001. http://www.booksense.com/people/archive/mchughmaureen.jsp.

# Research Sources

*Encyclopedias and Handbooks:* **AW, CA, CANR, ESF, SFW**

*Bibliographies:* **ARB, FF, SFAN**

## Biographies and Interviews

Lindow, Sandra and Michael Levy. Interview. *SFRA Review*. September–December 2001. 2–18. http://www.sfra.org/.
*Locus Online*. "Family Matters." October 1999. http://www.locusmag.com/1999/Issues/10/McHugh.html.
Nielsen Hayden, Patrick. "Interview: On Any Given Day." In *Starlight 3*. New York: Tor, 2001, 63–82.
Stansberry, Pat. Interview. *Strange Horizons*. September 9, 2002. http://www.strangehorizons.com/2002/20020909/mchugh.shtml.

## Criticism and Readers' Guides

Jenkins, Alice. "Knowing and Geography in Octavia Butler, Ursula K. Le Guin, and Maureen McHugh." *Journal of the Fantastic in the Arts*. 16(4) (2006): 320–334.
Kandel, Michael. "Twelve Thoughts, Not All Equally Important, on Reading Maureen F. McHugh's *China Mountain Zhang* and *Half the Day is Night*." *New York Review of Science Fiction*. 7(5) (1995): 21+.
O'Brien, Erin. "McHugh on *Mothers and Other Monsters*." *Angle: A Journal of Arts & Culture*. 22 (2005). http://www.anglemagazine.com/articles/McHugh_on_Mothers_and_Other_Mo_2318.asp.
Zhou, Yupei. "Beyond Ethnicity and Gender: *China Mountain Zhang*'s Transcendent Techniques." *Extrapolation*. 42 (2001): 374–383.

## Web Sites

*Maureen F. McHugh: Personal Web page*. Includes links to essays such as "Where I Get My Ideas," an excerpt from the novel *Mission Child* (1998), and personal musings. http://my.en.com/~mcq/.
*No Feeling of Falling*. Author Blog. http://maureenmcq.blogspot.com/.

# Vonda McIntyre (1948–   )

*Still, Stavin shivered when Mist touched his thin chest. . . . The cobra was four times longer than Stavin was tall. She curved herself in stark white loops across his swollen abdomen, extending herself, forcing her head toward the boy's face, straining against Snake's hands.*

*—"Of Mist, Grass and Sand" (1973)*

## Biography

Vonda Neel McIntyre was born in Louisville, Kentucky. She attended the University of Washington and was one of the first successful graduates of the Clarion Science Fiction writers' workshop. After a year of graduate work in genetics, she became a full-time writer, best known for "Of Mist, and Grass, and Sand" (1973) and *Dreamsnake*, her stories of a healer in a violent and superstitious post-apocalyptic world. *Dreamsnake* won the 1979 Hugo, Nebula, and Locus Awards for best novel. Both works reveal her skill in depicting strong female characters.

McIntyre is a keen supporter of sf fandom, and mentor to young writers. Her Web site contains a number of articles about the craft of writing, and resources for writers at all stages of their careers. McIntyre is also a regular contributor to the Star Trek saga, writing a number of movie tie-ins and novels, and coming up with the name "Hikaru" for the character of Mr. Sulu.

ALTERNATIVE HISTORY; APOCALYPSE AND AFTER; COLONIZATION OF OTHER WORLDS; FEMINISM; GENDER & SEXUALITY

## Major Works

*Novels*

*The Exile Waiting* (1975)
*Dreamsnake* (1978) **Hugo, Nebula, Locus Poll**
*Superluminal* (1983)
*The Bride* (1985)
*Barbary* (1986)
*The Moon and the Sun* (1997) **Nebula**
Star Trek: The Original Series: *The Entropy Effect* (1981), *Star Trek: The Wrath of Khan* (1982), *Star Trek III: The Search for Spock* (1984), *Star Trek IV: The Voyage Home* (1986), *Enterprise: The First Adventure* (1986), *Duty, Honor, Redemption* (2004)
Starfarers Quartet: *Starfarers* (1989), *Transition* (1991), *Metaphase* (1992), *Nautilus* (1994)
Star Wars: *The Crystal Star* (1994)

## Collections

*Fireflood and Other Stories.* New York: Houghton Mifflin, 1979.

## Short Stories

"Of Mist, Grass and Sand" (1973) **Nebula** http://www.vondanmcintyre.com/Fiction/
McIntyre-MistGrassSand.html.
"Aztechs" (1977)
"Steelcollar Worker" (1992)
"The Adventure of the Field Theorems" (1995) http://www.vondanmcintyre.com/
Fiction/FieldTheorems.html.
"Little Faces" (2005) http://www.vondanmcintyre.com/Fiction/McIntyre-LittleFaces.
html.

## Other Important Works

"A Modest Proposal . . . for the Perfection of Nature." *Nature.* March 3, 2005. http://
www.nature.com/nature/journal/v434/n7029/pdf/434122.pdf
"Pitfalls of Writing Science Fiction & Fantasy: General Useful Information &
Other Opinionated Comments." *Sff.net Site.* September 8, 2003. http://www.sff.
net/people/Vonda/Pitfalls.html.

# Research Sources

*Encyclopedias and Handbooks:* **AW, CA, CANR, ESF, MSSF, SFW**
*Bibliographies:* **FF, SFAN**

## Biographies and Interviews

*Cybling.* Interview. December 2000. http://www.cybling.com/artists/vonda.html.
*Locus Online.* "To Hollywood and Beyond." February 1998. http://www.locusmag.
com/1998/Issues/02/McIntyre.html.
O'Brien, Ulrika. "The Fannish Inquisition: Vonda McIntyre." *Trufen.net* (No date
given). http://trufen.net/article.pl?sid=05/04/13/237219&mode=nested.

## Criticism and Readers' Guides

Jameson, Frederic. "Science Fiction as a Spatial Genre: Vonda McIntyre's *The Exile
Waiting.*" In *Archaeologies of the Future.* New York: Verso, 2005. 296–313.
Wolmark, Jenny, "The Destabilisation of Gender in Vonda McIntyre's *Superlumi-
nal.*" In Rhys Garnett and R. J. Ellis, eds., *Science Fiction Roots and Branches,*
Basingstoke (UK): Macmillan, 1990, 168–182.
Wood, Diane S. "Breaking the Code: Vonda N. McIntyre's *Dreamsnake.*" *Extrapola-
tion.* 31 (1991): 63–72.
Wood, Diane S. "Family Ties in the Novels of Vonda N. McIntyre." *Extrapolation.* 29
(1988): 112–127.

*Web Sites*

*Vonda N. McIntyre.com.* Official Web site. With link to old Web site hosted by sfwa. http://www.vondanmcintyre.com/.
*Vonda N. McIntyre.* Carol Van Natta and Ann Harbour. May 2000. Includes an annotated bibliography. http://www.oz.net/~vonda/index.html.

# Walter M. Miller (1922–1996)

*Brother Francis produced a scrap of paper. . . . It was brittle with age and stained. The ink was faded. "Pound pastrami," Father Cheroki pronounced, slurring over some of the unfamiliar words, "can kraut, six bagels—bring home for Emma."*
                                                                    —*A Canticle for Leibowitz (1959)*

## Biography

*A Canticle for Leibowitz* (1959) was the single novel published by Walter M. Miller during a lifetime blighted by severe depression. A product of the nuclear anxiety of the 1950s, *Canticle* is also a novel that transcends its time, with its weird spirituality, stunning imagery, and clear, memorable prose.

Walter Michael Miller Jr. was born in New Smyrna Beach, Florida. After serving in the Army Air Corps during World War II, he resumed his education at the University of Texas, Austin, but did not complete his degree. He started a family, returned to Florida to live, converted to Roman Catholicism, and began writing. *A Canticle for Leibowitz* (1959) was a "fix up," assembled from three novellas. He never published another new novel or story in his lifetime, and in 1996, five months after the death of his wife, Walter M. Miller killed himself in Daytona Beach, Florida.

APOCALYPSE AND AFTER; FAR FUTURE; MYTHOLOGY & LEGEND; RELIGION

## Major Works

*Novels*

*A Canticle for Leibowitz* (1959) **Hugo**
*Saint Leibowitz and the Wild Horse Woman* (1997, completed by Terry Bisson)

*Collections*

*Dark Benediction.* (SF Masterworks) London: Gollanz, 2007. Includes some of Miller's best known short fiction, such as the 1951 title story, "Crucifixus Etiam" (1953) and "The Darfsteller" (1955—**Hugo**). Previous collections are *Conditionally Human* (1962) and *The View from the Stars* (1964).

*Other Important Works*

"Forewarning (an Introduction)." (1985) In Martin H. Greenberg, ed., *Beyond Armageddon*. Lincoln, NE: Univ. of Nebraska Press, 2006.

## Research Sources

*Encyclopedias and Handbooks:* **AW, BW, CA, CANR, ESF, MSSF, NNDB, SFW**

*Bibliographies:* **ARB, FF, SFAN**

Roberson, William H. and Robert L. Battenfeld. *Walter M. Miller, Jr.: A Bio-Bibliography*. Westport, CT: Greenwood, 1992.

Bibliography. Ed. Susan Stepney. July 1, 2007. University of York, Department of Computer Science, Unofficial Pages. http://www-users.cs.york.ac.uk/susan/sf/books/m/wltrmmll.htm.

*Biographies and Interviews*

Bisson, Terry. "A Canticle for Miller: or, How I Met Leibowitz and the Wild Horse Woman, But Not Walter M. Miller, Jr." *Locus*. December 1997. http://www.sff.net/people/tbisson/miller.html.

Garvey, John. "*A Canticle for Leibowitz*: A Eulogy for Walt Miller." *Commonweal*. April 5, 1996.

*Criticism and Readers' Guides*

Brians, Paul. *Study Guide*. May 29, 2007. Washington State University. http://www.wsu.edu:8080/~brians/science_fiction/canticle.html.

Cockrell, Amanda. "On This Enchanted Ground: Reflections of a Cold War Childhood in Russell Hoban's *Riddley Walker* and Walter M. Miller's *A Canticle for Leibowitz*. *Journal of the Fantastic in the Arts*. 15(1) (2004): 20–36.

Dunn, Thomas P. "To Play the Phoenix: Medieval Images and Cycles of Rebuilding in Walter Miller's *A Canticle for Leibowitz*." In Carl B. Yoke, ed., *Phoenix From the Ashes: The Literature of the Remade World*. New York: Greenwood, 1987, 105–116.

Olsen, Alexandra H. "Re-Vision: A Comparison of *A Canticle for Leibowitz* and the Novellas Originally Published." *Extrapolation*. 38 (1997): 135.

Roberts, Adam. "*A Canticle for Leibowitz:* SF Masterworks V." *Infinity Plus*. January 12, 2002. http://www.infinityplus.co.uk/nonfiction/canticle.htm.

Samuelson, D.N. *The Science Fiction Stories of Walter M. Miller, Jr*. Boston, MA: Gregg, 1978.

Samuelson, D.N. "The Lost Canticles of Walter M. Miller, Jr." *Science Fiction Studies*. 3 (1976): 3–26. http://www.depauw.edu/sfs/backissues/8/samuelson8art.htm.

Secrest, Rose. *Glorificemus: A Study of the Fiction of Walter M. Miller, Jr*. Lanham, MD: Univ. Press of America, 2002.

Seed, David. "Recycling the Texts of the Culture: Walter M. Miller's *A Canticle for Leibowitz." Extrapolation.* 37 (1996): 257–271.

Spencer, Susan. "Post-Apocalyptic Library: Oral and Literate Culture in *Fahrenheit 451 and A Canticle for Leibowitz." Extrapolation* 32 (1991): 331–343.

*Web Sites*

*A Canticle for Leibowitz, Soundtrack.* Composed and Performed by John Kannenberg. Nishi. 2005. "Possible soundtrack" for the novel. http://www.notype.com/nishi/releases/87/index.html.

# Michael Moorcock (1939–   )

*. . . we can, if we desire, change the course of planets, populate them with any kind of creature we wish, make our old sun burst with fresh energy or fade completely from the firmament. We control all. Nothing controls us!*
*—"Pale Roses" (1974)*

## Biography

As editor of *New Worlds* magazine, and the anthology *New Worlds Quarterly*, London-born Michael Moorcock was a moving force behind the 1960s "New Wave." His prodigious output includes rock songs, comics, screenplays, essays, and over seventy novels. Much of Moorcock's sf is played out in the "Multiverse," a kaleidoscope of alternate realities that interconnect and shift in time. The Multiverse has subsequently been used, with Moorcock's permission and encouragement, by numerous other writers in their own stories.

Since the later 1970s, Moorcock has broken out of the confines of sf. *Gloriana; or, The Unfulfill'd Queen* (1978) is alternative history, or perhaps Spenserian fantasy, dark, ironic, and enigmatic. His 1988 novel *Mother London*—generally considered to be his finest work—is neither science fiction nor fantasy at all, but contains sf touches, like telepathy and manifestations of psychic powers. Michael Moorcock currently lives with his wife Linda in Lost Pines, Texas.

ENTROPY; FANTASY; FAR FUTURE; GENDER & SEXUALITY; GOTHIC SF; IMMORTALITY; NEW WAVE; TIME TRAVEL

## Major Works

*Novels*

*The Sundered Worlds* (1965—aka *The Blood Red Game*)

Jerry Cornelius: *The Final Program* (1968), *A Cure for Cancer* (1971), *The English Assassin* (1972), *The Condition of Muzak* (1977) *The Great Rock'n'Roll Swindle* (1980)

*The Black Corridor* (1969, with Hilary Bailey)
*Behold the Man* (1969) **Nebula**
*Breakfast in the Ruins* (1972) http://www.revolutionsf.com/article.html?id=722.
Oswald Bastable: *The Warlord of the Air* (1971), *The Land Leviathan* (1974), and *The Steel Tsar* (1981)
The Dancers at the End of Time Trilogy: *An Alien Heat* (1972), *The Hollow Lands* (1974) and *The End of All Songs* (1976)
*The Transformation of Miss Mavis Ming* (1977)
*Gloriana* (1978)


## Collections

*Legends from the End of Time* (1977). Stone Mountain, GA.: White Wolf, 1999. Contains novellas such as *Pale Roses* (1974), *White Stars* (1975) and *Elric at the End of Time* (1975).
*The Cornelius Quartet* (1993). New York: Four Wall Eight Windows, 2001.
*The Dancers at the End of Time*. Stone Mountain, GA.: White Wolf, 1998.
*The Lives and Times of Jerry Cornelius: Stories of the Comic Apocalypse* (1976). New York: Four Wall Eight Windows, 2003. Includes Jerry Cornelius short stories from "The Peking Junction" (1969) to "Firing the Cathedral" (2002).


## Short Stories

"The Spencer Inheritance." (1997) http://www.theedge.abelgratis.co.uk/spencer.htm.
"Cheering for the Rockets" (1998) http://www.fantasticmetropolis.com/i/rockets/full/.
"Through the Shaving Mirror . . . or, How We Abolished the Future" (2001) http://www.fantasticmetropolis.com/i/mirror/.
"An Evening at Home" (2002) http://www.fantasticmetropolis.com/i/evening/.


## Other Important Works

"Epic Pooh (Why is the *Lord of the Rings* being widely read today?)" (1989) http://www.revolutionsf.com/article.php?id=953.
"An Excellence of Peake." *Fantastic Metropolis*. October 15, 2001. http://www.fantasticmetropolis.com/i/peake/.
"The Future of Science Fiction." *New York Review of Science Fiction*. 17(10) (2005): 1+
*Michael Moorcock's Multiverse*. Vertigo/DC Comics, 1999. An attempt to express the totality of the multiverse in graphic novel form.
"A New Literature for the Space Age." *New Worlds* 142 (May–June 1964): 2–3. Moorcock's first editorial for *New Worlds*, which set out his vision for what would become known as the New Wave.
"Starship Stormtroopers." Cienfuegos Press Anarchist Review, 1978. http://flag.blackened.net/liberty/moorcock.html.

"Triumph of the City." *Booksense* October 19, 2001. http://www.booksense.com/people/archive/moorcockm.jsp.

*Wizardry and Wild Romance: A Study of Epic Fantasy.* Revised edition. Austin, TX: MonkeyBrain, 2004.

*Writer's Talk: Michael Moorcock with Colin Greenland.* VHS Videocassette North-brooke, IL: The Roland Collection, 1989.

## Research Sources

*Encyclopedias and Handbooks:* **AW, CA, CANR, ESF, MSSF, NNDB, SFW**

*Bibliographies:* **ARB, FF, SFAN**

### Biographies and Interviews

*3am Magazone.* "Strange Connections – An Interview with Michael Moorcock." 2002. http://www.3ammagazine.com/litarchives/2002_jun/interview_michael_moorcock.html.

Auden, Sandy. "Chaotic Lives: An Interview with Michael Moorcock." *SF Site.* 2005. http://www.sfsite.com/05b/samm200.htm.

"The Bayley-Moorcock Letters: Old Farts by the Fire." *Fantastic Metropolis.* Part I—January 31, 2002. Part II—July 2003. http://www.fantasticmetropolis.com/i/bayley/.

Coombes, Mike. "An Interview with Michael Moorcock." *Internet Review of Science Fiction.* February 2005. http://www.irosf.com/q/zine/article/10115.

Hudson, Patrick. "Fifty Percent Fiction: Michael Moorcock Interviewed. *The Zone.* November 2005. http://www.zone-sf.com/mmoorcock.html.

Means, Loren. "Interview with Michael Moorcock." *Ylem Journal.* 25(10/12) (2005): 9–14. http://www.ylem.org/Journal/2005Iss10 & 12vol25.pdf.

Mondschein, Ken. "Michael Moorcock on Politics, *PUNK*, Tolkien, and Everything Else." *The Corporate MoFo.* December 18, 2005. http://www.corporatemofo.com/stories/Moorcock1.htm.

*Nightwaves.* Audio Interview. January 16, 2006. BBC3 Radio. http://www.multiverse.org/imagehive/v/mediahive/mp3z/nightwaves/.

### Criticism and Readers' Guides

Baker, Brian. "Ms. Found In a Bottle: Mr. Wells, Mr. Moorcock, and The Nomad of the Time Streams Trilogy." *Fantastic Metropolis.* February 21, 2002. http://www.fantasticmetropolis.com/i/msinbottle/.

Delville, Michel. "Pop Meets the Avant-Garde: Music and Muzak in Michael Moorcock's Jerry Cornelius Stories." In Michael A. Morrison, ed., *Trajectories of the Fantastic.* Westport, CT: Greenwood, 1997, 117–128.

Gardiner, Jeff. *The Age of Chaos: The Multiverse of Michael Moorcock.* The British Fantasy Society, 2002.

Greenland, Colin. *Michael Moorcock: Death Is No Obstacle*. Manchester (UK): Savoy, 1992.

————. *The Entropy Exhibition: Michael Moorcock and the British "New Wave" in Science Fiction*. London: Routledge, 1983.

Willett, Ralph. "Moorcock's Achievement and Promise in the Jerry Cornelius Books." *Science Fiction Studies*. 3 (1976): 75–79. http://www.depauw.edu/sfs/backissues/8/willett8art.htm.

### Web Sites

*Cartographer of the Multiverse*. Ian Davey. Sweet Despise. 2005. Fan site that explores Moorcock's work as an example of "dark literature." Among other useful links and resources, the full text of *A Caribbean Crisis, a Sexton Blake Story*, which was Moorcock's first published novel. http://www.eclipse.co.uk/sweetdespise/moorcock/.

*"The Edge's* Michael Moorcock Pages." *The Edge*. May 2004. Material from unavailable back issues or exclusive to *The Edge* online. http://www.theedge.abelgratis.co.uk/michaelmoorcockindex.htm.

Michael Moorcock (Author Detail). Hatchette Book Group. May 2008. Biographical details, interviews, excerpts, and essays. http://www.hachettebookgroupusa.com/Michael_Moorcock_(1015067)_AuthorInterview(1).htm.

*Moorcock's Miscellany—The Official Michael Moorcock Web site*. Author's blog, includes FAQs and other useful links. http://www.multiverse.org/.

*The Terminal Café*. Max Wilcox. June 2002. Novy Mir Productions. Attractive and very busy site, with many links to interviews and fan essays, but now seriously out of date. http://www.novymir.com.au/terminalcafe/intro.html.

# C.L. Moore (1911–1987)

*. . . somewhere back of history's first beginnings there must have been an age when mankind, like us today, built cities of steel to house its star-roving ships and knew the names of the planets in their own native tongues . . .*

*—"Shambleau" (1933)*

## Biography

Catherine Lucille Moore was born in Indianapolis, Indiana. Her first published story, "Shambleau" (1933), featuring the interplanetary bad-boy "Northwest Smith," was an immediate hit, establishing her as an author of sensual, vivid planetary romances. Her reputation was consolidated by sword and sorcery yarns featuring Jirel of Joiry, the first female swashbuckler hero. In 1940 she married writer Henry Kuttner, and they began writing together as "Lewis Padgett" (among at least seventeen other collaborative pen names), together specializing in science fiction with a touch of Lovecraftian horror.

Moore wrote almost no science fiction following Kuttner's untimely death in 1958; during the early 1960s, as "Catherine Kuttner," she wrote scripts for the classic television series such as *Maverick* and *77 Sunset Strip*. She was not forgotten by science fiction, however: in 1981 she was presented with the World Fantasy Award for Lifetime Achievement. She died on April 4, 1987 at her home in Hollywood, California.

ANDROIDS, CYBORGS AND ROBOTS; GENDER & SEXUALITY; GODS AND DEMONS; GOTHIC SF; SPACE OPERA

## Major Works

*Novels*

*Doomsday Morning* (1957)
. . . as Lewis Padgett (written with Henry Kuttner): *The Fairy Chessmen* (1946), *The Well of the Worlds* (1953), *The Time Axis* (1948), *Beyond Earth's Gates* (1954)
*Fury* (1947, as Lawrence O'Donnell)

*Collections*

*The Best of C.L. Moore*, edited by Lester Del Rey. Garden City, NY: Nelson/ Doubleday, 1975. Features a short essay by Moore about her work, "Afterword: Footnote to "Shambleau" . . . and Others."
*Black Gods and Scarlet Dreams*. London: Gollancz, 2002. An anthology of five Jirel of Joiry stories, plus Northwest Smith stories.
*Judgment Night: Facsimile Reproduction of the 1952 First Edition*. Mohegan Lake, NY: Red Jacket, 2004.

*Short Stories*

"Shambleau" (1933)
"The Bright Illusion" (1934)
"Mimsy Were the Borogoves" (1943, as Lewis Padgett)
"Clash By Night" (1943)
"No Woman Born" (1944)
"When the Bough Breaks" (1944)
"Vintage Season" (1946, as Lawrence O'Donnell)

# Research Sources

*Encyclopedias and Handbooks:* **AW, CA, CANR, ESF, MSSF, SFW**

*Bibliographies:* **ARB, FF, SFAN**

Utter, Virgil, Gordon Benson, and Phil Stephensen-Payne. *Catherine Lucille Moore & Henry Kuttner: A Marriage of Souls and Talent—A Working Bibliography*. Leeds (UK): Galactic Central, 1996.

## Biographies and Interviews

Bradley, Marion Z. "C.L. Moore: An Appreciation." *Locus*, (69) March 1988.
Del Rey, Lester. "Forty Years of C.L. Moore." In *The Best of C.L. Moore*. Garden City, NY: Nelson Doubleday, 1975.

## Criticism and Readers' Guides

Baccolini, Raffaella. "In-Between Subjects: C.L. Moore's *No Woman Born*." In Karen Sayer and John Moore, eds., *Science Fiction, Critical Frontiers*. New York: St. Martin's, 2000, 140–153.
Bredehoft, Thomas A. "Origin Stories: Feminist Science Fiction and C.L. Moore's 'Shambleau.'" *Science Fiction Studies* 24 (1997): 369–386.
Delahoyde, Michael. *Study Guide: Shambleau*. Feb. 4, 2006. Washington State University. http://www.wsu.edu/~delahoyd/sf/shambleau.html. A brief (but very sharp) analysis of key points of the story.
Gamble, Sarah. "'Shambleau . . . and others': The Role of the Female in the Fiction of C.L. Moore." In Lucie Armitt, ed., *Where No Man Has Gone Before: Women and Science Fiction*. London: Routledge, 1991, 29–49.
Mathews, Patricia. "C.L. Moore's Classic Science Fiction" In Tom Staicar, ed., *The Feminine Eye: Science Fiction and the Women Who Write It*. New York: Ungar, 1982, 14–24.
Shaw, Debra Benita. "No Woman Born': C.L. Moore's Dancing Cyborg." In *Women, Science and Fiction: The Frankenstein Inheritance*. New York: Palgrave, 2001.
Wymer, Thomas L. "Feminism, Technology, and Art in C.L. Moore's 'No Woman Born.'" *Extrapolation* 47 (2006): 51–65.

## Web Site

*Bodies and Identity: "No Woman Born." (The Frankenstein Project)*. Georgia Tech. February 28, 2004. Project by interdisciplinary group of students at Georgia Tech, using "No Woman Born" to illustrate Mary Shelley's literary legacy http:// frankenstein.lcc.gatech.edu/NoWomanBorn.html
*2004 Cordwainer Smith Foundation "Rediscovery" Award*. Rosana Lineberger Hart. *The Remarkable Science Fiction of Cordwainer Smith*. April 2005. http:// www.cordwainer-smith.com/kuttnermoore.htm. Praise from one sf classic to

another—announcement of the Cordwainer Rediscovery Award, written by the daughter of Cordwainer Smith.

# Larry Niven (1939–   )

*"First the sun explodes. . . . A flaming shock wave comes roaring over into the night side. It's closing on us right now. Like a noose . . . "*

*"Then we won't see the dawn. We won't even live that long."*
*—"Inconstant Moon" (1973)*

## Biography

Laurence van Cott Niven was born in Los Angeles. He graduated from Washburn University in Topeka, Kansas, with a BA in mathematics, and also did a year of graduate work at University of California, Los Angeles (UCLA). He quickly established a place for himself in the forefront of a hard sf renaissance, demonstrating an easy way with big scientific concepts and hard physics.

In recent years, Niven has been very successful working in collaborations, with authors such as Jerry Pournelle and Stephen Barnes. He opened up one of his Known Space scenarios—*The Man-Kzin Wars*—to other writers in a very successful shared-world anthology series about conflict with a vivious and cunning cat-like race. Niven is an intensely political writer, actively involved in advocacy for space exploration. He lives with his wife in the suburbs of Los Angeles and together they are active participants in the sf community.

ALIEN THREAT; COLONIZATION OF OTHER WORLDS; GALACTIC EMPIRES; HARD SF; LIBERTARIAN SF; WAR

## Major Works

*Novels*

The Ringworld series: *Ringworld* (1970—**Nebula, Hugo, Locus Poll**), *The Ringworld Engineers* (1979), *The Ringworld Throne* (1996), *Ringworld's Children* (2004)
*The Mote in God's Eye* (1974, with Jerry Pournelle)
*Inferno* (1976, with Jerry Pournelle)
*Lucifer's Hammer* (1977, with Jerry Pournelle)
*The Descent of Anasi* (1981, with Stephen Barnes)
Dream Park series (with Stephen Barnes): *Dream Park* (1981), *The Barsoom Project* (1989) and *The Voodoo Game* (1991)
The Smoke Ring series: *The Integral Trees* (1983—**Locus Poll**), *The Smoke Ring* (1987), and *Fallen Angels* (1991—with Jerry Pournelle and Michael F. Flynn, **Prometheus**) Excerpt: http://www.baen.com/library/.
*Achilles' Choice* (1991, with Stephen Barnes)

*The Gripping Hand* (1993, with Jerry Pournelle)
*Destiny's Road* (1997)
*Building Harlequin's Moon* (2005, with Brenda Cooper)
The Golden Road: *The Burning City* (2000) and *The Burning Tower* (2005)

## Collections

*Scatterbrain.* New York: Tor, 2003. Includes a selection of novel excerpts and short
    fiction, as well as essays such as "Introduction: Where Do I Get My Crazy Ideas?"
    to "Epilog: What I Tell Librarians."
Some recent story collections from Tales of Known Space are *Crashlander* (1994), and
    *The Draco Tavern* (2006). *N-Space* (1990) includes essays such as "The Alien in
    Our Minds" (1998) and stories not previously collected in book form.

## Short Stories

"The Coldest Place" (1964)
"Neutron Star" (1966) **Hugo**
"Inconstant Moon" (1971) **Hugo**
"The Hole Man" (1974) **Hugo**
"The Borderland of Sol" (1975) **Hugo**
"The Return of William Proxmire" (1989)
"The Missing Mass" (2000) **Locus Poll**

## Other Important Works

"Man of Steel, Woman of Kleenex." In Glenn Yeffeth, ed., *The Man from Krypton:
    A Closer Look at Superman.* Dallas, TX: BenBella, 2005, 51–58. http://www.
    rawbw.com/~svw/superman.html.
"The Words in Science Fiction." *The Craft of Science Fiction.* Edited by Reginald
    Bretnor. New York: Harper & Row, 1976, 178–194.

# Research Sources

*Encyclopedias and Handbooks:* **AW, CA, CANR, ESF, MSSF, NNDB,
SFW**

*Bibliographies:* **ARB, FF, SFAN**

Lambert, David and Carol Phillips. "Larry Niven's Bibliography." *Known Space.* 2007.
    http://www.larryniven.org/biblio/.

## Biographies and Interviews

Farrell, Shaun. Interview. *Shaun's Quadrant.* August. 2006. Far Sector. http://www.
    farsector.com/quadrant/interview-larryniven.htm.

Hughes, Aaron. "Larry Niven Interview." *Fantastic Reviews.* August 2004. http://www.geocities.com/fantasticreviews/niven_interview.htm.

James, Warren W. Interview. *Mike Hodel's Hour 25.* February 21, 2005. http://www.hour25online.com/Hour25_Previous_Shows_2005-02.html#larry-niven_2005-02-21.

Lilley, Ernest. Interview. *SFRevu.* August 2003. http://www.sfrevu.com/ISSUES/2003/0308/Larry%20Niven%20Interview/Review.htm.

McCarty, Michael. Interview. *SciFi.com.* September 13, 2004. http://www.scifi.com/sfw/interviews/sfw11420.html.

Wolfman, Marv. "Speaking with...Larry Niven." *SBC.* 2003. http://www.silverbulletcomicbooks.com/wolfman/103572529241628.htm.

*Criticism and Readers' Guides*

Hicks, James E. "Louis and Teela, Teela and Seeker: Sexual Relationships in Larry Niven's *Ringworld.*" *Extrapolation* 31 (1990): 148–159.

Stein, Kevin. *The Guide to Larry Niven's Ringworld.* New York: Baen, 1994.

*Web Site*

*Known Space: The Future Worlds of Larry Niven.* Ted Scribner et al. Fan Web site, sanctioned by Niven, that serves as semi-official source of information about Niven and Known Space. http://www.larryniven.org/.

*Larry Niven's Known Space.* Larry King. February 2004. Some links are out of date, but includes the *The Up To Date Known Space Chronology* by I. Marc Carlson, along with other useful chronologies. http://www.chronology.org/niven/.

*Ringworld Renderings.* Explanation of some of the technical (and visual) points of Ringworld. http://www.hellcrown.com/ringworld/.

# George Orwell [Eric Arthur Blair] (1903–1950)

> It was a bright cold day in April, and the clocks were striking thirteen...
> —*Nineteen Eighty-Four (1949)*

## Biography

Eric Arthur Blair's experience—birth in India, education at Eton; his time in the Indian Imperial Police, and fighting Fascism in Spain—equipped him with a keen socialist conscience, fragile health, and plentiful material for essays, novels, and investigative journalism. What he saw in Spain convinced him that fascism and Stalinist communism presented equal threats of a bleak, totalitarian future.

In 1944, as "George Orwell," his anti-Stalinist allegory *Animal Farm* was published, to critical and popular acclaim. But Blair's health was very poor, and he was in and out of hospitals for the last three years of his life. In spite of this, he managed to write *Nineteen Eighty-Four*, giving the world Big Brother, Room

101, Thought Police, and another word—"Orwellian"—for a nightmare future that was " . . . a boot stamping on a human face—forever." Eric Arthur Blair died in London, of the complications of tuberculosis, on January 21, 1950.

DYSTOPIAS; NEAR FUTURE; POLITICAL SF; PSYCHOLOGY

## Major Works

*Novels*

*Animal Farm* (1944)
*Nineteen Eighty-four* (1949)

## Collections

*Collected Essays, Journalism and Letters of George Orwell*. 3 Vols. Eds. Sonia Orwell and Ian Angus. Jaffrey, NH: Nonpareil, 2000.
*Essays*. Everyman's Library Classics. New York: Everyman/Alfred A. Knopf, 2002.

## Nonfiction

Unpublished Preface to *Animal Farm*. (1945). http://home.iprimus.com.au/korob/ Orwell.html.
"*George Orwell's 1984*." NBC Radio. August 27, 1949. National Broadcasting Company. http://greylodge.org/gpc/?p=78. Very early radio version, starring David Niven as Winston Smith.
"*1984*." *BBC Sunday Night Theatre*. British Broadcasting Corporation. 1954. Classic early televised version, starring Peter Cushing as Winston Smith.
*Nineteen Eighty-Four*. Umbrella Rosenblum Films. 1984. Film version, released to coincide with 1984, starring John Hurt, as Winston Smith, and Richard Burton as O'Brien.

## Research Sources

*Encyclopedias and Handbooks:* **AW, BW, CA, ESF, MSSF, NNDB, SFW, WS**

*Bibliographies:* **ARB, FF, SFAN**

Fenwick, Gillian. *George Orwell: A Bibliography*. New Castle, DE: Oak Knoll, 1998.
Pridmore, Donna J. Selective Secondary Bibliography. May 10, 2005. *Literary History*. http://www.literaryhistory.com/20thC/Orwell.htm.

## Biographies and Interviews

Bowker, Gordon. *George Orwell*. London: Little Brown, 2003.
Davison, Peter. *George Orwell: A Literary Life*. New York: St. Martin's, 1996.
Hammond, J.R. *A George Orwell Chronology*. New York: Palgrave, 2000.

James, Clive. "The Truthteller: George Orwell." *The New Yorker*. January 18, 1999.

Lucas, Scott. *George Orwell and the Betrayal of Dissent*. London: Verso, 2003.

Menand, Louis. "Honest, Decent, Wrong: The Invention of George Orwell" *The New Yorker*. January 27, 2003.

Meyers, Jeffrey. *Orwell: Wintry Conscience of a Generation*. New York: Norton, 2000.

Newsinger, John. *Orwell's Politics*. London: Macmillan, 1999.

Ross, John J. "Tuberculosis, Bronchiectasis, and Infertility: What Ailed George Orwell?" *Clinical Infectious Diseases*. 41(11) (2005): 1599–1603.

Shelden, Michael. *Orwell: The Authorized Biography*. London: Heinemann, 1991.

## Criticism and Readers' Guides

Aldiss, Brian. "The Downward Journey: Orwell's *1984*." In *The Detached Retina: Aspects of SF and Fantasy*. 92–100. Syracuse, NY: Syracuse Univ. Press, 1995.

Atwood, Margaret. "Orwell and Me." *Guardian Online*. June 16, 2003. http://arts.guardian.co.uk/features/story/0,978279,00.html.

Bloom, Harold. *George Orwell's Nineteen Eighty-Four*. New York: Chelsea House, 1996.

Brunsdale, Mitzi M. *Student Companion to George Orwell*. Westport, CT: Greenwood, 2000.

Fromm, Erich. "Negative Utopias and Orwell's Dark Vision." In Jesse G. Cunningham, ed., *Science Fiction*. San Diego, CA: Greenhaven, 2002, 108–117.

Gibson, William. "The Road to Oceania." *The New York Times*. June 25, 2003. http://www.netcharles.com/orwell/articles/col-rtoceania.htm.

Gleason, Abbott et al, eds. *On Nineteen Eighty-Four: Orwell and Our Future*. Princeton, NJ: Princeton Univ. Press, 2005.

Hitchens, Christopher. *Why Orwell Matters*. New York: Basic, 2002.

Hurst, L.J. "George Orwell in the World of Science Fiction." *L.J. Hurst Homepages*. December 1998. http://dialspace.dial.pipex.com/l.j.hurst/orwellsf.htm.

Lazaro, Alberto, ed. *The Road to George Orwell: His Achievement and Legacy*. New York: Peter Lang, 2001.

Pynchon, Thomas. "Foreword: The Road to *1984*." In *Nineteen Eighty-Four: Centennial Edition*. New York: Plume, 2003. http://www.themodernword.com/.

Rehnquist, William H. "1984." *Michigan Law Review*. 102 (2004): 981–987.

Rodden, John. *Scenes from an Afterlife: The Legacy of George Orwell*. Wilmington, DE: Intercollegiate Studies Institute, 2003.

## Web Sites

*Charles' George Orwell Links*. March 2007. Links to Orwell essays and full text of books as well as reviews, news articles, and images. In addition, there are hundreds of links to other Orwell Web sites. http://www.netcharles.com/orwell/.

*O. Dag's Orwell Project*. December 2004. Russian Web site with more links to the full text of essays and books, as well as interesting critical and biographical material. *George Orwell's Library* is a comprehensive online selection of Orwell's fiction and nonfiction, including: "Wells, Hitler and the World State" (1941), "Good Bad Books" (1945), and "Why I Write"(1946). http://orwell.ru/home.html.

*Orwell Reader.* Ed. Norman Ershler. One fan's thoughts on the work or Orwell, as well as useful links. http://www.theorwellreader.com/orwell.shtml.

# Marge Piercy (1936–    )

*We can only know what we can truly imagine. Finally what we see comes from ourselves.*

—Woman on the Edge of Time (1976)

## Biography

Marge Piercy was born in Detroit, Michigan. The family was extremely poor, and Piercy was the first in her family to attend college, winning various scholarships to support herself at the University of Michigan. Later, she received a fellowship to do an MA at Northwestern University.

Piercy was active in the civil rights movement, an early protestor against the war in Vietnam, and closely involved with the Students for a Democratic Society. Her work consistently raises issues of social justice and the equality of the sexes. *He, She and It* (1991) is set in a near-future world ruined by corporate greed. Piercy incorporates into the story elements of Jewish mysticism, particularly the legend of the Golem. Today, she is active in groups and organizations devoted to Jewish renewal, and lives on Cape Cod, Massachusetts with her third husband, Ira Wood.

DISABILITY & SF; FEMINISM; GENDER & SEXUALITY; TIME TRAVEL; UTOPIAS; WOMEN IN SF

## Major Works

*Novels*

*Dance the Eagle To Sleep* (1970)
*Woman on the Edge of Time* (1976)
*He, She And It* (1991, aka *Body of Glass*)

*Other Important Works*

"Active in Time and History." In William Zinsser, ed., *Paths of Resistance: The Art and Craft of the Political Novel.* Boston, MA: Houghton Mifflin, 1989, 89–123. http://www.margepiercy.com/essays/paths.htm.

Foreword. *Lost In Space: Probing Feminist Science Fiction and Beyond.* By Marleen Barr. Chapel Hill, NC: Univ. of North Carolina Press, 1993.

"In Your Name." *Monthly Review.* September 2004. http://www.monthlyreview.org/0904piercy.htm.

"Traveling Into Darkness (Introduction)." *The Last Man*. By Mary Shelley. New York: Bantam Books, 1994.

"Life of Prose and Poetry: An Inspiring Combination." Writers on Writing. *The New York Times*. December 20, 1999. http://www.margepiercy.com/essays/NYTLife. htm.

*Sleeping with Cats. A Memoir*. New York: Harper Perennial, 2002.

*So You Want to Write*. With Ira Wood. London: Piatkus, 2003.

"Love and Sex in the Year 3000." In Marleen S. Barr, ed., *Envisioning the Future: Science Fiction and the Next Millennium*. Middletown, NH: Wesleyan University Press, 2003, 131–145.

## Research Sources

*Encyclopedias and Handbooks:* **AW, BW, CA, CANR, ESF, MSSF, NNDB, SFW**

*Bibliographies:* **FF, SFAN**

Doherty, Patricia *Marge Piercy: An Annotated Bibliography*. Westport, CT: Greenwood, 1997.

### Biographies and Interviews

Podcast Interview. *Writers Voice*. March 2, 2007. Valley Free Radio. http://www.writersvoice.net/2007/03/podcast-marge-piercy/.

Swaim, Don. Interview. *Wired for Books*. 1984. WOUB Ohio University. http://wiredforbooks.org/margepiercy/.

Weinbaum, Batya. "Interview with Marge Piercy." *Femspec* 3(2) (2001): 101–103. http://www.margepiercy.com/interviews/kalliope.htm.

### Criticism and Readers' Guides

Armitt, Lucie. "Chronotopes and Cyborgs: Octavia Butler, Joanna Russ, Fay Weldon, and Marge Piercy." In *Contemporary Women's Fiction and the Fantastic*, 39–65. New York: St. Martin's, 2000.

Atwood, Margaret. "Marge Piercy: *Woman on the Edge of Time* and Living in the Open." In *Second Words: Selected Critical Prose*. Boston, MA: Beacon, 1984. 272–278.

Booker, M. Keith. "Woman on the Edge of a Genre: The Feminist Dystopias of Marge Piercy." *Science Fiction Studies*. 21 (1994): 337–350. http://www.depauw.edu/sfs/backissues/64/booker.htm.

Deery, June. "The Biopolitics of Cyberspace: Piercy Hacks Gibson." In Marleen S. Barr, ed., *Future Females, The Next Generation*. Lanham, MD: Rowman & Littlefield, 2000, 87–108.

Hicks, Heather. "Striking Cyborgs: Reworking the Human in Marge Piercy's *He, She and It*." In Mary Flanagan, and Austin Booth, eds., *Reload: Rethinking Women and Cyberculture*. Cambridge, MA: MIT, 2002, 85–106.

Keulen, Margarete. *Radical Imagination: Feminist Conceptions of the Future in Ursula Le Guin, Marge Piercy, and Sally Miller Gearhart.* New York: Peter Lang, 1991.

Martinson, Anna M. "Ecofeminist Perspectives on Technology in the Science Fiction of Marge Piercy." *Extrapolation.* 44 (2003): 50–68.

Morehouse, Barbara J. "Geographies of Power and Social Relations in Marge Piercy's *He, She and It.*" In Rob Kitchin and James Kneale, eds., *Lost in Space: Geographies of Science Fiction.* London: Continuum, 2002, 74–89.

Moylan, Tom. "Marge Piercy's Tale of Hope." In *Scraps of the Untainted Sky: Science Fiction Utopia Dystopia.* Boulder, CO: Westview, 2000. 247–272.

Sautter, Diane. "Erotic and Existential Paradoxes of the Golem: Marge Piercy's *He, She and It.*" *Journal of the Fantastic in the Arts.* 7(2/3) (1995): 255–268.

Shands, Kerstin W. *The Repair of the World: The Novels of Marge Piercy.* Westport, CT: Greenwood, 1994.

Shaw, Debra Benita. "Body of Glass: Marge Piercy and Sex in Cyberspace." In *Women, Science and Fiction: The Frankenstein Inheritance.* New York: Palgrave, 2001. 158–177.

### Web Sites

*Marge Piercy.com.* Official Web site. http://www.margepiercy.com/.

*Marge Piercy: Book Summaries, Chronology, Articles.* E.K. Sparks. March 2002. Clemson University. Good material on *He, She and It*, but other links are not active. http://hubcap.clemson.edu/~sparks/piercy/mpindex.html.

## Edgar Allan Poe (1809–1849)

*The great problem is at length solved! The air, as well as the earth and the ocean, has been subdued by science, and will become a common and convenient highway for mankind.*

*—"The Balloon-Hoax" (1844)*

## Biography

Today, Edgar Allan Poe is identified with horror fiction, and as the acknowledged father of the detective story. But his stories relied heavily on the science and technology of his time for their impact, and (like Mary Shelley) he made effective use of gothic conventions and contemporary angst about change and "progress."

The melodrama of Poe's life could be the plot of one of his wilder stories. Poe, the author of macabre and morbid tales of lost love and Gothic terrors, is also Poe, the drinker and gambler, who married his thirteen-year-old cousin, wandered the cities of the Eastern Seaboard in genteel literary poverty, and, at the age of forty, was discovered dying outside a bar in Baltimore. Some of this is even—almost—true. But Poe was also a thoughtful critic and literary professional who shaped attitudes to poetry and the short story in ways that endure to this day.

ANDROIDS, CYBORGS & ROBOTS; END OF THE WORLD; FANTASTIC VOYAGES; GOTHIC SF; PSYCHOLOGY; TIME TRAVEL

## Major Works

*Novels*

*The Narrative of A. Gordon Pym* (1837)

*Collections*

*The Science Fiction of Edgar Allan Poe*. Ed. Harold Beaver. London, Penguin English Library. 1976.

*Notable Short Stories*

All of the stories and essay of Edgar Allan Poe with sf themes are available on line at the Gutenberg Project: http://www.gutenberg.org/browse/authors/p#a481.
"MS Found in a Bottle" (1833)
"Hans Pfaall—A Tale" (1835)
"The Conversation of Eiros and Charmion" (1839) http://www.wondersmith.com/scifi/eiros.htm.
"The Facts in the Case of M. Valdemar" (1845)
"Some Words with a Mummy" (1845)
"Van Kempelen and his Discovery" (1849)

*Other Important Works*

"Eureka" (1848), subtitled "A Prose Poem," also subtitled as "An Essay on the Material and Spiritual Universe."
"Maelzels' Chessplayer" (1836) Essay that attempts to solve the real-life mystery of the chess-playing automaton, invented by Maelzel in 1769, which was touring the United States in the 1830s. http://www.geocities.com/Area51/Corridor/4220/maelzel.html#back2.
"Note about 'The Unparalleled Adventure of One Hans Pfaall.'" (1835, 1840). The 1840 edition included a very long note by Poe at the end.

## Research Sources

*Encyclopedias and Handbooks:* **AW, BW, ESF, MSSF, NNDB, SFW**

*Bibliographies:* **ARB, FF, SFAN**

Ehrlich, Heyward. "A Poe Webliography: Edgar Allan Poe on the Internet." *Poe Studies/Dark Romanticism*. 30 (1997): 1–26. http://andromeda.rutgers.edu/~ehrlich/poesites.html.

Ketterer, David. "The SF Element in the Work of Poe: A Chronological Survey." *Science Fiction Studies*. 1 (1974): 197–213. http://www.depauw.edu/sfs/backissues/3/ketter3bib.htm.

Pridmore, Donna J. Secondary Sources. *Literary History*. Revised March 2008. http://www.literaryhistory.com/19thC/Poe.htm. A selective bibliography of forty-three active links for Edgar Allan Poe. Not limited to science fiction themes.

## Biographies and Interviews

Kennedy, J. Gerald. *A Historical Guide to Edgar Allan Poe*. New York: Oxford University Press, 2001.

Meyers, Jeffrey. *Edgar Allan Poe: His Life and Legacy*. New York: Charles Scribner's Sons, 1992.

Quinn, Arthur Hobson. *Edgar Allan Poe: A Critical Biography*. Baltimore, MD: Johns Hopkins University Press, 1997.

Sova, Dawn B. *Edgar Allan Poe, A–Z: The Essential Reference to His Life and Work*. New York: Facts on File, 2001.

## Criticism and Readers' Guides

Burgoyne, Daniel. "Coleridge's 'Poetic Faith' and Poe's Scientific Hoax." *Romanticism on the Net*. February 2001. http://www.erudit.org/revue/ron/2001/v/n21/005960ar.html

Disch, Thomas. "Poe, Our Embarrassing Ancestor." In *The Dreams Our Stuff is Made Of*. New York: Touchstone, 1998. 32–56.

Egan, Jr., Ken. "Edgar Allan Poe and the Horror of Technology." *ESQ: A Journal of the American Renaissance*. 48 (2002): 187–208.

Franklin, H. Bruce. "Edgar Allan Poe and Science Fiction." In *Future Perfect: American Science Fiction of the Nineteenth Century*. New York: Oxford University Press, 1995. 87–95.

Grayson, Erik. "Weird Science, Weirder Unity: Phrenology and Physiognomy in Edgar Allan Poe." *Mode* 1 (2005): 56–77.

Moskowitz, Sam. "Poe's Influence on Science-Fiction." *Fantasy Commentator* 9 (1996): 24–32.

Tresch, John. "Extra! Extra! Poe Invents Science Fiction!" In Kevin J. Hayes, ed., *The Cambridge Companion to Edgar Allan Poe*. Cambridge: Cambridge University Press, 2002, 113–132.

Werner, James V. *American Flaneur: The Cosmic Physiognomy of Edgar Allan Poe*. New York: Routledge, 2004.

Westfahl, Gary. "The Jules Verne, H.G. Wells, Edgar Allan Poe Type of Story: Hugo Gernsback's History of Science Fiction." *Science Fiction Studies*. 19 (1992): 340–353.

## Web Sites

*The Edgar Allan Poe Society of Baltimore*. March 2008. Many pages of information about Poe's life and, specifically, Poe's life in Baltimore. http://www.eapoe.org/.

*Knowing Poe*. 2002. Maryland Public Television. Interactive Web site about "... the literature, life, and times of Edgar Allan Poe ... in Baltimore and beyond ... http:// knowingpoe.thinkport.org/default_flash.asp.

*PoeForward.com*. Brian Aldrich et al. March 2007. Very striking Web site "... dedicated to showcasing the work of artists who have been influenced by the mind and work of Edgar Allan Poe." Wide range of interesting material. http://poeblog.poeforward.com/?cat=42.

*The Poe Page*. M. Cullum. July 2002. Full text of various poems and stories. Some links to poems do not work, but most of the fiction links do. http://www.geocities. com/Area51/Corridor/4220/poe.html.

*Poe Studies Association*. Department of English. February 2008. Washington State University. Link to archive of newsletter, and other items of interest. http://www2. lv.psu.edu/PSA/.

# Frederik Pohl (1919–  )

> *There is no greater dark than the dark between the stars.*
> *—Heechee Rendezvous (1984)*

## Biography

Frederik George Pohl, Jr. was born in Brooklyn, New York. In high school, he met, and formed a lifelong friendship with Isaac Asimov and through him became a member of the "Futurians." Pohl served as editor of *Galaxy* and *If* magazines, and science fiction editor for Bantam Books. In these capacities, he has been able to encourage and publish a number of great sf writers.

Over a sixty-five-year career, Pohl has produced hundreds of books and stories. In the 1950s and 1960s he wrote ironic tales, such as *The Space Merchants* (1953, with Cyril Kornbluth), a dystopian satire of a world ruled by the advertising agencies. Currently, Frederik Pohl is in great demand as a public speaker, on science fiction and on his favorite causes and issues, such as the Democratic Party and world peace. He lives in the suburbs of Chicago with his wife, science fiction editor and scholar Dr. Elizabeth Anne Hull.

ALIENS; CITIES & SOCIETIES; COLONIZATION OF OTHER WORLDS; FANTASTIC VOYAGES; HUMOR AND SATIRE; POP CULTURE & MEDIA

## Major Works

*Novels*

*The Space Merchants* (1953, with C.M. Kornbluth)
*Search the Sky* (1954, with C.M. Kornbluth)
Undersea Eden trilogy (with Jack Williamson)—*Undersea Quest* (1954), *Undersea Fleet* (1955), *Undersea City* (1958)

*Gladiator at Law* (1955, with C.M. Kornbluth)
*Wolfbane* (1957, with C.M. Kornbluth)
Starchild trilogy (with Jack Williamson)—*The Reefs of Space* (1964), *Starchild* (1965),
   *Rogue Star* (1969)
*Man Plus* (1976, with Jack Williamson) Nebula
The Heechee series (with Jack Williamson): *Gateway* (1977—**Hugo, Locus Poll,**
   **Nebula**), *Beyond the Blue Event Horizon* (1980), *Heechee Rendezvous* (1984),
   *The Annals of the Heechee* (1987), *The Boy Who Would Live Forever: A Novel of*
   *Gateway* (2004)
*JEM: The Making of a Utopia* (1979)
*The Cool War* (1981)
*Black Star Rising* (1985)
*Outnumbering the Dead* (1991)
*O Pioneer!* (1998)


## Collections

*Our Best: The Best of Frederik Pohl and C. M. Kornbluth.* Riverdale, NY: Baen, 1987.
*Platinum Pohl.* New York: Orb, 2007. A selection which includes some of Pohl's best
   stories, such as "Servant of the People" (1983), "The Greening of Bed-Stuy"
   (1984), "Fermi and Frost" (1985—**Hugo**), and "The Day the Martians Came"
   (1988).


## Notable Short Stories

"The Gold At Starbow's End" (1972) **Locus Poll**
"The Meeting" (1972) **Hugo** A story which was written with C.M. Kornbluth in the
   1950s, but not published until twenty years after Kornbluth's death.
"Stopping at Slowyear" (1992)


## Other Important Works

"Creating Tomorrow Today: SF's Special Effects Wizards." In Danny Peary, ed.,
   *Omni's Screen Flights/Screen Fantasies: The Future According to Science Fiction*
   *Cinema.* Garden City, NY: Doubleday, 1984, 214–223.
"Edgar Rice Burroughs and the Development of Science Fiction." *Burroughs Bulletin*
   April 1992: 8–14.
"The Politics of Prophecy." In *Political Science Fiction*, 7–17. Columbia: University
   of South Carolina Press, 1997.
*Science Fiction in the Classroom.* With Elizabeth A. Hull. Video cassette. Plamer R.
   Chitester Fund/Idea Channel, 2000.
"Science Fiction: Stepchild of Science." *Technology Review* 97(7) (1994): 57–61.
"The Science Fiction Professional." *The Craft of Science Fiction.* edited by Reginald
   Bretnor. New York: Harper & Row, 1976, 292–311.

"The Study of Science Fiction: A Modest Proposal." *Science Fiction Studies.* 24 (1997): 11–16.
*The Way the Future Was: A Memoir.* New York: Ballantine, 1979.

## Research Sources

*Encyclopedias and Handbooks:* **AW, CA, CANR, ESF, MSSF, NNDB, SFW**

*Bibliographies:* **ARB, FF, SFAN**

Stephensen-Payne, Phil and Gordon R. Benson, Jr. *Fredrik Pohl: Merchant of Excellence, A Working Bibliography.* Albuquerque, NM: Galactic Central, 1989.

### Biographies and Interviews

Hull, Elizabeth Anne. "The Sharing of Worlds: A Dialogue." *Extrapolation* 30 (1989): 339–349.
Jenkins, Henry. James Patrick Kelly/Frederik Pohl in Discussion at MIT: September 18, 1997. (Edited version) *Media in Transition.* August 29, 1998. Massachusetts Institute of Technology. http://web.mit.edu/m-i-t/science_fiction/transcripts/pohl_kelly_index.html.
*Locus Online.* "Chasing Science." October 2000. http://www.locusmag.com/2000/Issues/10/Pohl.html.
McCarty, Michael. "How the Future Was." *Sci fi.com.* November 26, 2001. http://www.scifi.com/sfw/issue240/interview.html.
Wilson, Connie C. and Michael McCarty. "Frederik Pohl is Both the Boy Who Will Live Forever and the Man Who Sees Tomorrow." *Science Fiction Weekly.* May 29, 2006. http://www.scifi.com/sfw/interviews/sfw12818.html.

### Criticism and Readers' Guides

Clareson, Thomas. *Frederik Pohl.* Mercer Island, WA: Starmont, 1987.
Dunn, Thomas P. "Theme and Narrative Structure in Ursula K. Le Guin's *The Dispossessed* and Frederik Pohl's *Gateway.*" In Michael Collings, ed., *Reflections on the Fantastic.* Westport, CT: Greenwood, 1986, 87–96.
Hassler, Donald M. "Swift, Pohl, and Kornbluth: Publicists Anatomize Newness." In Donald M. Hassler and Clyde Wilcox, eds., *Political Science Fiction.* Columbia: University of South Carolina Press, 1997, 18–25.
McClintock, Michael. "The Problem of *Stopping at Slowyear.*" *Extrapolation* 38 (1997): 304–317.
Webster, Bud. "Anthropology 101: The Pohl Star." *New York Review of Science Fiction.* 14(5) (2002): 11+.

*Web Sites*

*Frederik Pohl.com.* Official Web site. http://www.frederikpohl.com/.
*Frederik Pohl Papers.* Syracuse University. Correspondence (1934–1968); manuscripts
   by Pohl and others (1947–1965); legal and financial papers (1917–1964); and
   published material. http://library.syr.edu/digital/guides/p/pohl_f.htm.

# Kim Stanley Robinson (1952–   )

> *We all want different things from Mars.*
>
> —*Red Mars (1992)*

## Biography

Kim Stanley Robinson was born in Waukegan, Illinois, and grew up in Southern
California. He was educated at University of California, San Diego, and at Boston
University; his doctoral thesis was published as *The Novels of Philip K. Dick.* A
recurring theme in all of his novels, however different they might seem on the
surface, is the struggle to survive in a hostile, alien environment—whether that
environment is the virgin canvas of the planet Mars, or the polluted biosphere of
the planet Earth.

Robinson was the first science fiction writer to win a National Science Foundation grant to study Antarctica, in preparation for his 1997 book of the same name;
he likens Antarctica to the environment that future pioneers will find on other
planets, and the experience of living and working there has deeply influenced his
fiction. He currently lives in Davis, California.

ALTERNATIVE HISTORY; ECOLOGY; MARS, MOON & THE PLANETS;
NEAR FUTURE; POLITICAL SF; SUSTAINABLE ALTERNATIVES

## Major Works

*Novels*

*Icehenge* (1984)
The Orange County Trilogy, the Three Californias: *The Wild Shore* (1984—**Locus
   Poll**); *The Gold Coast* (1988); *Pacific Edge* (1990)
*The Memory of Whiteness* (1985)
*A Short, Sharp Shock* (1990) **Locus Poll**
The Mars trilogy: *Red Mars* (1992—**BSF, Nebula**); *Green Mars* (1993—**Hugo, Locus
   Poll**); *Blue Mars* (1995—**Hugo, Locus Poll**)
*Antarctica* (1997)
*The Years of Rice and Salt* (2002) **Locus Poll**
   Excerpt: http://www.booksense.com/chapters/.

The Science in the Capital series: *Forty Signs of Rain* (2004); *Fifty Degrees Below* (2005); *Sixty Days and Counting* (2007).

## Collections

*The Martians*. New York: Spectra, 1999. **Locus Poll**. Includes supplementary material relating to the Mars Trilogy, such as the early novella "Green Mars" (1985), "Sexual Dimorphism," "A Martian Romance," and "Arthur Sternbach Brings the Curveball to Mars" (1999).
*Vinland the Dream and Other Stories*. New York: Voyager, 2002.
Earlier collections include *The Planet on the Table* (1986), *Escape from Kathmandu* (1989), and *Remaking History and Other Stories* (1994).

## Notable Short Stories

"The Blind Geometer" (1986) **Nebula**
"Before I Wake" (1989)
"Zurich" (1990)
"A History of the Twentieth Century, with Illustrations" (1991) http://www.infinityplus. co.uk/stories/history.htm
"A Martian Childhood" (1994)

## Other Important Works

"Cities in the Overshoot." *Para*doxa*. 2 (1996): 44–45.
*The Novels of Philip K. Dick*. Ann Arbor, MI: UMI Research, 1984.
"Pentalude: Science Fiction as Fantasy." In Milton T. Wolf, and Daryl F. Mallett, eds., *Imaginative Futures*. San Bernardino, CA: Borgo, 1995, 353–356.
"The Psychic Landscape." In Robin Wilson, ed., *Paragons: Twelve Master Science Fiction Writers Ply Their Craft*. New York: St. Martin's, 1996, 164–168.
"Review: Science in the Third Millennium." In Marleen S. Barr, ed., *Envisioning the Future: Science Fiction and the Next Millennium*. Middletown, CT: Wesleyan University. Press, 2003, 199–201.

# Research Sources

*Encyclopedias and Handbooks:* **AW, CA, CANR, ESF, SFW**

*Bibliographies:* **ARB, FF, SFAN**

Stephens, Christopher P. and Tom Joyce. *A Checklist of Kim Stanley Robinson*. Revised edition. Hastings-on-Hudson, NY: Ultramarine, 1991.

## Biographies and Interviews

Adams, John Joseph. Interview. *Science Fiction Weekly*. March 2007. http://www.scifi. com/sfw/interviews/sfw15203.html.

Crown, Sarah. "Future Tense." *Guardian Online.* September 14, 2005. http://books. guardian.co.uk/departments/sciencefiction/story/0,1569830,00.html.

Gunn, Moira. "Tech Nation: Audio Interview." *ITConversations.* January 2006. GigaVox Media Channel. http://www.itconversations.com/shows/detail935.html.

Interview. *Imagine Mars Project.* April 2002. The Planetary Society. http://mmp. planetary.org/artis/robik/robik70.htm.

James, Warren W. "Interview: Kim Stanley Robinson." *Mike Hodel's Hour 25: Science Fiction Radio for Southern California.* June 2001. http://www. hour25online.com/.

Lawrie, Duncan. "This is Year One: Kim Stanley Robinson." *Zone-sf.com.* November 2005. Pigasus Press. http://www.zone-sf.com/ksrobinson.html.

*New Mars.com.* "Interview: Like Nothing Else the World Has Seen." August 1999. Mars Society. http://www.newmars.com/archives/000013.shtml.

Rohn, Jennifer. Interview. *Lablit: The Culture of Science in Fiction & Fact.* February 4, 2007. http://www.lablit.com/article/208/.

Snider, John C. *SciFi Dimensions* Podcast. (Interview). April 2008. http://www. scifidimensions.com/podcast/2008/04/15/the-scifidimensions-podcast-5/.

*Space.com.* Interview. June 28, 2000. Imaginova Corp. http://www.space.com/ sciencefiction/kim_stanley_robinson_interview_000626.html.

## Criticism and Readers' Guides

Abbott, Carl. "Falling Into History: The Imagined Wests of Kim Stanley Robinson in the *Three Californias* and *Mars* Trilogy." *Western Historical Quarterly.* 34 (2003): 27–47.

Buhle, Paul. "Kim Stanley Robinson, Science Fiction Socialist." *Monthly Review: An Independent Socialist Magazine.* 54(3) (2002): 87–90.

Dynes, William. "Multiple Perspectives in Kim Stanley Robinson's *Mars* Series." *Extrapolation.* 42 (2001): 150–164.

Jameson, Frederic. "'If I can find one good city, I will spare the man:' Realism and Utopia in Kim Stanley Robinson's *Mars* Trilogy." In *Archaeologies of the Future.* New York: Verso, 2005. 393–416.

Moylan, Thomas P. "Utopia Is When Our Lives Matter: Reading Kim Stanley Robinson's *Pacific Edge.*" *Utopian Studies.* 6(2) (1995): 1–25.

Moylan, Tom. "Kim Stanley Robinson's Other California." In *Scraps of the Untainted Sky: Science Fiction Utopia Dystopia.* Boulder, CO: Westview, 2000. 203–222.

Stratton, Susan. "The Messiah and the Greens: The Shape of Environmental Action in *Dune* and *Pacific Edge.*" *Extrapolation.* 42 (2001): 303–316.

Swidorski, Carl. "Kim Stanley Robinson's Martian Vision." In Martha Bartter, ed., *The Utopian Fantastic.* Westport, CT: Praeger, 2004, 43–56.

## Web Sites

*Kim Stanley Robinson.net.* Official Web site. http://www.kimstanleyrobinson. net/.

*The Kim Stanley Robinson Encyclopedia.* April 2007. The Demimonde. Wiki-based encyclopedia dedicated to the works of Robinson. http://ksrwiki. philosophicalzombie.net/wiki/The_Kim_Stanley_Robinson_Encyclopedia.

*The Red, Green and Blue MarsSite.* Frans Blok. November 2002. Gorgeous virtual realization, by an "armchair terraformer," of the changes described in the mars series—maps of what Mars will look like as the series progresses. http://www. xs4all.nl/~fwb/rgbmars.html.

## If you enjoyed Kim Stanley Robinson...

Kim Stanley Robinson is a novelist of place: Antarctica, Mars, and post-apocalypse United States are all landscapes that he has shaped for his own devices. In his "Mars Trilogy," Robinson shows us how people shape Mars over a two hundred years period, and traces the social, political, and even philosophical impact of the choices that they make—on Mars, and on themselves.

## Then you might like...

*John Brunner.* Beginning with *Stand on Zanzibar* (1968), combined style and substance in four dystopian novels that depict futures rendered unlivable by scourges such as overpopulation and pollution. Some of Brunner's speculations, particularly about the Internet in *The Shockwave Rider* (1975), have a chilling ring of truth.

*Frank Herbert. Dune's* desert planet Arrakis is fully realized; the struggles and triumphs of the Messianic character, Paul Atriedes, and his dynasty cannot be disentangled from their landscape and Herbert's message—respect for the ecology and a plea for a sustainable lifestyle.

*Geoff Ryman.* Many of Ryman's stories consider the impact of change on fragile cultures and individuals. As a gay writer, he describes future threats and the possible horrors of progress in such a way that they echo gay concerns. But Ryman's stories cannot be "ring-fenced" (and ignored) by the population at large—his futures are ones that we all have to fear.

*Pamela Sargent.* Like Robinson's "Mars Trilogy," Sargent's "Venus" novels play out the personal dramas of real men and women against the background of the terraforming of Venus. In the Afterword to *Venus of Shadows*, Sargent says that science fiction should be " . . . as demanding in its depictions of characters and attention to literary values as it is with ideas . . . ."

*Peter Watts.* In the near future of the "Rifters Trilogy," the search for energy has led to the tapping of geothermal sources deep in the ocean. The series threatens (and delivers) earthquakes, tidal waves, and archaic monsters from the depths, unleashed by natural processes that the corporate elite exploit without understanding.

# Justina Robson (1968–   )

*Crouched obediently at the gate, like a giant cross between a crab and a
dog... engines cased in violet metal, connectors studded like warts over its
rhino-like surface. Blast damage and the streaks of old burn marks scored it.
The Heavy Angel Sisyphus Bright Angel was brutal and hideous to see.*

*—Natural History (2004)*

## Biography

In her debut novel, *Silver Screen*, one of the characters asks "Where does the life
end and the machine begin?" Justina Robson rings the changes on this question
in each of her intelligent, deeply thought-out novels. In *Silver Screen* and *Mappa
Mundi* (2001), the interface between life and machine is a computer link; in
*Natural History* (2004), genetic engineering has created human/machine hybrids
to do the dirty jobs in the universe.

Justina Louise Alice Robson was born in Leeds, in the North of England, and
studied philosophy and linguistics at the University of York. Before becoming a
full-time writer she worked as a secretary, technical writer, and yoga instructor.
She lives in Leeds with her partner and her young son.

ARTIFICIAL INTELLIGENCE; FANTASY; GENETICS & CLONING; NAN-
OTECHNOLOGY; POST-HUMAN

## Major Works

*Novels*

*Silver Screen* (1999)
*Mappa Mundi* (2001)
The Natural History novels: *Natural History* (2004), *Living Next Door to the God of
    Love* (2005)
Quantum Gravity novels: *Keeping It Real* (2006), *Selling Out* (2007)

*Notable Short Stories*

"Trésor" (1994)
"The Girl Hero's Mirror Says He's Not the One" (2007)

*Other Important Works*

"The American Planet: Kim Stanley Robinson's Martian Melting Pot." *Nova Express.*
    (Winter/Spring) 1998.

"Frelling Fantastic!" In Glenn Yeffeth, ed., *Farscape Forever! Sex, Drugs and Killer Muppets*, Smart Pop Series. Dallas, TX: BenBella, 2005, 1–14.

## Research Sources

*Encyclopedias and Handbooks:* **AW, CA**

*Bibliographies:* **FF, SFAN**

### Biographies and Interviews

Carter, Stuart. "23 Entirely Serious Questions." *Infinity Plus.* 2005. http://www.infinityplus.co.uk/nonfiction/intjr.htm.
*Locus Online.* "The Tao of SF." April 2006. http://www.locusmag.com/2006/Issues/04Robson.html.
Morgan, Cheryl. Interview. *Strange Horizons.* April 2003. http://www.strangehorizons.com/2003/20030421/robson.shtml.
Scalzi, John. "Femme Fatale Kung Fu Master." *Ficlets.* July 5, 2007. http://ficlets.com/blog/category/interviews.

### Criticism and Readers' Guides

Harrison, M. John. "Meat vs. Machine." *Guardian Online. June* 7, 2003. http://books.guardian.co.uk/reviews/sciencefiction/0,6121,971853,00.html.
Jones, Gwyneth. "High Jinks." *Guardian Online.* November 19, 2005. http://books.guardian.co.uk/review/story/0,1644978,00.html.
Mitchell, Kaye. "Bodies That Matter: Science Fiction, Technoculture, and the Gendered Body." *Science Fiction Studies.* 33 (2006): 109–128.

### Web Sites

*Justina Robson.com.* Official Web site www.justinarobson.com.

# Joanna Russ (1937–   )

> *For years I have been saying* Let me in, Love me, Approve me, Define me, Regulate me, Validate me, Support me. *Now I say* Move over.
> —*The Female Man (1975)*

## Biography

Joanna Russ is respected as a writer in the vanguard of feminist sf, as a critic and scholar, and as a sharp observer of the trends and assumptions in which science fiction—or writing of any kind—is created. Her work in the late 1970s brought issues of gender and sexuality to center stage. At WisCon, in May 2006, Samuel

Delany said of her that "[f]eminism works for Joanna Russ the way Marxism works for the great German writer Bertolt Brecht. It is something innate to the concerns, not something that can be dismissed."

Joanna Ruth Russ grew up in the Bronx, New York. She attended Cornell University, and received an MFA in Drama from Yale. Since then, she has taught at Cornell, SUNY at Binghamton, and the University of Washington. In recent years, her writing has been curtailed by chronic fatigue syndrome. She currently lives in Tucson, Arizona.

COLONIZATION OF OTHER WORLDS; GENDER & SEXUALITY; MYTHOLOGY & LEGEND; PSI POWERS; WOMEN IN SF

## Major Works

*Novels*

*Picnic on Paradise* (1968)
*And Chaos Died* (1970)
*The Female Man* (1975)
*We Who Are About To* (1977)
*The Two of Them* (1978)

*Collections*

Russ' short fiction is available in collections such as *The Adventures of Alyx* (1978), *The Zanzibar Cat* (1983), *(Extra)ordinary People* (1984), and *The Hidden Side of the Moon* (1987).

*Short Stories*

"When It Changed" (1972) **Nebula**
"The Mystery of the Young Gentleman" (1982)
"Souls" (1983) **Hugo, Locus Poll**

*Other Important Works*

"*A Boy and His Dog:* The Final Solution." *Frontiers: A Journal of Women's Studies* 1:1 (1975). http://www.ejumpcut.org/archive/.
*The Country You Have Never Seen: Essays and Reviews*. Liverpool, UK: Liverpool University Press, 2005. A collection that includes major essays such as "The Image of Women in Science Fiction" (1970), "Alien Monsters" (1977), "The Wearing Out of Genre Materials" (1971), and "Daydream Literature and Science Fiction" (1969).

*How to Suppress Women's Writing* (1983)

*Magic Mommas, Trembling Sisters, Puritans, and Perverts: Essays on Sex and Pornography* (1985)

"On Setting" In Robin Scott Wilson, ed., *Those Who Can: A Science Fiction Reader.* (1973) Reprint, New York: St. Martin's, 1996, 149–154.

"Recent Feminist Utopias." In Marleen S. Barr, ed., *Future Females: A Critical Anthology.* Bowling Green, OH: University Popular Press, 1981, 71–85.

"SF and Technology as Mystification." *Science Fiction Studies* 5 (1976): 250–260. http://www.depauw.edu/sfs/backissues/16/russ16.htm.

*To Write Like a Woman: Essays in Feminism and Science Fiction.* (1995) A collection that includes "*Amor Vincit Foeminam*, The Battle of the Sexes in SF." (1980), "On Mary Wollstonecraft Shelley" (1975), "What Can a Heroine Do? Or Why Women Can't Write" (1970)

"Towards an Aesthetic of Science Fiction." *Science Fiction Studies* 2 (1975): 112–119. http://www.depauw.edu/sfs/backissues/6/russ6art.htm.

## Research Sources

*Encyclopedias and Handbooks:* **AW, BW, CA, CANR, ESF, MSSF, NNDB, SFW**

*Bibliographies:* **ARB, FF, SFAN**

### Biographies and Interviews

Delany, Samuel. Interview. *Broad Universe.* 2007. http://www.broaduniverse.org/broadsheet/0702jrsrd.html.

Johnson, Charles. "A Dialogue: Samuel Delany and Joanna Russ on Science Fiction." *Callaloo: A Journal of African American and African Arts and Letters* 7(3) (1984): 27–35.

McCaffery, Larry. Interview. In *Across the Wounded Galaxies.* Urbana: University of Illinois Press, 1990. 176-210.

Perry, Donna. "Joanna Russ." In *Backtalk: Women Writers Speak Out.* New Brunswick, NJ: Rutgers University. Press, 1993. 287-311.

Willmer, J. Caissa. "Joanna Russ (1937–   )." *Contemporary Lesbian Writers of the United States: A Bio-Bibliographical Critical Sourcebook,* edited by Sandra Pollack and Denise D. Knight. Westport, CT: Greenwood, 1993, 481–489.

### Criticism and Readers' Guides

Ayres, Susan. "The 'Straight Mind' in Russ's *The Female Man.*" *Science Fiction Studies.* 22 (1995): 22–34. http://www.depauw.edu/sfs/backissues/65/ayres65art.htm.

Boulter, Amanda. "Unnatural Acts: American Feminism and Joanna Russ's *The Female Man.*" *Women: A Cultural Review* 10 (1999): 151–166.

Cortiel, Jeanne. *Demand My Writing: Joanna Russ, Feminism, Science Fiction.* Liverpool, UK: Liverpool University Press, 1999.

Delaney, Samuel R. "Orders of Chaos: The Science Fiction of Joanna Russ." In Jane Branham Weedman ed., *Women Worldwalkers: New Dimensions of Science Fiction and Fantasy.* Lubbock, TX: Texas Tech, 1985, 195–124.

Ferreira, Maria Aline Salgueiro Seabra. "Cloning and Biopower: Joanna Russ and Fay Weldon." In *I Am the Other: Literary Negotiations of Human Cloning*, 191–212. Westport, CT: Praeger, 2005.

Freedman, Carl. "*The Two of Them*: Joanna Russ and the Violence of Gender." In *Critical Theory and Science Fiction.* Hanover, NH: University Press of New England/Wesleyan University Press, 2000. 129–145.

Martins, Susana S. "Revising the Future in *The Female Man*." *Science Fiction Studies.* 32 (2005): 405–422.

Murphy, Patrick D. "The Left Hand of the Pilgrim: Joanna Russ's Contributions to Criticism." *New York Review of Science Fiction.* 2(6) (1990): 1+.

———. "Suicide, Murder, Culture, and Catastrophe: Joanna Russ's *We Who Are About To . . .* " In Nicholas Ruddick, ed., *State of the Fantastic: Studies in the Theory and Practice of Fantastic Literature and Film.* Westport, CT: Greenwood, 1992, 121–132.

Teslenko, Tatiana. *Feminist Utopian Novels of the 1970s: Joanna Russ & Dorothy Bryant.* New York: Routledge, 2003.

## Web Sites

*Guide to the Joanna Russ Papers.* University of Oregon Libraries. Correspondence and literary manuscripts. http://nwda-db.wsulibs.wsu.edu/findaid/ark:/80444/xv52000.

**If you enjoyed Joanna Russ . . .**
In 2006, Samuel Delany spoke of Joanna Russ' " . . . range and intensity of concern for the problems of women" (*WisCon 30 Interview*). In the 1960s, Russ wrote space opera with strong female characters; in the 1970s, her novels like *The Female Man* (1975) and stories like "We Who Are About To . . . " (1977) brought the issues of gender and sexuality to center stage.

**Then you might like . . .**
*Samuel R. Delany.* Novels such as *Babel-17, Triton: An Ambiguous Heterotopia*, and *Dhalgren* are potent blends of the conventions of space opera, and high philosophy, mythology, and language. Identity itself is often fluid in a Delany story: in a universe where one can change one's physical appearance, gender, and sexual orientation at will, what can you trust?

*Candas Jane Dorsey.* In *Black Wine* (1997) Dorsey weaves together the stories of five women of the same family to create a complex and human story about freedom, love, and the need to retain one's own identity. More recently, *A Paradigm of Earth* (2002), is a strong, character-driven tale that focuses on self-discovery.

*Nicola Griffith.* Like Russ, Griffith writes perceptively about how people interact, evolve and adapt to new circumstances. In *Ammonite* (1993), a human colony world where the men were wiped out by a virus is observed through the eyes of a female anthropologist. In *Slow River* (1995), the heiress of a wealthy and powerful biotech family must face her demons to survive.

***Naomi Mitchison***. The author of over 100 books, many of which used elements of fantasy and some mild elements of sf, to make political and satirical points. However, her *Memoirs of a Spacewoman* (1962), the story of a woman who becomes an intergalactic explorer and communicator with alien species, is a classic proto-feminist work.

***Marge Piercy***. All of Piercy's work—poetry, fiction and criticism—shares a focus on feminist and social concerns. *Woman on the Edge of Time* (1976) is a classic of feminist sf; *He, She and It* (1991) uses elements of Jewish mysticism, particularly the legend of the Golem, to depict a feminist response to a world ruined by corporate greed.

# *Geoff Ryman (1951–   )*

> Mae lived in the last village in the world to go on online. After that, everyone else went on Air.
>
> —*Air (2004)*

## Biography

Geoff Ryman's fiction considers the impact of change on societies and individuals—on the poor and disenfranchised, or on those who refuse to conform and are easily identified as nonconformist. Ryman is an informal spokesman of "Mundane sf," which challenges the genre to write about the future that is likely to happen, rather than galactic empires and faster-than-light drives.

Geoffrey Charles Ryman was born in Canada, near Toronto. His family moved to Los Angeles when he was eleven years old. In 1973, shortly after graduating from the UCLA, he moved to England, where he has lived ever since. Ryman worked for the Central Office of Information in London, in charge of the design of the official Web sites of the British Monarchy and 10 Downing Street. He is currently a member of the creative writing faculty of the Centre for New Writing at the University of Manchester, and has started a writing workshop in Cambodia.

GENDER & SEXUALITY; SUSTAINABLE ALTERNATIVES; MYTHOLOGY & LEGEND; NEAR FUTURE; POLITICAL SF; TECHNOLOGY

## Major Works

*Novels*

*The Warrior Who Carried Life* (1980)
*The Child Garden* (1989)

*Was* (1992)

*253—a Novel for the Internet about London Underground in Seven Cars and a Crash.*
October 8, 1997. www.ryman-novel.com. This interactive "Internet novel" was
issued in more traditional format in 1998 as *253: The Print Remix.*

*Lust: Or, No Harm Done* (2003)

*Air: Or, Have Not Have* (2004) **BSF, Tiptree**

*The King's Last Song* (2005)

## Collections

*Unconquered Countries: Four Novellas.* Introduction by Samuel R. Delany. New York:
St. Martin's, 1994. The novellas include **BSF** award winner *The Unconquered
Country* (1984).

## Notable Short Stories

"Love Sickness" (1987) **BSF**

"Pol Pot's Beautiful Daughter" (2006) http://www.sfsite.com/fsf/fiction/gr01.htm.

## Other Important Works

BORÉAL 2007 Guest of Honor Speech. Montreal April 29, 2007. Mundane.sf.
September 16, 2007. http://mundane-sf.blogspot.com/2007/09/take-third-star-
on-left-and-on-til.html.

*The Transmigration of Timothy Archer.* Stage play. Based on novel by Philip K. Dick—
winner of 1984 British Science Fiction Award for Dramatic Presentation.

"The World on a Train." *BBC News.* British Broadcasting Corporation. 9 August 9,
2005. http://news.BBC.co.uk/2/hi/uk_news/magazine/4132482.stm.

"Writing after the Slaughter: Geoff Ryman on Cambodian Writers." *Guardian Online.*April 8, 2006. http://books.guardian.co.uk/review/story/0,1749101,00.html.

# Research Sources

*Encyclopedias and Handbooks:* **AW, CA, CANR, ESF, SFW**

*Bibliographies:* **ARB, FF, SFAN**

## Biographies and Interviews

*Chronicles Network.* "Geoff Ryman Interview, in Four Parts." June 2006. http://www.
chronicles-network.com/forum/11294-geoff-ryman-interview-in-four-
parts.html.

*Copydesk.* "200 Words with Geoff Ryman." August 11, 2001. http://www.copydesk.
co.uk/200/ryman.shtml.

Grossman, Wendy. "Underground Fiction." *Salon.* March 20, 1997. http://archive.
salon.com/march97/21st/london970320.html.

*Locus Online.* "Geoff Ryman: The Mundane Fantastic." January 2006. http://www.
locusmag.com/2006/Issues/01Ryman.html.

Reed, Kit. Interview. *Infinity Plus.* August 2004. http://www.infinityplus.co.uk/nonfiction/intgr.htm.

### Criticism and Readers' Guides

Canaan, Howard. "The Pressures of History and Fiction in Geoff Ryman's *Was.*" *Journal of the Fantastic in the Arts*, 13 (2003): 218–225.

Cheney, Matthew. "Pol Pot's Fantasized Daughter." *Strange Horizons.* August 13, 2007. http://www.strangehorizons.com/2007/20070813/cheney-c.shtml.

Colombino, Laura. "Negotiations with the System: J.G. Ballard and Geoff Ryman Writing London's Architecture." *Textual Practice.* 20 (2006): 615–635.

Flynn, Richard. "Imitation Oz: The Sequel as Commodity." *The Lion and the Unicorn*, 20 (1996): 121–131.

Hantke, Steffen. "'There's No Place Like Home': Geoff Ryman's *Was* and Turner's Myth of National Childhood." *49th Parallel: An Interdisciplinary Journal of North American Studies.* 4 (2000). http://www.49thparallel.bham.ac.uk/back/issue4/hantke.htm.

# Pamela Sargent (1948–   )

> How strange, I think objectively, that our lives are such that discomfort, pain, sadness and hatred are so easily conveyed and so frequently felt.
> *—"Gather Blue Roses" (1971)*

## Biography

Pamela Sargent was born in Ithaca, New York. Reading science fiction offered her an escape from difficult family circumstances, particularly a time as a teenager when she was briefly institutionalized. She eventually acquired an MA in classical philosophy from the State University of New York (SUNY) at Binghamton, New York.

Sargent's first important impact on science fiction was in the role of editor, when she persuaded a publisher to produce a volume of sf by women, about women. *Women of Wonder* (1975) established Sargent's credentials as a serious critic and advocate of feminist sf. In her own fiction, the personal dramas of real men and women are played out against the background of big ideas.

Pamela Sargent lives near Albany, in upstate New York, with her partner, the sf author George Zebrowski. Together, they have collaborated on several novels in the Star Trek Universe. She lectures on science fiction, historical fiction, and science fiction by women at high schools, colleges, all over the world.

CHILDREN IN SF; COLONIZATION OF OTHER WORLDS; GENETICS & CLONING; MARS, MOON & THE PLANETS; WOMEN IN SF

# Major Works

## Novels

*Cloned Lives* (1976)
*Sudden Star* (1979)
The Watchstar Trilogy: *Watchstar* (1980), *Eye of the Comet* (1984), *Homesmind* (1984)
*The Golden Space* (1982)
*The Alien Upstairs* (1983)
Seed Trilogy (in progress): *Earthseed* (1983) and *Farseed* (2007)
*The Shore of Women*. (1986)
The Venus Trilogy: *Venus of Dreams* (1986), *Venus of Shadows* (1988), *Child of Venus*(2001)
*Alien Child* (1988)
Star Trek: The Next Generation: *A Fury Scorned* (1996, with George Zebrowski)
Classic Star Trek: *Heart of the Sun* (1997), *Across the Universe* (1999), and *Garth of Izar* (2003)

## Collections

*The Best of Pamela Sargent*. Ed. Martin H. Greenberg. Chicago, IL: Academy, 1987.
*The Mountain Cage and Other Stories*. Decatur, GA: Meisha Merlin, 2002.
*Thumbprints*. Intro. James Morrow. Urbana, IL: Golden Gryphon, 2004.

## Short Stories

"Gather Blue Roses" (1972)
"Danny Goes to Mars" (1992) **Nebula, Locus Poll**

## Other Important Works

Guest of Honor Speech. Wiscon. March 2, 1991.http://www.wiscon.info/downloads/sargent.pdf.
"The Historical Novelist and History." *Para*doxa*. 1 (1995) 363–374.
Introduction. *Women of Wonder: Science Fiction Stories by Women about Women*. Ed. Pamela Sargent. New York, Vintage Books, 1975.
"Jewish Enough" *Femspec*. 4(2) (2004): 83–89.
"The Martians Among Us." In Glenn Yeffeth, ed., *The War of the Worlds: Fresh Perspectives on the H.G. Wells Classic*. Dallas, TX: BenBella, 2005, 173–180.
"A SciFi Case History." *Science Fiction Studies*. July 1997. http://www.depauw.edu/sfs/review_essays/sargent7.htm.
"The Writer as Nomad." In Maxim Jakubowski and Edward James, eds., *The Profession of Science Fiction: SF Writers on Their Craft and Ideas*. New York: St. Martin's, 1992, 111–119.
"Women in Science Fiction." In *Women of Wonder: The Contemporary Years*. San Diego, CA: Harcourt Brace, 1995.

## Research Sources

*Encyclopedias and Handbooks:* **AW, CA, CANR, ESF, MSSF, SFW**

*Bibliographies:* **ARB, FF, SFAN**

Elliot, Jeffrey M. and Boden Clarke. *The Work of Pamela Sargent: An Annotated Bibliography & Literary Guide.* 2nd ed. San Bernardino, CA: Borgo, 1996.

Engel-Cox, Jill, ed. Bibliography. Pamela Sargent Official Web site. September 2005. http://www.engel-cox.org/sargent/bibliog.htm.

### Biographies and Interviews

Engel, Jill. "Letters from Upstate New York: A Correspondence with Pamela Sargent." *Nova Express.* Winter 1991. http://www.engel-cox.org/sargent/intrview.htm.

———. "Pamela Sargent: The Millennium Interview." December 2000–April 2001. http://www.engel-cox.org/sargent/interview2001.htm.

Melloy, Kilian. "Woman of Wonder: Pamela Sargent Has Left Her Thumbprints Across the Face of Modern SF." *Science Fiction Weekly.* November 8, 2004. http://www.scifi.com/sfw/interviews/sfw11615.html.

Wilson, Alyce. Interview. *Wild Violet.* Winter 2005. http://www.wildviolet.net/heavenhell/pamela_sargent.html.

### Criticism and Readers' Guides

Bishop, Michael. "Saluting Pamela Sargent." In Martin H. Greenberg, ed., *The Best of Pamela Sargent.* Chicago, IL: Academy Chicago, 1987.

Hassler, Donald M. "Ambivalences in the Venus of Pamela Sargent." *Extrapolation.* 38 (1997): 150–156.

Morrissey, Thomas J. "Pamela Sargent's SF for Young Adults: Celebrations of Change." *Science Fiction Studies.* 16 (1989): 184–190.

Reid, Suzanne Elizabeth. "Feminism and Science Fiction: Pamela Sargent." In *Presenting Young Adult Science Fiction.* New York: Twayne, 1998. 101–119.

### Web Sites

*Pamela Sargent.* Author's blog and details about her publications. http://www.engel-cox.org/sargent/index.html.

# Melissa Scott (1960–   )

> *Quinn Lioe walked the galliot down the sky, using the shaped force fields of the sails as legs, balancing their draw against the depth of gravity here in the planet's shadow.*
>
> —*Burning Bright (1993)*

# Biography

Melissa Scott's science fiction may deal in the familiar territory of plucky space captains and endearing cyberpunk tough-girls, but the care that she puts into the character, background, and soul of her stories raises her space opera and cyberpunk above the common level, and gives them heart. Many of her protagonists are gay, lesbian, bisexual, or transgendered, and she has repeatedly won Lambda Literary Awards for her positive depiction of gay and transgendered characters.

Melissa Scott was born and spent most of her childhood in Little Rock, Arkansas. She was educated at Harvard, and Brandeis University, where her doctoral thesis was on ancient military strategy. She lives in Portsmouth, New Hampshire, until recently with her partner and coauthor Lisa A. Barnett. Since the latter's death of breast cancer on May 2, 2006, Scott's writing has been a moving account of loss and adjustment following the death of a loved one.

ARTIFICIAL INTELLIGENCE; CYBERPUNK; GENDER & SEXUALITY; POPULAR CULTURE; VIRTUAL REALITY; WOMEN IN SF

# Major Works

*Novels*

*The Game Beyond* (1984)
The Silence Leigh Trilogy: *Five-Twelfths of Heaven* (1985), *Silence in Solitude* (1986) and *The Empress of Earth* (1987)
*The Kindly Ones* (1987)
*Dreamships* (1992)
*Burning Bright* (1993)
*Trouble and Her Friends* (1994)
Star Trek: Deep Space Nine: *Proud Helios* (1995)
*Shadow Man* (1995)
*Night Sky Mine* (1996)
*Dreaming Metal* (1997)
Star Trek: Voyager: *The Garden* (1997)
*The Jazz* (2000)

*Notable Short Stories*

"The Carmen Miranda Gambit" (1990, with Lisa A. Barnett)
"The Sweet Not-Yet" (2003)
"Mr. Seeley" (2006)

*Other Important Works*

*Conceiving the Heavens: Creating the Science Fiction Novel.* Portsmouth, NH: Heinemann, 1997.

"Building a World. (Lecture)" *Odyssey: The Fantasy Writing Workshop.* http://www. sff.net/odyssey/scott.html.

## Research Sources

*Encyclopedias and Handbooks:* **AW, BW, CA, CANR, ESF, SFW**

*Bibliographies:* **ARB, FF, SFAN**

### Biographies and Interviews

*Diverse Universe.* "An Interview with Melissa Scott." September 2003. http://www. spacedoutinc.org/DU-17/MelissaScottInterview.html.
*Locus Online.* "Melissa Scott: Masks and Metaphors." January 1999. http://www. locusmag.com/1999/Issues/01/Scott.html.
McCartin, Jeanné. "A New Page in Sci-fi Writer's Life." *Seacoast Online.* May 20, 2007. http://www.seacoastonline.com/apps/pbcs.dll/article?AID=/20070520/ ENTERTAIN/705200308/-1/rss51.

### Criticism and Readers' Guides

Mitchell, Julie. "Of Cyber Gods and Aliens." *Lesbian Review of Books.* 6(3) (2000): 3–5.
Schleifer, Paul C. "Fear of the 'Other' in Melissa Scott's *Dreamships.*" *Extrapolation.* 35(1994): 312–318.
Shainblum, Mark. Review: *Conceiving the Heavens. SFsite.com.*1997. http://www. sfsite.com/04b/con31.htm.

### Web Sites

*Melissa Scott.* Official Web site, which includes information about her writing and creative writing classes. http://www.pointsman.net/mpage/mainpage.html.

# Robert Sheckley (1928–2005)

> *"Someone is dancing on our grave," said Charleroi. His gaze lifted to include the entire earth. "This will make a fine mausoleum."*
> — *"Zirn Left Unguarded, the Jenghik Palace in Flames, John Westerley Dead" (1972)*

## Biography

Robert Sheckley's genius—for he *was* a genius—was for plausible madness, the sort of humor in which the reader recognizes the unsettling grain of truth within the laugh.

Sheckley was born in Brooklyn, New York, and grew up in New Jersey. He was the author of several hundred short stories and fifteen novels; during his most prolific period, he used various pen names to disguise the fact that so many of his stories filled whole issues of sf magazines. His work was translated into many languages, and it remains especially popular in Russia and Eastern Europe. In April 2005, he had to undergo open-heart surgery after becoming ill at an international sf convention in Kiev, Ukraine. Sheckley appeared to be recovering, but on December 9, 2005, following surgery for a brain aneurysm, he died in a Poughkeepsie, New York, hospital.

GODS AND DEMONS; HUMOR AND SATIRE; IMMORTALITY; POP CUL-
TURE & MEDIA; SEX & TABOOS

## Major Works

*Novels*

*Immortality, Inc.*, (1958, orig. *Time Killer*)
*The Status Civilization* (1960)
*Journey Beyond Tomorrow* (1962—aka *The Journey of Joenes*)
*Mindswap* (1966)
*Dimension of Miracles* (1968)
*Crompton Divided* (1978)
*Futuropolis* (1978)
*Bill, the Galactic Hero on the Planet of Bottled Brains* (1990, with Harry Harrison)
*Bring Me the Head of Prince Charming* (1991, with Roger Zelazny)
*Godshome* (1999, with David G. Hartwell)
*In A Land Of Clear Colors* (2005)

*Collections*

*The Collected Short Fiction of Robert Sheckley*: Vols *1–5*. Eugene, OR: Pulphouse, 1992.
*Dimensions of Sheckley: The Selected Novels of Robert Sheckley*. Framingham, MA: NESFA, 2002.
*The Masque of Mañana*. Framingham, MA: NESFA, 2005. Over forty examples of Sheckley's short fiction, including "Shall We Have a Little Talk?" (1953) and "What is Life?" (1977).

*Notable Short Stories*

"The Demons" (1953) http://www.lesekost.de/HHL139D.htm.
"The Prize of Peril" (1958)
"Zirn Left Unguarded, The Jenghik Palace in Flames, John Westerley Dead" (1972)
"Reborn Again" (2004) http://www.infinitematrix.net/stories/index.html.

*Other Important Works*

Introduction. *Pane Burro e Paradossina*. Roberto Quaglia. October 1996. http://www.robertoquaglia.com/rs_intro.html.

"Philosophy & Science Fiction: A View of a Personal Reality." *Greenwich Village Gazette*. March 2000. http://www.nycny.com/columns/sheckley/SHECKLEY3-00.html.

"The Search for the Marvellous." In Peter Nicholls, ed., *Science Fiction at Large: A Collection of Essays, by Various Hands, About the Interface between Science Fiction and Reality*. London: Gollancz, 1976, 185–198.

## Research Sources

*Encyclopedias and Handbooks:* **AW, CA, CAAS, CANR, ESF, MSSF, SFW, WS**

*Bibliographies:* **ARB, FF, SFAN**

*Biographies and Interviews*

Jonas, Gerald. Obituary. *New York Times*. December 10, 2005. http://www.sheckley.com/.

*Locus Online*. "Robert Sheckley: Still Laughing." September 2003. http://www.locusmag.com/Archives.html.

Priest, Christopher. Obituary. *Guardian*. December 20, 2005. http://www.guardian.co.uk/news/2005/dec/20/guardianobituaries.booksobituaries1.

Rusch, Kristine Kathryn. Obituary. *Internet Review of Science Fiction*. June 2006. http://www.irosf.com/q/zine/article/10277.

Urell, Bob. "Other Dimensions: An Afternoon with Robert Sheckley." *Singularity*. 2003. http://www.sfsite.com/map3.htm.

Wingrove, David. "'I am a bill collector disguised as a tree, said the bill collector disguised as a tree': An Interview with Robert Sheckley." *Vector*. 89 (1978): 10–20. http://members.tripod.com/~sheckley/intv78a.htm.

*Criticism and Readers' Guides*

Aldiss, Brian W. "Why They Left Zirn Unguarded: The Stories of Robert Sheckley." *This World and Nearer Ones*, 59–63. Kent, OH: Kent State University Press, 1981.

Faber, Michel. "Close Encounters." *Guardian Online*. February 1, 2003. http://books.guardian.co.uk/departments/sciencefiction/story/0,886325,00.html.

Horwich, David. "Irony and Misunderstanding in the Stories of Robert Sheckley." *Strange Horizons*. September 25, 2000. http://www.strangehorizons.com/2000/20000925/Article_Sheckley_Horwich.shtml

Sallis, James. "Revisiting Sci-fi's Neglected Hero and Others." *Boston Globe*. December 12, 2005. http://www.grasslimb.com/sallis/GlobeColumns/globe.11.sheckley.html.

Special Robert Sheckley Issue. *Vector* 89 (Sep/Oct 1978).

Stephenson, Gregory. *Comic Inferno: The Satirical Work of Robert Sheckley*. San Bernardino, CA: Borgo, 1997.

### Web Sites

*Sheckley.com*. Official Web site. Includes two downloadable TV interviews with Sheckley, both dated Summer 2004. http://www.sheckley.com/.

*My Private Robert Sheckley Pictures and Video Collection*. Roberto Quaglio. January 2008. Tribute site maintained by an Italian fan who became a close friend of Sheckley. Includes poignant photos of Sheckley on his Ukrainian trip, before his final illness. http://www.robertoquaglia.com/foto/fotoindexsheckley. html.

# Mary Wollstonecraft Shelley (1797–1851)

*Time is no more, for I have stepped within the threshold of eternity . . .*
                                                           *—The Last Man (1826)*

## Biography

Mary Wollstonecraft was weeks short of her nineteenth birthday when she created two of the most enduring archetypes of science fiction, and of the modern age: the monster created by the man of science, and the "creator" who pays the ultimate price for refusing to take responsibility for his creation. Since its anonymous publication in 1818, *Frankenstein* has developed a life of its own, with countless film and stage versions, sequels and homages, reworkings and retellings. This is a testament to the power of Shelley's story, and the lasting impact that it has had on the popular imagination.

Mary Wollstonecraft was born in London, the daughter of notorious authors and free thinkers. At age sixteen, she ran away with the poet Percy Byshe Shelley. After his death by drowning in 1822, she continued to write stories with recognizable sf themes. She died in London, at the age of fifty-three, of a brain tumor.

ANDROIDS, CYBORGS & ROBOTS; END OF THE WORLD; GOTHIC SF; MONSTERS

## Major Works

*Novels*

*Frankenstein* (1818)

*The Last Man* (1826)

 *Frankenstein, The Last Man* and other works by Shelley are available online, at various Web sites such as http://www.gutenberg.org/.

*Collections*

*The Mary Shelley Reader.* Eds. Betty T. Bennett and Charles E. Robinson. Oxford (UK): Oxford University Press, 1990.
*The Mortal Immortal: The Complete Supernatural Short Fiction of Mary Shelley.* San Francisco, CA: Tachyon, 1996. Includes stories with sf elements such as "Valerius: The Reanimated Roman" (1819), "The Mortal Immortal" (1833), and "Roger Dodsworth: The Reanimated Englishman" (published in 1863).

*Other Important Works*

Author's Introduction. *Frankenstein.* London, 1831. Rpt. London: Penguin, 1992. 5–10.
"Author's Preface." *Frankenstein.* London, 1818. http://www.4literature.net/Mary_Wollstonecraft_Shelley/Frankenstein/.
The Letters of Mary Wollstonecraft Shelley. Ed. Betty T. Bennett. Baltimore, MD: Johns Hopkins University Press, 1980.
Mary Shelley's Journal. Ed. Frederick L. Jones. Norman: University of Oklahoma Press, 1947. Excerpts: http://www.english.uga.edu/~232/mws.letand jour.html

## Research Sources

*Encyclopedias and Handbooks:* **AW, BW, ESF, LE, MSSF, NNDB, SFW**

*Bibliographies:* **ARB, FF, SFAN**

Garrett, Martin. *A Mary Shelley Chronology.* New York: Palgrave, 2002.
Lawson, Shannon. "Mary Wollstonecraft Shelley Chronology & Resource Site." *Romantic Circles.* June 1999. University of Maryland. http://www.rc.umd.edu/reference/chronologies/mschronology/mws.html.
Voller, Jack G. "Mary Shelley." *The Literary Gothic.* February 3, 2007. http://www.litgothic.com/Authors/mshelley.html.

*Biographies and Interviews*

Bennett, Betty T. and Stuart Curran, eds. *Mary Shelley in Her Times.* Baltimore, MD: Johns Hopkins University Press, 2000.
Buss, Helen M. et al. *Mary Wollstonecraft and Mary Shelley: Writing Lives.* Waterloo, Ontario: Wilfrid Laurier University Press, 2001.
Hoobler, Dorothy and Thomas Hoobler. *The Monsters: Mary Shelley and the Curse of Frankenstein.* Boston, MA: Little, Brown, 2006.
Nichols, Joan K. *Mary Shelley, Frankenstein's Creator: First Science Fiction Writer.* Berkeley, CA: Conari, 1998.
Spark, Muriel. *Mary Shelley: A Biography.* New York: Dutton, 1987.
Williams, John. *Mary Shelley: A Literary Life.* New York, London: Macmillan, 2000.

## Criticism and Readers' Guides

Aldiss, Brian. "Science Fiction's Mother Figure." *The Detached Retina: Aspects of SF and Fantasy.* Syracuse, NY: Syracuse University Press, 1995. 52–86.

Aldiss, Brian with David Wingrove. "On the Origin of Species: Mary Shelley." In James Gunn and Matthew Candelaria, eds., *Speculations on Speculation: Theories of Science Fiction.* Lanham, MD: Scarecrow, 2005, 163–204.

Badalamenti, Anthony F. "Why did Mary Shelley Write *Frankenstein?*" *Journal of Religion & Health.* 45 (2006): 419–439.

Botting, Fred, ed. *New Casebooks: Frankenstein by Mary Shelley.* New York: St. Martin's, 1995.

Bradshaw, Michael. "Mary Shelley's *The Last Man* (The End of the World as We Know It)." In Derek Littlewood, ed., *Impossibility Fiction: Alternativity, Extrapolation, Speculation.* Amsterdam, The Netherlands: Rodopi, 1996, 163–176.

Fuller, Sarah C. "Reading the Cyborg in Mary Shelley's *Frankenstein.*" *Journal of the Fantastic in the Arts.* 14 (2003): 217–227.

Ketterer, David. "Frankenstein's 'Conversion' from Natural Magic to Modern Science—and a *Shifted* (and Converted) Last Draft Insert." *Science Fiction Studies.* 24 (1997): 57–78. http://www.depauw.edu/sfs/backissues/71/ketterer71art.htm.

Lomax, William. "Epic Reversal in Mary Wollstonecraft Shelley's *The Last Man:* Romantic Irony and the Roots of Science Fiction." In Michele K. Langford, ed., *Contours of the Fantastic.* Westport, CT: Greenwood, 1990, 7–18.

Morrison, Lucy et al. *A Mary Shelley Encyclopedia.* Westport, CT: Greenwood, 2003.

Oates, Joyce Carol. "Frankenstein's Fallen Angel." *Critical Inquiry.* 10 (1984): 543–555.

Parrinder, Patrick. "From Mary Shelley to *The War of the Worlds:* The Thames Valley Catastrophe." In David Seed, ed., *Anticipations: Essays on Early Science Fiction and its Precursors.* Syracuse, NY: Syracuse University Press, 1995, 58–74.

Purinton, Marjean D. "Mary Shelley's Science Fiction Short Stories and the Legacy of Wollstonecraft's Feminism." *Women's Studies.* 30 (2001): 147–175.

Rowen, Norma. "The Making of Frankenstein's Monster: Post-Golem, Pre-Robot." In Nicholas Ruddick, ed., *State of the Fantastic: Studies in the Theory and Practice of Fantastic Literature and Film.* Westport, CT: Greenwood, 1992, 169–178.

Russ, Joanna. "On Mary Wollstonecraft Shelley." In *To Write Like a Woman: Essays in Feminism and Science Fiction.* Bloomington: Indiana University Press, 1995. 120–132.

Stableford, Brian. "*Frankenstein* and the Origins of Science Fiction." In David Seed, ed., *Anticipations: Essays on Early Science Fiction and its Precursors.* Syracuse, NY: Syracuse University Press, 1995, 46–57.

Wolf, Leonard, ed. *The Essential Frankenstein: The Definitive, Annotated Edition of Mary Shelley's Classic Novel.* New York: Plume 1993.

## Web Sites

*Mary Wollstonecraft Shelley.* Ashton Nichols. *Romantic Natural History.* December 2002. Dickinson College.Web site which surveys relationships between literary works and natural history before Darwin's *On the Origin of Species* (1859). Includes a reproduction of "An Early Review of *Frankenstein*" from *The British Critic* of April 1818. http://users.dickinson.edu/~nicholsa/Romnat/mwshelley. htm.

*Frankenstein: Penetrating the Mysteries of Nature.* U.S. National Library of Medicine. February 2002. Exhibition which looks Mary Shelley's world and how her creation blurs the line of what we consider "acceptable" science. http://www.nlm. nih.gov/hmd/frankenstein/frankintrod.html.

*My Hideous Progeny: Mary Shelley's Frankenstein.* Cynthia Hamburg. September 2007. Fan site containing " . . . everything you have ever wanted to know about Mary Shelley;" part of the designer's MA thesis on the functionality of literary Web sites. Interesting page on Gothic literature and possible influences on Shelley. http://home-1.worldonline.nl/~hamberg/.

*Mary Wollstonecraft Shelley.* Andreas Teuber. November 2000. Brandeis University. Web site for an undergraduate class, with links to a wide variety of information about Shelley's life and work. http://people.brandeis.edu/~teuber/shelleybio. html.

*Review. The Gentleman's Magazine. April 1818.* Transcript of a contemporary review, which seems to be scrambling for something nice to say: " . . . many parts of it are strikingly good, and the description of the scenery is excellent . . . " (The reviewer may have been laboring under the misapprehension that P.B. Shelley wrote the book.) http://www.english.upenn.edu/Projects/knarf/Reviews/gentmag.html.

# Lucius Shepard (1947–  )

*Even if it is death . . . in this place death might last longer than our old lives.*
—*"The Sun Spider" (1987)*

## Biography

Lucius Taylor Shepard was born in Lynchburg, Virginia, and "raised up hard," as he describes it, by an abusive and demanding father in Daytona Beach, Florida. The young man ran away from home at age fifteen, working his way around Europe, North Africa and Asia. In a Locus interview in 2001, he describes his work as " . . . mainstream, I guess, but it's weird." It also consistently reflects, in setting and spirit, his abiding love affair with Central and South America, an affinity that dates from the days when he would visit Cuba, Mexico, and Guatemala with his mother, a Spanish teacher.

Lucius Shepard currently lives in Vancouver, Washington. He also writes nonfiction: in the early 1980s, he worked as a freelance journalist reporting on the civil war in El Salvador. He writes on sport, particularly boxing, and is also a regular movie reviewer for *The Magazine of Fantasy & Science Fiction* and electricstory.com.

DRUGS & ALTERED CONSCIOUSNESS; FANTASY; GOTHIC SF; MYTHOL-
OGY & LEGEND; PSI POWERS; WAR

## Major Works

*Novels*

*Green Eyes* (1984)
*Life During Wartime* (1987)
*The Scalehunter's Beautiful Daughter* (1988) **Locus Poll**
*The Father of Stones* (1989) **Locus Poll**
*Kalimantan* (1990)
*The Golden* (1993) **Locus Poll**
*AZTECHS* (2003)
*Viator* (2004)
*Softspoken* (2007)

*Collections*

*The Best of Lucius Shepard*. Burton, MI: Subterranean, 2008. Includes highlights from
    previous collections, such as "Salvador" (1984) **Locus Poll**, "R & R" (1986—
    Nebula, Locus Poll), "Radiant Green Star" (2000—**Locus Poll**), " and "Jailwise"
    (2003).
Other collections by Shepard are *The Jaguar Hunter* (1987—**Locus Poll**), *Beast of the
    Heartland and Other Stories* (1999), and *Eternity and Other Stories* (2005).

*Notable Short Stories*

"The Night of White Bhairab" (1984) http://www.electricstory.com/.
"The Jaguar Hunter" (1985) http://www.infinityplus.co.uk/stories/jaguarhunter.htm.
"The Sun Spider" (1987)
"Barnacle Bill the Spacer" (1992)—**Hugo, Locus Poll**
"Stars Seen Through Stone" (2007) http://www.sfsite.com/fsf/fiction/ls01.htm.

*Other Important Works*

"Dark, Darker, Darko." *Fantasy & Science Fiction*. April 2002. http://www.sfsite.com/
    fsf/2002/ls0204.htm.
"eXcreMENt." *Fantasy & Science Fiction*. December 2000. Other "Exclusive Movie
    Reviews" can be found at *Electric Story.com*: http://www.electricstory.com/
    reviews/lsreviews.aspx.
"God is in the Details." In Robin Wilson, ed., *Paragons: Twelve Master Science Fiction
    Writers Ply Their Craft*. New York: St. Martin's, 1996, 195–205.
Introduction. *Brighten to Incandescence*. By Michael Bishop. Urbana, IL: Golden
    Gryphon, 2003.
*Sports & Music*. Shingletown, CA: Mark V. Ziesing, 1994.
*Weapons of Mass Seduction*. Wilsonville, OR: Wheatland, 2005.

## Research Sources

*Encyclopedias and Handbooks:* **AW, CA, CANR, ESF, SFW**

*Bibliographies:* **ARB, FF, SFAN**

Contento, William G. "Lucius Shepard: A Bibliography." *Magazine of Fantasy and Science Fiction.* 100(3) (2001): 85–88.

### Biographies and Interviews

Blaschke, Jayme L. "Interview: Lucius Shepard." *Strange Horizons* January 5, 2004. http://www.strangehorizons.com/2004/20040105/shepard.shtml.

Gevers., Nick. Interview. *SciFi.com.* April 2003. http://www.scifi.com/sfw/issue314/interview.html.

Kelly, James Patrick. "How to Talk to Lucius Shepard." *Essays/Appreciations.* 1995 (?) Jim Kelly.com. http://www.jimkelly.net/.

Martini, Adrienne. "An Interview with Lucius Shepard." *Bookslut.com.* December 2004. http://www.bookslut.com/features/2004_12_003799.php.

Vander Meer, Jeff. "Prolific and Prodigious." *Rain Taxi.* Winter 2004. http://vanderworld.blogspot.com/2005/07/lucius-shepard.html.

### Criticism and Readers' Guides

Blackmore, Tim. "Talking the Talk, Walking the Walk: The Role of Discourse in Joe Haldeman's 'The Monster' and Lucius Shepard's 'Delta Sly Honey.'" *Journal of the Fantastic in the Arts.* 6 (1994): 191–202.

Daniel, Tony. "Dat Wascally Wabbit: The Influence of *Song of the South* on Lucius Shepard." *New York Review of Science Fiction.* 2(9) (1990): 7+

Gomel, Elana. "From Dr. Moreau to Dr. Mengele: The Biological Sublime." *PoeticsToday.* 21 (2000): 393–421.

Matthews, Aaron. "Lucius Shepard: Borges, Influence and References." *Jorge Luis Borges: The Garden of Forking Paths.* January 2004. The Modern Word. http://www.themodernword.com/borges/borges_infl_shepard.html.

### Web Sites

*Lucius Shepard.com.* Official Web site http://lucius-shepard.com/.

# Robert Silverberg (1935–   )

> *Today you liquidated about 50,000 Eaters in Sector A, and now you are spending an uneasy night. You and Herndon flew east at dawn, with the green-gold sunrise at your backs, and sprayed the neural pellets over a thousand hectares along the Forked River.*
>
> —*"Sundance" (1969)*

# Biography

Robert Silverberg was born in Brooklyn, New York. He attended Columbia University, and it was while he was an undergraduate there that his first novel was published. From the mid-1960s to the mid-1970s, he took advantage of his popularity among sf readers to write more challenging stories: stories that paid far more attention to depth of character and social background, stories that experimented with form and content, and harkened back to the modernist literature he had studied at Columbia—in effect, his own personal "New Wave."

Robert Silverberg has been a professional writer since he was twenty years old. In 1956, he was awarded a Nebula as "Most Promising New Author," the youngest recipient of that award; he has won major sf awards in six consecutive decades (from the 1950s to the 2000s). He lives in Oakland, California with his wife Karen Haber, who is also an sf writer and scholar.

ALIEN THREAT; COLONIZATION OF OTHER WORLDS; ENTROPY; FANTASY; PSYCHOLOGY; RELIGION; TIME TRAVEL

# Major Works

*Novels*

*Revolt on Alpha C* (1955)
*To Open the Sky* (1967)
*Thorns* (1967)
*Nightwings* (1969) **Hugo**
*Downward to the Earth* (1970)
*A Time of Changes* (1971) **Nebula**
*The Book of Skulls* (1972)
*Dying Inside* (1972).
The Majipoor series: including *Lord Valentine's Castle* (1980—**Locus Poll**), *Majipoor Chronicles* (1982), *Valentine Pontifex* (1983), *The Mountains of Majipoor* (1995)
*Kingdoms of the Wall* (1992)
*The Alien Years* (1998)
*Roma Eterna* (2003)

*Collections*

*Phases of the Moon: Stories from Six Decades*. Burton, MI: Subterranean, 2004.
Includes a selection of the very best stories of Silverberg's long career: "The Road to Nightfall" (1958), "Passengers" (1968—**Nebula**), "Sundance" (1969), "Good News from the Vatican" (1971—**Nebula**), "Born with the Dead." (1974—**Locus Poll, Nebula**), "Sailing to Byzantium" (1985—**Nebula**).
*To Be Continued: The Collected Stories of Robert Silverberg*. Burton, MI., Subterranean, 2006.

*Notable Short Stories*

"Gilgamesh in the Outback" (1986) **Hugo**
"Secret Sharer" (1988) **Locus Poll**
"Enter a Soldier. Later, Enter Another" (1989) **Hugo**

*Other Important Works*

"How We Work: Robert Silverberg." In Brian W. Aldiss and Harry Harrison, eds., *Hell's Cartographers: Some Personal Histories of Science Fiction Writers.* London: Weidenfeld, 1975, 213–217.

Introduction to "Sundance." *Those Who Can: A Science Fiction Reader* (1973), Robin Scott Wilson, ed. New York: St. Martin's, 1996. 149–154.

Introduction. *Virtual Unrealities: The Short Fiction of Alfred Bester.* Edited, with Byron Preiss and Keith R.A. DeCandido. New York: Vintage Books, 1997.

Introduction. *The War of the Worlds: Fresh Perspectives on the H.G. Wells Classic,* edited by Glenn Yeffeth. Dallas, TX: BenBella, 2005, 1–14.

*Reflections and Refractions: Thoughts on Science Fiction, Science, and Other Matters* (1997)

"Reflections: The Conquest of Space." *Asimov's Science Fiction.* April 2003.Dell Magazines. http://www.asimovs.com/_issue_0304/ref.shtml.

*Science Fiction 101: Where to Start Reading and Writing Science Fiction* (2001)

## Research Sources

*Encyclopedias and Handbooks:* **AW, CA, CANR, ESF, MSSF, NNDB, SFW**

*Bibliographies:* **ARB, FF, SFAN**

Clareson, Thomas D. *Robert Silverberg: A Primary and Secondary Bibliography.* Boston, MA: G.K. Hall, 1983.

*Biographies and Interviews*

Freund, Jim. Interview. *Hour of the Wolf.* September 7, 1997. WBAI New York. http://www.hourwolf.com/chats/silverberg.html.

Huddleston, Kathie. Interview. *Science Fiction Weekly.* August 5, 2002. http://www.scifi.com/sfw/issue276/interview.html.

Hunt, Stephen. "Hot Spice and Majipoor." *SF Crowsnest.* July 2002. http://www.computercrowsnest.com/sfnews2/02_july/news0702_2.shtml.

Lalumière, Claude. "A Brief History of Robert Silverberg." *Locus Online.* October 13, 2004. http://www.locusmag.com/2004/Reviews/10_LalumiereOnSilverberg.html.

"One Word at a Time." *Locus.* March 2004. http://www.locusmag.com/2004/Issues/03Silverberg.html.

## Criticism and Readers' Guides

Bee, Robert. "Galaxy Magazine and Robert Silverberg's Development as a Writer." *Internet Review of Science Fiction*. February 2008. http://www.irosf.com/q/zine/article/10393.

Chapman, Edgar L. *The Road to Castle Mount: The Science Fiction of Robert Silverberg*. Westport, CT: Greenwood, 1999.

Dudley, Joseph M. "Transformational SF Religions: Philip Jose Farmer's *Night of Light* and Robert Silverberg's *Downward to the Earth*." *Extrapolation*. 35 (1994): 342–350.

Elkins, Charles L. and Martin Harry Greenberg, eds. *Robert Silverberg's Many Trapdoors: Critical Essays on His Science Fiction*. Westport, CT: Greenwood, 1992.

Flodstrom, John. "Enlightening the Alien Savages: Colonialism in the Novels of Robert Silverberg." In Elisabeth Anne Leonard, ed., *Into Darkness Peering: Race and Color in the Fantastic*. Westport, CT: Greenwood, 1997, 159–170.

Saciuk, Olena. "The Aztecs, Turks, and Incas Have It: Robert Silverberg's Playful Alternate Histories." In Edgar L. Chapman and Carl B. Yoke, eds., *Classic and Iconoclastic Alternate History Science Fiction*. Lewiston, NY: Edwin Mellen, 2003, 123–140.

Stableford, Brian M. "The Metamorphosis of Robert Silverberg." In *Outside the Human Aquarium: Masters of Science Fiction*. San Bernardino, CA: Borgo, 1995, 37–48.

## Web Sites

*The Quasi-Official Robert Silverberg Web site*. Jon Davis, ed. March 2007. According to an introductory note by Silverberg, " . . . as close to an official site as I'm ever going to have . . . " http://www.majipoor.com/.

*The Worlds of Robert Silverberg*. Yahoo! Groups. June 2008. Web site discussion forum for devoted fans. http://groups.yahoo.com/group/theworldsofrobertsilverberg/.

# Dan Simmons (1948–   )

> *In twentieth-century Old Earth, a fast food chain took dead cow meat, fried it in grease, added carcinogens, wrapped it in petroleum based foam, and sold nine hundred billion units. Human beings. Go figure.*
>
> —*Hyperion* (1989)

## Biography

Dan Simmons was born in Peoria, Illinois, and was educated at Wabash College in Indiana, and Washington University in St. Louis, Missouri. For eighteen years he wrote in his spare time while teaching elementary school, in Missouri, Buffalo, New York, and Colorado. As a national language arts consultant, he made the

"Writing Well" curriculum that he developed for his own Sixth-grade class available to schools across the country.

Simmons uses allusions to classic writers to enhance the depth and substance of his science fiction, horror, and historical narratives. The first two volumes of the Hyperion Cantos take their titles, and some of their rich mythic texture, from poems by Keats. In 1995, Wabash College awarded him an honorary doctorate for his contributions to education and writing. He lives with his wife and daughter along the Front Range of Colorado.

GALACTIC EMPIRES; GODS AND DEMONS; MONSTERS; MYTHOLOGY & LEGEND; NANOTECHNOLOGY; POSTHUMAN

## Major Works

### Novels

*Song of Kali* (1985)
*Phases of Gravity* (1989)
The Hyperion Cantos: *Hyperion* (1989—**Hugo**), *The Fall of Hyperion* (1990), *Endymion* (1995), *The Rise of Endymion* (1997)
The Ilium series: *Ilium* (2003), *Olympos* (2005)
*The Terror* (2007)

### Collections

*Prayers to Broken Stones* (1991). London: Dark Harvest, 1997.
*LoveDeath*. New York: Warner, 1993. Includes **Locus Poll** winning stories "Entropy's Bed at Midnight" (1990) and "Death in Bangkok" (1993).
*Worlds Enough and Time: Five Tales of Speculative Fiction*. Burton, MI: Subterranean, 2002. Includes the Hyperion story "Orphans of the Helix" (1999—**Locus Poll**)

### Other Important Works

*Going After the Rubber Chicken, Three Guest of Honor Speeches* (1991)
*Summer Sketches* (1992)
"Writing Well: Installments One through Seven." Dan Simmons.com. http://www.dansimmons.com/writing_welll/writing.htm.

### Research Sources

### Encyclopedias and Handbooks: **AW, CA, CANR, ESF, NNDB**

### Bibliographies: **ARB, FF, SFAN**

### Biographies and Interviews

Lilley, Ernest. Interview. *SFRevu*. July 2003. http://www.sfrevu.com/ISSUES/2003/0307/Dan%20Simmons%20Interview/Review.htm.

*SF World.com.* Interview. February 6, 2007. http://www.sffworld.com/mul/218p0. html.

Shindler, Dorman T. "The Outsider." *Salon.* February 27, 2002. http://dir.salon.com/ story/books/int/2002/02/27/simmons/index.html.

Schweitzer, Darrell, ed. "Dan Simmons Interview." In *Speaking of the Fantastic.* Holicong, PA: Wildside, 2002, 158–171.

Silver, Steven H. "A Conversation with Dan Simmons." *SF Site.* July 2003. http:// www.sfsite.com/09b/ds160.htm.

### Criticism and Readers' Guides

Clute, John. "On the Cusp of Far." In Damien Broderick, ed., *Earth Is But a Star: Excursions through Science Fiction to the Far Future.* Crawley: University of Western Australia Press, 2001, 151–163.

Killheffer, Robert. "The Fallout of *Hyperion.*" *New York Review of Science Fiction.* 3(2) (1990): 14+.

Palmer, Christopher. "Galactic Empires and the Contemporary Extravaganza: Dan Simmons and Iain M. Banks." *Science Fiction Studies.* 26 (1999): 73–90. http://www.depauw.edu/sfs/backissues/77/palmer77.htm.

Sheehan, Bill. "The Void and the Word: Dan Simmons' Complete Hyperion Cantos." *Nova Express.* 5(1) (1998). http://home.austin.rr.com/lperson/hyperion.html.

Webb, Janeen. "Simmons and Powers: Postmodernism to Post-romanticism." In Alliene R. Becker, ed., *Visions of the Fantastic.* Westport, CT: Greenwood, 1996, 139–148.

### Web Sites

*Dan Simmons.com.* Official Web site. http://www.dansimmons.com/.

*Dan Simmons.* Sean Ware, ed. December 2003. Fan Web site, with links to reviews and interviews, including a 1990 interview with the site editor. http://www.erinyes. org/simmons/.

# *"Smith Cordwainer" [Paul Linebarger] (1913–1966)*

> *She did not know it, but therewith unborn futures reeled out of existence, rebellion flamed into coming centuries, people and underpeople died in strange causes, mothers changed the names of unborn lords, and starships whispered back from places which men had not even imagined before.*
> — *"The Dead Lady of Clown Town" (1964)*

## Biography

Paul Myron Anthony Linebarger was born in Milwaukee, Wisconsin, but spent his childhood in Asia and Europe as his father, a lawyer and political activist, advocated for the aims of Sun Yat-sen and the Chinese revolution of 1911. Linebarger became a freelance intelligence officer for the CIA, and advisor to presidents on Asian affairs. He was fluent in six languages, and a pioneer of the science of psychological warfare.

As Cordwainer Smith, he wrote about the Instrumentality of Mankind, a nightmarish far future of genetically modified slave-animals, and elaborate feudal hierarchies. The style and substance reflect Linebarger's easy familiarity with Eastern philosophy and mythology. Toward the end of his life, he became a devout Episcopalian, and began to add layers of religious allegory to his tales of the Instrumentality.

Paul Linebarger died suddenly of a heart attack in 1966, in Baltimore, Maryland. He is buried in Arlington National Cemetery, in Washington DC.

COLONIZATION OF OTHER WORLDS; FAR FUTURE; GENETICS & CLONING; IMMORTALITY; MYTHOLOGY & LEGEND; PSI POWERS; RELIGION

## Major Works

*Novels*

*The Planet Buyer* (1964)
*The Underpeople* (1968)
*Norstrilia* (1975)

*Short Stories*

"Scanners Live in Vain" (1950)
"The Game of Rat and Dragon" (1955)
"Alpha Ralpha Boulevard" (1961)
"Mother Hitton's Littul Kittons" (1961)
"The Ballad of Lost C'mell" (1962).
"The Dead Lady of Clown Town" (1964)

*Collections*

*The Rediscovery of Man: The Complete Short Science Fiction of Cordwainer Smith.* James A, ed. Mann. Framingham, MA: NESFA, 1993. Thirty-three Cordwainer Smith stories, two previously unpublished.
*We the Underpeople*. Riverdale, NY: Baen, 2006.
*When the People Fell*. Riverdale, NY: Baen, 2007.

*Other Important Works*

*The Political Doctrines of Sun Yat-Sen: An Exposition of San Min Chu I* (1937)
*Government in Republican China* (1938)

The China of K'ai-shek: A Political Study (1941)
Psychological Warfare (1948)
Prologue and Epilogue. Space Lords. (1965) (New York: Ace, 1984).

## Research Sources

Encyclopedias and Handbooks: **AW, CA, CANR, ESF, MSSF, NNDB, SCFW, SFW, WS**

Bibliographies: **ARB, FF, SFAN**

Bennett, Mike. A Cordwainer Smith Checklist. Polk City, IA: Chris Drumm, 1991.

### Biographies and Interviews

Biography. Arlington National Cemetary Web site. Michael Robert Patterson, ed. November 2005. http://www.arlingtoncemetery.net/linebarg.htm.

Elms, Alan C. "The Creation of Cordwainer Smith." Science Fiction Studies. 11 (1984): 264–283. Although this is an older article, and may be challenging to find, it contains a very thorough (and even amusing) narrative of Linebarger's early life—well worth reading.

———— "The Thing from Inner Space: John W. Campbell, Robert E. Howard, Cordwainer Smith." In Uncovering Lives: The Uneasy Alliance of Biography and Psychology. New York: Oxford UP, 1994, 103–116.

### Criticism and Readers' Guides

Brooks, Alasdair. "Under Old Earth: Material Culture, Identity, and History in the Work of Cordwainer Smith." In Miles Russell, ed., Digging Holes in Popular Culture: Archaeology and Science Fiction. Oxford (UK): Oxbow, 2002, 77–84.

Cramer, Kathryn. Introduction to "No, No, Not Rogov!" The Ascent of Wonder. New York: Tor, 1994. http://ebbs.english.vt.edu/exper/kcramer/anth/Rogov.html.

Elms, Alan C. "Between Mottile and Ambiloxi: Cordwainer Smith as a Southern Writer." Extrapolation. 42 (2001): 124–136.

————"Painwise in Space: The Psychology of Isolation in Cordwainer Smith and James Tiptree, Jr." In Gary Westfahl, ed., Space and Beyond. Westport, CT: Greenwood, 2000, 131–142.

Gorsch, Robert. "Re-mythologizing Outer Space with C.S. Lewis and Cordwainer Smith." In Gary Westfahl, ed., Space and Beyond. Westport, CT: Greenwood, 2000, 123–130.

Hellekson, Karen L. The Science Fiction of Cordwainer Smith. Jefferson, NC: McFarland, 2001.

Le Guin, Ursula. "Thinking about Cordwainer Smith." In The Wave in the Mind: Talks and Essays on the Writer, the Reader, and the Imagination. Boston, MA: Shambhala, 2004.

Lewis, Anthony R. *Concordance to Cordwainer Smith*. Cambridge, MA: New England Science Fiction Association, 2000.

McGuirk, Carol. "The Rediscovery of Cordwainer Smith." *Science Fiction Studies*. 28 (2001): 161–200.

McIntyre, Angus. "Cats, Cruelty and Children: Idealism and Morality in the Instrumentality of Mankind." *Outsider*. 2001. http://www.raingod.com/angus/Writing/Essays/Literary/Smith.html.

Turner, Alice K. "The Crimes and the Glories of Cordwainer Smith." In Damien Broderick, ed., *Earth Is But a Star: Excursions through Science Fiction to the Far Future*. Crawley: University of Western Australia Press, 2001, 325–332.

VanderMeer, Jeff. "Cordwainer Smith (Blog essay)." *Ecstatic Days*. October 20, 2007. http://www.jeffvandermeer.com/2007/10/20/cordwainer-smith/.

### Web Sites

*Cordwainer Smith Unofficial Biography Page*. Alan C. Elms. Biographical and bibliographical information by a Linebarger scholar, as well as a secondary bibliography of Professor Elms' extensive research on Smith/Linebarger and his work. http://www.ulmus.net/ace/menus/ace_s5_c7_b0_d0_x.html.

*The Remarkable Science Fiction of Cordwainer Smith*. Rosana Hart. Hart works, ed. Official Web site maintained and edited by Linebarger's daughter. http://www.cordwainersmith.com.

*The Universe of Cordwainer Smith*. Corby Waste, ed. 160th Century Worldtours. January 2007. The Fourth Millennium. Very entertaining virtual reality "tour" of Cordwainer Smiths' universe, including the editor's CGI images of Norstrilia, Mother Hitton's farm, and other settings from Smith's stories. http://www.fourth-millennium.net/cordwainer-vr/cs-index.html.

# E.E. "Doc" Smith (1890–1965)

*To any profound thinkers in the realms of Science who may chance to read this story, greetings . . .*

—*The Skylark of Space (1928)*

## Biography

Edward Elmer Smith was born in Sheboygan, Wisconsin, and grew up there and in Idaho, on a farm near the Pend d'Oreille River. He had a doctorate in Chemical Engineering from George Washington University, and worked all his life as a food technologist. His writing career began when a neighbor suggested he write a story set in outer space. (Previously, sf had been firmly rooted on a future version of Earth or, at best, within the Solar System.) "Doc" Smith did just that—and invented "space opera."

"Doc" Smith painted his interstellar adventures with broad brushstrokes. In his essay "The Epic of Space," he admitted that " . . . [my] characters get away from me and do exactly as they damn please." The Edward E. Smith Memorial—the Skylark Award, which the New England Science Fiction Association presents to one who has contributed significantly to science fiction—is named in his honor. He died in Seaside, Oregon, August 31, 1965.

ALIENS; GALACTIC EMPIRES; GENETICS & CLONING; PSI POWERS; SPACE OPERA

## Major Works

*Novels*

The Skylark series: *The Skylark of Space* (1928, with Lee Hawkins Garby), *Skylark Three* (1930), *Skylark of Valeron* (1934), *Skylark DuQuesne* (1965)
The Lensman series: *Galactic Patrol* (1937), *Triplanetary: A Tale of Cosmic Adventure* (1934), *Gray Lensman* (1939), *Second Stage Lensman* (1941), *Children of the Lens* (1947), *The Vortex Blaster* (1941—aka *Masters of the Vortex*), *First Lensman* (1950)
*Spacehounds of IPC* (1931)

*Collections*

*Chronicles of the Lensmen (The Lensmen Series, Volume 1)*. Baltimore, MD: Old Earth Books, 1998.
*Chronicles of the Lensmen (The Lensmen Series, Volume 2)*. Baltimore, MD: Old Earth Books, 1998.
*The Skylark of Space*. Introduction by Vernor Vinge. Rockville, MD: Wildside, 2007.

*Other Important Works*

"The Epic of Space." In Lloyd Arthur Eshbach, ed., *Of Worlds Beyond: The Science of Science Fiction Writing*. Reading, PA: Fantasy Press, 1947.
*Have Trenchcoat—Will Travel*. Lloyd Arthur Eshbach, ed. Chicago, IL: Advent, 2001.
Introduction. *Man of Many Minds*. By E. Everett Evans. Fantasy, 1953.
Worldcon Guest of Honor Speech. Chicon I. Sept. 1, 1940. *Worldcon Guest of Honor Speeches*. Mike Resnick and Joe Siclari, eds. ISFiC, 2006.

## Research Sources

*Encyclopedias and Handbooks:* **AW, CA, CAAS, ESF, MSSF, NNDB, SFW, WS**

*Bibliographies:* **ARB, FF, SFAN**

Lucchetti, Stephen C. *"Doc"—First Galactic Roamer: A Complete Bibliography and Publishing Checklist of Works by and about E.E. "Doc" Smith*. Framingham, MA: NESFA, 2004.

*Biographies and Interviews*

Heinlein, Robert A. "Larger than Life: A Memoir in Tribute to Dr. Edward E. Smith." In *Expanded Universe*. New York: Ace, 1982.
Warner, Harry. "Edward E. Smith—A Biography." *Spaceways*. June 1939. http://fanac. org/fanzines/Spaceways/Spaceways1-06.html.

*Criticism and Readers' Guides*

Ellik, Ron and Bill Evans. *The Universes of E.E. Smith*. Chicago, IL: Advent, 1966.
Harken, Leigh Anna. "E.E. 'Doc' Smith's *Triplanetary*." *Bison Books Blog*. March 16, 2006. University of Nebraska Press. http://nebraskapress.typepad.com/ university_of_nebraska_pr/2006/03/ee_doc_smiths_t.html.
King, Larry. "The Lensmen: FAQ." *Space Monkey Science Fiction Timeline*. November 27, 1994. http://chronology.org/noframes/lens/.
Murphy, Derryl. "Interstellar Conflict Across Time: Military and Structural Similarities and Differences Throughout the History of Space Opera." *Strange Horizons*. July 7, 2003. http://www.strangehorizons.com/2003/20030707/space_opera.shtml.
Sanders, Joe. "Spaceman in Homespun." *Science Fiction Studies*. 32 (2005): 208–210.

*Web Sites*

*Z9M9Z: A Lensman Web Site*. Ethan Fleischer. April 2007. Pariah Press. Attractive and well-organized fan Web site, with FAQs, forums, and news. http://www. ethanfleischer.com/lensman/main.htm.

# *Norman Spinrad (1940–   )*

> *The saddest day of your life isn't when you decide to sell out. The saddest day of your life is when you decide to sell out and nobody wants to buy.*
> —*Bug Jack Barron (1969)*

## Biography

Norman Richard Spinrad was born and raised in the Bronx, New York, and attended the prestigious Bronx School of Science. At the City College of New York he cycled through various majors—from engineering to chemistry, with a few creative writing classes—before graduating in 1961 and embarking on a writing career.

Spinrad is a challenging writer, who refuses to go easy on the reader. *Bug Jack Barron* (1969), a proto-cyberpunk tale of a cynical, exploitative talk-show host, was turned down by various publishers because of explicit language and graphic sexuality, and denounced in the British House of Commons. (The *Encyclopedia of Science Fiction* describes it as "not particularly shocking" by today's standards.)

Norman Spinrad has twice been elected President of the Science Fiction and Fantasy Writers of America (SFWA), once from 1980 to 1982 and again from 2001 to 2002. Since the late-1980s, he has lived in Paris, France.

ALTERNATIVE HISTORY; CYBERPUNK; ECOLOGY; ENTROPY; END OF THE WORLD; POP CULTURE & MEDIA; SEX & TABOOS

# Major Works

*Novels*

*The Solarians* (1966)
*The Men in the Jungle* (1967)
*Bug Jack Barron* (1969)
*The Iron Dream* (1972)
*A World Between* (1979)
*The Void Captain's Tale* (1983)
*Little Heroes* (1987)
*Russian Spring* (1991)
*Greenhouse Summer* (1999)
*He Walked Among Us* (2003)
      http://www.scifidimensions.com/Oct05/hewalked.htm.

*Collections*

Spinrad collections include *The Last Hurrah of the Golden Horde* (1970), *No Direction Home* (1975), *Other Americas* (1988), and *Deus X and Other Stories* (2003).

*Notable Short Stories*

"The Last of the Romany" (1963)
"Carcinoma Angels" (1967)
"Riding the Torch" (1974)
"The Fat Vampire" (1993)
      http://ourworld.compuserve.com/homepages/normanspinrad/fat.htm.

*Other Important Works*

"Building a Starfaring Age." In *Writing Science Fiction & Fantasy*, edited by The Staff of *Analog & Isaac Asimov's Science Fiction Magazine*. New York: St. Martin's Griffin, 1993, 185–199.
"The Doomsday Machine." *Star Trek: The Original Series*. Episode # 35. October 20, 1967.
Introduction. *A Canticle for Leibowitz*. By Walter M. Miller, Jr. Boston, MA: Gregg, 1975.

Introduction. *Modern Science Fiction.* Garden City, NY: Doubleday, 1974.
Introduction. *We Can Remember It for You Wholesale.* By Philip K. Dick. New York: Carol, 1990.
"Rubber Sciences." *The Craft of Science Fiction.* edited by Reginald Bretnor. New York: Harper & Row, 1976, 54–70.
*Science Fiction in the Real World* (1990).
"Science Fiction in the Real World—Revisited" In *Science Fiction and Market Realities,* edited by George Slusser et al. Athens: University of Georgia Press, 1996, 20–35.
"Star Trek in the Real World." In David Gerrold and Robert J. Sawyer, eds., *Boarding the Enterprise: Transporters, Tribbles and the Vulcan Death Grip in Gene Roddenberry's Star Trek.* Dallas, TX: Benbella, 2006, 17–32.
*Staying Alive: A Writer's Guide* (1983)
"Where I Get My Crazy Ideas." In Maxim Jakubowski and Edward James, eds., *The Profession of Science Fiction: SF Writers on Their Craft and Ideas.* New York: St. Martin's, 1992, 95–100.

## Research Sources

*Encyclopedias and Handbooks:* **AW, CA, CANR, ESF, MSSF, NNDB, SFW**

*Bibliographies:* **ARB, FF, SFAN**

### Biographies and Interviews

Chester, Tony. "More than Human: Panel Discussion with Charles Stross, Colin Greenland and Norman Spinrad." *Mexicon 5: The Science Fact and Science Fiction Concatenation.* May 1994. http://www.concatenation.org/interviews/morethanhuman.html.
Lohr, Michael. "Druid King Norman Spinrad." *The Zone Online.* November 2005. http://www.zone-sf.com/nospinrad.html.
Snider, John C. Interview. *SciFi Dimensions.* June 2001. http://www.scifidimensions.com/Oct01/normanspinrad.htm.
"Spinrad VideoBlog on History Of Doomsday." *The Trek Movie Report.* February 10, 2007. SciFanatic Network. http://trekmovie.com/2007/02/10/spinrad-videoblog-on-history-of-doomsday/.
Strickland, Galen. Profile. *The Templeton Gate.* 2004. http://templetongate.tripod.com/spinrad.htm.

### Criticism and Readers' Guides

Le Guin, Ursula K. "On Norman Spinrad's *The Iron Dream.*" *Science Fiction Studies.* 1 (1973): 41–44. http://www.depauw.edu/sfs/backissues/1/leguin1art.htm.
Moorcock, Michael. *"Bug Jack Barron* by Norman Spinrad—An Introduction." *The Edge.* June 17, 2003. http://www.theedge.abelgratis.co.uk/bugjackbarron.htm.

Notkin, Debbie. "Forbidden Sex and Uncontrollable Obsession: Sex in the Writings of Norman Spinrad." *New York Review of Science Fiction.* 1(2) (1988): 1+.

*Web Sites*

*Norman Spinrad.* Official Web site. http://ourworld.compuserve.com/homepages/normanspinrad/.

# Olaf Stapledon (1886–1950)

*Two lights for guidance. The first, our little glowing atom of community, with all that it signifies. The second, the cold light of the stars . . .*
                                                    —*Star Maker (1937)*

## Biography

William Olaf Stapledon was born in on the Wirral peninsula in England, near Liverpool. He attended Balliol College, Oxford, and eventually earned a PhD in philosophy from the University of Liverpool. He served with the Friends' Ambulance Unit in France and Belgium during World War I, an experience that confirmed his life-long pacifism. He began writing fiction as a way of bringing his philosophical ideas to a wider audience. In dealing with subjects like genetic engineering, terraforming, and "transhumanism"—the use of genetics and technology to enhance human life—he was far ahead of his time, and authors such as Arthur C. Clarke, Brian Aldiss, and Stanisław Lem cite him as an influence.

In addition to his science fiction, Stapledon wrote and lectured extensively on philosophy, ethics, and pacifism. On September 6, 1950, he died suddenly of a heart attack at his home in Caldy, Wirral.

APOCALYPSE AND AFTER; FAR FUTURE; GENETICS & CLONING; GODS & DEMONS; POST-HUMAN; SUPERMAN

## Major Works

*Novels*

*Last and First Men: A Story of the Near and Far Future* (1930)
*Last Men in London* (1932)
*Odd John: A Story between Jest and Earnest* (1935)
*Star Maker* (1937)
*Sirius: A Fantasy of Love and Discord* (1944)
> All of the above novels are available online at Project Gutenberg, Australia. http://www.gutenberg.net.au/.

## Collections

*Far Future Calling: Uncollected Science Fiction and Fantasies of Olaf Stapledon.* Sam Moskowitz, ed. Philadelphia, PA: O.Train, 1979. Includes the essay "Interplanetary Man?" (1948) and an authorized biography.
*An Olaf Stapledon Reader.* Robert Crossley, ed. Syracuse, NY: Syracuse University Press, 1997.

## Notable Short Stories

The following short stories are available at Project Gutenberg. http://www. gutenberg.net.au/plusfifty-n-z.html#letterS.
"The Seed and the Flower" and "The Road to the Aide Post" (1916)
"A World of Sound" (1936)
"Arms Out of Hand" (1946)
"East is West" (published 1979)
"A Modern Magician" (date unknown).

## Other Important Works

*A Modern Theory of Ethics: A Study of the Relations of Ethics and Psychology* (1929)
*Talking Across the World: The Love Letters of Olaf Stapledon and Agnes Mille, 1913–1919.* Robert Crossley, ed. Hanover, NH: University Press of New England, 1987.
*The Opening of the Eyes* (1954)

# Research Sources

*Encyclopedias and Handbooks:* **AW, CA, ESF, MSSF, SFW, WS**

*Bibliographies:* **ARB, FF, SFAN**

Satty, H.J. and C.C. Smith. *Olaf Stapledon: A Bibliography.* Westport, CT: Greenwood, 1984.

## Biographies and Interviews

Fiedler, Leslie A. *Olaf Stapledon, a Man Divided.* Oxford: Oxford University Press, 1983.
Philmus, Robert M. "Undertaking Stapledon." *Science Fiction Studies.* 11 (1984). http://www.depauw.edu/sfs/review_essays/philm32.htm.

## Criticism and Readers' Guides

Aldiss, Brian. "The Immanent Will Returns—2" In *The Detached Retina: Aspects of SF and Fantasy.* Syracuse, NY: Syracuse University Press, 1995. 37–45.

Crossley, Robert. *Olaf Stapledon: Speaking for the Future*. Liverpool, UK: Liverpool University Press 1994.

Lem, Stanislaw. "On Stapledon's *Last and First Men*." *Science Fiction Studies*. 13 (1986): 272–291.

————. "On Stapledon's *Star Maker*." In Damien Broderick, ed., *Earth is But a Star: Excursions through Science Fiction to the Far Future*. Crawley: University of Western Australia Press, 2001, 1–8.

McCarthy, Patrick A. "The Genesis of *Star Maker*." *Science Fiction Studies*. 31 (2004): 25–42.

McCarthy, Patrick A, Charles Elkins, and Martin Harry Greenberg, eds. *The Legacy of Olaf Stapledon: Critical Essays and an Unpublished Manuscript*. Westport, CT: Greenwood, 1989.

*Web Sites*

*The Olaf Stapledon Archive*. University of Liverpool Library. An index to the personal and professional papers of Stapledon, spanning his career. http://www.sfhub.ac. uk/Stapledon.htm.

*The Olaf Stapledon Online Archive*. February 2008. Online text, in full, of stories, essays, poetry, and nonfiction—work that is difficult to find elsewhere. http: //www.geocities.com/olafstapledon_archive/index.html.

*2001 Cordwainer Smith Foundation "Rediscovery" Award*. Rosana Lineberger Hart. The Remarkable Science Fiction of Cordwainer Smith. September 2007. http://www.cordwainer-smith.com/stapledon.htm. Praise from one sf classic to another—announcement of the winner of the first Cordwainer Rediscovery Award, written by the daughter of Cordwainer Smith.

# *Neal Stephenson (1959– )*

> *Hiro is approaching the Street. It is the Broadway, the Champs Elysees of the Metaverse. It is the brilliantly lit boulevard that can be seen, miniaturized and backward, reflected in the lenses of his goggles. It does not really exist.*
>
> *—Snow Crash (1992)*

## Biography

Neal Town Stephenson was born in Fort Meade, Maryland. He attended Boston University, first as a Physics major and then, when he found that it would allow him to spend more time on the university mainframe, as a Geography major. Novels such as *Snow Crash* and *The Baroque Cycle*, in their different ways, reflect his keen interest in mathematics, technology, and the history of science. Neal Stephenson is one of the "new breed" of sf writers who has moved science fiction away from space rockets and laser blasters, and more toward a consideration of our current relation with science, and the evolution of ideas.

When time allows, Stephenson writes about technology for publications such as *Wired*, and works as an advisor for "Blue Origin," a company funded by Jeff Bezos to develop a manned suborbital launch system. He also serves on the advisory board of the Science Fiction Museum in Seattle. He lives near Seattle, Washington.

ARTIFICIAL INTELLIGENCE; CYBERPUNK; LANGUAGE; NANOTECHNOLOGY; VIRTUAL REALITY

## Major Works

*Novels*

*Snow Crash* (1992)
*Interface* (1994, as "Stephen Bury", with his uncle J. Frederick George)
*The Diamond Age: or a Young Lady's Illustrated Primer* (1995)
*Cobweb* (1996, as "Stephen Bury", with his uncle J. Frederick George)
*Cryptonomicon* (1999)
The Baroque Cycle: *Quicksilver* (2003), *The Confusion* (2004), *The System of the World* (2004)

*Notable Short Stories*

"Spew" (1994) http://wired-vig.wired.com/wired/archive/.
"The Great Simoleon Caper" (1995) http://kuoi.asui.uidaho.edu/~kamikaze/Text/simoleon.html.
"Jipi and The Paranoid Chip" (1997) http://www.vanemden.com/books/neals/jipi.html.

*Other Important Works*

"Global Neighborhood Watch." *Wired*. 1998. http://www.wired.com/wired/scenarios/global.html.
*In the Beginning . . . Was the Command Line* (1999)
"In the Kingdom of Mao Bell." *Wired*. February 1994. http://www.wired.com/wired/archive/.
"Mother Earth Mother Board." *Wired*. December 1996. http://www.wired.com/wired/archive/.
"Turn On, Tune In, Veg Out." *New York Times*. June 17, 2005.

## Research Sources

*Encyclopedias and Handbooks:* **AW, CA, CANR, ESF, NNDB, SFW**

*Bibliographies:* **ARB, FF, SFAN**

*Biographies and Interviews*

Godwin, Mike. "Neal Stephenson's Past, Present and Future." *Reason*. February 2005. http://www.reason.com/news/show/36481.html.

Leonard, Andrew. "The Summit of Mount Stephenson." *Salon.* September 22, 2004. http://dir.salon.com/story/tech/books/2004/09/22/system/index.html? source=search&aim=/tech/books.

Levine, Robert. "Neal Stephenson Rewrites History." *Wired.* September 2003. http:// www.wired.com/wired/archive/11.09/history.html.

McClellan, Jim. "Neal Stepehenson, the Interview." *The Guardian.* November 4, 2004. http://www.guardian.co.uk/technology/2004/nov/04/onlinesupplement.

Miller, Laura. "Neal Stephenson: The Salon Interview." *Salon.* April 2004. http://dir.salon.com/story/books/int/2004/04/21/stephenson/index.html?source= search&aim=/books/int.

Miller, Robin. "Neal Stephenson Responds with Wit and Humor." *Slashdot.* October 20, 2004.

Open Source Technology Group. http://interviews.slashdot.org/interviews/04/10/20/ 1518217.shtml?tid=192&tid=214&tid=126&tid=11.

## Criticism and Readers' Guides

Blackmore, Tim. "Agent of Civility: The Librarian in Neal Stephenson's *Snow Crash*." *Simile* 4(4) (2004). http://www.utpjournals.com/simile/simile.html.

Brigg, Peter. "The Future as the Past Viewed From the Present: Neal Stephenson's *The Diamond Age*." *Extrapolation.* 40 (1999): 116–124.

Grassian, Daniel. "Discovering the Machine in You: The Literary, Social, and Religious Implications of Neal Stephenson's *Snow Crash*." *Journal of the Fantastic in the Arts.* 12 (2001): 250–267.

Heuser, Sabine. "Neal Stephenson's Metaspace." In *Virtual Geographies: Cyberpunk at the Intersection of the Postmodern and Science Fiction.* Amsterdam, The Netherlands: Rodopi, 2003, 171–190.

Jones, Gwyneth. "The Boys Want to Be with the Boys: Neal Stephenson's *Snow Crash*." In *Deconstructing the Starships.* Liverpool, UK: Liverpool University Press, 1999, 146–152.

Kendrick, Michelle. "Space, Technology and Neal Stephenson's Science Fiction." In Rob Kitchin and James Kneale, eds., *Lost in Space: Geographies of Science Fiction.* London: Continuum, 2002, 57–73.

Longan, Michael and Tim Oakes. "Geography's Conquest of History in *The Diamond Age*." In Rob Kitchin and James Kneale, eds., *Lost in Space: Geographies of Science Fiction.* London: Continuum, 2002, 39–56.

## Web Sites

*Neal Stephenson.* Official Web page. www.nealstephenson.com.

*Neal Stephenson.* Personal Homepage. Links to stories, essays, and a photogallery. http://web.mac.com/nealstephenson/Neal_Stephensons_Site/Home.html.

*Cryptonomicon.com.* Avon Books. May 2003. Publicity Web site for the book, with quotes from review and downloadable version of essay "In the Beginning was the Command Line." http://www.cryptonomicon.com/praise.html.

*Hiro Worship Page.* Mark Damon Hughes. July 2001. Fan site, with links to Stephenson work that is not available elsewhere. http://kuoi.asui.uidaho.edu/~kamikaze/Text/snowcrash.php.

# Charles Stross (1964–  )

*It's a hot summer Tuesday, and he's standing in the plaza in front of the Central Station with his eyeballs powered up and the sunlight jangling off the canal . . .*
                                                    —*Accelerando (2005)*

## Biography

Charles David George Stross was born in Leeds, in West Yorkshire, England. He is a qualified pharmacist, with a postgraduate degree in Computer Science, and prior to becoming a full-time writer in 2003, he worked as a technical author, freelance journalist, programmer, and pharmacist. He has also written for and about role-playing games, and some of the creatures he devised have been officially adopted for *Dungeons & Dragons.*

Stross' work was first published in the late 1980s, but his name was made in 2001 by a series of novellas that would become the fix-up novel *Accelerando* (2005). Stross' stories deftly juggle the impact of technological change on individuals and societies, the political and the personal. Like a number of current British science fiction writers, his fiction has a "genre-bending" quality: his sf has distinct elements of fantasy and Lovecraftian horror. He lives in Edinburgh, Scotland, with his wife Feórag NicBhride.

ALIEN THREAT; NANOTECHNOLOGY; POSTHUMAN; SPACE OPERA; TECHNOLOGY

## Major Works

*Novels*

Timelike Diplomacy series*: Singularity Sky* (2003), *Iron Sunrise* (2004)
*Accelerando* (2005) **Locus Poll** http://www.accelerando.org/copyright/.
"Laundry" series*: The Atrocity Archives* (2004), *The Jennifer Morgue* (2006)
The Merchant Princes series: T*he Family Trade* (2004), *The Hidden Family* (2005), *The Clan Corporate* (2005), *The Merchants' War* (2007)
*Glasshouse* (2006)
*Halting State* (2007)
*Saturn's Children* (2008)

*Collections*

*Toast: And Other Rusted Futures.* Rockville, MD: Cosmos, 2002. Title novella and previously unpublished "The Concrete Jungle" (**Hugo**—available on line at http://www.goldengryphon.com/Stross-Concrete.html). Also includes introduction ("Charlie's Demons") by Ken MacLeod.

## Short Stories

Charles Stross is a staunch supporter of Creative Commons, and much of his work is available freely online. For links, see http://www.freesfonline.de/authors/Charles_Stross.html.
*Scratch Monkey* (1993) http://www.antipope.org/charlie/fiction/monkey/index.html.
"A Colder War" (2002) http://www.infinityplus.co.uk/stories/colderwar.htm.
"Unwirer" (2004) with Cory Doctorow. http://craphound.com/unwirer/archives/000006.html.

## Other Important Works

"Civil Liberties in Cyberspace." *Computer Shopper* (Dennis Publishing Ltd.). 89 (1995). http://www.antipope.org/charlie/journo/civil-lib.html.
"The High Frontier, Redux." *Charlie's Diary.* June 16, 2007. The Autopope Zone. http://www.antipope.org/charlie/blog-static/2007/06/the_high_frontier_redux.html.
"Life's a Game and Then You Die." *PlayerVox.* March 27, 2007. Beta GuildCafe. http://www.guildcafe.com/Vox/04071-Stross-Lifes-a-Game.html.
*The Web Architect's Handbook* (1996)

# Research Sources

*Encyclopedias and Handbooks:* **AW, CA, NNDB**

*Bibliographies:* **ARB, FF, SFAN**

## Biographies and Interviews

"Charles Stross Uploads his Mind to HardSF.net." *Hardsf.net.* June 28, 2006. http://www.hardsf.net/?mode=8&id=1.
Chester, Tony. "More than Human: Panel Discussion with Charles Stross, Colin Greenland, and Norman Spinrad." *Mexicon 5: The Science Fact and Science Fiction Concatenation.* May 1994. http://www.concatenation.org/interviews/morethanhuman.html.
Kemble, Gary. "Charles Stross: Keeping Life Interesting." *Articulate.* July 31, 2006. Australian Broadcasting Company. http://www.abc.net.au/news/arts/articulate/200607/s1700770.htm.
Lilley, Ernest. "Interview with Charles Stross." *SFRevu* April 7, 2005. http://sfrevu.com/Review-Id.php?id=2715.
*Locus Online.* "Fast Forward." January 2005. http://www.locusmag.com/2005/Issues/01Stross.html.
Lohr, Michael. "Searching for Scottish Ghosts, Stardust and Causality Violations: An Interview with Charles Stross." *Internet Review of Science Fiction.* March 2006. http://www.irosf.com/q/zine/article/10260.

Scalzi, John M. Interview. *By the Way . . .* Dec. 6, 2006. http://journals.aol.com/
   johnmscalzi/bytheway/.

*Criticism and Readers' Guides*

Empson, Martin. "Electric Reading: Free Downloads Benefit Artists and the Public."
   *Socialist Review.* November 2005. http://www.socialistreview.org.uk/article.php?
   articlenumber=9612. Article that focuses on Stross' success in using Creative
   Commons to make a living from writing.
Rucker, Rudy. "Notes on Clarles Stross's Accelerando." *New York Review of Science
   Fiction* 18(3) (2005): 1+.

*Web Sites*

*The Autopope Zone.* Official Web site. http://www.antipope.org/charlie/.

## *Arkady Strugatsky (1925–1991) and Boris Strugatsky (1931–   )*

> *"Part dreamer,"* continued the prosecutor, *"part adventurer."*
>
> *"That's no longer a profession, replied Mac. "It is, if I may say so, simply a trait possessed by any decent scientist."*
>
> *"And decent politician."*
> *"A rare combination of words,"* quipped Mac.
>
> *—Prisoners of Power (1969)*

## Biography

The Brothers Strugatsky are the best known, most widely translated Russian science fiction authors in the world. They began to write together in the late-1950s, using allegory, social satire, and the conventions of Russian folktales to express their disillusionment with the Soviet system. Their humor and ingenuity makes it possible for readers anywhere to relate to the universal experience of the "little man" struggling for survival, meaning, and dignity against overwhelming forces.

Arkady Natanovich Strugatsky and Boris Natanovich Strugatsky were born in the Soviet Union, and grew up in Leningrad. For most of his life Arkady was a translator and language teacher; Boris was trained as an astronomer and worked as a computer mathematician at the Pulkovo Observatory in Leningrad. Their writing partnership ended on October 23, 1991 when Arkady Strugatsky died of a chronic heart condition. Since the death of his brother, Boris Strugatsky continues to write science fiction, under the name "S. Vititsky."

FANTASY; FIRST CONTACT; HUMOR AND SATIRE; NEAR FUTURE; POLITICAL SF; SPACE OPERA

# Major Works

*Novels*

Noon Universe stories: *Noon: 22nd Century* (1962), *Escape Attempt* (1962), *Far Rainbow* (1963), *Hard to Be a God* (1964), *Prisoners of Power* (aka *The Inhabited Island*, 1971), *Beetle in the Anthill* (1980), *The Time Wanderers* (1986)
*Monday Begins on Saturday* (1965)
*The Snail on the Slope* (1965)
*Tale of the Troika* (1968)
    An excerpt can be found in *Politicizing Magic: An Anthology of Russian and Soviet Fairy Tales*. Marina Balina et al., eds. Evanston, IL: Northwestern University Press, 2005. 316–344.
*The Second Martian Invasion* (1968)
*Roadside Picnic* (1972)
*Definitely Maybe: A Manuscript Discovered Under Unusual Circumstances* (1977)

*Short Stories*

"Destination: Amaltheia." (1960, trans. Leonid Kolesnikov). http://www.kuzbass.ru/moshkow/koi/STRUGACKIE/engl_amal.txt.
"The Gigantic Fluctuation." (1962, trans. Gladys Evans). http://www.lib.ru/STRUGACKIE/r_fluct_engl.txt
"The Visitors" (1979) In Roger DeGaris, ed. and tr., *Aliens, Travelers, and Other Strangers (Best of Soviet Science Fiction)*. London: Macmillan, 1984.

*Other Important Works*

*Stalker.* Dir. Andrei Tarkovsky. Mosfilm, 1979. Based on *Roadside Picnic*; the text of the screenplay, written with director Andrei Tarkovsky, can be found in *Collected Screenplays*, translated by William Powell and Natasha Synessios. London: Faber, 1999. 373–416.
"Working for Tarkovsky." (BNS) *Science Fiction Studies* 31 (2004): 418–420.
"Working with Andrei [Tarkovsky] on the Script of *Stalker.*" (ANS) Trans. Sergei Sossinsky. From *About Andrei Tarkovsky, Memoirs and Biographies* (1990). http://www.acs.ucalgary.ca/~tstronds/nostalghia.com/TheTopics/Stalker/strugatsky.html.

# Research Sources

*Encyclopedias and Handbooks:* **AW, BW, CA, CAAS, ESF, MSSF, SFW**

*Bibliographies:* **FF, SFAN**

Borisov, V. "English Language Bibliography (Primary and Secondary Sources)" *The Brothers Strugatsky*. Alexandr Usov, ed. http://www.rusf.ru/abs/english/index.htm.

Sofka, Mike. Bibliography. February 2004. Rensselaer Polytechnic Institute. http://www.rpi.edu/~sofkam/lem/abs.html.

*Biographies and Interviews*

Gopman, Vladimir. "Science Fiction Teaches the Civic Virtues: An Interview with Arkadii Strugatsky." *Science Fiction Studies* 18 (1991): 1–10. http://www.depauw.edu/sfs/interviews/Gopman53interview.htm.

Howell, Yvonne. *Arkady Strugatsky: Obituary. Science Fiction Studies* 19 (1992): 150.

Ivanova, Vera and Mikhail Manykin. "Stalkers of Russian Science Fiction—the Strugatsky Brothers." *Russian InfoCenter.* August 16, 2006. Moscow State University. http://www.russia-ic.com/culture_art/literature/230/.

Suvin, Darko. "Strugatski Remembrance." *Extrapolation.* 44 (2003): 224–226.

Vishnevsky, Boris. "Boris Strugatsky: We Cannot Do It Any Other Way Yet." *The Moscow News.* August 2004. http://english.mn.ru/english/issue.php?2004-22-19.

*Criticism and Readers' Guides*

Airaudi, Jesse T. *"Hard To Be a God*: The Political Antiworlds of Voznesensky, Sokolov, and the Brothers Strugatsky." In Alliene R. Becker, ed., *Visions of the Fantastic.* Westport, CT: Greenwood, 1996, 63–70.

Boer, Roland. "Pawing Through Garbage: On the Dialectics of Dystopia in Lamentations and the Strugatsky Brothers." In *Knockin' on Heaven's Door: The Bible and Popular Culture.* New York: Routledge, 1999. 110–129.

Csicsery-Ronay, Istvan, Jr. "Towards the Last Fairy Tale: On the Fairy-Tale Paradigm in the Strugatskys' SF, 1963–1972." *Science Fiction Studies.* 13 (1993): 1–41.

———— "Zamyatin and the Strugatskys: The Representation of Freedom in *We* and *The Snail on the Slope.*" In Gary Kern, ed., *Zamyatin's We: A Collection of Critical Essays.* Ann Arbor, MI: Ardis, 1988, 236–258.

Gomel, Elana. "The Poetics of Censorship: Allegory as Form and Ideology in the Novels of Arkady and Boris Strugatsky." *Science Fiction Studies.* 22 (1995): 87–105. http://www.depauw.edu/sfs/backissues/65/gomel65art.htm.

Howell, Yvonne. *Apocalyptic Realism: The Science Fiction of Arkady and Boris Strugatsky.* New York: Peter Lang, 1994.

Lem, Stanislaw. "About the Strugatsky's *Roadside Picnic.*" In *Microworlds.* Orlando, FL: Harvest/Harcourt Brace, 2006, 243–278.

Potts, Stephen W. *The Second Marxian Invasion: The Fiction of the Strugatsky Brothers.* San Bernardino, CA: Borgo, 1991.

Simon, Erik. "The Strugatskys in Political Context." *Science Fiction Studies.* 31 (2004): 378–406.

*Web Sites*

*The Brother Strugatsky.* Alexandr Usov. January 1998. Very professional Russian fan Web site (pages in English and Russian), which includes a bibliography and information about Strugatsky-based movies. Three Strugatsky novels and one novella are available as a downloads. http://www.rusf.ru/abs/english/index.htm.

# Theodore Sturgeon (1918–1985)

*After a time you may find that having is not so pleasing a thing, after all, as wanting. It is not logical, but it is often true.*

*—"Amok Time," Star Trek (1967)*

## Biography

Born Edward Hamilton Waldo, on Staten Island, New York, he was renamed "Ted Sturgeon" when he was adopted by his austere and demanding stepfather. At age seventeen, he ran away and joined the Merchant Marine, and during three years at sea, he began to write, churning out mainstream adventure, science fiction, and romance. His stories are peopled with outcasts and youngsters whose powers and talents are underestimated and reviled.

At one time, Sturgeon was the most anthologized author alive; according to The Encyclopedia of Science Fiction, " . . . he was a powerful and generally liberating influence in post-WWII US sf." He wrote a number of *Star Trek* episodes, notable for introducing crucial elements of Trek lore, such as *pon farr*, the Vulcan mating ritual, and the "Prime Directive." Theodore Sturgeon died on May 8, 1985, of pneumonia brought on by chronic lung disease, in Eugene, Oregon.

ALIENS; CHILDREN IN SF; GENDER & SEXUALITY; POSTHUMAN; PSI POWERS; SEX & TABOOS

## Major Works

*Novels*

*The Dreaming Jewels* (1950, aka *The Synthetic Man*)
*More Than Human* (1953)
*The Cosmic Rape* (1958)
*Venus Plus X* (1960)
*Some of Your Blood* (1961)

*Collections*

*The Complete Short Stories of Theodore Sturgeon* (edited by Paul Williams. Berkeley, CA: North Atlantic Books): Eleven volumes, which cover Sturgeon's career: *The Ultimate Egoist*: 1937 to 1940 (1994, foreword by Ray Bradbury), *Microcosmic God*: 1940 to 1941 (1995), *Killdozer*: 1941 to 1946 (1996), *Thunder and Roses*: 1946 to 1948 (1997), *The Perfect Host*: 1948 to 1950 (1998), *Baby is Three*: 1950 to 1952 (1999), *Saucer of Loneliness*: 1953 (2000, foreword by Kurt Vonnegut),

*Bright Segment*: 1953 to 1955 (2002), *And Now the News* . . . :1955 to 1957 (2003), *The Man Who Lost the Sea* (2005), *The Nail and the Oracle* (2007)

## Notable Short Stories

"Killdozer!" (1944)
"If All Men Were Brothers, Would You Let One Marry Your Sister?" (1967)
"Slow Sculpture" (1970) **Hugo, Nebula**
"Case and the Dreamer" (1973)

## Other Important Works

"Future Writers in a Future World." *The Craft of Science Fiction*, edited by Reginald Bretnor. New York: Harper & Row, 1976, 89–103.
Introduction. *Roadside Picnic* and *Tale of the Troika*, by Arkady and Brois Strukatsky. New York: Macmillan, 1977, viii.
"Science Fiction, Morals, and Religion." In Reginald Bretnor, ed., *Science Fiction, Today and Tomorrow; A Discursive Symposium*. New York: Harper & Row, 1974, 98–115.
"Theodore Sturgeon on Philip Dick." In D. Scott Apel, ed., *Philip K. Dick: The Dream Connection*. San Jose, CA: Permanent Press, 1987, 288–289.
"Why So Much Syzygy?" In Damon Knight, ed., *Turning Points: Essays on the Art of Science Fiction*. New York: Harper & Row, 1977, 269–272.

## Research Sources

*Encyclopedias and Handbooks:* **AW, CA, CAAS, CANR, ESF, MSSF, SFW, WS**

*Bibliographies:* **ARB, FF, SFAN**

Stephensen-Payne, Phil and Gordon R. Benson, Jr. *Theodore Sturgeon: Sculptor of Love and Hate, A Working Bibliography*. Albuquerque, NM: Galactic Central, 1989.

### Biographies and Interviews

Aldiss, Brian. "Sturgeon—The Cruelty of the Gods." (Obituary) In *The Detached Retina: Aspects of SF and Fantasy*. Syracuse, NY: Syracuse University Press, 1995. 87–91.
Duncan, David. "The Push from Within: The Extrapolative Ability of Theodore Sturgeon." *Phoenix*. University of Tennessee. 1979. http://www.physics.emory.edu/~weeks/misc/duncan.html.
Hartwell, David G. "An Interview with Theodore Sturgeon (2 parts)." *New York Review of Science Fiction*. 1(7 & 8) 1989.

Salmonson, Jessica Amanda. "Regarding Ted Sturgeon (1918–1985)." *Aunt Violet's Book Museum*. 2000. http://www.violetbooks.com/REVIEWS/jas-sturgeon.html.

## Criticism and Readers' Guides

Clute, John. "Eros in the Age of Machines: Why Did Theodore Sturgeon's Great Love Stories Languish in the Ghetto of Science Fiction?" *Salon*. November 15, 2000. http://archive.salon.com/books/feature/2000/11/15/sturgeon/index.html.
Delany, Samuel. "Sturgeon." In *Starboard Wine: More Notes on the Language of Science Fiction*. Pleasantville, NY: Dragon, 1984.
Hartwell, David G. "Middle High Sturgeon." *New York Review of Science Fiction*. 16(5) (2004): 20+.
Menger, Lucy. *Theodore Sturgeon (Recognitions)*. New York: Frederick Ungar, 1981.
Merril, Judith. "A [Real?] Writer—Homage to Ted Sturgeon." *Fantasy & Science Fiction*. October/November 1999.
Spinrad, Norman. "Sturgeon, Vonnegut and Trout." In *Science Fiction in the Real World*. Carbondale: Southern Illinois University. Press, 1990, 167–181.
Stableford, Brian. "Schemes of Salvation: The Literary Explorations of Theodore Sturgeon." In *Outside the Human Aquarium: Masters of Science Fiction*. San Bernardino, CA: Borgo, 1995, 117–125.
Sturgill, Jeremiah. Exploring Theodore Sturgeon through Analysis of "Die, Maestro, Die" *Internet Review of Science Fiction*. November 2004. http://www.irosf.com/q/zine/article/10099.

## Web Sites

*The Theodore Sturgeon Literary Trust*. March 2007. Information about the Complete Strugeon project, and other re-releases of Sturgeon's work. Links to all know online reviews of Sturgeon's work. http://www.physics.emory.edu/~weeks/sturgeon/.
*The Theodore Sturgeon Page*. Eric Weeks. February 2008. Reviews, articles, and links to personal reminiscences of Sturgeon. http://www.physics.emory.edu/~weeks/misc/sturgeon.html.

# Sheri S. Tepper (1929–  )

*Then I tumbled back down the rock wall into the bottom of the cavern to lie face down on the stones, weeping miserably and feeling that never, never, in my fifteen years of life had I been understood by anyone at all.*
*After which I went and raised up the dead.*

*—King's Blood Four (1983)*

## Biography

Sheri Tepper was born near Littleton, Colorado. She worked for Rocky Mountain Planned Parenthood for twenty years, eventually becoming its Executive Director. As well as her science fiction and fantasy, Tepper has also written two well-received horror novels (as "E.E. Horlak") and detective stories (as "A.J. Orde" and "B.J. Oliphant"). She currently operates a guest ranch with her husband Gene Tepper in Santa Fe, New Mexico.

Although Tepper was writing poetry and children's stories as early as 1963, her writing career began in earnest in the early 1980s, with a burst of creativity that included *The Gate to Women's Country* (1988). This was her first wholly sf work, and immediately recognized as one of the great feminist science fiction novels of the 1980s. Since then, Tepper has kept up a steady stream of inventive and challenging novels about the abuse of power, and the ultimate triumph of the powerless.

ALIENS; APOCALYPSE AND AFTER; CHILDREN IN SF; FANTASY; FEMINISM; GENDER & SEXUALITY; UTOPIAS

## Major Works

*Novels*

*The Land of True Game* (a trilogy of trilogies)
"Peter": *King's Blood Four* (1983), *Necromancer's Nine* (1983), *Wizard's Eleven* (1984)
"Mavin Manyshaped": *The Song of Mavin Manyshaped* (1985), *The Flight of Mavin Manyshaped* (1985), *The Search for Mavin Manyshaped* (1985)
"Jinian": *Jinian Footseer* (1985), *Dervish Daughter* (1986), *Jinian Star-Eye* (1986)
*The Revenants* (1984)
*After Long Silence* (1987, aka *The Enigma Score* in the U.K.)
The Awakeners: *NorthShore* (1987), *SouthShore* (1987)
*The Gate to Women's Country* (1988)
The Arbai Trilogy: *Grass* (1989), *Raising the Stones* (1990), *Sideshow* (1992)
*A Plague of Angels* (1993)
*Shadow's End* (1994)
*Gibbon's Decline & Fall* (1996)
*Family Tree* (1997)
*Six Moon Dance* (1998)
*The Fresco* (2000)

*Collections*

*The True Game* (1985) New York: Ace, 1996. Single-volume edition of the "Peter" stories.

*Other Important Works*

"The Power of Art." *sffworld.com* 2002. http://www.sffworld.com/authors/t/tepper_sheri/articles/powerofart.html.

## Research Sources

*Encyclopedias and Handbooks:* **AW, CA, CANR, ESF, NNDB, SFW**

*Bibliographies:* **ARB, FF, SFAN**

Bibliography. *Novel Reflections.* http://www.novelreflections.com/authors/sheri-tepper/bibliography.php.

*Biographies and Interviews*

*Fresh Air from WHYY.* Radio Interview. April 24, 2002. National Public Radio. http://www.npr.org/templates/story/story.php?storyId=1142218.
*Locus Online.* "Speaking to the Universe." September 1998. http://www.locusmag.com/1998/Issues/09/Tepper.html.

*Criticism and Readers' Guides*

Jones, Gwyneth. "Plague of Angels: The Fiction of Sherri Tepper." In *Deconstructing the Starships: Science, Fiction, and Reality.* Liverpool, UK: Liverpool University Press, 1999. 178–183.
Jowett, Lorna. "The Female State: Science Fiction Alternatives to the Patriarchy—Sheri Tepper's *The Gate to Women's Country* and Orson Scott Card's Homecoming Series." In Karen Sayer and John Moore, eds., *Science Fiction, Critical Frontiers.* New York: St. Martin's Press, 2000, 169–192.
Pearson, Wendy. "After the (Homo)Sexual: A Queer Analysis of Anti-Sexuality in Sheri S. Tepper's *The Gate to Women's Country.*" *Science Fiction Studies.* 23 (1996): 199–226.
Reid, Robin Anne. "'Momutes': Momentary Utopias in Tepper's Trilogies." In Martha Bartter, ed., *The Utopian Fantastic.* Westport, CT : Praeger, 2004, 101–108.
Wilson, Tamara. "Beyond Personal Introspection: Classroom Response to Sherri Tepper's *The Gate to Women's Country.*" In Martha Bartter, ed., *The Utopian Fantastic.* Westport, CT: Praeger, 2004, 123–128.

*Web Sites*

*Sheri S. Tepper.* Atlanta and Jan Schmidt, eds. May 2007. http://www.sheri-s-tepper.com.

# "James P. Tiptree, Jr." [Alice Hastings Bradley Sheldon] (1915–1987)

*"For Christ's sake, Ruth, they're aliens!"*
*"I'm used to it," she says absently.*

*—"The Women Men Don't See" (1973)*

## Biography

Alice Hastings Bradley Sheldon was born in Chicago, Illinois, and spent much of her childhood in Africa and India with her author/adventurer parents. With her husband, Huntingdon Sheldon, she was involved in U.S. Army Air Intelligence, and the development of the CIA. After retiring from the service in the late 1950s, she began writing science fiction under the pseudonym "James P. Tiptree Jr." (a name acquired from a jar of marmalade).

Tiptree's work reconciles the style and spirit of space opera with the darker, deeper alienation of the New Wave. Various critics have detected her influence on cyberpunk. Her greatest works appearing during the 1970s, and a subsequent dropping off of quality and control was due to her declining health, and that of her husband. In 1987, she shot and killed him, and then herself, in their home in McLean, Virginia.

ALIENS; ENTROPY; FEMINISM; GENDER & SEXUALITY; PSYCHOLOGY; VIRTUAL REALITY; WOMEN IN SF

## Major Works

*Novels*

*Up the Walls of the World* (1978)
*Brightness Falls from the Air* (1985)
*The Starry Rift* (1986)

*Collections*

*Her Smoke Rose Up Forever*. San Francisco, CA: Tachyon, 2004. Selected stories from Tiptree's earlier collections *Ten Thousand Light Years From Home* (1973), *Warm Worlds and Otherwise* (1975), and *Star Songs of an Old Primate* (1978). The Introduction, by John Clute, is available online at http://davidlavery.net/Tiptree/.

*Notable Short Stories*

"The Last Flight of Doctor Ain" (1969) http://mtsu32.mtsu.edu:11072/3050/Stories/Two_by_Tiptree.pdf.

"Love is the Plan, the Plan is Death" (1973) **Nebula**
"The Girl Who Was Plugged In" (1974) **Hugo**
"Houston, Houston, Do You Read?" (1976) **Hugo, Nebula**
"The Screwfly Solution" (1977, as "Racoona Sheldon") **Nebula** http://mtsu32.mtsu.
    edu:11072/3050/Stories/Two_by_Tiptree.pdf.
"Beyond the Dead Reef" (1983) **Locus Poll**
"The Only Neat Thing to Do" (1985) **Locus Poll**

## Other Important Works

"Dear Starbear: Letters Between Ursula K. Le Guin and James Tiptree Jr." Philips,
    Julie, ed. *Fantasy & Science Fiction* 111(3) (2006): 77–115.
*Meet Me at Infinity: The Uncollected Tiptree*. Edited by David Hartwell. New York: Tor,
    2000. Thirty-five essays and stories, including "Everything But the Signature Is
    Me" (1979), "Review of Ursula K. Le Guin's *The Lathe of Heaven*" (1975), "With
    Tiptree Through the Great Sex Muddle" (1975), "A Woman Writing Science
    Fiction and Fantasy" (1988), "Do You Like it Twice?" (1972, as Alice Sheldon),
    and "The Lucky Ones" (1946, as Alice Bradley).
*Neat Sheets: The Poetry of James Tiptree, Jr.* San Francisco, CA: Tachyon, 1996.

# Research Sources

*Encyclopedias and Handbooks:* **AW, CA, CANR, ESF, MSSF, SCFW, SFW, WS**

*Bibliographies:* **ARB, FF, SFAN**

Stephensen-Payne, Phil and Gordon Benson Jr. *James Tiptree Jr., A Lady of Letters: A
    Working Bibliography*. Polk City, IA: Galactic Central, 1988.

## Biographies and Interviews

Elms, Alan C. "The Psychologist Who Empathized with Rats: James Tiptree, Jr. as
    Alice B. Sheldon, PhD." *Science Fiction Studies*. 31 (2004): 81–96.
Itzkoff, Dave. "Alice's Alias." *New York Times Book Review*. August 20, 2006: 1+.
Philips, Julie. *James Tiptree, Jr.: The Double Life of Alice B. Sheldon*. New York: St.
    Martin's, 2006.
Siegel, Mark. "Love Was the Plan, the Plan was . . . A True Story About James Tiptree,
    Jr." *Foundation*. Winter 1988/1989. http://davidlavery.net/Tiptree/.

## Criticism and Readers' Guides

Hicks, Heather J. "Whatever It Is That She's Since Become: Writing Bodies of Text
    and Bodies of Women in James Tiptree, Jr.'s 'The Girl Who Was Plugged In' and
    William Gibson's 'The Winter Market.'" *Contemporary Literature* 37 (1996):
    62–93.

Larbalestier, Justine. "I'm Too Big, But I Love to Play: Stories about James Tiptree Jr." In *The Battle of the Sexes in Science Fiction*. Middletown, CT: Wesleyan University Press, 2002, 180–202.

Lefanu, Sarah, "Who is Tiptree, What Is She?" In *In the Chinks of the World Machine: Feminism and Science Fiction*. London: Women's, 1988, 105–129.

Pearson, Wendy. "(Re)reading James Tiptree Jr.'s 'And I Awoke and Found Me Here on the Cold Hill Side.'" In Justine Larbalestier, ed., *Daughters of Earth: Feminist Science Fiction in the Twentieth Century*. Middletown, CT: Wesleyan University Press, 2006, 160–189.

Shaw, Debra Benita. "'Your Haploid Heart': James Tiptree, Jr. and Patterns of Gender." In *Women, Science and Fiction: The Frankenstein Inheritance*. New York: Palgrave, 2001, 107–127.

Siegel, Mark Richard. *James Tiptree Jr.* Starmont Reader's Guide 22. San Bernardino, CA: Borgo, 1984.

## Web Sites

*James Tiptree, Jr. World Wide Web Site*. David Lavery. July 2006. A thorough and well-designed site that includes extensive biographical and bibliographical information. http://davidlavery.net/Tiptree/.

*James Tiptree, Jr.: The Double Life of Alice B. Sheldon*. Julie Phillips. January 2007. Site to publicize Phillips' biography of Tiptree. Further Reading and Links section is especially interesting. http://www.julie-phillips.com/.

**If you enjoyed James Tiptree Jr...**

Alice Sheldon was a unique voice in science fiction: "proto-punk" in style and attitudes, full of rage and humor, she proved that women sf writers could play with the big boys. "Several themes interpenetrate JT's best work—sex, exogamy, identity, feminist depictions of male/female relations, ecology, death—but the greatest of these is death." (**ESF**).

**Then you might like...**

*Alfred Bester*. Like Tiptree, Bester was the master of slang and a richly imagine future. His writing remains so fresh and modern, fifty years after it was written, that he is periodically claimed by the "latest new thing" as one of their own: proto-New Wave, proto-cyberpunk, proto-slipstream. In *The Stars My Destination* and *The Demolished Man*, Bester combined action with insights, and single-handedly moved the genre away from the cardboard characterizations of the Golden Age.

*Samuel R. Delany*. Novels such as *Babel-17*, *Triton: An Ambiguous Heterotopia*, and *Dhalgren* are potent blends of the conventions of space opera, and high philosophy, mythology, and linguistics. Identity itself is often fluid in a Delany story: in a universe where one can change one's physical appearance, gender, and sexual orientation at will, what can you trust?

*Harlan Ellison*. Like Tiptree, Ellison is best known for his stories "dramatizing situations of extreme alienation" (**AW**). Stories such as "Pretty Maggie Moneyeyes" and "Jeffty is Five" reflect a mistrust of technology as a cure for all ills, the value of strong emotions of all sorts, and the importance of myth, both personal and universal.

**Doris Piserchia.** Darkly comic, imaginative fiction, by an author with interesting biographical parallels to Sheldon: service in the U.S. Navy during the 1950s, followed by a Master's degree in educational psychology. Between 1966 and 1983, thirteen novels and nearly a score of short stories include metaphysical time travel (*Mister Justice*, 1973) and escapist yarns (*Spaceling*, 1978; *Star Rider*, 1973); like Tiptree, her work is action packed, thoughtful, and ambitious.

**Sheri Tepper.** Like Tiptree, whose "most effective stories seem motivated by outrage" (**AW**), Tepper has channeled her anger about issues such as the abuse of power and the exploitation of nature into novels such as *The Gate to Women's Country* (1988), *Grass* (1989), and *The Fresco* (2000).

# A.E. Van Vogt (1912–2000)

*Cunning came, understanding of the presence of these creatures. This, Coeurl reasoned for the first time, was a scientific expedition from another star. Scientists would investigate, and not destroy. Scientists would refrain from killing him if he did not attack. Scientists, in their way, were fools.*
*—The Voyage of the Space Beagle (1939)*

## Biography

Alfred Elton van Vogt grew up on a farm in a Mennonite community in Manitoba, Canada. During the Depression, while he worked as a truck driver, and later as a statistical clerk at the Canadian Department of National Defence, he dreamed of making his name and fortune by writing. During the 1940s, van Vogt wrote a vast number of short stories, which he later patched together into novels such as *Slan* (1946) and *The Voyage of the Space Beagle* (1950), a process he called a "fix-up." In the 1950s, he became involved briefly with L. Ron Hubbard, Scientology and Dianetics, a form of psychoanalysis that offered to unleash the individual's potential to become the very sort of superman depicted in his novels.

At the end of his life, A.E. van Vogt suffered from Alzheimer's disease, although he continued writing and reworking old material. On January 26, 2000, he died of pneumonia in Los Angeles.

ALIENS; CHILDREN IN SF; GENETICS & CLONING; GODS AND DEMONS; MONSTERS; PSI POWERS; SUPERMEN

## Major Works

*Novels*

Null-A: *The World of Null-A* (1945), *The Pawns of Null-A* (1956—aka *The Players of Null-A* (1966), *Null-A Three* (1985—aka *Null A-3*). An excerpt from *The World of Null-A* is available online at http://vanvogt.www4.mmedia.is/nullA1chapter. htm.

*Slan* (1946)

*The Weapon Makers* (1947)

*The Voyage of the Space Beagle* (1950) Fix-up, consisting of short stories "Black Destroyer" (1939), "Discord in Scarlet" (1939) and "M 33 in Andromeda" (1943)

*The Weapon Shops of Isher* (1951) Fix-up, consisting of short stories "The Seesaw" (1941), "The Weapon Shop" (1942) and "The Weapon Shops of Isher" (1949)

*The Silkie* (1969)

*Children of Tomorrow* (1970)

*The Battle of Forever* (1971)


## Collections

*Futures Past: The Best Short Fiction of A.E. van Vogt.* San Francisco, CA: Tachyon, 1999.

*Transfinite: The Essential A.E. van Vogt.* Framingham, MA: NESFA, 2003.


## Other Important Works

*Reflections of A.E. van Vogt: The Autobiography of a Science Fiction Giant.* Lakemont, GA: Fictioneer, 1975.


# Research Sources

*Encyclopedias and Handbooks:* **AW, CA, CAAS, CANR, ESF, MSSF, NNDB, SFW, WS**

*Bibliographies:* **ARB, FF, SFAN**

Stephensen-Payne, Phil and Ian Covell. *A.E. van Vogt: Master of Null-A, A Working Bibliography.* Leeds (UK): Galactic Central, 1997.


## Biographies and Interviews

Drake, H.L. *A.E. van Vogt: Science Fantasy's Icon.* Lancaster, PA: H.L. Drake, 2002.

Drake, H.L. Interview. *Science Fiction Review.* 1977. http://www.angelfire.com/art/ megathink/vanvogt/vanvogt_interview.html.

Elliot, Jeffrey M. "A.E. Van Vogt: A Writer with a Winning Formula." In *SF Voices No. 3*. San Bernardino, CA: Borgo, 1980. 30–40. http://vanvogt.www4.mmedia. is/jeff.htm.

*Guardian Online.* Obituary. February 1, 2000. http://books.guardian.co.uk/news/ articles/0,131148,00.html.

*Locus Online.* Appreciations & Obituary. (Anderson, Bradbury, Clarke, Ellison, et al.) January 2000, 66–68.

Von Puttkamer, Jesco. "The Childlike Enthusiasm and Unmatched Imagination of A.E. van Vogt." *Space.com*. January 28, 2000. Imaginova Corp. http://www.space.com/ sciencefiction/books/van_vogt_tribute_000128.html.

Weinberg, Robert. "An Astounding Interview with A.E. Van Vogt." (unpublished interview for *Astounding* magazine.) 1980. http://www.home.earthlink.net/~ icshi/Interviews/Weinberg-1980.html.

### Criticism and Readers' Guides

Bloom, Harold. "A.E. Van Vogt." In *Science Fiction Writers of the Golden Age*. New York: Chelsea House, 1995, 188–203.

Jameson, Frederic. "The Space of Science Fiction: Narrative in Van Vogt." In *Archaeologies of the Future*. New York: Verso, 2005, 314–327.

Rossi, Umberto. "The Game of the Rat: A.E. Van Vogt's 800-Word Rule and P.K. Dick's *The Game-Players of Titan*." *Science Fiction Studies* 31 (2004): 207–226.

Sharp, William H. "A.E. Van Vogt and the World of Null-A." *Etc: A Review of General Semantics*. 63(1) (2006): 2–19.

### Web Sites

*Icshi: The A E. Van Vogt Information Site*. Isaac Willcott. March 2008. Enthusiastic and thorough fan Web site, which features links to reading guides, plot summaries, and other information. http://www.home.earthlink.net/~icshi/.

*The Weird Worlds of A.E. Van Vogt*. Magnus Axelsson. January 2007. Fan site, which brings together a wide variety of interesting information, including essays such as "Introduction to the World of Null-A" by James Gunn (1987), "Man Beyond Man: The Early Stories of A.E. Van Vogt" by Alexei Panshin, and "Oh, the Humanity of A.E. van Vogt's Monsters: Reorienting Critics and Readers to the van Vogt Method" by Trent Walters (2005). http://vanvogt.www4.mmedia.is/index.htm.

# John Varley (1947–  )

*I sat on her rented bed to get my breath. There were car keys and cigarettes in her purse, genuine tobacco, worth its weight in blood. I lit six of them, figuring I had five minutes of my very own. The room filled with sweet smoke. They don't make 'em like that anymore.*

*—"Air Raid" (1977)*

## Biography

John Herbert Varley grew up in Texas, in Fort Worth and near Port Arthur. He briefly attended Michigan State University on a National Merit scholarship, but dropped out and spent six years traveling, from San Francisco to Woodstock and back again, before he decided to become a science fiction writer.

Varley's "Eight Worlds" sequence of novels and stories, in which mankind has been driven from Earth and forced to colonize the less attractive real estate of the Solar System, was well ahead of its time in considering the possibilities of biological enhancements. Many of the variations on old sf tropes that he worked effortlessly into his very earliest fiction—the gender-bending, the gritty, survive-at-all-costs attitude, and the strong female protagonists—quickly became standard; everyone was doing it and thus it is easy to forget that Varley did it first. He currently divides his time between Portland, Oregon, and an RV parked along California's central coast.

DISABILITY IN SF; GENDER & SEXUALITY; GENETIC ENGINEERING & CLONING; MARS, MOON & THE PLANETS; POST-HUMAN; WOMEN IN SF

## Major Works

*Novels*

*The Ophiuchi Hotline* (1977)
*Millennium* (1983)
The Gaea Trilogy: *Demon* (1984), *Wizard* (1980), *Titan* (1979—**Locus Poll**)
The Metal series: *Steel Beach* (1992) and *The Golden Globe* (1998—**Prometheus**)
*Red Thunder* (2003)
*Mammoth* (2005)
*Red Lightning* (2006)

*Collections*

*The John Varley Reader*. New York: Berkeley, 2004. **Locus Poll** Includes "Picnic on Nearside" (1974), "Overdrawn at the Memory Bank" (1976), "Air Raid" (1977), "In the Hall of the Martian Kings" (1977), and five new stories. Among Varley's other collections are *The Persistence of Vision* (1978—**Nebula**) and *The Barbie Murders* (1980—**Locus Poll**).

*Notable Short Stories*

"The Persistence of Vision" (1978) **Nebula, Hugo, Locus Poll**
"The Barbie Murders" (1978) **Locus Poll**
"Blue Champagne" (1981) **Locus Poll**
"The Pusher" (1981) **Hugo, Locus Poll**
"Press ENTER []" (1984) **Hugo, Locus Poll, Nebula**

## Research Sources

*Encyclopedias and Handbooks:* **AW, CA, CANR, ESF, MSSF, NNDB, SFW**

*Bibliographies:* **ARB, FF, SFAN**

*Biographies and Interviews*

Farrell, Shaun. Interview. *Shaun's Quadrant.* July 2005. Far Sector.com. http://www.
farsector.com/quadrant/interview-johnvarley.htm.
Interview. *Xero Magazine* 1(4) (1996). http://www.xeromag.com/varley.html.
"John Varley: The Wonderful Alarming Future." *Locus Online* October 2004. http:
//www.locusmag.com/2004/Issues/10Varley.html.
Lilley, Ernest. Interview. *SFRevu* May 2003. http://www.sfrevu.com/ISSUES/2003/
0305/Feature%20-%20John%20Varley/Interview.htm.

*Criticism and Readers' Guides*

Delaney, Samuel R. "Zelazny, Varley, Gibson—and Quality." In *Shorter Views: Queer
Thoughts & the Politics of the Paraliterary.* Hanover, NH: Wesleyan University
Press, 1999, 271–291.
Kollmann, Judith J. "John Varley's Women." *Extrapolation* 29 (1988): 65–75.
Kramer, R. "The Machine in the Ghost: Time and Presence in Varley's *Millennium*."
*Extrapolation* 32 (1991): 156–169.
Vint, Sherryl. "Both/And: Science Fiction and the Question of Changing Gender. (De-
lany's *Trouble on Triton* and Varley's *Steel Beach*)." *Strange Horizons* February
18, 2002. http://www.strangehorizons.com/2002/20020218/both_and.shtml.

*Web Sites*

*John Varley.net.* Official Web site, including a *"recipe du jour."* http://www.varley.net/.
*Gaea, The Mad Titan.* Jack Eggers. March 2005. Tribute to the Gaea series, with
maps and photoshopped images illustrating the texts. http://www.ammon-ra.com/
gaea/.
*Varley Vade Mecum.* Doug Eigsti. February 2007. Fictionados Book Club. Ready
reference for John Varley fans, with essays and illustrations demonstrating the
interconnectedness of John Varley's "Eight Worlds" stories, and links to various
other (sometimes outdated) sites. http://www.freewebs.com/herbboehm/.

**If you enjoyed John Varley ...**
In Varley's "Eight Worlds" sequence, in novels like *Steel Beach* and the "Gaea"
trilogy, sex changes are routine, and cloning (legal or otherwise) offers the
opportunity to have multiple versions of the same character. Varley effortlessly
rejuvenated many of the tropes of classic sf: "urgent and risk-taking ... he understood the imaginative implications ..." (**ESF**)

**Then you might like ...**
*Samuel Delany.* Novels such as *Babel-17, Triton: An Ambiguous Heterotopia,*
and *Dhalgren* are potent blends of the conventions of space opera, and high
philosophy, mythology, and linguistics. Identity itself is often fluid in a Delany
story: in a universe where one can change one's physical appearance, gender, and
sexual orientation at will, what can you trust?

*Justina Robson*. As Varley did in the 1970s, with characters whose cloned existences stretch the definition of identity to the limit, Robson uses characters who are wired up by computer interface and "enhanced" beyond all recognition by genetic engineering to ask, as she does in her 1999 novel *Silver Screen*, "Where does the life end and the machine begin?"

*Bruce Sterling*. Author of the Shaper/Mechanist universe of stories, which includes *Schismatrix* (1985) and the excellent "Swarm" (1982), in which 23rd century warring factions of humanity clash over augmentation by genetics or prosthetics. Like Varley, Sterling's clever extrapolation of current trends and possible technology add up to a richly textured, and very believable, future world.

*Michael Swanwick*. Like Varley, he writes well-crafted stories that take the conventional territories of sf—a well-imagined and complex solar system (*Vacuum Flowers*, 1987), the far-flung corners of the galaxy (*Stations of the Tide*, 1991), and the distant past (*Bones of the Earth*, 2002)—and in his hands they become something altogether more complicated.

*James Tiptree, Jr.* A master of the short-story form, Tiptree's work demonstrates that sf can "square" various circles—reconciling "hard" technology with "soft" psychology, the masculine with the feminine. Like Varley, in short stories such as "Houston, Houston, Do You Read?" (1976) and "The Only Neat Thing to Do" (1985), Tiptree reconciles the style and spirit of space opera with a darker, deeper alienation.

## Jules Verne (1828–1905)

*I wanted to see what no one had yet observed, even if I had to pay for this curiosity with my life.*

*—Twenty Thousand Leagues under the Sea (1870)*
*translated by Walter James Miller and Frederick Paul Walter (1993)*

### Biography

Jules Gabriel Verne was born in Nantes, in France, the son of an attorney. He spent some years as a genteel failure in Paris, writing ponderous historical novels, until his publisher saw a gap in the market for *voyages extraordinaires*, and encouraged Verne to write them. Eventually he wrote more than sixty such "scientific romances," drawing upon his fascination with geography and science, and giving the world something new and memorable—the technological adventure.

Verne's final years were clouded by ill health and some bitterness that he did not receive the recognition he felt he deserved from the French literary establishment. But he never lost his spark, and the sense that he was doing something worth remembering. Jules Verne died of the complications of chronic diabetes at his home in Amiens, on Boulevard Longueville (now Boulevard Jules-Verne), on March 24, 1905.

FANTASTIC VOYAGES; MONSTERS; TECHNOLOGY

## Major Works

*Novels*

Many of Verne's titles are available on Project Gutenberg, in French, English, and other languages. http://www.gutenberg.org/browse/authors/v#a60.
*A Journey to the Centre of the Earth* (1864)
*From the Earth to the Moon* (1865)
*Twenty Thousand Leagues Under the Sea* (1869)
*From the Earth to the Moon . . . and a Trip Around It* (1870)
*Around the World in Eighty Days* (1873)
*The Begum's Fortune* (1879)
*Floating Island* (*L'Île à hélice*, 1895—aka *Propeller Island*)
*The Chase of the Golden Meteor* (1908—aka *The Meteor Hunt*)

*Short Stories*

"A Drama in the Air" (1851)
"Master Zacharius, or The Clockmaker Who Lost His Soul" (1854)
"In the Year 2889" (1889)
"The Eternal Adam" (1910) A "posthumously discovered" story, there are suspicions that this may have been written by Verne's son, Michel.

*Other Important Works*

"Edgard Poë [sic] et ses oeuvres." *Musée des Familles* (April 1864). Highly edited English version, "The Bizarre Genius of Edgar Poe," translated by I.O. Evans. In Peter Haining, ed., *The Jules Verne Companion*. London: Pictorial, 1978, 26–30.
*The Discovery of the Earth* (1878)

## Research Sources

*Encyclopedias and Handbooks:* **AW, BW, CA, ESF, LE, MSSF, NNDB, SFW, WS**

*Bibliographies:* **ARB, FF, SFAN**

Kytasaari, Dennis. "*Les Voyages Extraordinaires*: The Works of Jules Gabriel Verne, Feb 8, 1828 to Mar 24, 1905." *Jules Verne—Links of Interest*. July 13, 2006. http://epguides.com/djk/JulesVerne/works.shtml.

Dehs, Volker, Jean-Michel Margot and Zvi Har'El. "The Complete Jules Verne Bibliography." *Zvi Har' El's Jules Verne Collection*. June 2007. http://jv.gilead.org.il/biblio/.

## Biographies and Interviews

Butcher, William. *Jules Verne: The Definitive Biography*. New York: Thunder's Mouth, 2006.
Sherard, Robert H. "Jules Verne Re-Visited." *T.P.'s Weekly* October 9, 1903. http://jv.gilead.org.il/sherard2.html. A contemporary interview.
Teeters, Peggy. *Jules Verne: The Man Who Invented Tomorrow*. New York: Walker, 1992.
Verne, Jean Jules. (Verne's grandson). *Jules Verne: A Biography*. Translated and abridged by Roger Greaves. New York: Taplinger, 1976.

## Criticism and Readers' Guides

Brown, Eric. *The Extraordinary Voyage of Jules Verne*. Hornsea (UK): PS, 2005.
Butcher, William. "Jules Verne, Prophet or Poet?" National Institute for Statistics and Economic Studies. November 17, 1984. *Publications de l'INSEE*. http://home.netvigator.com/~wbutcher/articles/prophetorpoet.htm.
Debus, Allen A. "Reframing the Science in Jules Verne's *Journey to the Center of the Earth*." *Science Fiction Studies*. 33 (2006): 405–420.
Derbyshire, John. "Jules Verne, Father of Science Fiction." *New Atlantis*. Spring 2006. http://www.thenewatlantis.com/archive/12/derbyshire.htm.
Evans, Arthur B. "The 'New' Jules Verne." *Science Fiction Studies*. 22 (1995): 35–46. http://www.depauw.edu/sfs/backissues/65/evans65art.htm.
Harpold, Terry. "Reading the Illustrations of Jules Verne's *Voyages Extraordinaires*: The Example of Le Superbe Orenoque." *ImageTexT: Interdisciplinary Comics Studies*. Summer 2006. http://www.english.ufl.edu/imagetext/archives/v3_1/harpold/.
Krystek, Lee. "Jules Verne: An Author Before His Time?" *The Museum of Unnatural Mystery*. 2002. http://www.unmuseum.org/verne.htm.
Renzi, Thomas C. *Jules Verne on Film: A Filmography of the Cinematic Adaptations of His Works, 1902 through 1997*. Jefferson, NC: McFarland, 2004.
Rose, Mark. "Filling the Void: Verne, Wells, and Lem." *Science-Fiction Studies*. 8 (1981): 121–142. http://jv.gilead.org.il/sfs/rose.art.html.
*Science Fiction Studies*. Jules Verne Centenary Issue. 32 (2005).
Unwin, Timothy. *Jules Verne: Journeys in Writing*. Liverpool, UK: Liverpool University Press, 2005.

## Web Sites

*A Jules Verne Centennial: 1905–2005*. Norman Wolcott and Martin R. Kalfatovic. Smithsonian Institution Libraries. December 2005. Smithsonian collection of Verne material. http://www.sil.si.edu/OnDisplay/JulesVerne100/index.htm.

*The Jules Verne Collecting Resource Page.* Andrew Nash. October 14, 2007. Complete
list of Jules Verne titles, texts of contemporary obituaries, and links to other useful
sites. http://www.julesverne.ca/index.html.
*Verne Moon Gun.* Mark Wade. November 17, 2007. Encyclopedia Astronautica.
Hypothesis on the design of Verne's Moon gun, based on clues in the text.
http://www.astronautix.com/lvs/julongun.htm
*The North American Jules Verne Society.* Andrew Nash. March 2007. Web site of
Society based in Akron, Ohio, which aims to promote interest in Jules Verne and
his writings. Secondary-source bibliography of member's publications on Verne,
and index to quarterly Society newsletter. http://www.najvs.org/.
*Verne's Nautilis.* Michael & Karen Crisafulli. January 2006. Design of the *Nautilis*,
based on clues in the texts. http://home.att.net/~karen.crisafulli/nautilus.html.

# *Vernor Vinge (1944–   )*

> *... there was another reason for the present state of affairs, a reason that went
> back to the Moon Lander and Adventure games at the "dawn of time": it was
> simply a hell of a lot of fun to live in a world as malleable as the human
> imagination.*
>
> *—"True Names" (1981)*

## Biography

Vernor Vinge has twice changed the landscape of modern science fiction. His
1981 novella "True Names" is widely credited with introducing the concept of
cyberspace and making cyberpunk possible. And in 1993, in a paper he presented
to a NASA symposium on the future, he defined the moment when, as he sees
it, sentient computers, computer/human interfaces, or enhanced transhumans will
accelerate technological progress beyond current understanding—the Singularity.
Vinge's fiction dramatizes the challenges that ordinary human will face in these
changed landscapes.

Vernor Steffen Vinge was born in Waukesha, Wisconsin. He has a PhD in
Mathematics from the University of California at San Diego, and from 1972
he was Professor of Mathematics at San Diego State University. During the
1970s he was married to Joan D. Vinge, author of space fantasies such as *The
Snow Queen*. In 2002, he retired from teaching to devote himself full-time to his
writing.

ARTIFICIAL INTELLIGENCE; FIRST CONTACT; LIBERTARIAN SF; NEAR
FUTURE; SPACE OPERA; POST-HUMAN; VIRTUAL REALITY

## Major Works

*Novels*

*Grimm's World* (1969)

*The Witling* (1976)
*The Peace War* (1984)
*Marooned In Realtime* (1986) **Prometheus**
*A Fire Upon the Deep* (1992) **Hugo**
*A Deepness in the Sky* (1999) **Hugo, Prometheus**
*Rainbow's End* (2006) **Hugo, Locus Poll**

## Collections

*The Collected Stories of Vernor Vinge.* New York: Orb, 2001. Includes "Bookworm, Run!" (1966) and "Fast Times at Fairmont High" (2001—**Hugo**)

## Short Stories

"True Names" (1981)
"The Ungoverned" (1985) http://www.webscription.net/chapters/1416520724/1416520724__4.htm.
"The Cookie Monster" (2003) **Hugo, Locus Poll** http://www.analogsf.com/0310/cookie.shtml.

## Other Important Works

Introduction. *Skylark of Space*, by E.E. "Doc" Smith. Lincoln: University of Nebraska Press, 2007.
"The Singularity." Talk to VISION-21 Symposium. NASA Lewis Research Center. Ohio Aerospace Institute, March 30–31, 1993. http://hem.passagen.se/replikant/vernor_vinge_singularity.htm.
"What If the Singularity Does NOT Happen?" *The Long Now Foundation Seminar.* February 15, 2007. http://www.longnow.org/projects/seminars/.

# Research Sources

*Encyclopedias and Handbooks:* **AW, BW, CA, CANR, ESF, NNDB, SFW**

*Bibliographies:* **ARB, FF, SFAN**

## Biographies and Interviews

Blaschke, Jayme Lynn. Interview. *Strange Horizons.* September 15, 2003. http://www.strangehorizons.com/2003/20030915/vinge.shtml.
Farrell, Shaun. Interview. *Far Sector.com.* April 2006. http://www.farsector.com/quadrant/interview-vinge.htm.
Hind, John. Interview. *The Observer.* (London) Dec. 29, 2002. http://observer.guardian.co.uk/magazine/story/0,11913,865638,00.html.
*IT Conversations.* "Accelerating Change 2005." (Audio Interview). September 17, 2005. Giga Vox Media. http://www.itconversations.com/shows/detail711.html.

Means, Loren. Interview. *YLEM Journal,* 23(4) (2003): 4–7. http://www.ylem.org/Journal/2003Iss04vol23.pdf.

*Small World.* Podcast Interview. June 9, 2006. http://smallworldpodcast.com/?p=409.

### Criticism and Readers' Guides

Frenkel, James, ed. *True Names . . . And the Opening of the Cyberspace Frontier.* New York: Tor, 2001. Eleven essays, which spell out the influence of the short story "True Names" on fact and fiction. Introduction by Vernor Vinge.

### Web Sites

*Singular Vernor Vinge Page.* Damien Sullivan. December 2007. Mindstalk. Basic, unadorned fan Web site with very useful links. http://mindstalk.net/vinge/.

# Kurt Vonnegut (1922–2007)

*So it goes.*

—*Slaughterhouse-Five (1969)*

## Biography

Kurt Vonnegut, Jr. was born in Indianapolis. In 1944, as a U.S. Prisoner of war in Nazi Germany, he survived the bombing of Dresden. His experience provided the basis for *Slaughterhouse-Five,* now considered as one of the best American novels of the 20th century.

Following the war, Vonnegut studied anthropology at the University of Chicago, and then worked as a crime reporter, publicist, and car salesman while trying to establish his writing career. Vonnegut's fiction makes extensive use of comfortable old sf conventions—time travel, visiting aliens, automated dystopias, misguided inventions, and fake religions—to achieve something new and important. His unique role in 20th century American literature was to demonstrate that the familiar tropes of pulp science fiction had a part to play in expressing the inexpressible. Kurt Vonnegut died at the age of eighty-four on April 11, 2007, in New York City, after a fall at his East Side Manhattan home.

ANTHROPOLOGY; HUMOR AND SATIRE; RELIGION; TIME TRAVEL; WAR

## Major Works

*Novels*

*Player Piano* (1952)
*The Sirens of Titan* (1959)
*Cat's Cradle* (1963)

*Slaughterhouse-Five* (1969). The complete title is *Slaughterhouse-Five; or, The Children's Crusade: A Duty-Dance with Death, by Kurt Vonnegut, Jr., a Fourth-Generation German-American Now Living in Easy Circumstances on Cape Cod (and Smoking Too Much) Who, as an American Infantry Scout* Hors de Combat, *as a Prisoner of War, Witnessed the Fire-Bombing of Dresden, Germany, the Florence of the Elbe, a Long Time Ago, and Survived to Tell the Tale: This Is a Novel Somewhat in the Telegraphic Schizophrenic Manner of Tales of the Planet Tralfamadore, Where the Flying Saucers Come From.* HarperAudio version available online at http://town.hall.org/radio/HarperAudio/
*Breakfast of Champions; or, Goodbye Blue Monday!* (1973)
*Galápagos: A Novel* (1985)
*Timequake* (1997)


## Collections

*Welcome to the Monkey House: A Collection of Short Works* (1968) An enhanced version of the collection *Canary in a Cathouse* (1961); includes eleven additional stories and the frequently anthologized "Harrison Bergeron" (1961).
*Bagombo Snuff Box: Uncollected Short Fiction.* New York: Berkley, 2000.
*Armageddon in Retrospect.* New York: Putnam, 2008. Uncollected stories and essays spanning Vonnegut's career.


## Other Important Works

*Between Time and Timbuktu: A Space Fantasy* (1972) National Educational Television Network, Playhouse production: a "collage" of Vonnegut's work. Author's Preface to the printed screenplay is available in the Archives on The Vonnegut Web, http://www.vonnegutweb.com/.
*Breakfast of Champions.* Flying Hearts Films, 1999.
*Fates Worse than Death: An Autobiographical Collage of the 1980s* (1991)
*God Bless You, Dr. Kevorkian* (1999)
*Harrison Bergeron.* Atlantic Films Ltd., 1995.
*In These Times.* http://www.inthesetimes.com/. Regular newspaper column, that includes "Kurt Vonnegut vs. the !&#*!@" (Interview, 2003), "Cold Turkey" (2004), "Requiem for a Dreamer" (Vonnegut Interviews Kilgore Trout) (2004).
*A Man Without a Country* (2005)
*Slaughterhouse-Five.* Universal Pictures, 1972.


# Research Sources

*Encyclopedias and Handbooks:* **AW, BW, CA, CANR, ESF, LE, MSSF, NNDB, SFW, WS**

*Bibliographies:* **ARB, FF, SFAN**

## Biographies and Interviews

Allen, Rodney, ed. *Conversations with Kurt Vonnegut.* Jackson: University Press of Mississippi, 1988.

Brinkley, Douglas. "Vonnegut's Apocalypse." *Rolling Stone.* August 24, 2006. http://www.rollingstone.com/politics/story/11123162/kurt_vonnegut_says_this_is_the_end_of_the_world

Hayman, David, et al. "Kurt Vonnegut: The Art of Fiction No. 64." *The Paris Review.* Spring 1977. http://www.theparisreview.org/viewinterview.php/prmMID/3605.

"The Infinite Mind Interview with Kurt Vonnegut Live from Second Life." (and other video clips). *Video.Google.* September 22, 2006. http://video.google.com/videoplay?docid=-2140455044291565033.

*The Long View.* "Kurt Vonnegut Judges Modern Society." January 23, 2006. National Public Radio. http://www.npr.org/templates/story/story.php?storyId=5165342.

*NOW: Arts and Culture.* "Kurt Vonnegut." October 7, 2005. Public Broadcasting System. http://www.pbs.org/now/arts/vonnegut.html.

Reed, Peter J. and Marc Leeds, eds. *The Vonnegut Chronicles: Interviews and Essays.* Westport, CT: Greenwood, 1996.

Wasserman, Harvey. "Kurt Vonnegut's 'Stardust Memory.'" *The Free Press.* March 4, 2006. http://freepress.org/columns/display/7/2006/1326.

## Criticism and Readers' Guides

Bloom, Harold, ed. *Kurt Vonnegut's Cat's Cradle.* Philadelphia, PA: Chelsea, 2002.

Boon, Kevin A., ed. *At Millennium's End: New Essays on the Work of Kurt Vonnegut.* Albany: State University of New York Press, 2001.

Davis, Todd F. *Kurt Vonnegut's Crusade or, How a Postmodern Harlequin Preached a New Kind of Humanism.* Albany: State University. of New York Press, 2006.

Klinkowitz, Jerome. *The Vonnegut Effect.* Columbia: University of South Carolina Press, 2004.

Leeds, Marc. *The Vonnegut Encyclopedia: An Authorized Compendium.* Westport, CT: Greenwood, 1995.

Lessing, Doris. "Vonnegut's Responsibility." *New York Times.* February 4, 1973. http://www.nytimes.com/books/97/09/28/lifetimes/vonnegut-lessing.html.

Marvin, Thomas F. *Kurt Vonnegut: A Critical Companion.* Westport, CT: Greenwood, 2002.

Morse, Donald E. *The Novels of Kurt Vonnegut: Imagining Being an American.* Westport, CT: Praeger, 2003.

Reed, Peter J. *The Short Fiction of Kurt Vonnegut.* Westport, CT: Greenwood, 1997.

Thomas, P.L. *Reading, Learning, Teaching Kurt Vonnegut.* New York: Peter Lang, 2006.

Wharton, David Michael. "Dubious Truths: An Examination of Vonnegut's *Cat's Cradle.*" *Strange Horizons* March 24, 2003. http://www.strangehorizons.com/2003/20030324/truths.shtml.

*Web Sites*

*Kurt Vonnegut Corner.* Mark Vit. January 2007. Collection of student essays on Vonnegut (enthusiastic, but mixed quality), quotes, a photo gallery, and a section devoted to Kilgore Trout. http://www.geocities.com/Hollywood/4953/vonn.html.

*Vonnegut.com.* Official Web site: beautiful, illustrated with weird and wonderful pictures, and, since April 2007, featuring touching testimonials from family and friends. http://www.vonnegut.com/.

*The Vonnegut Web.* Chris Huber. February 2005. "[T]he most expansive, yet wholly unauthorized, Kurt Vonnegut site in the cosmos. . . . pages on each of his novels as well as all manner of detail on the man's life and work." Archive includes 1965 *New York Times* article "On Science Fiction," and an extremely thorough bibliography. http://www.vonnegutweb.com/.

# H.G. Wells (1866–1946)

*Yet across the gulf of space, minds that are to our minds as ours are to those of the beasts that perish, intellects vast and cool and unsympathetic, regarded this earth with envious eyes, and slowly and surely drew their plans against us.*
*—War of the Worlds (1898)*

## Biography

Herbert George Wells was born in Bromley, Kent, the son of working class parents. He escaped the treadmill of the British class system through a liberal, scientific education, and his writing reflects these early experiences: faith in the literal possibilities of evolution, an abiding hatred of arrogance, and desire to eradicate the injustices and hypocrisies of his world.

Wells had an uncanny knack in his fiction of predicting the worst that the 20th century would throw at mankind—chemical warfare, the tank, aerial bombardment of civilian populations, and the use of atomic weapons—and this gave him a reputation as the "voice of the future." His later fiction was more utopian—the future as he thought it could be, or should be. H.G. Wells died in London on August 13, 1945, only days after the future he warned us about unleashed some of its terrible power on Hiroshima and Nagasaki.

ALIEN THREAT; GENETICS & CLONING; MARS, MOON & THE PLANETS; POLITICAL SF; TIME TRAVEL; TECHNOLOGY; UTOPIAS

## Major Works

*Novels*

*The Time Machine* (1895)
*The Invisible Man* (1897)

*The Island of Doctor Moreau* (1896)
*War of the Worlds* (1898)
*When the Sleeper Wakes* (1899)
*The First Men on the Moon* (1901)
*The Shape of Things to Come* (1933)
All of H.G. Wells' novels are available online at Project Gutenberg http://www.
gutenberg.org/ and the Online Library of the University of Adelaide, Australia.
http://etext.library.adelaide.edu.au/w/wells/hg/.

## Collections

*The Door in the Wall, and Other Stories* (1911) This early collection varies items of sf
interest such as the title story, "The Star" (1897), and "The Country of the Blind"
(1904). It is available online, at the Web site of the Library of the University of
Adelaide, Australia. http://etext.library.adelaide.edu.au/w/wells/hg/.
*Selected Stories of H.G. Wells*. Ed. Ursula Le Guin. New York: Modern Library, 2004.
Divided into sections on Visionary and Technologicial/Predictive Science Fiction,
Horror, and Fantasies.

## Short Stories

"The Crystal Egg" (1899) http://etext.lib.virginia.edu/toc/modeng/public/WelCrys.
html
"The Land Ironclads" (1903) http://www.zeitcom.com/majgen/60w-1_landironclads.
html

## Other Important Works

*Experiment in Autobiography: Discoveries and Conclusions of a Very Ordinary Brain
since 1866* (1934)
*H.G. Wells's Literary Criticism*. Eds. Patrick Parrinder and Robert M. Philmus.
Brighton, England: Harvester, 1980. Wells' book reviews, and essays on his
contemporaries.
*The New World Order* (1940) http://www.theforbiddenknowledge.com/hardtruth/
new_world_order_hgwells.htm.
*A Short History of the World* (1922) http://www.bartleby.com/86/.
"Utopias." Australian Broadcasting Company. January 19, 1939. *Science Fiction Studies* 9 (1982): 117–121. http://www.depauw.edu/sfs/documents/wells1.htm.
"Woman and Primitive Culture." (1895) *Science Fiction Studies* 8 (1981): 35–37.
http://www.depauw.edu/sfs/documents/wells2.htm

# Research Sources

*Encyclopedias and Handbooks:* **AW, BW, CA, ESF, MSSF, NNDB,
SFW, WS**

## Bibliographies: ARB, FF, SFAN

"An H.G. Wells Bibliography." *The H.G. Wells Society of the Americas.* July 2004. http://www.hgwellsusa.50megs.com/bibliography.html.

## Biographies and Interviews

Austin, Mary. "An Appreciation of H.G. Wells, Novelist." *American Magazine.* 72 (1911). http://etext.lib.virginia.edu/toc/modeng/public/AusWell.html.

Chesterton, G.K. "Mr. H.G. Wells and the Giants." *Heretics.* (1905). Hendrickson Christian Classics 2007. http://www.cse.dmu.ac.uk/~mward/gkc/books/heretics/ch5.html.

Creek, Dave. "H.G. Wells: Creature of the Twilight." *Internet Review of Science Fiction.* July 2005. http://www.irosf.com/q/zine/article/10167.

Foot, Michael. *H.G.: The History of Mr. Wells.* Washington, DC: Counterpoint, 1995.

Hammond, J.R. *An H.G. Wells Chronology.* New York: St. Martin's, 1999.

Langford, David. "The History of Mr. Wells." *Fortean Times.* 199 (2005). http://www.ansible.co.uk/writing/ft-wells.html.

Wells, G.P., ed. *H.G. Wells in Love: Postscript to an Experiment in Autobiography.* Boston, MA: Little, Brown, 1984. Notes for the unpublished second volume of Wells' autobiography, edited and annotated by his son.

West, Anthony. *H.G. Wells: Aspects of a Life.* New York: Random House, 1984. http://wiredforbooks.org/anthonywest/. Anthony West (1914–1987) was Wells' son by Rebecca West. Also see West's radio interview with Don Swaim for *Wired for Books.* 1984. WOUB Online. http://wiredforbooks.org.

## Criticism and Readers' Guides

Beresford, J.D. *H.G. Wells: A Critical Study.* Rockville, MD: Wildside, 2005.

Brians, Paul. *Study Guides: The War of the Worlds.* June 13, 1995. Washington State University. http://www.wsu.edu:8080/~brians/science_fiction/warofworlds.html.

Ferguson, Niall. "H.G. Wells Warned Us of How It Would Feel to Fight a 'War of the World.'" *The Daily Telegraph* (London). July 24, 2005. http://www.telegraph.co.uk/opinion/main.jhtml?xml=/opinion/2005/07/24/do2402.xml.

Gornick, Vivian. "The Beginning of Wisdom: On Reading H.G. Wells." *Boston Review.* January/February 2007. http://www.bostonreview.net/BR32.1/gornick.html.

Hammond, J.R. *A Preface to H.G. Wells.* New York: Longman, 2001.

Hammond, John R. *H.G. Wells' The Time Machine: A Reference Guide.* Westport, CT: Greenwood, 2004.

Higgins, David M. "An Ingenious Use of Scientific Patter: The Great War and the Science Fiction of H.G. Wells." *Strange Horizons* March 13, 2006. http://www.strangehorizons.com/2006/20060313/wells-a.shtml.

Holmsten, Brian and Alex Lubertozzi, eds. *The Complete War of the Worlds: Mars Invasion of Earth from H.G. Wells to Orson Welles.* Napierville, IL: Sourcebooks, 2001.

Kirchwey, Freda . "When H.G. Wells Split the Atom: A 1914 Preview of 1945." *The Nation.* August 18, 1945. http://www.thenation.com/doc/19450818/wells.

Lem, Stanislaw. "H.G. Wells's *War of the Worlds.*" In Rhys Garnett and R. J. Ellis, eds., *Science Fiction Roots and Branches.* Basingstoke, England: Macmillan, 1990, 18–29.

Levy, David M. and Sandra J. Peart. "Eugenics Rides a Time Machine: H.G. Wells' Outline of Genocide." *Reason.* March 26, 2002. http://www.reason.com/news/show/32537.html.

Miller, John J. "War of the Worldviews: H.G. Wells Was a Sci-Fi Pioneer, But His Political Ideas Were Abominable." *Opinion Journal.* June 21, 2005. *The Wall Street Journal.* http://www.opinionjournal.com/la/?id=110006849.

McMillan, Gloria, ed. *Wells and His Worlds: Wells and His Box. Welcome to Hypertext Classics.* University of Arizona. 2002. http://www.u.arizona.edu/~gmcmilla/menu.html. Essays and links relating to *The Time Machine.*

Orwell, George. "Wells, Hitler and the World State." *Horizon.* August 1941. http://orwell.ru/library/reviews/wells/english/e_whws.

Parrinder, Patrick. "History in the Science Fiction of H.G. Wells." *Cycnos* 22(2) (2006). http://revel.unice.fr/cycnos/document.html?id=615.

Parrinder, Patrick. *Shadows of the Future: H.G. Wells, Science Fiction, and Prophecy.* Liverpool, UK: Liverpool University Press, 1995.

Philmus, Robert M. "The Strange Case of *Moreau* Gets Stranger." *Science Fiction Studies* 19(2) (1992): 248–250. http://www.depauw.edu/sfs/backissues/57/philmus57art.htm.

Rayward, W. Boyd. "H.G. Wells's Idea of a World Brain: A Critical Re-Assessment." *Journal of the American Society for Information Science.* 50 (1999): 557–579. http://people.lis.uiuc.edu/~wrayward/Wellss_Idea_of_World_Brain.htm.

Slusscr, George et al, eds. *H.G. Wells's Perennial Time Machine: Selected Essays from the Centenary Conference.* Athens: University of Georgia Press, 2001.

Stover, Leon. *The Annotated H.G. Wells.* Jefferson, NC: McFarland, 2002.

Wagar, W. Warren. *H.G. Wells: Traversing Time.* Middletown, CT: Wesleyan University Press, 2004.

Willis, Martin T. "Edison as Time Traveler: H.G. Wells's Inspiration for his First Scientific Character." *Science Fiction Studies.* 26 (1999): 284–294. http://www.depauw.edu/sfs/backissues/78/willis78art.htm.

Yeffeth, Glenn. *The War of the Worlds: Fresh Perspectives on the H.G. Wells Classic.* Dallas, TX: BenBella, 2005.

## Web Sites

*The H.G. Wells Society.* Portal to the Web sites of the organization dedicated to "promoting and encouraging an active interest in and appreciation of the life, work, and thought of H.G. Wells." Links to the H.G. Wells Society, the Americas, and the Wellsian, official journal of the society. http://www.hgwellsusa.50megs.com/.

*Eve of the War.* Anthony Pearson et al. August 2007. The Web site of Jeff Wayne's 1978 musical version of *The War of the Worlds*, featuring special effects, artwork, and notes about adaptation from book to stage. Worth a visit, if only to hear the actor Sir Richard Burton read selections from the novel. http://www.eveofthewar. com.au/default.html.

*H.G. Wells' The War of the Worlds.* 2004 Pendragon Pictures. Notes and visuals from "the first and only authentic movie adaptation of the classic novel." Unlike the 1953 and 2005 Hollywood versions, this production remains entirely faithful to Wells' narrative, characters, and setting. The Web site offers a very interesting contrast to the more famous Hollywood adaptations. http://www. pendragonpictures.com/WOTWKEY.html.

*Invasion: The Historical Perspective.* John Gosling. July 2007. Tribute to the 1938 Orson Welles radio broadcast. http://www.war-ofthe-worlds.co.uk/.

*The Time Machine Project.* Don & Mary Coleman. November 2007. Tribute to the 1960 movie version, directed by George Pal. Enthusiastic Wells section, with a biography, photo gallery, text of the *New York Times* obituary for Wells, and full text of "The Chronic Argonauts," the 1888 precursor to *The Time Machine*, originally published by the Royal College of Science in a student journal edited by Wells. http://www.colemanzone.com/Time_Machine_Project/.

# Kate Wilhelm (1928–  )

*Somewhere a star was going nova, a black hole was vacuuming space, a comet was combing its hair.*

*—"Mrs. Bagley Goes to Mars" (1978)*

## Biography

Kate Wilhelm was born Katie Gertrude Meredith in Toledo, Ohio, and grew up in Kentucky. Her fiction is firmly rooted in real life: it is very rare for her to stray off with aliens on other planets. Instead, her wonders are found in the deceptively ordinary "heart land" locations of Ohio and Oregon, and her horrors happen in familiar laboratories and family kitchens

Wilhelm is well known as mentor and teacher to young sf writers. She and her late husband, Damon Knight, helped to found the Clarion Writers Workshop and hosted the first Milford Writer's Conferences at their home in Milford, Pennsylvania, as get-togethers for their friends in the world of science fiction. In the year 2000, all four winners of Nebula Awards for fiction were her former students. Since the mid-1980s, she has been concentrating on thrillers and detective fiction. She lives in Eugene, Oregon.

DRUGS & ALTERED CONSCIOUSNESS; GENETIC ENGINEERING & CLONING; IMMORTALITY; WOMEN IN SF

## Major Works

*Novels*

*The Clone* (1965, with Theodore L. Thomas)
*The Killer Thing* (1967)

*The Year of the Cloud* (1970, with Theodore L. Thomas)
*Margaret and I* (1971)
*Where Late the Sweet Birds Sang* (1976) **Hugo, Locus Poll**
*The Clewiston Test* (1976)
*Juniper Time* (1979)
*Crazy Time* (1988)
*Death Qualified: A Mystery of Chaos* (1991)

## Collections

Wilhelm's short sf is available in collections *The Downstairs Room* (1968), *The Infinity Box* (1975), *And the Angels Sing* (1992), and *Children of the Wind: Five Novellas* (1989)

## Short Stories

"The Planners" (1968) **Nebula**
"April Fool's Day Forever" (1970)
"Forever Yours, Anna" (1987) **Nebula**
"The Girl Who Fell into the Sky" (1986) **Nebula**

## Other Important Works

*A Flush of Shadows* (1995) Five novellas from Wilhelm's "Constance and Charlie" mysteries, some of which have sf or fantastic elements.
*The Hills Are Dancing* (1986) with Richard Wilhelm.
"On Point of View." In Robin Scott Wilson, ed., *Those Who Can: A Science Fiction Reader.* New York: St. Martin's Press, 1996, 149–154.
*Storyteller: Writing Lessons and More from 27 Years of The Clarion Writers' Workshop* (2005) Excerpt "My Silent Partner" available online: http://www.sfsite.com/01b/sp216.htm.

# Research Sources

*Encyclopedias and Handbooks:* **AW, BW, CA, CANR, ESF, MSSF, SFW**

*Bibliographies:* **ARB, FF, SFAN**

Contento, William G. "Kate Wilhelm Bibliography." *Fantasy & Science Fiction.* 101(3) (2001): 71 l.

## Biographies and Interviews

Thielemans, Johan. "Interview with Damon Knight and Kate Wilhelm." In Luk de Vos, ed., *Just the Other Day: Essays on the Suture of the Future.* Antwerp, The Netherlands: EXA, 1985, 395–397.

Van Gelder, Gordon. "Kate Wilhelm: An Appreciation" *Fantasy & Science Fiction.* December 2001. http://www.sfsite.com/fsf/2001/gvg0109.htm.

Wood, Susan. "Kate Wilhelm Is a Writer." Introduction. *The Mile-Long Spaceship*, by Kate Wilhelm. Boston, MA: Gregg, 1980.

### Criticism and Readers' Guides

Cramer, Kathryn. "The Planners." In David G. Hartwell and Kathryn Cramer, eds., *The Ascent of Wonder.* New York: Tor, 1994. http://ebbs.english.vt.edu/exper/kcramer/anth/Planners.html.

Hopkinson, Nalo. "If all birds were of a feather, would you let one marry your sister? (Kate Wilhelm's *Where Late the Sweet Bird Sang*)" October 5, 1998. http://www.scifi.com/sfw/issue80/books.html#wl.

Lukin, Josh. "Cold War Masculinity in the Early Work of Kate Wilhelm." In Justine Larbalestier, ed., *Daughters of Earth: Feminist Science Fiction in the Twentieth Century.* Middletown, CT: Wesleyan University Press, 2006, 97–129.

### Web Sites

*Kate Wilhelm.com.* Web site endorsed by the author, with bibliography and list of awards and nominations. http://www.katewilhelm.com/.

## Connie Willis (1945–   )

*The past is beyond saving. Surely that was the lesson the history department sent me all this way to learn.*

—*"Fire Watch" (1982)*

### Biography

Connie Willis writes widely loved and admired novels about, among other things, time travel, in which the travelers must learn the hard way that history is populated with real people. For all their wit and humor, stories like "Fire Watch" (1982) and *Doomsday Book* (1992), based on the misadventures of historians from a near-future Oxford, resonate with the real sadness at the very core of the concept of time travel: the past is dead and gone, and nothing can be done about *that*.

Constance Elaine Trimmer Willis was born in Denver, Colorado. When she was twelve years old, her mother died in childbirth, a terrible event, which, in interview after interview, she says shaped her as a person and as a writer. Willis has a BA in English and Education from the University of Northern Colorado. She was the first author to win Nebulas in all the four fiction categories. She lives with her family in Greeley, Colorado.

ANTHROPOLOGY; HUMOR AND SATIRE; IMMORTALITY; NEAR FUTURE; TIME TRAVEL

# Major Works

## Novels

*Lincoln's Dreams* (1987)
*Doomsday Book* (1992) **Hugo, Nebula**
*Uncharted Territory* (1994)
*Remake* (1994) **Locus Poll**
*Bellwether* (1996) **Locus Poll**
*To Say Nothing of the Dog* (1997) **Hugo, Locus Poll**
*Passage* (2001) **Locus Poll** Excerpt: http://www.booksense.com/chapters/willispas sage.jsp.

## Collections

*The Winds of Marble Arch and Other Stories: A Connie Willis Compendium.* Burton, MI: Subterranean, 2007. Includes the **Hugo** winning 1999 title story, and "A Letter from the Clearys" (1982—**Nebula**), "The Last of the Winnebagos" (1988—**Hugo, Nebula**), "At the Rialto" (1989—**Nebula**), "Even the Queen" (1992—**Hugo, Locus Poll, Nebula**), "The Soul Selects Her Own Society: Invasion and Repulsion: A Chronological Reinterpretation of Two of Emily Dickinson's Poems: A Wellsian Perspective" (1996—**Hugo**), and "Newsletter" (1997—**Locus Poll**). Earlier collections are *Fire Watch* (1984) and *Impossible Things* (1993).

## Notable Short Stories

"Fire Watch" (1982) **Hugo, Nebula** http://www.infinityplus.co.uk/stories/firewatch. htm.
"Close Encounter" (1993) **Locus Poll**
"Death on the Nile" (1993) **Hugo**
"Just Like the Ones We Used to Know" (2003) http://www.asimovs.com/_issue_0501/ justliketheones.shtml.
"Inside Job" (2005) **Hugo** http://www.asimovs.com/_issue_0604_5/insidejob.shtml.

## Other Important Works

"Learning to Write Comedy, or Why It's Impossible and How to Do It." In *Writing Science Fiction & Fantasy,* edited by the Staff of *Analog & Isaac Asimov's Science Fiction Magazine.* New York: St. Martin's Griffin, 1993, 76–90.
"Science in Science Fiction: A Writer's Perspective." In Jack H. Stocker, ed., *Chemistry and Science Fiction.* Washington, DC: American Chemical Society, 1998, 21–34.
"2006 Worldcon Guest of Honor Speech." *SFRevu.* September 1, 2006. http://sfrevu. com/Review-id.php?id=4426.
"Women's Lib, 'The Liberation,' and the Many Other Liberations of Science Fiction." In Connie Willis and Sheila Williams, eds., *A Woman's Liberation: A Choice of Futures by and About Women.* New York: Warner/Aspect: 2000.

## Research Sources

*Encyclopedias and Handbooks:* **AW, CA, CANR, ESF, NNDB, SFW**

*Bibliographies:* **ARB, FF, SFAN**

### Biographies and Interviews

Hennessey-DeRose, Christopher and Michael McCarty. "Connie Willis—*To Say Nothing Of the Dog.*" *The Zone Online.* November 24, 2005. http://www.zone-sf.com/conniewillis.html.

Jenkins, Henry. Connie Willis/Nalo Hopkinson in Discussion at MIT: March 6, 2000. (Edited version) *Media in Transition.* August 29, 1998. Massachusetts Institute of Technology. http://web.mit.edu/m-i-t/science_fiction/.

*Locus Online.* "Connie Willis: The Facts of Death." January 2003. http://www.locusmag.com/2003/Issue01/Willis.html.

McCarty, Michael. "Connie Willis." In *Giants of the Genre: Interviews with Science Fiction. Fantasy and Horror's Greatest Talents.* Holicong, PA: Wildside, 2003, 121–127.

### Criticism and Readers' Guides

Kessel, John. "'A Letter from the Cleary's' and the Science Fiction Audience." *Short Form.* June 1989. http://www4.ncsu.edu/~tenshi/Clearywhite.html.

Shulman, Polly. "Tempting Fate." *Salon.com.* December 23, 1999. http://www.salon.com/books/feature/1999/12/23/sf_willis/index.html.

Slonczewski, Joan. "Bells and Time." In Milton T. Wolf and Daryl F. Mallett, eds., *Imaginative Futures.* San Bernardino, CA: Borgo, 1995, 161–166.

### Web Sites

*Connie Willis.net.* Official Web site. http://www.sftv.org/cw/.

*The Connie Willis Homepage.* Elisabeth McMahon. March 22, 1999. Fan site, with interesting links. http://www.geocities.com/Wellesley/5595/willis/willis.html.

**If you enjoyed Connie Willis ...**

Connie Willis has been called science fiction's P.G. Wodehouse; novels like *Lincoln's Dreams* (1987), *Doomsday Book* (1992), and *Passages* (2002) are written with wit and good humor, populated with characters who are very real, and serious situations that belie the lightness of her touch.

**Then you might like ...**

*Terry Bisson.* Like Willis, a consummate storyteller, who manages to deal with serious themes while being hilariously funny. Unlike Connie Willis, Bisson has tended to roam freely through the tropes of sf, such as alternative history (*Fire on the Mountain*, 1990), space travel (*Voyage to the Red Planet*, 1990), and social satire (*Pirates of the Universe*, 1996).

***Jack Finney***. In *Time and Again*, an "illustrated novel" in which the hero uses autohypnosis to transport himself back to New York City of the 1880s, Finney tapped into a powerful human yearning for tranquility and nostalgia as characters seek escape from a dangerous future, or a boring, unpleasant present. The effect was enhanced by Finney's careful research, and eye for the past.

***Mary Gentle***. Beginning with *Golden Witchbreed* (1983), Mary Gentle has made a career of fiction that slips the bonds of sf and fantasy. In *Ash: A Secret History* (2000), a potent blend of sword and sorcery style and alternative history, a female mercenary fights across a Europe that is not quite what we remember from history class, where Carthage never fell and Golems man the castle ramparts.

***Harry Turtledove***. Master of the alternative history, Turtledove has reimagined the American Civil War (*The Guns of the South*, 1992), the Spanish Armada (*Ruled Britannia*, 2002), and World War II (*Days of Infamy*, 2004). A historian, with a PhD in Byzantine history (*Agent of Byzantium*, 1987), Turtledove knows his subject well enough to have a lot of fun with it.

***Jo Walton***. *Farthing* (2006) is the first volume in the "Small Change" trilogy, a "country house murder mystery" set in an alternative England, which has made peace with Hitler. Walton's previous novels are reimaginings of Roman Britain (*The King's Peace*, 2000) and a Victorian melodrama, with dragons (*Tooth and Claw*, 2003). Like Willis, Walton's work is notable for its versatility and dry wit.

# Gene R. Wolfe (1931– )

*We believe that we invent symbols. The truth is that they invent us; we are their creatures, shaped by their hard, defining edges.*
> —*The Shadow of the Torturer (1980)*

## Biography

Gene Rodman Wolfe was born in New York City. After a brief spell at Texas A & M University, he was drafted to fight in the Korean War. Following his military service, he graduated from the University of Houston and became an industrial engineer. For many years he worked in that field, developing industrial processes (such as the one used to produce Pringle potato chips), and acted as editor of a professional engineering journal before he retired to write full-time.

Authors such as Neil Gaiman and Patrick O'Leary cite Gene Wolfe as an inspiration, and he is often credited as one of the great stylists of science fiction. A convert to Catholicism, Wolfe's writing is suffused with the moral attitudes and quandaries derived from his faith as well as a love of language, thoughtful plotting, and complicated narrative sense. He currently lives in Barrington, Illinois, a suburb of Chicago.

CHILDREN IN SF; FAR FUTURE; GODS AND DEMONS; LANGUAGE; MESSIAHS; MYTHOLOGY & LEGEND; RELIGION

## Major Works

*Novels*

*The Fifth Head of Cerberus* (1972)
The Briah Cycle, The Book of the New Sun: *The Shadow of the Torturer* (1980—**BSF**), *The Claw of the Conciliator* (1981—**Nebula, Locus Poll**), *The Sword of the Lictor* (1982—**Locus Poll**), *The Citadel of the Autarch* (1983)
*Free Live Free* (1984)
The Briah Cycle, The Book of the Long Sun: *Nightside the Long Sun* (1993), *Lake of the Long Sun* (1994), *Caldé of the Long Sun* (1994), *Exodus From the Long Sun* (1996)
The Briah Cycle, The Book of the Short Sun: *On Blue's Waters* (1999), *In Green's Jungles* (2000), *Return to the Whorl* (2001)

*Collections*

*The Island of Doctor Death and Other Stories and Other Stories* (1980)
Some subsequent Wolfe collections are *The Young Wolfe* (1992), *Strange Travelers* (2000), *Innocents Aboard* (2004), and *Starwater Strains* (2005).

*Notable Short Stories*

"The Island of Doctor Death and Other Stories" (1970)
"The Death of Doctor Island" (1973) **Nebula, Locus Poll**
"Seven American Nights" (1978)
"The Arimaspian Legacy" (1987) http://www.infinityplus.co.uk/stories/arimaspian.htm.
"Under Hill" (2002) http://www.infinitematrix.net/stories/shorts/under_hill.html.
"Memorare" (2007) http://www.sfsite.com/fsf/fiction/gw01.htm.

*Other Important Works*

"The Best Introduction to the Mountains." *Interzone*. December 2001. http://home.clara.net/andywrobertson/wolfemountains.html.
"The Profession of Science Fiction." In Maxim Jakubowski and Edward James, eds., *The Profession of Science Fiction: SF Writers on Their Craft and Ideas*. New York: St. Martin's Press, 1992, 131–139.

# Research Sources

*Encyclopedias and Handbooks:* **AW, BW, CA, CANR, ESF, MSSF, NNDB, SFW**

*Bibliographies:* **ARB, FF, SFAN**

Stewart, Perrin. "Master of the House of Pens: Bibliography." February 1997. Clemson University. http://hubcap.clemson.edu/~sparks/wolfpage.html.

## Biographies and Interviews

Andre-Driussi, Michael. "Gene Wolfe: The Man and His Work." *Fantasy & Science Fiction.* April 2007. http://www.sfsite.com/fsf/toc0704.htm.

Gevers, Nick. "A Magus of Many Suns: An Interview with Gene Wolfe." *SF Site.* January 2002. http://sfsite.com/03b/gw124.htm.

Gevers, Nick, et al. "Some Moments with the Magus: An Interview with Gene Wolfe." *Infinity Plus.* December 2003. http://www.infinityplus.co.uk/nonfiction/intgw.htm.

Huddleston, Kathie. "Gene Wolfe Invites Readers to Vacation on His Science-Fiction Islands." *SciFi.com.* February 25, 2002. http://www.scifi.com/sfw/interviews/sfw8152.html.

*Locus Online.* "The Wolfe & Gaiman Show." September 2002. http://www.locusmag.com/2002/Issue09/GaimanWolfe.html.

## Criticism and Readers' Guides

Andre-Driussi, Michael. *Lexicon Urthus: A Dictionary for the Urth Cycle.* San Francisco, CA: Sirius, 1994.

Blackford, Jenny. "Reading Gene Wolfe's *Return to the Whorl.*" *New York Review of Science Fiction.* 15(11) (2003): 9+.

Borski, Robert. *The Long and Short of It: More Essays on the Fiction of Gene Wolfe.* New York: iUniverse, 2006.

———. *Solar Labyrinth: Exploring Gene Wolfe's Book of the New Sun.* New York: iUniverse, 2004.

——— and Michael Andre-Driussu. *Cicerone Sinister: A Guide to Gene Wolfe's The Fifth Head of Cerberus.* Albany, CA: Sirius, 2001.

Gevers, Nick. "Five Steps Towards Briah: Gene Wolfe's *The Book of the Long Sun.*" *Nova Express.* Fall/Winter 1998. http://home.austin.rr.com/lperson/briah.html.

Gordon, Joan I. *Gene Wolfe.* Mercer Island, WA: Starmont, 1986.

Locey, Kathryn. "Three Dreams, Seven Nights, and Gene Wolfe's Catholicism." *New York Review of Science Fiction.* 8(11) (1996): 1+.

Palmer, Stephen. "Severian as Christ-figure." *Vector.* August 1991. http://members.bellatlantic.net/~vze2tmhh/sevchrist.html.

Wright, Peter. *Attending Daedalus: Gene Wolfe, Artifice and the Reader.* Liverpool, UK: Liverpool University Press, 2003.

*Web Sites*

*Gene Wolfe Fan Site.* Paul Duggan. March 2007. Links to essays by and about Wolfe, fan Forum, and news. http://members.bellatlantic.net/~vze2tmhh/wolfe.html.

*Fantasy & Science Fiction: Special Gene Wolfe Section.* April 2007. The essays by Neil Gaiman and Michael Swanwick, written specially for this tribute edition, are available in full online. http://www.sfsite.com/fsf/toc0704.htm.

*Map of the Whorl: Elucidations of the Suns.* March 2006. Glossary of terms, characters, and places in the Wolfe volumes *The Fifth Head of Cerberus, The Soldier Novels*, The Book of the Long Sun, and The Book of the Short Sun. http://www.urth.org/whorlmap/.

*Ultan's Library: A Journal of the Study of Gene Wolfe.* Jonathan Laidlow & Nigel Price. March 2007. News, articles, and reference materials. http://www.ultan.org. uk/index.html.

*Urth List.* E-mail discussion group about the works of Gene Wolfe. Archived discussion from 1997 to present. http://www.urth.net/.

# John Wyndham (1903–1969)

*When a day that you happen to know is Wednesday starts off by sounding like Sunday, there is something seriously wrong somewhere.*

*—The Day of the Triffids (1951)*

## Biography

John Wyndham Parkes Lucas Beynon Harris grew up in a suburb of Birmingham, in England, where his father practiced law. His parents' marriage collapsed spectacularly when he was eight years old; John was packed off to a succession of boarding schools, and never saw his father again. His first stories were pulp space operas, juveniles, ghost, and detective fiction, but following World War II, there was a radical change in both his style and subject matter. John Benyon Harris became "John Wyndham," and, in novels like *The Day of the Triffids*, depicted fantastic catastrophes happening to ordinary people. Wyndham recognized the horror possibilities in the complicated threads that connect our modern world.

Toward the end of his life, Wyndham lived in Hampshire, just outside the grounds of Bedales School, the one place he had been happy after the collapse of his family. He died there on March 12, 1969.

APOCALYPSE AND AFTER; CHILDREN IN SF; ECOLOGY; MONSTERS; NEAR FUTURE; PSI POWERS

## Major Works

*Novels*

*The Day of the Triffids* (1951)
*The Kraken Wakes* (1953)

*The Chrysalids* (1955)
*The Midwych Cuckoos* (1957)
*Trouble with Lichen* (1960)
*Chocky* (1968)

## Collections

*Consider Her Ways and Others* (1961) (London: Penguin, 1970).

# Research Sources

*Encyclopedias and Handbooks:* **AW, BW, CA, CAAS, CANR, ESF, MSSF, NNDB, SFW**

*Bibliographies:* **ARB, FF, SFAN**

Stephensen-Payne, Phil. *John Wyndham: Creator of the Cozy Catastrophe.* Leeds (UK): Galactic Central, 2001.

## Biographies and Interviews

BBC Four. TV Interview (1960). *The Lost Decade—1945–1955 (People).* January 2007. BBC Four.co.uk. http://www.bbc.co.uk/bbcfour/lostdecade/.
Bleiler, E.F. "Luncheon with John Wyndham." *Extrapolation.* 25 (1984): 314–317.
Ketterer, David. "John Wyndham and the Sins of His Father: Damaging Disclosures In Court." *Extrapolation.* 46 (2005) 163–188.
Obituary. *Times* (London) March 12, 1969. http://www.gcwillick.com/Spacelight/obit/wyndhamo.html.

## Criticism and Readers' Guides

Clareson, Thomas D. and Alice S. Clareson, "The Neglected Fiction of John Wyndham: 'Consider Her Ways,' *Trouble with Lichen* and *Web.*" In Rhys Garnett and R.J. Ellis, eds., *Science Fiction Roots and Branches.* Basingstoke, UK: Macmillan, 1990, 88–103.
Davies, Sue. "The Long and Wyndham Road." *SF Crowsnest.com.* 2003. http://www.computercrowsnest.com/sfnews2/03_sept/news0903_10.shtml.
Hurst, L.J. "Remembrance of Things to Come? *Nineteen Eighty-Four* and *The Day of the Triffids Again.*" *Vector.* No date. http://dialspace.dial.pipex.com/l.j.hurst/firstpar.htm.
Hurst, L.J. "'We Are the Dead:' *The Day of the Triffids* and *Nineteen Eighty-Four.*" *Vector.* 133 Aug/Sept 1986. http://dialspace.dial.pipex.com/l.j.hurst/weredead.htm.
Ketterer, David. "The Genesis of the Triffids." *New York Review of Science Fiction.* 16(7) (2004): 11+.
Salyer, Jerry. "Self against Other: Isolation and Community in *The Midwich Cuckoos.*" 3 (2006). http://www.irosf.com/q/zine/article/10323.

Sawyer, Andy. "A Stiff Upper Lip and a Trembling Lower One: John Wyndham on Screen." In I.Q. Hunter, ed., *British Science Fiction Cinema*. New York: Routledge, 1999, 75–87.

Thomas, G.W. "John Benyon Harris: The Early Pulp SF of John Wyndham." *The Zone Online*. November 2005. Pigasus Press. http://www.zone-sf.com/jbhwyndham. html.

## Web Sites

*The John Wyndham Archive*. Andy Sawyer. SF Hub. 2005. University of Liverpool. Catalogue of archives, with finding aid. http://www.sfhub.ac.uk/Wyndham.htm.

*"Return of the Triffids:" The John Wyndham Archive*. University of Liverpool Art Gallery. February 1999. Exhibition of art, illustrations, and other documents. http://www.liv.ac.uk/~asawyer/triffid2.html.

**If you enjoyed John Wyndham...**

Wyndham has been dismissed as the master of the middle-class, "cozy catastrophe." But his signature themes—ecological disasters, alien invasion, genetic mutations, and nuclear war, all brought on or made worse by a potent combination of mankind's blindness and arrogance—would seem to be just about right for the fraught opening years of the 21st century.

**Then you might like...**

*John Brunner*. He combined style and substance in four dystopian novels that depict futures rendered unlivable by scourges such as overpopulation and pollution, beginning with *Stand on Zanzibar* (1968). Some of Brunner's speculations, particularly about the Internet in *The Shockwave Rider* (1975), have a chilling ring of truth.

*John Christopher*. Considered Wyndham's great rival, with novels like *No Blade of Grass* (1956; orig. *The Death of Grass*), and *A Wrinkle in the Skin* (1965). While Wyndham tended to relieve the doom and gloom with a "stiff upper lip" faith in the ability of his ordinary heroes to survive in spite of everything, Christopher's scenarios hold no such promises of salvation. He also wrote a number of well-regarded Young Adult novels, with similar themes.

*Pat Frank*. Although he is not specifically identified as a science fiction author, Frank wrote three novels in the later 1940s and 1950s that deal with fears of nuclear contamination and the collapse of society after nuclear war. In the most famous—*Alas, Babylon* (1959)—residents of a small Florida town learn to adapt and survive in the aftermath of nuclear Armageddon.

*Kim Stanley Robinson*. In the Mars Trilogy, ordinary people reshape a planet. In his recent "Capital Code" series, the planet being "terraformed" is not Mars, but Earth, as politicians and scientists are forced to confront the impact of global warming. In *The Wild Shore*, first of the Orange County series, survivors try to rebuild civilizations following nuclear holocaust.

**George R. Stewart.** In his single sf novel, *Earth Abides* (1949), most of humanity is wiped out by a plague. Isherwood Williams, one of a tiny minority of immune survivors, raises a family and tries to hold on to something of the civilization that was lost. Some outdated attitudes, but deeply moving in its cool, scientific depiction of the man-made world crumbling away, and returning to nature.

# Roger Zelazny (1937–1995)

> *I'm a baitman. No one is born a baitman, except in a French novel.... How I got that way is barely worth the telling and has nothing to do with neo-exes, but the days of the beast deserve a few words, so here they are.*
> —*"The Doors of His Face, The Lamps of His Mouth" (1965)*

## Biography

Roger Joseph Zelazny was born in Euclid, Ohio, near Cleveland. Shortly after he was awarded an MA in Elizabethan and Jacobean drama from Columbia University, his novelette, "A Rose for Ecclesiastes," was nominated for a Hugo Award. But it was some years before he was able to give up his job with the Social Security Administration in Baltimore, and write full-time.

Zelazny is a leading figure of the American New Wave. His work broke the traditional mold of American science fiction: sometimes allusive and lyrical, sometimes making wise-cracking references to pop culture, he experimented with elements of mainstream fiction, borrowing from mythic traditions such as Greek, Egyptian, Hindu, and Native American, making unapologetic references to classic prose and poetry of the late nineteenth and early twentieth centuries.

In 1975, Zelazny moved to Santa Fe, New Mexico with his family. He died there in 1995, of kidney failure due to lung cancer.

GENDER & SEXUALITY; GODS & DEMONS; MARS, MOON & THE PLANETS; MYTHOLOGY & LEGEND; NEW WAVE; SEX & TABOOS

## Major Works

*Novels*

*This Immortal* (1965, originally *. . . and Call Me Conrad*) **Hugo**
*The Dream Master* (1966)
*Lord of Light* (1967) **Hugo**
*Isle of the Dead* (1969)
*Damnation Alley* (1969)

*Doorways in the Sand* (1976)
*Roadmarks* (1979)
*Eye of Cat* (1982)
*Deus Irae* (1976, with Philip K. Dick)
*Psychoshop* (1998, with Alfred Bester) This is a doubly posthumous novel: finished by
  Zelazny after the death of Alfred Bester, it was published after Zelazny's death.

## Collections

*The Doors of His Face, The Lamp of His Mouth, and Other Stories* (1971). New York:
  iBooks, 2005.
Other Zelazny collections are *My Name is Legion* (1976), and *Unicorn Variations*
  (1983—**Locus Poll**)

## Short Stories

"A Rose for Ecclesiastes" (1963)
"The Doors of His Face, The Lamp of His Mouth" (1965) **Nebula**
"He Who Shapes" (1965) **Nebula**
"The Man Who Loved the Faoili" (1967)
"Home is the Hangman" (1975) **Hugo, Nebula**
"Unicorn Variation" (1981) **Hugo**
"24 Views of Mt. Fuji, by Hokusai" (1985) **Hugo**
"Permafrost" (1986) **Hugo**

## Other Important Works

"Fantasy and Science Fiction: A Writer's View." In George E. Slusser and Eric S.
  Rabkin, eds., *Intersections: Fantasy and Science Fiction*. Carbondale: Southern
  Illinois University Press, 1987, 55–60.
*The Illustrated Roger Zelazny* (1979)
"Stand on Zanzibar: The Novel as Film." In Thomas D. Clareson, ed., *SF: The Other
  Side of Realism*. Bowling Green, OH: Bowling Green University Popular Press,
  1971, 181–185.
*Writing Science Fiction: Roger Zelazny*. Audio cassette. Wichita, KS: The Writer's
  Voice, 1973, 1975. http://zelazny.corrupt.net/audio/WritersVoice.html.

# Research Sources

*Encyclopedias and Handbooks:* **AW, BW, CA, CAAS, CANR, ESF,
MSSF, NNDB, SFW, WS**

*Bibliographies:* **ARB, FF, SFAN**

Stephens, Christopher P. *A Checklist of Roger Zelazny*. Hastings-on-Hudson, NY:
  Ultramarine, 1993.

Stephensen-Payne, Phil. *Roger Zelazny: Master of Amber; A Working Bibliography*. Albuquerque, NM: Galactic Central, 1991.

## Biographies and Interviews

Bisson, Terry. "Roger Zelazny: An Appreciation." 1996 World Fantasy Program Book. http://www.sff.net/people/TBisson/zelazny.html.
Dowling, Terry and Keith Curtis. "A Conversation with Roger Zelazny." *Science Fiction: A Review of Speculative Literature*. 1(2) (1978): 11–23. http://zelazny.corrupt.net/19780408int.html.
Martin, George R.R. "In Memoriam: Roger Zelazny, Lord of Light." *GRRM—The Official Web site of George R. R. Martin*. June 1995. http://www.georgerrmartin.com/musings-roger.html.
Nizalowski, John. "An Interview with Roger Zelazny." *New York Review of Science Fiction*. 18(7) (2006): 1+.
Wilgus, Neal. "Lord of the Shadows, Jack of Light." In *Seven by Seven: Interviews with American Science Fiction Writers of the West and Southwest*. San Bernardino, CA: Borgo, 1996, 93–107.

## Criticism and Readers' Guides

Delaney, Samuel R. "Zelazny, Varley, Gibson—and Quality." In *Shorter Views: Queer Thoughts & the Politics of the Paraliterary*. Hanover, NH: University Press of New England/Wesleyan University Press, 1999, 271–291.
Hartwell, David G. "Home is the Hunter: Roger Zelazny and 'Home is the Hangman.'" *New York Review of Science Fiction*. 9(1) (1996): 21+.
Lindskold, Jane M. *Roger Zelazny*. New York: Twayne, 1993.
Sanders, Joseph. "Dancing on the Tightrope: Immortality in Roger Zelazny" In Carl B. Yoke and Donald M. Hassler, eds., *Death and the Serpent: Immortality in Science Fiction and Fantasy*. Westport, CT: Greenwood, 1985, 135–144.
Sanders, Joseph. "The Forms I Move to Meet: Roger Zelazny's '24 Views of Mt. Fuji, by Hokusai.'" *New York Review of Science Fiction*. 8(5) (1996): 1+.
Wymer, Thomas L. "'Comes Now the Power': Roger Zelazny's Transformation of Romantic Poetic Themes." *Extrapolation*. 40 (1999): 320–324.
Yoke, C.B. *Roger Zelazny*. Mercer Island, WA: Starmont, 1979.

## Web Sites

*24 Views of Mt. Fuji*. Tim Eagen. January 2004. Zelazny's Hugo-winning novella was inspired by these Hokusai prints. http://www.stmoroky.com/reviews/gallery/hokusai/24views.htm#fuji06.
*Zelazny.corrupt.net*. Norris Thomlinson. March 2008. Links to appreciations, interviews, photos, and other information. http://zelazny.corrupt.net/.

# Major Awards

There are a number of awards given every year for the best science fiction novels, novellas, novelettes, and short stories, for services to the world of sf, and for career achievement. Most are sponsored by organizations of writers and/or fans. A comprehensive index to all major awards can be found at http://www.locusmag.com/SFAwards/. This includes information about the awards themselves—who sponsors them, who is eligible to vote, as well as issues and controversies. Information about winners and nominees can be accessed by prize, by author, or by year.

In this volume, the following major award winners are noted in each author entry:

## Hugo Awards (http://www.wsfs.org/hugos.html)

Science Fiction Achievement Award, named after Hugo Gernsback, founder of *Amazing Stories* magazine in 1926, and widely regarded as the "father" of the science fiction genre. Awarded annually by the World Science Fiction Society (WSFS) for over fifty years in various categories, including best books, stories, dramatic works, professional, and fan activities. Voters represent the committed fan and professional sf community, with paid memberships to the annual World Science Fiction Conventions.

*"Retro Hugos"* were introduced in 1996 to recognize retroactively works and people eligible fifty years prior to a current World Science Fiction Convention. They've been awarded only three times, in 1996, 2001, and 2004.

## Nebula Awards (http://www.sfwa.org/awards/)

Presented by professionals to professionals, they were created in the mid-1960s, by the Science Fiction Writers of America, as the basis for annual anthologies that would contribute to the income of the organization. Annual ballot of members, among them most of the leading writers of science fiction and fantasy, selects the year's best novel, novella, novelette, and short story from among those eligible.

## Locus Poll Awards (http://www.locusmag.com/SFAwards/)

Presented to winners of *Locus Magazine*'s annual readers' poll. Established in the early 1970s to provide recommendations and suggestions to Hugo Awards voters. Over the decades, the Locus Awards have often drawn more voters than the Hugos and Nebulas combined.

## The James Tiptree, Jr. Award (http://www.tiptree.org/)

Annual literary prize for "science fiction or fantasy that explores and expands the roles of women and men . . . " Founded by sf authors Pat Murphy and Karen Joy Fowler, as a memorial to Alice B. Sheldon, otherwise known as James Tiptree, Jr.

## British Science Fiction Awards (http://www.bsfa.co.uk/bsfa/website/awards.aspx)

Sponsored by the British Science Fiction Association, this is awarded each year at the annual Eastercon convention to best book, short fiction, media, and artist. Novels must be published in the United Kingdom, but short fiction may appear anywhere.

Some other prestigious sf awards (and date of inception) are:

*John W. Campbell Memorial Award*: 1973—Best sf novel published in the United States. Judged award, limited to novel. (Not to be confused with the John W. Campbell Award for Best New Writer.) http://www.ku.edu/~sfcenter/campbell. htm.

*Arthur C. Clarke Award*: 1987—Best sf novel published each year in the United Kingdom (not necessarily by a British writer). Juried award, sponsored by Sir Arthur C. Clarke. http://www.clarkeaward.com/.

*Damon Knight Memorial Grand Master Award*: 1975—Presented by the Science Fiction and Fantasy Writers of America, to a living author for a lifetime's achievement in sf and/or fantasy. http://www.sfwa.org/awards/grand.htm.

*The Philip K. Dick Award*: 1983—Best original paperback published each year in the United States. http://ebbs.english.vt.edu/exper/kcramer/PKDA.html.

*The Skylark*: 1966—Officially the "Edward E. Smith Memorial Award for Imaginative Fiction," given annually by the New England Science Fiction Association, for significant contribution to sf in the spirit of the writer E.E. "Doc" Smith.

# General Bibliography

## Encyclopedias and Handbooks

Barron, Neil. *Anatomy of Wonder*. 5th ed. Westport, CT: Libraries Unlimited, 2004.

Clute, John and Peter Nicholls, ed. *The Encyclopedia of Science Fiction*. Revised ed. New York: Orbit, 1999.

Magill, Frank N., ed. *Survey of Science Fiction Literature*. Englewood Cliffs, NJ: Salem, 1979.

Sabella, Robert. *Who Shaped Science Fiction?* Commack, NY: Kroshka, 2000.

Tixier, Diana, ed. *Strictly Science Fiction*. Englewood, CO: Libraries Unlimited, 1999.

Westfahl, Gary, ed. *The Greenwood Encyclopedia of Science Fiction and Fantasy: Themes, Works, and Wonders*. Westport, CT: Greenwood, 2005.

———. *Science Fiction Quotations: From the Inner Mind to the Outer Limits*. New Haven, CT: Yale University Press, 2005.

## Guides to Biography

Bleiler, Everett Franklin. *Science Fiction Writers*. New York: Scribners, 1982. Critical studies of the major authors from the early nineteenth century to the early 1980s.

*Contemporary Authors*. Detroit, MI: Gale Research, 1981–current. *Also available online*—check availability with your school or library.

*Contemporary Authors, Autobiography Series*. Detroit, MI: Gale Research, 1984–1999. Thirty volumes, each containing about twenty autobiographical essays written exclusively for the series.

*Contemporary Authors, New Revision Series*. Detroit, MI: Gale Research, 1981–current.

Harris-Fain, Darren, ed. *British Fantasy and Science-Fiction Writers before World War I* (*Dictionary of Literary Biography 178*). Detroit, MI: Gale, 1997.

―――. *British Fantasy and Science-Fiction Writers, 1918–1960* (*Dictionary of Literary Biography 255*). Detroit, MI: Gale, 2002.

―――. *British Fantasy and Science-Fiction Writers Since 1960.* (*Dictionary of Literary Biography 261*). Detroit, MI: Gale, 2002.

Pedersen, Jay. *St. James Guide to Science Fiction Writers.* Detroit, MI: St. James, 1996.

## *Short Story Collections*

*The James Tiptree Award Anthology.* Ed. Karen Joy Fowler, Pat Murphy, et al. Various editions. San Francisco, CA: Tachyon. Prize-winning works of fantasy and science fiction that explore gender roles and the role of women.

*Nebula Awards Showcase 2007.* Various editors, various editions. New York: Roc/Penguin. This annual publication, as chosen by the Science Fiction and Fantasy Writers of America, brings together the best of the year's stories as well as essays and commentary on the current state of the genre.

*The Year's Best Science Fiction.* Ed. Gardner Dozois. Various annual editions. New York: St. Martin's Griffin. Personal favorites by the veteran editor, compiled from stories published in magazines and anthologies during the preceding year.

## *Some "Frequently Cited" Sources*

Barr, Marleen. *Lost In Space: Probing Feminist Science Fiction and Beyond.* Chapel Hill: University of North Carolina Press, 1993.

Bloom, Harold, ed. *Classic Science Fiction Writers.* New York: Chelsea House, 1995.

Disch, Thomas. *The Dreams Our Stuff Is Made Of.* New York: Touchstone, 1998.

Donawerth, Jane. *Frankenstein's Daughters: Women Writing Science Fiction.* Syracuse, NY: Syracuse University Press, 1997.

Greenland, Colin. *The Entropy Exhibition: Michael Moorcock and the British "New Wave" in Science Fiction.* Boston, MA: Routledge & Kegan Paul, 1983.

Gunn, James. *The Science of Science-Fiction Writing.* Lanham, MD: Scarecrow, 2000.

Jones, Gwyneth. *Deconstructing the Starships: Science, Fiction, and Reality.* Liverpool, UK: Liverpool University Press, 1999.

Lefanu, Sarah. *In the Chinks of the World Machine: Feminism and Science Fiction.* London: Women's, 1988.

Nicholls, Stan. *Wordsmiths of Wonder: Fifty Interviews with Writers of the Fantastic.* London: Orbit, 1993.

Platt, Charles. *Dream Makers: The Uncommon People Who Write Science Fiction.* New York: Berkley, 1980.

Resnick, Mike, and Joe Siclari, eds. *Worldcon Guest of Honor Speeches.* Deerfield, IL: ISFiC, 2006. http://www.isficpress.com/worldcon_goh_speeches.asp. From "Doc" Smith in 1940 to Vernor Vinge in 2002.

Roberts, Adam. *The History of Science Fiction.* London: Palgrave Macmillan, 2005.

Seed, David, ed. *A Companion to Science Fiction.* Malden (UK): Blackwell, 2005.

Stover, Leon. *Science Fiction from Wells to Heinlein*. Jefferson, NC: McFarland, 2002.
Whissen, Thomas Reed. *Classic Cult Fiction: A Companion to Popular Cult Literature*.
New York: Greenwood, 1992.

# Web Sites

## Bibliographies

*Alpha Ralpha Boulevard*. September 2006. http://www.catch22.com/SF/ARB/. Bibliographic Web site, with links.

*Archive of Science Fiction*. December 2001. CyberSpace Spinner. http://www.hycyber.
com/SF/. Not a pretty site, and seems to be dormant since 2001, but extremely
useful: comprehensive bibliographies, list of authors' pseudonyms, and cinema
archive.

*Fantastic Fiction*. April 2008. http://www.fantasticfiction.co.uk/. Bibliographies for
over 4000 British and American authors, including science fiction. Some entries
include portraits and biographical statements. Bibliographies include titles and
images of book jackets of selected primary works (books and stories written by
the author). Generally reliable, but has occasional glitches (for instance, in many
cases, short story collections are listed as "novels").

*Feminist Science Fiction, Fantasy and Utopia*. Laura Quilter. June 2007. http://
feministsf.org/. Complex bibliography that lists cites and describes sf and critical
works from a feminist perspective. Includes a wiki of author information.

*Internet Speculative Fiction Database*. April 2008. http://www.isfdb.org/. Open-
content collaborative bibliographic database for science fiction, fantasy, and
horror. Bibliographic data, award listings, magazine, anthology, and collection
content listings, and forthcoming books. Hosted by the Cushing Library Science
Fiction and Fantasy Research Collection at Texas A&M University.

*Uchronia: The Alternative History List*. Robert B. Schmunk. April 2008. http://www.
uchronia.net/. A bibliography of over 2800 novels, stories, essays, and other
printed material involving "allohistory," or the "what ifs" of history.

## Fiction, Full Text Online

*Free Speculative Fiction Online* Richard Cissée. 2008. http://www.freesfonline.de/
index.html. Includes links to free, full text fiction from a variety of science fiction
writers. This site *does not* link to sites that violate the authors' copyright.

*Project Gutenberg*. April 2008. http://www.gutenberg.net/index.shtml. Project Gutenberg is one the largest digital collections of uncopyrighted works. Includes a
search interface for locating the text of a specific author or title. Tends to be better
for early writers.

*SciFiction*. SciFi Channel.com. http://www.scifi.com/scifiction/archive.html. As of
June 2007, Scifi.com announced that it would no longer be hosting this excellent

Web site, which brought together a wide range of classic and contemporary science fiction short stories, full text, with the permission of authors or their estates. However, as of April 2008, the above URL still works, as do the links for the individual stories. It is necessary to be patient, as pages take a little longer than usual to load.

## General Sources on Writers and Writings

*Books and Writers: Authors' Calendar.* Petri Liukkonen and Ari Pesonen. August 2007. Pegasos. http://www.kirjasto.sci.fi/calendar.htm Finnish literary Web site, organized by author's birthdates, with detailed biographical entries and selected bibliographies.

*Contemporary Writers.com.* British Arts Council. http://www.contemporarywriters. com/. Up-to-date profiles of some of the UK and the Commonwealth's most important living writers—biographies, bibliographies, critical reviews, prizes, and photographs.

*Internet Book List.* Steven Jeffery. February 2008. http://www.iblist.com/. Database of information about authors and titles. Useful search feature by genre, subject, and type of book and short story.

*Library Thing.com.* Tim Spaulding. http://www.librarything.com/. "...the world's largest book club..." Find people with similar tastes, by entering what you're reading—or your whole library. Includes Author Chat, and tallies of popular titles.

*Reader's Advice.com.* February 2008. http://www.readersadvice.com/. Database site, which features almost 10,000 fiction authors in almost 500 subgenres. Administered by Janet Kerns, a retired librarian based in Oklahoma, and has a wide-ranging "search by theme" feature.

## Indexes and Databases

*Access My Library.* April 2008. The Gale Group. http://www.accessmylibrary.com/. Free access to millions of articles in Thomson Gale databases for patrons of public and school libraries. *Available online with a library card; check if your local library is registered.*

*Annual Bibliography of English Language and Literature.* Modern Humanities Research Association. http://collections.chadwyck.com/marketing/home_abell.jsp. Indexes scholarly articles on English language, literature, and film. *Available by subscription; check your local library for availability.*

*The Gnooks Literature-Map.* Marek Gibney. http://www.gnooks.com/. A "self-adapting community system" based on the *gnod engine* (a database that makes connections based on user input, and "learns" as it searches). Intriguing—and hypnotic! Makes some interesting and unexpected connections.

*Literature Resource Center.* Thomson Gale. *Links through library homepages.* Incorporates materials from the Dictionary of Literary Biography series, as well as other printed reference series published by Gale. *Available online by subscription; check your local library for availability.*

*Modern Language Association International Bibliography.* Modern Language Association. http://www.mla.org/bibliography. Indexes scholarly articles on English and non-English language, literature, film, cultural studies, folklore, and linguistics. Published in print and online. *Available by print and online by subscription; check your local library for availability.*

*Notable Names DataBase.* Soylent Communications. http://nndb.com/. "Intelligence aggregator" (or "Who's Who?") that tracks the activities of noteworthy people—living and dead.

*SciFan.com.* Olivier Travers and Sophie Bellais. March 2008. http://www.scifan.com/. Comprehensive bibliographic database of sf and fantasy writers, focused on organizing the author data into series and themes. Links to relevant Web sites.

*Science Fiction and Fantasy Research Database.* Hal W. Hall. October 2007. Texas A&M University. http://library.tamu.edu/cushing/sffrd/default.asp. ". . . Online index to historical and critical items about science fiction, fantasy, and horror." Encompasses and updates Hal W. Hall's classic *Science Fiction and Fantasy Reference Index* series.

*SF: If You Like This, Then You'll Like That.* The Ultimate Science Fiction Web Guide. Ed. Jonathan Vos Post. February 2004. Magic Dragon Multimedia. An extensive list of themes, with titles ranging from the earliest "proto-sf" to the late 1990s. http://www.magicdragon.com/UltimateSF/thisthat.html.

*Themes/Genres in Science Fiction: An idiosyncratic and woefully incomplete list.* Ed. Kathleen L. Fowler. June 2002. http://phobos.ramapo.edu/~kfowler/sfthemes. html. Extremely knowledgeable—a wide range of reading possibilities. Unfortunately (as the subtitle warns us), work on the list appears to have been abandoned, and the final few links are not active. (And they would have been interesting ones!)

## Interviews

*Fast Forward.* March 2008. DG Productions. http://www.fast-forward.tv/ Online archives for "Fast Forward," an interview program featuring fantasy and science fiction authors. Includes and archive of video interviews, special reports, and book reviews.

*Hour of the Wolfe.* April 2008. http://www.hourwolf.com/toc.html. Web site of sf radio program broadcast live over WBAI (99.5 FM) in New York City on Saturday mornings, for the past thirty-five years. Includes audio files, transcripts, and links.

*Media in Transition Archive.* 2000. Massachusetts Institute of Technology. http://web. mit.edu/m-i-t/science_fiction/index.html. Articles and interviews, by various sf writers and others, on Media and Imagination.

*Mike Hodel's Hour 25.* December 2007. http://www.hour25online.com/. Online archives for this long-running science fiction/fantasy radio interview show. Audio files.

*Wired for Books.* April 2007. Ohio University Telecommunications Center. http:// wiredforbooks.org. Radio interviews with various sf authors. Audio files.

## Magazines and Journals

(*All Web sites last visited April 2008*)

*Analog Science Fiction and Fact.* http://www.analogsf.com/. Web site of the classic sf magazine, with links to articles from current issues, some short fiction available in full online, FAQs and archives.

*Bookslut.com.* http://www.bookslut.com/. Monthly Web magazine and daily blog dedicated to those who love to read. Often features items of interest to sf readers.

*Extrapolation: A Journal of Science Fiction and Fantasy.* http://www.morganprinting. org/recentExtrapo.html. " . . . the first [journal] to publish academic work on science fiction and fantasy."

*Fantastic Metropolis.* Ed. Luís Rodrigues. http://www.fantasticmetropolis.com/. Occasional online magazine, last updated in January 2006. Editorial board includes, L. Timmel Duchamp, Michael Moorcock, and Jeff VanderMeer.

*The Guardian* (London) *Online: Science fiction, Fantasy and Horror.* http://books. guardian.co.uk/departments/sciencefiction/front/0,,95684,00.html. The book review section of the quality London newspaper, which makes article and reviews available online.

*Infinite Matrix.* Ed. Eileen Gunn. January 2007. Matrix.net. http://www.infinitematrix. net/. Online magazine, published from August 2001 to January 2006 (and April 2006). Archive essays, excerpts, and complete stories available in full.

*Infinity Plus.* Ed. Keith Brooke. August 2007. http://www.infinityplus.co.uk/. British Web site featuring articles, author interviews, and some original fiction from science fiction and fantasy authors.

*The Internet Review of Science Fiction.* April 2008. Quintamid LLC. http://www.irosf. com/index.qsml. Current monthly sf and fantasy magazine.

*January Magazine.* April 2008. http://www.januarymagazine.com/SFF/SFF.html. Includes reviews, author interviews. Coverage extends to science fiction, fantasy, mystery, mainstream, children's books, and non-fiction.

*LOCUS Online.* April 2008. http://www.locusmag.com/. Includes author interviews, book reviews, and news about the science fiction, fantasy, and horror publishing industry. Web site includes a variety of resources, including excerpts of published interviews and listings for major awards in science fiction, fantasy, and horror.

*The Magazine of Fantasy and Science Fiction.* http://www.sfsite.com/fsf/. Original stories and novellas, and index to all issues since 1998.

*New York Review of Science Fiction and Fantasy.* February 2008. Dragon Press. http:// davidghartwell.typepad.com/nyrsf/2008/02/editorial-iss-1.html. Includes author interviews, reviews, and critical articles on science fiction, fantasy, and horror. Online index to all issues since 1988.

*SF Revu.* Ed. Ernest Lilley. April 2008. http://www.sfrevu.com/. Monthly online magazine: news, book reviews, and columns of U.S. and UK interest.

*Science Fiction and Fantasy News.* Dag Rambrout, Gary Wassner, et al. April 2008. http://sffworld.com/. Volunteer site, run from Norway, which includes interviews, articles, news, and reviews.

*Science Fiction Studies.* Istvan Csicsery-Ronay, Jr. February 2008. DePauw University. http://www.depauw.edu/sfs/. Scholarly articles on science fiction and fantasy literature, published three times a year, as well as some author interviews. The Web site includes abstracts and *free* online full text from issues that were published at least one year ago.

*SciFi Dimensions*. Ed. John C. Snider. http://www.scifidimensions.com/. Monthly online science fiction magazine offering interviews, articles, and reviews plus original fiction and commentary.

*Some Fantastic*. Ed. Matthew Appleton. February 2008. http://www.somefantastic.us/. Bimonthly, e-published crit-zine focused on science fiction, fantasy, and horror in literature and film.

*Strange Horizons*. Ed. Susan Marie Groppi. April 2008. http://www.strangehorizons. com/. Weekly Web-based magazine of and about speculative fiction.

*The Zone Online*. 2008. Pigasus Press. http://www.zone-sf.com/home.html. Online author interviews and profiles, critical articles, essays, plus media reviews. Published nine issues in print format, which included original fiction.

## Organizations and Conventions

*The New England Science Fiction Association*. (NESFA) http://www.nesfa.org/. Founded in 1967, one of the oldest science fiction clubs in New England. Organizes the long-running, annual Boskone convention, and NESFA Press.

*Obituary Archive*. http://www.sfwa.org/News/obits.htm.

*Science Fiction and Fantasy Writers of America, Inc.* http://www.sfwa.org/ The Science Fiction and Fantasy Writers of America sponsors the yearly Nebula Awards. Its Web site includes a variety of resources for writers as well as readers.

*Science Fiction Oral History Association*. November 2006. http://www.sfoha.org/. Non-profit organization that maintains an archive of audio and video recordings of historic people and events related to science fiction and fantasy. Archive catalog online.

*Science Fiction Research Association*. http://www.sfra.org/. "the oldest professional organization for the study of science fiction and fantasy literature, and film."

*Science Fiction and Fantasy Writers of America, Inc.* http://www.sfwa.org/ The Science Fiction and Fantasy Writers of America sponsors the yearly Nebula Awards. Its Web site includes a variety of resources for writers, as well as readers.

*The Speculative Literature Foundation*. http://www.speclit.org/index.php. Volunteer-run, nonprofit organization dedicated to promoting the interests of readers, writers, editors, and publishers in the speculative literature community.

*World Science Fiction Society/World Science Fiction Convention* http://www. worldcon.org/. The World Science Fiction Society sponsors the yearly Hugo Awards as well as the yearly World Science Fiction Convention.

## Portals and Home Pages

*Locus Online*. http://www.locusmag.com/Links/Portal.html. Links to any and all Web sites the sf and fantasy fan could possibly wish for: 'zines, blogs, forums, authors' Web sites, et al. If it is on the Web, it is here, and if it isn't here, there are links to half-a dozen other link collection Web sites. Includes a section for closed or dormant sites, and "fun."

*SF Site*. http://www.sfsite.com/home.htm. The home page for science fiction and fantasy. Includes author interviews (extensive index), articles, and reviews. Index of reviews. http://www.sfsite.com/map3.htm

*Sci Fi Channel*. http://www.scifi.com/. Includes author interviews, reviews, and articles about fantasy and science fiction literature and media. Weekly newsletter http://www.scifi.com/sfw/.

*SciFiPedia (wiki encyclopedia)* http://scifipedia.scifi.com/index.php/Main_Page.

*Science Fiction Citations*. Ed. Jesse Sheidlower, Jeff Prucher, and Malcolm Farmer. January 2008. http://www.jessesword.com/sf/home. Fascinating site maintained by the Editor at Large of the Oxford English Dictionary (OED), which aims to provide accurate definitions, and first know use dates, for science fiction terms. The project grew out of regular work that was being done for the OED's reading programs, and each entry supplies a basic definition, the history of this project's research on the term, and quotes supporting the earliest known use, gathered for OED.

*Science Fiction-Related Materials*. Paul Brians. October 2006. Washington State University. http://www.wsu.edu/~brians/science_fiction/. Study guides for various sf novels, bibliographies, and other links.

*Spacelight*. George C. Willick. March 2008. http://www.gcwillick.com/Spacelight/index.html. "Vital statistics and personal data for the golden age writers of pulp magazine, stories, and paperback books . . . " Includes much interesting information not available elsewhere, such as original obituaries.

*Templeton Gate*. Galen Strickland. http://templetongate.tripod.com/mainpage.htm. Fan Web site, collecting essays on various sf writers.

*The Ultimate Science Fiction Web Guide*. Ed. Jonathan Vos Post. November 2004. Magic Dragon Multimedia. http://www.magicdragon.com/UltimateSF/SF-Index. html.

# Lists of Authors by Type

Some authors are known for revisiting the same themes again and again (think Connie Willis' fascination with time travel, or C.S. Lewis' use of sf to illustrate Christian ideals). Other sf writers—Robert A. Heinlein, for example—in their long and varied careers, covered so many of the themes, tropes, and plotlines of sf that it is almost an exercise in futility to try to pin them down to half-a-dozen or so.

Modeled closely on The Checklist of Themes in Clute and Nicholls' *The Encyclopedia of Science Fiction*, the following "subject tags" are not meant to pin down authors, all of whose works are far more rich and complicated than half a dozen words can describe. Rather, they are intended to *suggest connections*—sometimes, I hope, unexpected ones—and give readers some ideas about other authors they might enjoy.

## *Aliens*

| | | |
|---|---|---|
| Adams, Douglas | Knight, Damon | Tepper, Sheri S. |
| Butler, Octavia E. | Lethem, Jonathan | Tiptree Jr., James |
| Jones, Gwyneth | Pohl, Frederik | Van Vogt, A.E. |
| Kelly, James Patrick | Smith, E.E. "Doc" | |

## *Alien Threat*

| | | |
|---|---|---|
| Brunner, John | Finney, Jack | Silverberg, Robert |
| Card, Orson Scott | Haldeman, Joe | Stross, Charles |
| Disch, Thomas M. | Niven, Larry | Wells, H.G. |

## Alien Worlds

Aldiss, Brian
Anderson, Poul
Banks, Iain M.

Bishop, Michael
Burroughs, Edgar Rice
Cherryh, C.J.

Greenland, Colin
Lem, Stanislaw
McHugh, Maureen F.

## Alternative History

Chiang, Ted
Dick, Philip K.
Goonan, Kathleen Ann

Harrison, Harry
McIntyre, Vonda
Robinson, Kim Stanley

Spinrad, Norman

## Androids, Cyborgs, and Robots

Asimov, Isaac
Čapek, Karel
Cherryh, C.J.
Dick, Philip K.

Goonan, Kathleen Ann
Lem, Stanislaw
Moore, C.L.
Poe, Edgar Allan

Shelley, Mary
　Wollstonecraft

## Anthropology

Bishop, Michael
Gloss, Molly

Hoban, Russell
Le Guin, Ursula K.

Vonnegut, Kurt
Willis, Connie

## Apocalypse and After

Atwood, Margaret
Bova, Ben
Brackett, Leigh
Bradbury, Ray
Brin, David

Charnas, Suzy McKee
Harrison, M. John
Hoban, Russell
McIntyre, Vonda
Miller, Walter M.

Stapledon, Olaf
Tepper, Sheri S.
Wyndham, John

## Artificial Intelligence

Adams, Douglas
Banks, Iain M.
Cadigan, Pat
Clarke, Arthur C.
Gibson, William

Goonan, Kathleen Ann
Jones, Gwyneth
L'Engle, Madeleine
MacLeod, Ken
Robson, Justina

Scott, Melissa
Stephenson, Neal
Vinge, Vernor

## Children in SF

Bear, Greg
Clarke, Arthur C.
Heinlein, Robert A.
Kelly, James Patrick

L'Engle, Madeleine
Sargent, Pamela
Sturgeon, Theodore
Tepper, Sheri S.

Van Vogt, A.E.
Wolfe, Gene R.
Wyndham, John

# Cities and Societies

Bishop, Michael
Harrison, M. John

McHugh, Maureen F.
Pohl, Frederik

# Colonization of Other Worlds

Baxter, Stephen
Blish, James
Cherryh, C.J.
Gloss, Molly
Le Guin, Ursula K.

Lethem, Jonathan
McCaffrey, Anne
McIntyre, Vonda
Niven, Larry
Pohl, Frederik

Russ, Joanna
Sargent, Pamela
Silverberg, Robert
Smith, Cordwainer

# Cyberpunk

Cadigan, Pat
Doctorow, Cory

Gibson, William
Scott, Melissa

Spinrad, Norman
Stephenson, Neal

# Disability and SF

Bujold, Lois McMaster
Keyes, Daniel

McCaffrey, Anne
Piercy, Marge

Varley, John

# Drugs and Altered Consciousness

Dick, Philip K.
Huxley, Aldous

Lethem, Jonathan
Shepard, Lucius

Wilhelm, Kate

# Dystopias

Atwood, Margaret
Bradbury, Ray
Brunner, John

Burgess, Anthony
Charnas, Suzy McKee
Disch, Thomas M.

Huxley, Aldous
Knight, Damon
Orwell, George

# Ecology

Ballard, J.G.
Brunner, John
Harrison, Harry

Herbert, Frank
Robinson, Kim Stanley
Spinrad, Norman

Wyndham, John

# End of the World

Adams, Douglas
Disch, Thomas M.
Finney, Jack

Knight, Damon
Poe, Edgar Allan

Shelley, Mary
    Wollstonecraft
Spinrad, Norman

## *Entropy*

Aldiss, Brian
Ballard, J.G.
Dick, Philip K.
Disch, Thomas M.

Ellison, Harlan
Harrison, M. John
Moorcock, Michael
Silverberg, Robert

Spinrad, Norman
Tiptree Jr., James

## *Fantastic Voyages*

Adams, Douglas
Bester, Alfred
Blish, James

Burroughs, Edgar Rice
L'Engle, Madeleine
Poe, Edgar Allan

Pohl, Frederik
Verne, Jules

## *Fantasy*

Bradley, Marion Zimmer
Burroughs, Edgar Rice
Delany, Samuel R.
Greenland, Colin
Harrison, M. John

Hoban, Russell
McCaffrey, Anne
Moorcock, Michael
Robson, Justina
Shepard, Lucius

Silverberg, Robert
Strugatsky, Arkady &
   Boris
Tepper, Sheri S.

## *Far Future*

Aldiss, Brian
Banks, Iain M.
Baxter, Stephen
Blish, James

Harrison, M. John
Herbert, Frank
Miller, Walter M.
Moorcock, Michael

Smith, Cordwainer
Stapledon, Olaf
Wolfe, Gene R.

## *Feminism*

Atwood, Margaret
Bradley, Marion Zimmer
Charnas, Suzy McKee

Le Guin, Ursula K.
McIntyre, Vonda
Piercy, Marge

Tepper, Sheri S.
Tiptree Jr., James

## *First Contact*

Bova, Ben
Haldeman, Joe
MacLeod, Ken

Strugatsky, Arkady and
   Boris
Vinge, Vernor

## *Galactic Empires*

Anderson, Poul
Asimov, Isaac
Bradley, Marion Zimmer

Brunner, John
Bujold, Lois McMaster
Herbert, Frank

Niven, Larry
Simmons, Dan
Smith, E.E. ("Doc")

## *Gender and Sexuality*

Bradley, Marion Zimmer
Butler, Octavia E.
Charnas, Suzy McKee
Delany, Samuel R.
Le Guin, Ursula K.
McHugh, Maureen F.

McIntyre, Vonda
Moorcock, Michael
Moore, C.L.
Piercy, Marge
Russ, Joanna
Ryman, Geoff

Scott, Melissa
Sturgeon, Theodore
Tepper, Sheri S.
Tiptree Jr., James
Varley, John

## *Genetic Engineering and Cloning*

Atwood, Margaret
Blish, James
Brin, David
Bujold, Lois McMaster
Cherryh, C.J.
Haldeman, Joe

Herbert, Frank
Huxley, Aldous
Kelly, James Patrick
Robson, Justina
Sargent, Pamela
Smith, Cordwainer

Smith, E.E. "Doc"
Stapledon, Olaf
Van Vogt, A.E.
Varley, John

## *Gods and Demons*

Chiang, Ted
Clarke, Arthur C.
Farmer, Philip José
Lewis, C.S.

Moore, C.L.
Sheckley, Robert
Simmons, Dan
Stapledon, Olaf

Van Vogt, A.E.
Wolfe, Gene R.
Zelazny, Roger

## *Gothic SF*

Aldiss, Brian
Bishop, Michael
Bradbury, Ray

Moorcock, Michael
Moore, C.L.
Poe, Edgar Allan

Shelley, Mary
  Wollstonecraft
Shepard, Lucius

## *Hard SF*

Anderson, Poul
Baxter, Stephen
Bear, Greg

Bova, Ben
Brin, David
Clarke, Arthur C.

Haldeman, Joe
Niven, Larry
Stross, Charles

## *Humor and Satire*

Adams, Douglas
Anderson, Poul
Bester, Alfred
Bishop, Michael
Bradbury, Ray
Bujold, Lois McMaster

Čapek, Karel
Dick, Philip K.
Harrison, Harry
Huxley, Aldous
Knight, Damon
Lem, Stanislaw

Pohl, Frederik
Sheckley, Robert
Strugatsky, Arkady &
  Boris
Vonnegut, Kurt
Willis, Connie

## Immortality

| | | |
|---|---|---|
| Anderson, Poul | Moorcock, Michael | Wilhelm, Kate |
| Doctorow, Cory | Sheckley, Robert | |
| Farmer, Philip José | Smith, Cordwainer | |

## Language

| | | |
|---|---|---|
| Burgess, Anthony | Hoban, Russell | Wolfe, Gene R. |
| Delany, Samuel R. | Stephenson, Neal | |

## Libertarian SF

| | | |
|---|---|---|
| Anderson, Poul | Heinlein, Robert A. | Vinge, Vernor |
| Bear, Greg | MacLeod, Ken | |
| Brin, David | Niven, Larry | |

## Mars, Moon and The Planets

| | | |
|---|---|---|
| Asimov, Isaac | Burroughs, Edgar Rice | Sargent, Pamela |
| Bova, Ben | Heinlein, Robert A. | Varley, John |
| Brackett, Leigh | Lewis, C.S. | Wells, H.G. |
| Bradbury, Ray | Robinson, Kim Stanley | Zelazny, Roger |

## Messiahs

| | | |
|---|---|---|
| Card, Orson Scott | Heinlein, Robert A. | Wolfe, Gene R. |
| Dick, Philip K. | Herbert, Frank | |

## Monsters

| | | |
|---|---|---|
| Shelley, Mary Wollstonecraft | Simmons, Dan | Verne, Jules |
| | Van Vogt, A.E. | Wyndham, John |

## Mythology and Legend

| | | |
|---|---|---|
| Butler, Octavia E. | Gloss, Molly | Shepard, Lucius |
| Čapek, Karel | Hoban, Russell | Simmons, Dan |
| Chiang, Ted | Jones, Gwyneth | Smith, Cordwainer |
| Delany, Samuel R. | L'Engle, Madeleine | Wolfe, Gene R. |
| Ellison, Harlan | Miller, Walter M. | Zelazny, Roger |
| Farmer, Philip José | Ryman, Geoff | |

## Nanotechnology

Bear, Greg
Brin, David
Gibson, William
Goonan, Kathleen Ann

MacLeod, Ken
Robson, Justina
Simmons, Dan
Stephenson, Neal

Stross, Charles
Vinge, Vernor

## Near Future

Burgess, Anthony
Cadigan, Pat
Doctorow, Cory
Gibson, William
Jones, Gwyneth
Knight, Damon

Lethem, Jonathan
McHugh, Maureen F.
Orwell, George
Robinson, Kim Stanley
Ryman, Geoff

Strugatsky, Arkady &
   Boris
Vinge, Vernor
Willis, Connie
Wyndham, John

## New Wave

Aldiss, Brian
Ballard, J.G.
Delany, Samuel R.

Disch, Thomas M.
Ellison, Harlan
Harrison, M. John

Moorcock, Michael
Zelazny, Roger

## Overpopulation

Brunner, John
Burgess, Anthony

Harrison, Harry
Silverberg, Robert

## Political SF

Čapek, Karel
Doctorow, Cory
Ellison, Harlan
Farmer, Philip José

Jones, Gwyneth
Le Guin, Ursula K.
Lem, Stanislaw
MacLeod, Ken
Orwell, George

Robinson, Kim Stanley
Ryman, Geoff
Strugatsky, Arkady &
   Boris
Wells, H.G.

## Pop Culture

Ballard, J.G.
Cadigan, Pat
Dick, Philip K.
Doctorow, Cory

Gibson, William
Lethem, Jonathan
Pohl, Frederik
Scott, Melissa

Sheckley, Robert
Spinrad, Norman

## Post-Human

McCaffrey, Anne
Robson, Justina
Stapledon, Olaf

Stross, Charles
Sturgeon, Theodore
Varley, John

Vinge, Vernor

## Psi Powers

Bester, Alfred
Bradley, Marion Zimmer
Butler, Octavia E.
Herbert, Frank

McCaffrey, Anne
Russ, Joanna
Shepard, Lucius
Smith, Cordwainer

Smith, E.E. "Doc"
Sturgeon, Theodore
Van Vogt, A.E.
Wyndham, John

## Psychology

Bester, Alfred
Burgess, Anthony
Kelly, James Patrick
Keyes, Daniel

Knight, Damon
Lem, Stanislaw
Orwell, George
Poe, Edgar Allan

Silverberg, Robert
Tiptree Jr., James
Zelazny, Roger

## Religion

Blish, James
Card, Orson Scott
Gloss, Molly
L'Engle, Madeleine

Lewis, C.S.
Miller, Walter M.
Silverberg, Robert
Smith, Cordwainer

Vonnegut, Kurt
Wolfe, Gene R.

## Sex and Taboos

Ballard, J.G.
Delany, Samuel R.
Ellison, Harlan
Farmer, Philip José

Heinlein, Robert A.
Huxley, Aldous
Jones, Gwyneth
Lethem, Jonathan

Sheckley, Robert
Spinrad, Norman
Sturgeon, Theodore
Zelazny, Roger

## Space Opera

Asimov, Isaac
Banks, Iain M.
Bova, Ben
Brackett, Leigh
Cherryh, C.J.

Delany, Samuel R.
Greenland, Colin
Moore, C.L.
Pohl, Frederik
Smith, E.E. "Doc"

Stross, Charles
Strugatsky, Arkady &
   Boris
Vinge, Vernor

## Supermen

Bear, Greg
Bester, Alfred

Keyes, Daniel
Stapledon, Olaf

Van Vogt, A.E.

## Sustainable Alternatives

Gloss, Molly
Kelly, James Patrick

McHugh, Maureen F.
Robinson, Kim Stanley

Ryman, Geoff

## Technology

| | | |
|---|---|---|
| Doctorow, Cory | McCaffrey, Anne | Stross, Charles |
| Kelly, James Patrick | Poe, Edgar Allan | Wells, H.G. |
| MacLeod, Ken | Ryman, Geoff | |

## Time Travel

| | | |
|---|---|---|
| Anderson, Poul | Moorcock, Michael | Vonnegut, Kurt |
| Bishop, Michael | Piercy, Marge | Willis, Connie |
| Finney, Jack | Silverberg, Robert | |

## Utopias

| | | |
|---|---|---|
| Clarke, Arthur C. | Le Guin, Ursula K. | Tepper, Sheri S. |
| Huxley, Aldous | Piercy, Marge | Wells, H.G. |

## Virtual Reality

| | | |
|---|---|---|
| Cadigan, Pat | Kelly, James Patrick | Stephenson, Neal |
| Card, Orson Scott | Scott, Melissa | Tiptree Jr., James |
| Haldeman, Joe | Spinrad, Norman | Vinge, Vernor |

## War

| | | |
|---|---|---|
| Bujold, Lois McMaster | Haldeman, Joe | Shepard, Lucius |
| Card, Orson Scott | Heinlein, Robert A. | Vonnegut, Kurt |
| Cherryh, C.J. | Niven, Larry | |

## Women in SF

| | | |
|---|---|---|
| Bradley, Marion Zimmer | Piercy, Marge | Tiptree Jr., James |
| Charnas, Suzy McKee | Russ, Joanna | Varley, John |
| Greenland, Colin | Sargent, Pamela | Wilhelm, Kate |
| McCaffrey, Anne | Scott, Melissa | |

# Index

## About the Author

MAURA HEAPHY has her BA from Marymount Manhattan College, in New York, and an MA in politics from Lancaster University, in the United Kingdom. She is a Senior Lecturer at The Ohio State University, Columbus, Ohio, where she teaches fiction writing, business writing, and science fiction. She is married to Richard Dutton, and they have two daughters, Kate and Claire. Photo © PICS, Powell OH, 2007.